Organic
Flower Gardening

Organic
Flower Gardening

By
Catharine Osgood Foster

Illustrations by Erick Ingraham
Photographs by Bob Griffith and T. L. Gettings

Rodale Press, Inc., Emmaus, Pa. 18049

Printed in the United States of America on recycled paper

Book design by Repro Art Service

Library of Congress Cataloging in Publication Data

Foster, Catharine Osgood, 1907-
    Organic flower gardening.

    Bibliography: p.
    Includes index.
    1. Flower gardening. 2. Organic gardening. I. Title.
SB405.F78   635.9'1'58   75-25666
ISBN 0-87857-105-1 (Hardcover)
ISBN 0-87857-208-2 (Paperback)

      4   6   8   10   9   7   5

For

Barbara Beecher, a very knowledgeable and talented gardener

Contents

PART 1

Getting Ready
for
Flowers

Garden Housekeeping

The reasons for being an organic gardener and refraining from using poisonous sprays are all very obvious if you are growing fruits and vegetables. Every summer when we begin to harvest our first lettuce and radishes in our Vermont garden, my husband, Tom, and I are thankful once again that we have healthy plants we don't have to scrub to get rid of the contaminating things that may be on the produce one buys at a supermarket.

With our flower gardening the reasons for using the methods of organic gardening are just as serious, though they do not focus on making plants edible—except that I do grow nasturtiums I put in the salad, and do use daylilies for fritters and rose hips for jam and tea. The herbs we grow we know we are going to harvest for flavoring though we grow these primarily as pest repellents and because they make such neat hedges for edging a garden of annuals or such decorative potted plants for the terrace.

WHY YOU NEED TO BE A GOOD GARDEN HOUSEKEEPER

We have other very good reasons for refraining from using poison sprays. One is for the sake of the bees, wasps and other beneficial insects and butterflies which aid in pollinating the plants when they frequent the ones that are in flower. In fact, an excellent plan for any garden—whether for vegetables or for ornamentation—is to set out honey plants especially intended to attract bees to your place. Another good reason is to protect the birds that you want to come in for their lovely and entertaining presence in the garden and for their invaluable aid as insect-consumers. Plants attractive to bees and to birds are suggested in the chapter, *Gardening Techniques*, and the enormous capacities of birds to eat up invading insects are described there.

Perhaps the most important reason for being an organic gardener is that you avoid starting chain reactions in the environment from poisonous chemical sprays and dusts you might introduce or other chemicals whose effects can spread all over your garden or your entire area. Such chemicals have been known to build to dangerous, lethal concentrations. Sprays and weedkillers even drift in the air, and float down into streams and ponds, to poison many other living things besides the few weeds intended as the original target. A sight I hate to see is the wilting, browning row of plants alongside a railroad, cornfield or a utility company right-of-way, devastated by weedkillers because the owners thought that some weeds in such places would be detrimental to their operation. Before people discovered the side-effects, weedkillers were greeted as a substitute for the man with a scythe who had up to then taken care of the invasions of plants that really did interfere with the utility wires or the roadside lines of vision.

Just a few years ago I visited a small backyard flower and vegetable garden that had been ruined by the drift of a weedkiller sprayed one windy evening from a passing work train by the company the local railroad hired to clear the banks of their line. The owner of the garden was morose and resentful as he showed me what had happened. He had expected to enjoy the flowers and eat quite a lot of food that summer besides the harvest he had planned to help get his family through the winter. There were only a few gardens affected along that route, but any number of stream banks (and probably streams) had been sprayed, and the effect on the fish and aquatic stream bed population was undoubtedly rather potent, too.

Good garden housekeeping does not involve the use of poisons that will have such harmful environmental effects. No matter how neat something may look, the health and cleanliness of the life network of organisms that make up a garden is not well served by these chemicals. Even in container gardening, even in the case of plants which spend part of the year in the house, I believe the gardener should take the same precautions. Though the chemicals used indoors will not necessarily get into the natural cycles as rapidly and powerfully as they do from open-garden application, you still can let loose undesirable substances into the large, long interlocking nets of biological reactions which we find in all life that supports itself from the soil. And that is all life as we know it—from the soil to plants in one complex step; and from

plants to the food they make which is the basis of all food there is.

USE ORGANIC FERTILIZERS AND SPRAYS

The best garden housekeeping will involve methods which enhance and support the life networks of interrelationships. In the soil it will involve taking care of all the minerals, water, humus, air and other components of the soil, and all the microorganisms which live in the soil; and in the plants themselves, all the living systems essential to survival, from the root hairs down in the soil up to the pores in the leaf where some of the water so vitally necessary to plant life is finally expelled into the air. For all these reasons the plant environment needs nurturing, fertilizing and renewal. And natural methods are the most appropriate, most cooperative and the best. There are on the market, or available on your own land, a great many excellent, reliable organic fertilizers and plant materials for making organic sprays which will do the job you want done with efficiency, long-lasting benefits, and no unfavorable after-effects. And with a little knowledge of botanicals you can make your own sprays, as described in the chapter, *Gardening Techniques.*

INTERPLANT IN A MULTIPURPOSE GARDEN

Since a garden itself and many plants within it should serve several purposes at once, one very fine step to take in areas which need protection from pests is to mix in pest-repellent and pest-resistant plants along with the more vulnerable flowers in the perennial and annual border and under shrubs. Old-time gardeners, as is explained in the chapter, *Old-Fashioned Gardens,* did exactly this. One example is feverfew, well known now as a repellent. It was a favorite ornamental, too, and a medicinal herbaceous plant used in many colonial gardens in this country. So was its cousin, camomile. Both are examples of multipurpose plants, and when in bloom they attract bees. Both these plants have escaped, or gone wild from cultivated gardens, and have spread since colonial days so that now we often see them growing along a roadside, even where soil is very poor.

In primitive societies today, where people still make harmonious gardens of all sorts of flowering plants mixed all together, the gardeners put the repellents such as Datura or Jimson weed in amongst the edible, cosmetic, medicinal and ceremonial plants where the repellents act to ward off pests. People in this country today have learned to use Datura to repel Japanese beetles, especially from white roses, which are particularly susceptible to that pest. And the white trumpets, often called angels' trumpets, go very well with the white roses.

A multiple-purpose garden is, then, lovely and harmonious, lovely and edible, lovely and bird-attracting, lovely and pest-repellent all at once. It can, in addition, be a garden for perfume, for dye plants, shade trees, for white flower forms to see and smell at night, for leisure, exercise, games, for cook-outs or just for the relaxing pleasure of working outdoors in the sunshine or cool of the evening to take care of the plants that grow there. Some of the appeals of design are discussed in the chapter about planning and landscaping, where it is implied that an ornamental garden is, above all, as the Elizabethans called it, a Garden of Pleasure. If you have a pool, your garden is for you, the fish, the frogs, and the dragonflies, too. And your garden, like all your land, is for the multitudes of beneficial microorganisms whose activities keep the soil alive and well. If you have chosen to have a Japanese garden, it is for your solace and for the peace of mind of anyone who comes to it.

Even a small corner with one flowering shrub and a few petunias is for you, the bees and wasps, the toads and earthworms, and for all of the gardens, no matter how multiple they actually are, they are of course for the plants themselves.

OIKONOMOI

In Greek, the word "oikonomoi" means housekeeping. The sound of the word has softened now into words like "economy" and "ecology," and the word suggests that garden housekeeping is done not, therefore, just for aesthetic or useful reasons; it is also done for the sake of the whole living environment, the whole house of the outdoors that we live in. The life in the soil, in the branches of the trees, in the yard, in the plants, bees, birds and small animals who live in the house of the environment are all involved in what the organic gardener wants to take care of, to cooperate with. I don't think garden housekeeping should be confined to a narrow aim of neatness, geometrical control or the sacrifice of other forms of life to an exquisite trim perfection of plants devoid of all spots, holes or nibbles. Once in a while in the past such an aim of neatness has caught up some gardeners. But I see no sense in gardening in that combative nature-defying way. And I see no sense in submitting to the influence of the glamorous ads that show spotless, nail-polished riders on lawnmowers, acting as though what they really want is a plastic garden that never has a blemish and never changes. These gardeners look as though they couldn't bear to have their hands in the dirt, for their hands are as white as swans. The pictures make you think that the aim of all the mowing, clipping and spraying advocated by such ads is some sort of immobilization of the growing plants into something as lifeless as a plastic hedge or plastic flower, or perhaps something like that painted grass in certain cities in the Southwest which certainly never varies its color with the seasons. Natural structures come and go with ease, submitting without pride—unlike man-made systems—to the overall whole, feeding into it and taking from it, and at last succumbing as the living household requires. I think organic gardeners prefer that way of doing to the aim of becoming immobilized and geometrical. It is an exciting housekeeping, to keep in touch with the changes, the seasons, the whole cycle of variations, and to enlarge your involvement by enlarging—not reducing and limiting—the many purposes you can have for an ornamental garden. And not being combative.

EXPERIMENTING

You can always try out new things. Your love of experiment can be fulfilled by growing one variety of flower in several different soils or in several different exposures in order to test out which one is best. You can move them in and out of different degrees of sun or shade to see just where they like it best, and you can try out different mulches, or different varieties, sizes, colors, or textures of plants to see what works best for your garden or what suits you and your family best. One useful experiment to try is to test out different ways of leaving some of the pungent weeds in your garden as long as they do not stifle small plants. You might find that some of them work wonders in repelling some pest that had previously haunted a place nearby. Or after mid-July you might try leaving a whole groundcover of weeds to act as a mulch, as some vegetable gardeners have done. Compost piles lead to a lot of experimenting, especially when you get the habit of scavenging for every kind of organic matter you can lay your hands on, or push into the trunk of your car.

After you have established the kinds of plants that do well in your garden and the methods you

need to use to keep them in good shape, you may want to experiment with additional kinds of gardens. In the chapters toward the end of the book there are suggestions for water gardens, rock gardens, seaside gardens, old-fashioned gardens, rose gardens and gardens in the shade. Any year you can try out new arrangements for your outdoor living area, your terrace or patio garden, and improve the relations between your indoor and outdoor plants, especially if you have a picture window or a glass wall that provides for a close interchange.

And there is always more to do for your soil, and more to learn about the structure and vital systems in the soil as well as in your plants, as is discussed in the next chapter.

WARNINGS

Experimenting is a good thing, up to a point. You can get too enthusiastic as many gardeners know from experience, and then be swamped with a big, unmanageable undertaking on your hands, or an exploding population of tenacious, rampant plants. In fact, if you are given a strange plant by a well-meaning friend who tells you it does very well, beware. Back away from the generosity of all gardeners who say they have lots of something and can easily spare a few plants for you. If you do take some, however, put them in a tub for a year or two until you see how they behave. If they show signs of spreading rampantly by underground stems or stolons, or if they self-seed all over the place, you'd better bury them in the middle of the compost heap. Maybe you do know of a place where you can keep spreading plants under control, or maybe you have a need for some groundcovers that are of value because they do spread by underground means. Sections in later chapters concerning groundcovers will give you information about which ones will spread that way.

I have had neighbors—and you may have,

too—who have complained and begged for help in methods to get rid of Star-of-Bethlehem, crown vetch, or Hall's Japanese honeysuckle. Plants like these can take over and ruin whatever plan of balance and mutual aid you want in your garden. In fact, like the effect of eucalyptus in some areas of the globe, they can create a biological desert, unsuitable for anything else to grow. Many catalogues and books entice you to buy such plants because they are "easy to establish," "easy to grow" and so on. But they are the devil to get rid of, and in the long run can cause you a lot more work than you anticipated unless you can put them between a big stone wall and a driveway where they cannot spread. Never put them in a border.

But even so, even while you are fighting the invaders, you cannot, as the poet says, "live among growing things and still think small, petty thoughts." You can't help marveling at the plants' wonderful resources for tenacity, their age-old adaptability, their splendid color, fine glossy leaves, or their exquisite flower form and overwhelmingly sweet scents.

Obviously no gardener will be so foolish as to plant nothing but delicate, susceptible flowers, and then do nothing to protect them from the ravages of wind, weather, pests or from subtle but insidious changes in the soil which they cannot withstand. And I'd say there are certain plants to avoid unless you are already an experienced and watchful organic gardener. One would be the hybrid tea rose. Choose instead some of the climbers or *Rosa rugosa*, which are much more resistant to invaders, and which bloom luxuriantly all summer as well as forming rose hips of high vitamin content that make such good jam and tea. In *Rosa rugosa* you have a multipurpose plant in itself. Besides all those virtues, it is attractive to birds, makes an excellent windbreak, and sheds leaves valuable for the compost heap, so it is a paradigm, or could be, for all organic gardeners.

Other warnings are given in later chapters. It is all very well to know what to do in a garden, but rather important to know what not to do, too.

SPECIAL PLEASURES OF KEEPING HOUSE OUTDOORS

When I was quite young, my mother used to send me out into the yard to clear out and fix up rooms between the big roots of the large trees there, make furniture from pieces of bark, and dolls to live in these rooms out of flowers. This was a multipurpose activity because it did something to develop habits of clearing up dirt, but what was more important to me was the love it gave me for taking care of things outdoors and for the natural materials you work with when you do. When you are quietly busy out there, the house of the yard has birds coming in and going out, and you get to know their travel routes, their songs and their characteristic flights and flitters. I know one woman who says that her main reason for loving gardening is that it gives her a chance to get to know the birds who live there. You can also watch chipmunks, bees and butterflies and best of all, as a flower gardener, you learn which plants are the ones the bees like to come to, and which ones the chipmunks are willing to stay away from.

As a young neighbor of mine says, "I like the feeling outdoors in my garden of being a sensuous, observing creature, as specific and unalienated as the flowers I am working with. I like to watch the good praying mantises arrive from behind the irises in the garden next door or any of the other busy, working creatures, and feel that I am not alone. Then I can go indoors, where I really am alone, but feel great for the rest of the day." She thinks that working outdoors in an organic garden does something like that for her husband, too. But in addition he satisfies his virile handyman instincts by making pits for the compost, hauling around big bags of leaves or dried manure or taking over the big jobs of pruning the shrubs and snagging out the crabgrass.

We all feel in the garden something of the humility that comes from knowing we belong to the Earth's web of life, larger than ourselves, and not just to the web of mechanical gadgets and systems, as though we were caught in corporate influences too remote and too big to understand or combat. Everything is alive in a garden. The soil itself is teeming with microscopic life. The delight of observing and learning about all the wonderful happenings of nature is reason enough, some gardeners say, for keeping right on with it—no matter how many other purposes it serves.

All the practical hints and explanations in the chapters that follow are invitations to get out in the garden and learn more. The hint to grow marigolds for nematode control and the explanation that these plants ooze something into the soil that wards off those tiny, invisible worms might have been astounding to our ancestors. But today we find such news perfectly acceptable and believable, because we are all well acquainted with the fact, now, that important events take place all the time at a microscopic level. We are able to think now in terms, for instance, of twelve parts per million, for we have heard that this minute dosage has been enough to start a chain reaction of DDT build-up which can grow serious enough to kill salmon or thin down the shell of an osprey's egg to tissue paper thickness. And on the other side of the picture, for

beneficial effects, I have read that a dosage of the same minute size of the essence of allyl derived from garlic has been enough to control the mosquitoes spawning in the mud beside a lake in California, and in this case with no lethal after-effects on other species. Nevertheless, without understanding the particulars of how these natural marigold and garlic potencies worked, our ancestors, or some of them, did use such plants in their gardening and now, of course, modern organic gardeners do, too.

These are just a few of the myriad instances of the interconnections between living things and the influence all things have on each other which you learn about and take part in when you garden. As the great California naturalist, John Muir, said, "There are no harsh dividing lines in nature. Glaciers blend with the snow and the snow blends with the thin invisible breath of the sky. . . There are no stiff, frigid, strong partition walls betwixt us and heaven. There are blendings as immeasurable and untraceable as the edges of melting clouds." I often think of the air as the environment we mostly live in; and it enters us and becomes part of our inner environment every time we breathe. And that kind of time, living time, is different from clock time. It is not linear, and you do not have to wear a watch to know it. In the garden you know it, for gardens go by seasonal, sunlight and starlight time, and even the complex ticking of spiritual time in the mysterious webwork of ever-renewing living relationships that go on and on in the garden.

Soil, Water and Plant Growth

To start with, many soils are not of garden quality, so include soil improvement in your plans from the beginning. Though you can't control sun, wind and rain, you certainly can buffer your soil so it is able to take care of the impact of all such natural forces better and better as the seasons go by. Keep it up, and the improvements will help the soil, both in your lifetime and later.

What I love most about good garden topsoil is that it is alive, teeming with living forms, visible and invisible, and that it has, as it were, its own breathing system and pores, a circulatory system of water and soil solution, and even what you could call a digestive system carried on by the beneficial soil bacteria. A gardener who loves the living fabric of the soil will give it the care it needs, open it up for good circulation, know the soil as a process, a continual happening, and will feed it—seeing that it has enough organic matter to make its structure crumbly and friable and keeping the soil healthy and productive. (We do not, by the way, feed plants—even though we talk as though we could—for plants make their own food. But we can feed the soil with minerals and organic matter for the population of microorganisms which provide nutrients, enzymes and antibiotics to be taken up by the root

hairs or exchanged in the mysterious and wonderful interchange of carbohydrates and proteins and other materials between fungi and roots called the mycorrhizal association.)

Topsoil has millions of these small creatures in it that make these things happen through millions of biophysical changes and biochemical events every day. Aeons ago and still going on today is the gradual evolving of rock into fine particles that make up the soil as we know it. Scientists have studied soil types for a good many years and have devised several methods for categorizing them. One indicates the size of the predominant particles, usually listed in eight classes. But what they amount to are three general types: sandy soil, silts or loam soils, and clay soils, with the loam soils having humus in them, too. Your soil will be one of these, and you should set out to improve it, especially if it is a sandy or clay soil.

SANDY SOIL

This kind of soil obviously has larger particles in it and feels gritty when you rub it between your fingers. It has more space between particles for water to run through and air to get in, so it tends to become dry very quickly after a rain and to warm up easily in the spring. The air that goes into a porous soil provides oxygen for many chemical reactions and for bacterial decomposition of organic matter, and also nitrogen. Plants cannot use that nitrogen directly and normally rely on bacterial action for its conversion to usable nitrates. Though in very sandy soils the soil solution drains out all too quickly, the rain or irrigation water in sandy soils takes up nutrients, cools and waters your plants, and provides the hydrogen and oxygen for the biochemical events which sustain life in the soil. If your soil is below par because it is too sandy, add compost both fine and finished, and partly finished, as well as other coarser organic materials like leaves, peat moss, ground bark, grass clippings, shredded corncobs and other mulch materials dug in. These will help to prevent leaching of valuable nutrients and enable the comparatively infertile, fast-drying sand to hold the water and save the nutrients. It will also improve the structure of the soil, giving it more crumbliness, will fill in some of the air spaces, moderate the temperature in hot weather, and increase all the biochemical exchanges. Sandy soils are valuable, however, in that they rarely get puddled and waterlogged, and they warm up quickly in the spring—facts that make them excellent for tulips and other spring bulbs which do poorly in cold, wet soils.

CLAY

Clay soils stay damp and cold much longer after the snow melts and drain less easily. Since their particles are many times smaller than sand particles, clay soils have many more surfaces to hold nutrients and to hold twice as much water twice as long. These tiny surfaces are especially useful because the nutrient particles which adhere to them are right there ready to be taken up by the root hairs. The soil solution has picked up calcium, magnesium, potassium and sodium ions released from minerals in the soil in the form of exchangeable cations, lodging them where the roots can get at them. When the root hair takes up a calcium ion, for example, it releases two hydrogen ions in the soil solution. When nitrates, sulfates or phosphates are taken up, on the other hand, the roots release hydroxyl or OH ions. Humus surfaces also take part and are essential to these processes. The pH of the soil, or the rating we give it designating its acidity or alkalinity, estimates the number of hydrogen ions, the H in that term standing for hydrogen. And this is why we add lime or calcium when a soil is acid, or when too many hydrogen ions are on the loose in the soil solution. Clay soils are more likely to get that way.

Clay soils also need humus and organic matter for air, warmth and especially to improve internal drainage and keep the water from running off after rains. Humus will hold nearly four times as much water from run-off as will a heavy clay. It also prevents compaction and then, after rains dry off, a hard, baked, cracked condition of the soil. If you ever do see such a condition in your garden, get to work and add organic matter, compost or humus—after breaking up the soil, that is. When leaching occurs from clay soils, the alkaline bases wash out, and soil becomes more and more acid, as it has in most of the cool, humid Northeast since the virgin forests were cut down. It is a good thing, nevertheless, for a soil solution to be somewhat acid, for then it acts on the remaining minerals and bits of rock, causing them to break down and be more available for the microorganisms and biochemical exchanges in the soil, and eventually for the plants.

SILT AND LOAM

The loam soil which the gardener aims for has a good deal of silt in it, plus the organic matter and enough clay and sand particles to give it good texture and structure. The organic matter will have many tiny bits of humus as well as all degrees of decomposing matter, animal and plant both, from a daily renewal from the dying microogranisms and other larger inhabitants of the garden. The weeds and larger plant materials you work into the soil eventually decompose, too, into humus. This humus content, besides helping to make the soil chemicals and enzymes available to plants, improves the water-retaining capacity of the soil by its sponginess, but helps drainage by being porous and less water-retentive than clay. And humus in itself is an indispensable food for the bacteria that do much of the work of the living soil, and for the beneficial earthworms. It even feeds pests like slugs who will eat it in preference to the live plants we want to protect in the garden.

IDEAL STRUCTURE

A good fertile loam soil feels soft and oily when you rub it between your fingers, will hold together for a minute in a loose lump when you squeeze it, but will fall as crumbly bits when you drop it back on the ground. It is said to have good crumbs, granules or aggregates. What holds an aggregate together is not only the colloidal character of the surfaces of clay and humus particles, but also little bits of root and decayed leaves, threads or hyphae of various fungi, the secretions of slimy stuff from earthworms and maybe slugs or snails, residual gums and resins left after the decomposition of vegetation and the invisible bodies of the countless bacteria and fungi alive in the soil.

Amazingly enough, the amount of humus is not as great as one would expect. In an average soil it is estimated that the mineral content is 45 per cent, the organic content 5 per cent, and the air and water 25 per cent each. The organic content in gardens of organic gardeners and farmers often rises to 10 or 12 per cent, and this includes both the compost, manure, and organic fertilizers used and all the live and dead bodies of the soil inhabitants. Too much fresh organic matter, such as plant residues and manure, like too much air in the soil, can cause nitrogen loss, evidently because the bacteria multiply and consume so much they rob the soil. Nitrogen loss can also come from too much water, which depletes mineral nutrients and then slows down nitrogen release to low levels.

(In all considerations of the comparative values of organic and chemical gardening methods, it should be mentioned, I think, that old Justus von Liebig who thought up chemical gardening 150 years ago lived in a day when bacteria had not even been discovered, and the whole miracle of invisible biological life in the soil was not even imagined—except by a few intuitive eccentrics who said plants lived on humus, but who couldn't conceive of micro-organisms as we know them today. Back in the beginning of the last century people used to have a close, direct relationship with the soil and their gardens; they really believed in humus and its power to benefit plants. But then that conviction was all swept aside and called superstition, and we lost that old close relation, that love of the soil when the age of chemical and mechanical farming and gardening came upon us.)

LAYERS

From the bed rock on up through the layers of the soil there are gradations and character-istics which benefit the plants in your garden and help give them their bloom.

The rock itself is little by little eaten away, contributing minerals to the upper layers. Deep-rooted big trees get down to it, help invade the rock, bring up into their systems the needed minerals and then deposit them on the upper level in the fall of leaves.

Next there are smaller stones and gravelly

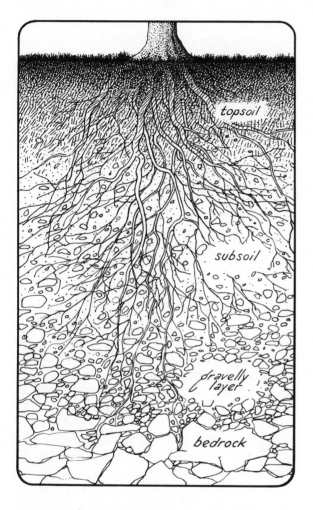

layer is one called subsoil, usually well pulverized mineral materials, but lacking in humus, microorganisms and earthworms or any other creatures who exist on organic matter. It is hard, pale-colored, and sometimes literally impenetrable unless you use heavy machinery to break it up. It turns to hardpan, as can happen in clayey soils which have been plowed to the same depth year after year or with adobe soils in the West, which need soaking for four or five days before you can even get a fork down into them. Conditions like these usually mean that you should break through somehow and fill trenches with gravel to reach down to the gravelly layer beneath to improve drainage. If you don't, your garden will be ruined by run-off rainwater (or sprinkled water) and you'll have to convert to potted plants and hanging baskets.

The top layer, the topsoil, is dark, humusy and full of life, so it is the layer you especially care for and try to improve. In potting mixtures you improve clay soils by adding sand, but outdoors this method is not often used except when you dig up a whole bed for new perennials and annuals. But organic matter is always added, and this is valuable for both structure and nutrients—especially if it has been composted.

layers which are good for drainage and for the spread and stabilizing of the water table, which is continually being tapped by plants for their transpiration process consisting of the up-pull of water through the roots, up the trunk into the branches and leaves and finally out the pores of the leaves. Roots reaching down to such deep levels also recycle the rich supply of minerals into the upper layers of the soil when the leaves turn to leafmold (or to good black compost you will return to the garden).

Above the gravel and just below the topsoil

THE IMPORTANT NUTRIENTS

Nitrogen, phosphorus and potassium are still considered important nutrients for plants, but we know enough nowadays about the vital importance of tiny quantities of things, even in parts per million when they are poisonous or absent, to make it obvious to gardeners that all 15 chemical elements needed by plants are really needed. Though Liebig's kind of analysis was done by burning the plant and analyzing the ash, today's biologically more savvy scientists analyze a living plant, and when they do, they find that the compounds going up in the sap are 95 per cent organic compounds.

The 15 elements needed are: carbon (C), hydrogen (H), and oxygen (O)—all found in many compounds—plus nitrogen (N), phosphorus (P), potassium (K), sulfur (S), calcium (Ca), magnesium (Mg), and iron (Fe)—all known since the end of the nineteenth century; and those more recently discovered as necessary: boron (B), copper (Cu), manganese (Mn), zinc (Zn) and the still rather mysterious molybdenum (Mo), whose function is not yet understood. Plants also have a curious habit of taking up elements which they may not use at all, such as chlorine, sodium and silicon—though our grandmothers and great-grandmothers were glad to have the silicon in the horse-tail plants that they used for scrub brushes before we had chore-boy metal scrubbers. I have a hunch that the scratchy silicon may function as a pest-repellent, for the horse-tail plant is sometimes recommended for that purpose. Even arsenic, barium, bromine, aluminum, colbalt, gold, mercury and selenium have been found in plants, but there's no proof that these were used by the plant or necessary to its metabolism. Perhaps some of the unknown causes of plants' vigor come from one or more of these elements as well as from the vitamins and hormones and even antibiotics which plants are believed to get from the soil. (A very good reason for not using poisons on the soil is the chance you run of killing off such beneficial substances.)

It is well to note such facts—and especially lack of facts—because it is worth knowing what we have already discovered and it is essential, I believe, for gardeners to be aware of the vastness and intricacy of all we have not yet come to understand. It promotes respect for nature, and a goodly amount of respect and reverence for the wonderful and reliable processes in nature is just about as necessary for successful gardening as a grasp of the basic facts. These facts have for the last century or so been thought of in categories of living and non-living elements, so called. But scientists today are bio-chemists in their thinking, regarding things in much more biological terms than did the 18th and early 19th century chemists (and promoters of chemical fertilizers). And once we are into biological areas we know there is a lot we do not know.

DEFICIENCIES AND SOME CURES

There are signs to watch for when you need to take care of certain deficiencies. If there is not enough nitrogen, your plants lose their normal green color and look pale and flimsy. Since nitrogen is needed for the formation of proteins and for photosynthesis, add such high-nitrogen materials as cottonseed meal (7 per cent), hoof and horn meal (10 per cent), blood meal (13-15 per cent), alfalfa meal (10-12 per cent) or well-rotted manure which is relatively quite a bit lower in nitrogen (.5-.8 per cent). The time to watch for nitrogen deficiency is soon after you have added green organic matter to the soil (or if you inadvertently add manure that is too raw and fresh). The bacteria get so busy digesting and decomposing those materials that they use up even the nitrogen in the soil as well as that in the fresh materials for their metabolism.

A phosphorus deficiency can be suspected when you see the growth of young plants slow down, when the leaves get reddish or purplish underneath, or weak and are easily attacked by insects and disease. You need phosphorus for the health of your plants, for good strong roots and for nice, bright-colored flowers. Give bone meal, more organic matter, rock phosphates, and all sorts of marine products, such as fish meal, seaweeds, wastes from shellfish factories and sludge. Most of those can well be composted first, especially if you find they attract animals when used directly. Also in the compost heap put six inches of green leaves, weeds, clippings to every two inches of manure, and use the compost on the garden as soon as it is broken down. Flowers need a pound of finely ground rock phosphate every three or four years for each ten square feet of garden.

That method is good for potassium deficiency, too. You know you have this when you see the leaves in poor shape at the edges, turning dark or brown and curling. Wood ashes help to cure this condition, and so do greensand and granite dust, finely ground potash rocks, flyash, vetch and alfalfa hay, and many other kinds of hay, old potatoes, tobacco stems, straw and dried manure, especially goat and sheep if you can get it. Some of these can also be processed through the compost heap, but not wood ashes which leach out too easily. Use those directly on the soil. (Wood ashes are good insect and slug repellents, too, if you happen to need them for such a cause.) Calcium helps to make potassium available.

Calcium, though widely present in the soil, can be reaching your plants in inadequate amounts. If growth is slow and stems seem too thick and woody, add finely ground dolomitic limestone. Use of other limes may lead to a build-up which can lock up phosphorus and magnesium. (Slaked lime and quicklime are never to be used.) Finely ground oyster shells, marl and marble are other possibilities. And a treatment every four or five years ought to be sufficient (at ½ pound per square yard). Make a soil test or send a sample to your County Agent or university Extension Service office to be sure what you need.

Yellowed leaves, especially on acid-loving plants like heaths and azaleas, may be the sign of iron deficiency. Though iron in the soil is in most areas plentiful, the deficiency in your plants is likely to come from too much calcium in the soil. If you have limed it too much, counteract the condition by adding manure, dried blood or tankage of some other high-nitrogen material to bring the soil back to a more favorable pH condition, to neutral, that is, or to the slightly acid condtion which most garden plants prefer. Though chemical gardeners slap in the aluminum sulfate to make soil more acid, organic gardeners prefer to use peat moss, oak leaves, pine needles, rotted pine and oak sawdust and bark to increase the nitrogen content. Some gardeners of both kinds use finely powdered sulfur.

Magnesium, like calcium, helps to make potassium available, It is present in all cholorphyl cells which make plants green, and aids in the plant's use of nitrogen. If the lower leaves of a plant turn yellow but keep their green veins, that may be a sign that you should give some judicious doses of dolomitic limestone. A constant program of compost-feeding, however, will probably never make that necessary.

For other elements such as boron, copper, zinc and manganese, manure and compost are good sources, as well as old bits of metal and annual autumn supplies of leaves from trees with deep roots, for those leaves have in them just about all the elements. Even before your garden has a chance to get any such deficiencies, give it treatments that will assure good supplies of nutrients.

GROW LEGUMES

In fact, before you start the garden at all, a cover crop of some legume is a good thing to grow for a year. If you want a flowery one, try one of the lupines, for instance *Lupinus hartweggi*, varieties 'Harlequin', 'Attraction' or the pretty 'Rose Queen.' There are also *L. angustifolius*, in blue and *L. luteus*, in yellow, if you prefer those colors. Broadcast the seed, mow when the growth is lush, and lightly disk the plant material into the top two or three inches of the soil, where the bacteria and fungi will go to work and release the nutrients and convert them into forms your plants will be able to use. If you will settle for a clover instead of the more decorative lupines, use sweet clover, *Melilotus alba*, which sends roots way down into the soil and builds up a wonderful supply of fertility. (And you will enjoy all the bees that come when it is in flower.) Even as early as the first half of this century an agronomist at the University of Missouri was testing crops as nitrogen suppliers to the soil. These tests revealed that sweet clover was far and away the best, with the power to add half a ton of nitrogen per acre to the soil. If inoculated, legumes can add as much nitrogen as would ten tons of manure per acre. As living fibers they are able to give twice the benefits to the soil that inert powders of chemical fertilizer could give, and legumes consume none of the five tons of coal necessary to burn for the manufacture of a ton of nitrogen fertilizer converted from the air.

❀OTHER SOIL CONDITIONS❀
BAD FOR FLOWERS

In addition to nutrient deficiencies, your plants can suffer from such conditions as poor drainage, too much manure, too much peat, or too little air. Iris, for instance, has to have good drainage or it will get crown rot; and if the soil is too rich that can happen, too. Use only a little bone meal, wood ashes and ground rock phosphate and no manure. Peonies suffer if they have been mulched with peat. It may not show up for a year or so, but it is much better to use side dressings of well-rotted manure and a little bone meal, but never let those materials touch the crown of the plants. Too rich a soil is bad for camellias, so avoid blood meal for them and use only small amounts of well-rotted manure or compost. Almost any plants will have a hard time if the soil around them has been walked on or worked when too wet, for that compacts the soil and sends the air out of it. Or plants that just

grow by paths that get heavy use have their roots killed when the air is finally tramped out of the soil around them.

WEEDS AS INDICATORS

Even before you have a soil test, you can judge something about the acidity of your soil from the kinds of weeds which grow there. Not from moss. It's an old wives' tale that moss indicates an acid soil. (It indicates a poor soil, very low in nutrients.) In fact, when you are looking around for a place to put some new acid-loving plants, the weeds will give you a hint: bent grasses grow where it is acid, and so do meadow foxtails, daisies, mouse-ear hawkweed, the corn chrysanthemum (*C. segetum*, often called corn marigold in England) knawel in eastern states and corn spurry in the Pacific Northwest, sheep's sorrel, sow thistle, coltsfoot and nettles. It may also be acid where you see many volunteers of Johnny-jump-up.

For alkaline preference in plants, indicators include white mustard, clustered bellflower, musk thistle, black knapweed, Queen Anne's lace, corn salad, salad burnet and henbane.

BACTERIA

Soil is said to be like a bank with a vast bankroll of nutrients which are released from the supply only by the right conditions. The bacteria you need are attuned to these conditions. If you plan for acid soil, you hope for bacteria native to acid woodsy places.

❀WHAT TO DO FOR PLANTS NEEDING❀
ACID SOIL

Azaleas, rhododendrons, blueberry bushes, gardenias and hydrangeas all prefer a soil with pH ratings of 4.5 for the azaleas and blueberries, and up to pH 6.5 for the others. If you are going to plant an acid-loving shrub or border of shrubs, it is best to dig out the entire garden to a depth of 18 inches and fill in the whole area with a new mixture. Use one part clean, sharp sand, one part ordinary garden loam; and three parts acid peat—and be sure to get the imported kind which is acid from a wild flower nursery or other supply house. Test the mixture for its pH, and if, for azaleas and rhododendrons it does not test about pH 5.5, add rotted sawdust from pines or oaks or rotted ground bark until the right degree is reached. (Some people also use sulfur, especially in the West where the soils are alkaline. To bring a soil testing pH 7.5 to pH 5.5 you need five pounds of sulfur per 100 square feet, except in areas where there is a lot of air pollution with sulfur in it and where you will need less. I get the pure flowers of sulfur at the drug store because I have no objection to using this chemical. Maybe you do. I know other organic gardeners who use it as an insecticide or repellent, and to repel mice.)

If there are limestone ledges beneath the spot where you want to grow acid-loving plants, you may need to make a bin with a bottom to keep the lime from seeping in. Or if you plan to put acid-loving plants next to a house foundation, line the sides with plastic or pine wood to prevent such seepage.

Since the castings of earthworms include quite a bit of calcium picked up and ejected from their digestive systems, it is best to bar them from the area where you want to grow acid plants. If you do not build a bin, you can keep them from coming into the acid area by laying down one to two inches of cinders on the bottom of the hole. This is especially important if there is limy material nearby, which they will just bring in and deposit if you do not keep them out. And do not use bone meal or wood ashes, for both have lime.

Also test your town water, and if it is about pH 7.2, use rainwater for your acid-loving plants. Each year test the water again; and each

year test your made soil for acid-loving plants. When needed, add more acid peat and, if you don't object to using it, sulfur. Leaf mold, especially from oaks and pines, is good to add yearly, too. And in general, do not cultivate these plants, but keep them mulched with acid materials such as those mentioned. If you don't plan for it, and have the normal garden bacteria, you will find that these acid soils leach potassium and magnesium and that the phosphates are locked up. Then too much iron and aluminum is released and the bacteria you wanted are inactivated. To bring them back, you need to add the finely ground dolomitic lime. This will also help the soil structure, as does gypsum— especially if you have worked on it first, if it tends to be rather sticky clay soil, or if you live at the seaside and have just had a tidal wave. What the calcium helps to do in the soil also, is to get the potash out of bondage with silica so that the potassium salts can go into the soil solution and then to the roots of your plants. Wherever there are acid soils, the potash supply needs replacement, even though an unfortunately small amount of it may be used.

Both acid and alkaline soils are modified by the addition of organic matter which can often bring it to a neutral or slightly acid condition of pH 6.5 to pH 7, which is what most garden flowers prefer—with the exception of certain woodland and rock garden plants. The organic matter you add can be in the form of peat moss, either worked in or as a mulch; leaf mold; salt hay or other hay; woodchips, sawdust, ground bark or shavings; and other plant residues such as cocoa shells, shredded corncobs, buckwheat shells and many, many others.

❧HOW TO ADD HUMUS❧

1. <u>Peat moss.</u> This conditioner is available to gardeners and is partially decomposed sphagnum moss from bogs, swamps or other wet

places. Sphagnum grows with shoots up to a foot tall, with a green tip and all the rest beige or brownish but undecayed because the water where it grows is so acid and sterile. The shoots contain large cells which can hold up to 20 times their own weight in water, and this is the ability you want to get when you buy peat moss. Most of the foreign peat is acid; domestic peat is more alkaline. Canadian peat, often shipped to this country (along with its ticks, too) is likely to be rather acid, so test the pH rating if you expect to use it where plants prefer a more alkaline condition, such as coral bells, primrose or toadflax. Very acid peat moss, good for azaleas and heathers, can have a pH as low as 3.6. It is best to soak the peat moss before you add it to your soil and incorporate it at the rate of one to three, or one inch to each three inches of soil you condition. Add a cupful of finely ground dolomitic limestone to each bushel if the acidity needs correcting. Added bone meal and blood meal help to make peat more of a fertilizer, for in itself it has little nutrient value.

WARNING: When it is dry, peat moss acts as a wick and draws water out of the soil. Always bury it for best results, as you always bury peat pots, for they, too, will dry where exposed to the air and draw the water right out of the very place where you want it preserved. Peat moss used as a mulch must also be well watered before using and kept moist on the soil side. Some surface drying does not hurt, but the underside if dry will also act as a wick and dry out the soil when you least want that.

2. Reed-sedge peat. It is much coarser and more likely to have weed seeds and sticks in it than that which comes from sphagnum moss. It is more matted, has more little roots in it, and sometimes you see pieces of the stems of cattails and arrowhead in it, and bits that look like fern stems. It will help to aerate your soil because of this coarseness and will provide some slow-release nutrients. For best results, again, it is a good idea to add some bone meal, blood meal, dried fish scraps, seaweed and other nutrients. A bale weighing approximately 100 pounds will make a one-inch layer over 300 square feet. A good mulch is often three inches deep, so use three bales. This peat, too, conditions the soil as it slowly decays and adds humus—if watered, that is.

3. Leaf mold. This is just about the best additive and mulch you can use to improve your soil. Save all the leaves you rake off your lawn, shred them if you can, compost them, and dig them into the soil. They do not always have to be composted or shredded, and can be dug in at any time when you won't hurt the roots of plants. Fall is a good time.

WARNING: Beware of maple and poplar leaves for a winter mulch because they can mat and make an airless, even icy cover over your garden. Always compost those first, if you can, or mix them with hay or straw. Norway maple leaves should never be used without long-time composting for they have an alkaloid in them which is not good for other plants.

Because leaves from big trees are rich in all the minerals and nutrients which their big roots have brought up from deep rich layers of the earth, the values of leaf mold, or partly decayed leaves are both nutritious and physically helpful to the soil. Light, airy leaves such as pine needles and oak leaves are sometimes wasted because people think of them as *too* acid. They are not. Use them when you can. Just add a little lime unless of course you are using them with plants of the heath family. These and the leaves of many other trees can simply be raked into the garden beneath a hedge or into the area around a tree or onto the flower border and used as a mulch and soil conditioner. The great thing about pine needles is that they decay so slowly you can rake them off one bed, store them in a pile, and use them later on another bed if you want to. White pine needles are fluffier than needles of other varieties, and make good mulches for rhododendrons and azaleas especially.

4. Salt hay. This is a splendid mulch and soil conditioner, if you can get it. It is sold in garden centers in some communities and if you live near the seacoast, you can sometimes find it just floating in the estuaries, there for the taking. Its advantage over regular hay is that there are no weed seeds, which you have to combat if you use any other hay but the first cutting. That usually goes to the livestock, however, because it is the best for them, too. Both hays—and straw, also—need to be applied three to four inches deep so that in addition to their soil-conditioning properties they will also serve as mulch. Because common hay is not very pretty and because it invites mice to come in and nest, it is not often used on flower gardens except as a late winter mulch in difficult areas. A season of composting will reduce hay to more manageable conditions, and then it can be shredded and incorporated in the soil any time you wish.

5. Sawdust. Though rather a funny, light tan color at first, is an excellent soil additive and mulch, and it will turn dark in time. At some sawmills you can get already weathered sawdust which won't have that odd color. Do not put it on top of the soil in a layer more than an inch or an inch and half thick because it may cake. The other hazard is the nitrate loss in the soil that can come with using sawdust, both when you use it as mulch and when you incorporate it in the soil. To avoid this add a cup of blood meal, cottonseed meal or other high-nitrogen fertilizer to each ten square feet of soil before you apply the sawdust. People say you mustn't use sawdust because it is *too* acid. What they are actually referring to, in most cases, is this aftermath of sawdust application if a high-nitrogen fertilizer is not applied at the same time. What happens is that the bacteria use up so much of the soil's nitrogen in decomposing the

sawdust that the plants nearby suffer as they do from other deficiencies of nitrogen in acid soils.

6. Wood chips, shavings, ground bark. These materials are made up of pieces big enough so that the bacteria do not work on them with such acidity to deplete the nitrogen supplies in the soil. It is, however, advisable to add a good supply of fertilizer along with the woody material. Here with these additives, since they decompose more slowly, all the three main elements are needed: nitrogen, phosphorus and potassium. A combination of dried blood, incinerator ash and tobacco stems would be good. But if those are hard to get, use greensand, granite dust and phosphate rock. A good fish fertilizer is highly recommended for the three elements, if you are free of opossums, who are quite fond of fish emulsion. Of all these humus-making materials I like ground bark best because it is an attractive color and works slowly and perpetually into the earth.

7. Cocoa and buckwheat shells. I also like to use these dark-colored materials because they look rich and dark. I especially like the rich, chocolatey brown of the cocoa shells. But they do cake sometimes and get filled up with fungus growth. It helps to mix them with peat moss, and to use them only in sunny places so that the excess moisture which makes the fungi flourish will be absorbed or dissipated. Buckwheat shells seem to stay drier and not cake so much. Another precaution in using either of these for a mulch is to use only a thin layer and begin working it into the soil whenever it gets wet. This does not, therefore, give you much weed protection, but it will be just as good for your soil.

8. Sunflower seed hulls. Inadvertently we have a very good mulch and soil conditioner under all our bird feeders, especially where the bird feed goes more to squirrels than to the birds. In fact under one feeder above one of our stone walls, it softened the soil so much the wall began

to heave, though I must admit that chipmunks lived in that wall and stored I don't know how many stolen seeds in their secret hiding places up and down their runways. We have peonies below that wall and I always enjoy coming to the sunflower seed area every spring when I am weeding behind the peonies because the roots slip out as though they were coming from pure excelsior rather than soil.

9. Shredded corncobs. A lot of flower gardeners refuse to use corncobs—as they refuse to use unrotted sawdust—because they are so light colored. One way to use them, however, if you live in a cold climate, is in the late fall, just before the snow comes. After the ground has frozen well, put down the layer of corncobs and then, if you wish, cover that layer with evergreen boughs. In the spring, if you still don't like the color, take them off and compost them, or scratch them in after the ground thaws, and let the soil stay open to the sun until it is dry and warm. Then add a dark-colored summer mulch.

WARNING: In any case, no matter what mulch you use, and what soil-conditioning organic matter you use, don't just dump it on and then go away and forget about it. Look it over to see whether a fungus has got in. Look under it to see what's happening. Find out, if you use hay, for instance, whether the mice have moved in and are getting ready to eat your tulip bulbs or other plants. Keep track of the little plants growing in areas where you have dug in leaves or a lot of weeds or grass clippings. If they are spindly and pale, go down in and break up any wads of organic matter that are causing it.

10. Compost. Compost, therefore, is the best of all the humus materials you can use. None of those hazards can result from it, for it is so mild and well-balanced, so near to good rich loam itself that it doesn't threaten your garden at all.

❧ HOW TO MAKE COMPOST ❧

Making compost can be great fun, and it can satisfy many of your instincts for hoarding, saving, scavenging and for prettying things up when you apply it to the garden. There are lots of scientific things to know about it and some strict, logical rules to follow if you want to make it scientifically. But you can also make it almost any old way, and can come out with a fine product you'll be glad to use on any garden, worked into the soil, or spread around as top dressing near your prize plants.

MATERIALS TO USE

The materials to use, whether you make it in a bin, a pit, a pile or a plastic bag, are the same—all the organic materials you can get, but in a proportion between the ones high in carbon as compared to those high in nitrogen. If you make it in a plastic bag, you rely on an anaerobic, or airless, process because the bacteria which convert the raw materials to compost do not use air. (Instead of decomposing the materials, they putrefy it and the smell is rather awful while in process. It's best to wait until the whole bagful is composted before you open it.) All other composting is aerobic, for it uses air because the bacteria need the oxygen for their decomposition of the grass and lettuce and weeds and radish tops and all other organic materials you take to the heap to be composted.

You can scavenge for materials not only in your own yard and kitchen but all over town. Go to dairy farms to get manure, bedding and spent hay that has gone bad for some reason. Go to chicken farms, too, and if you can get feathers as well as chicken bedding or droppings, do so, for they have a high nitrogen content: 15 per cent as compared to 1 to 2 per cent in the chicken manure. Get sludge from secondary sewage treatment plants (or Milorganite, put out by the city of Milwaukee from their plant) and find or start a municipal leaf pile. If there is none, beg the big plastic bags people put out by the road in fall when they have raked their leaves, and take them home for your pile. Hair from beauty parlors is high in nitrogen, and so are fish scraps from a fish wharf, or things you can buy such as hoof and horn meal, fish meals, cottonseed meal, blood meal, sunflower seed oil cake. And use any legume hays you can get such as alfalfa hay, clover hay or vetch.

In your own yard, grass clippings and all sorts of green materials put on the compost heap are beneficial to promote the carbon/nitrogen ratio most conducive to good processing of the heap. The final ratio, when all is finished and ready to use, should be about 10/1. Materials you put in are higher than that, for the carbon has not yet been worked on by the composting bacteria and fungi to reduce it. Grass clippings start out with a 25/1 ratio; manure and bedding with 23/1; legumes such as pea pods or pea vines, bean vines or soybean shells with 15/1, as is also the ratio for straight dog manure and other farm animal manures without the bedding. Woodier and more fibrous vegetable materials like pine needles, hay, straw, sawdust or corncobs run much higher, with carbon content up to 50, 60, even 100 or 300 to 500 to one in the carbon/nitrogen ratio.

For a well-balanced compost fertilizer you also need materials high in phosphorus and potassium. Of course many plant residues including leaves from tall trees will have good supplies of these, but especially good ones for phosphorus include bone meal, fish scraps and ground rock phosphate. (Avoid superphosphate which is a commercial fertilizer which encourages sulfur-using bacteria at the expense of the ones you want to have in your pile, and which has had some of the rock phosphate's trace elements inactivated, such as boron, nickel and zinc.) The sludge will also provide nearly 8 per

cent phosphorus, if you can get that to compost. And composting is a very good precautionary measure for sludge, if you are nervous about using it.

Potassium is fairly high in wood ashes, seaweed, cocoa shells, and in fish scraps. Greensand and granite dust are also good sources. But do not use wood ashes, for all the goodness will leach away in the rainy spells. Save it to use directly on the garden, not only for fertilizer but also for an insect invasion you want to get rid of.

Since the main point about humus in the soil is the organic content, the fibers and bacteria are as important or more important than the mineral and chemical content. Some people have an impulse to put lime on a heap—perhaps in some notion that it will keep the pile sweet. It is a poor practice. Don't do it. For it will cause a loss of nitrogen, and certainly of all the elements you provide your plants, nitrogen is about the most important. You often see, and will see in this book, the advice to use well-rotted manure for a fertilizer. In many a compost heap, use manure that is as fresh as you can get it, or manure that at least has been kept under a tarp and prevented from losing its nitrogen. Though it has been known for several centuries that weathered manure was less effective than unleached manure, I still see, when I drive around my town, the farmers' piles stacked out in the rain and all weathers losing their goodness to the ground below. Better to get some of the ground's good rich earth and put that on your compost heap.

Earth is an important ingredient of the heap. In piling it up, if you do so by layers, every third or fourth layer can be of good garden soil. Or if you make a heap from daily garbage, as some people do, scatter earth over it each day. One question that often arises about garbage is whether or not to include animal matter along with vegetable matter. I've heard one pretty good scientist (and his wife) claim that if you cover meat scraps with earth each time you add them, there is no objection to using them. I believe there are still a few objections, and one of them is that any melted fat — or fat that is going to melt in hot weather — will coat the organic fibers and make it hard for the bacteria to get at them to decompose them. Fat-reducing organisms will turn up, but they are not the ones that work on fibers, and it is thought, in fact, that they replace or overwhelm the fiber-reducing ones, much as the sulfur-reducing bacteria replace the others when the chemical fertilizer superphosphate is used by gardeners who are not organic gardeners.

HOW TO LAYER A HEAP

Though as I said before you can make a compost heap any old way and just toss out materials and let nature take over and decompose them, that method is usally pretty slow. Gardeners like Sam Ogden, author of the *Step-by-Step Guide to Organic Vegetable Growing*, have three bins into which they toss their vegetable wastes, but they leave each to ripen for

a year before using the fine black compost that results. A layered heap will decompose more quickly, and you are more likely to have a carbon/nitrogen ratio favorable to quick and efficient decomposition.

Start on bare earth, so that the bacteria can get up in, and the earthworms, too, after the heap has cooled.

Next put down a layer of twigs and small branches, so that the air can circulate and help provide necessary oxygen for the bacteria to oxidize and decompose the materials.

Over this layer put some vegetable matter coarse enough so it won't fall through, and fibrous enough to supply carbonaceous materials. This layer might include hay, straw, coarse weeds, leaves (preferably shredded), farm or stable bedding, vegetable garden residues like bean vines, garbage like pea pods or apple cores.

Next put a layer of manure or other high-nitrogen material such as Milorganite or other activated sludge. Untreated or raw sewage is too dangerous to use because the heat necessary to kill the pathogens or harmful germs may not be reached when your pile gets working

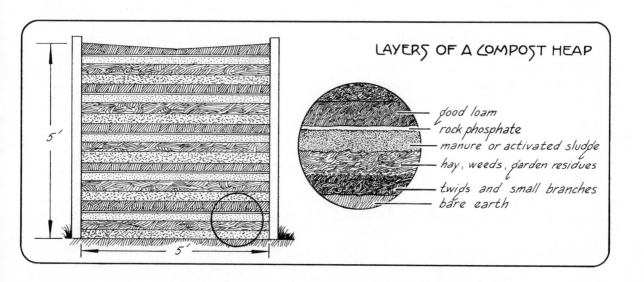

LAYERS OF A COMPOST HEAP

— good loam
— rock phosphate
— manure or activated sludge
— hay, weeds, garden residues
— twigs and small branches
— bare earth

and decomposing, and there may be industrial or pesticide wastes such as DDT or copper, cadmium or zinc in large amounts, and detergents that are not biodegradable.

On the high-nitrogen layer you can sprinkle some rock phosphate and greensand or granite dust, shredded seaweed or other sources of nutrients, and then put on your layer of good loam. With the good loam, if you wish to add an activator, you may do so. The activator may be an herbal or bacterial kind, and those who use them say they help to speed up and modulate the working of the pile. I do not use them because I seem to get plenty of bacterial action from the organisms provided by the air, soil, and materials I put in the heap. My sister-in-law, who lives in a neighborhood where she believes it is better to make her heap only from leaves and weeds, does use it, along with some dried blood or alfalfa meal for extra nitrogen, and she gets excellent results.

Then repeat the layers, until you have a good-sized pile. The best size is considered to be about five feet wide and five feet tall. This is large enough for the center to heat up when the bacteria get going, and small enough to be convenient for turning. Either when finished, or as you go along, sprinkle the materials with water so that the consistency, in general, is like a wrung-out sponge: damp but not wet. Some people also put a pole or so down in the heap which they later pull out, or insert a wire cylinder which they leave, to insure that enough air gets in.

TURNING THE PILE

Your next job is to turn the pile, after it has shrunk to about half size and has begun to warm up in the middle. Put the outer, undecomposed materials into the middle and the inside, warmed-up materials on the outside for the new arrangement. The turning will get more air in; sprinkle if the heap has got dry. You can tell it is too dry if it has turned gray, for that means that fungi are taking over where the bacteria should be working. If it is soggy, limy and smelly, that means the anaerobic bacteria are taking over where the aerobic bacteria should be working. Whenever that begins to happen, turn the heap at once to get air in. A well made, properly aired heap does not smell. And that is why, if you have a box of loam so you can add good earth after each layer of vegetable refuse, or non-fat meat scraps, you can make compost in a milk carton on your kitchen counter, as some people do.

ABOUT THE PATHOGENS (AND PESTS)

A compost pile heats up to somewhere between 140° and 160° or even 170°, though that may be a bit high for some of the beneficial microorganisms. Actually more than just some bacteria do the work, for at certain stages fungi and creatures half way between fungi and bacteria called actinomycetes do some of the work, and the bacteria themselves are divided into those who can stand the heat and those who work when it is cooler. You can read all about them in Clarence G. Golueke's *Composting/A Study of the Process and its Principles*, published by Rodale Press in 1972. This book tells about the pathogens — all put in terms of Centigrade temperatures, but I will put them in Fahrenheit for this book.

When your heap has reached a temperature of 130°, the salmonella germs stop growing, and after it has reached and stayed at 140° for twenty minutes they will die. Even at 130° to 135°, if the heap stays that hot, they will die. One investigator found that no salmonella of four varieties survived after 14 days of composting; and another that these germs were rendered harmless within five or six days.

By the time the heap reaches 150° it will kill typhoid, paratyphoid and dysentery germs.

Anthrax requires three weeks at 140°, and hepatitis much longer. Up here in Vermont we say: leave the pile to work all winter. *Streptococcus pyogenes*, according to Golueke, will die in ten minutes when the heat is 130°. Weed seeds are killed at temperatures between 140° and 150°.

I go into all this to solace some of the people who think they would like to start composting but are still afraid to for one reason or another. Prepared, activated sludge like Milorganite is processed at 200° so there is nothing to fear. A well-aired, well-made home heap can heat up to the safe levels, too, but be sure that all the materials, both outside and inside have a chance to heat up. You want them all to heat up, anyhow, for the heat is the result of the oxidation being carried on by the microorganisms, and it is that oxidation which is transforming the old weeds, residues and manures into the fine, fluffy, soft, rich end-product which is your compost.

Other pests people are afraid of are dogs, cats, raccoons, opossums and perhaps rats. I have never seen a rat on my heap and I know countless people who never have, either. And the same goes for flies. There are two reasons: first, the heat and second, the fact that you cover the materials with soil. We are not always assiduous in doing this, but the fact that we do not put out meat scraps or fat keeps the dogs and cats away who are very bored by items like coffee grounds, orange peel slurry made by putting the pieces of peel through a blender, or the outside leaves of lettuce. The raccoons, I guess, do come. But I'd rather have them eat lettuce out there than corn or my pet plants in the garden.

HOW TO USE COMPOST

Every plant in the flower garden can benefit by applications of compost. In preparing the bed, goodly amounts of even half-completed compost can be dug in to enrich the soil. A handful can be put into any hole you dig for a perennial or annual plant. Flowering shrubs or trees you plant are greatly benefited not only by the good supply of long-lasting nutrients in the compost you add to the big planting hole, but also by the yearly or semi-yearly topdressing you can add.

Topdressing on your flower plants is highly beneficial, and I also like to use a mulch of compost, which look even better than the coarser dark brown mulches because it is so blackish and fine-grained itself. If you want a very showy border for the day of the garden tour or your most special guests, put a few bushels of compost through a screen and spread it around on your gardens. And of course, if you keep using compost and other organic materials in your garden soil for a number of years, all your soil will turn to that wonderful dark, soft consistency which is characteristic of the best compost. It is aesthetically very pleasing as well as thoroughly nutritious for your plants. I find that the really fairly small amount of work involved in running compost heaps is well worth all the effort.

And don't forget that whatever organic mulches you use are also sources of compost because in the bottom layer, where it is in contact with the soil and where it is just moist enough and airy enough, the bacteria will work and keep making a good compost fertilizer that feeds down into the soil and to the roots of your plants. This is one reason why it is better to rake leaves around the base of your shrubs to let them compost there over the winter, and even through the year, than to haul them all away—even if you do shred them to put on a compost heap.

All these kinds of humus and compost are what the organic flower gardener uses to get thriving plants and fine blooms. They feed the soil as no other substances can, as we have learned from experience. But a garden also needs water.

❧WATER❧

It may seem a truism to say a garden needs water, but I have not found many people who think of water as a fertilizer the way I do. As I mentioned when I was describing the soil solution, the hydrogen and hydroxyl ions from the H and OH or H_2O of water are essential to many of the processes providing nutrients to plants. But even more important, perhaps, is the wonderful capacity of water to take certain substances into solution. And water goes into the plant according to at least two systems, so you can say, I think, that the physiology and the very life of the plant depend on what water is and does as it goes into and out of the plant and as it is used in its many processes.

TURGOR PRESSURE

A plant can stay upright, rigid, and well supplied with water all the time by means of the column of water that stretches from the water table below the surface of the earth up through the interstices between soil particles, into the root hairs, up the roots, stalks, stems, into the leaves where it is finally evaporated at the tiny pores on the backs of leaves called stomata. The continual pull of the evaporation and loss of water at the top keeps drawing the water up into the plant from the sources below. Of course, the woody texture and its hard lignin fibers hold up a tree, but herbaceous plants, if they lose turgor pressure, are no longer swollen with water and they wilt, as we know quite well when we neglect our house plants or when we see what happens to shallow-rooted seedlings outdoors on a hot day. And besides, that column of water brings nutrients for use by the plant, making its processes possible. Especially important, of course, is the plant's food-making process, which begins in the green leaf with photosynthesis.

This uptake of water from the soil and

evaporation from the leaf is called transpiration, and it goes on all the time except when a plant is trying to recover from wilt by shutting its pores, and at night and other times when it is dormant or partially so. The evaporation is especially important when it is hot, for the cooling effect of evaporation helps to cool off the plant and keep it from being singed by the sun. In the desert, plants have adapted to the conditions of dryness and transpire relatively little; instead they are protected by very tough cell walls and succulent structures for storing water. So if your yard or patio is dark and dry—or if you have reasons for not watering your plants very much—plan to grow those coming from areas where transpiration is limited.

PHOTOSYNTHESIS

The pores in the leaf are also necessary for admitting air, with its supplies of oxygen and carbon dioxide used by the plant in its main metabolic events. The one that is far and away the most important—and, after all, the most miraculous event in nature—is photosynthesis, the making of living food out of nonliving materials by tiny green structures in the leaf's cells called chloroplasts. There must be the green in these leaf parts, and there must be light for this miracle to happen. Its elegant and simple essence is:

$$6\ CO_2 + 6\ H_2O + 674\ kg\ calories \longrightarrow C_6H_{12}O_6 + 6\ O_2$$

This means that carbon dioxide plus water plus calories of sun energy react to yield sugar and oxygen. Even though this is an oversimplified version, it gives the clue to the basic fact of plant life: that air and water are absolutely necessary, and that with the aid of all the other processes, substances, enzymes and so on that go on in a plant, the plant is somehow enabled to make its own food—and then, of course, to provide the food thereafter for the entire food chain, including ourselves.

The heat comes from the sun, in the form of light, or from some reflection of that heat, or some electrical duplicaton of it in a fluorescent bulb, such as Vitalite, the one I recommend as most near in its wave lengths to sunlight.

OTHER FUNCTIONS OF WATER

Though just about everything you do in your garden for your plants is to aid and promote the process of photosynthesis, you also are promoting some other events and processes, too. As a solution, carrying nutrients, enzymes, sugars, starches and proteins, water is said to translocate, and the translocation may be impelled by various gradients caused by the movement from an area of greater to lesser concentration, or lesser to greater; by osmosis or by other hydrostatic and adsorptive forces. Some water is held chemically in the molecules of carbohydrates and proteins.

Water permeates, suffuses nearly all the phases of a plant. It can even travel up through the nonliving tissues such as heart wood in a shrub or tree and then be moved by living cells nearby to areas where it is used for the plant's needs.

Sap, as we call it, also picks up and transports or translocates nutrients as well as sugars which can move down to points of lower concentrations, even way down in the root or tuber or bulb, where they can be stored for use by the peonies, iris or tulips the following year. When the upper portions of the plant need food, the low concentration there induces the sugars to move from areas of higher concentration (in a source-sink relationship). This is the usual kind of streaming in a plant, and is healthy unless it harbors viruses that also move rapidly from one part of a plant to another and infect it.

PHOSPHATES

When phosphates, for example, go up the xylem or woody cells of the cambium of a stem and then down the phloem, or living cells of that layer, they tend to be present in increased amounts for periods up to two weeks. After that, if there is no increase in supplies, the phosphates are in a decline. Experiments using tracers to follow the movement of phosphates reveal that these nutrients go up the transpiration stream and then travel all around the plant in the phloem. It was once thought that salts went to the xylem, or woody cells in the cambium, because the liquid there is usually acid (and attracts the alkaline salts). At that time studies showed that the contents of a salty sap stream moved around the plant 30 times in an hour in a pattern closely related to the movement of oxygen into the roots at the bottom of the plant and of carbon dioxide out at the top.

It is not yet known, however, how the water and salts entering the plant relate to the oxygen intake and carbon dioxide exit. But it is believed that the movement does occur in relation to the oxygen pressure, and is controlled by the oxygen in the soil which has come from the atmosphere and is subject to atmospheric pressures. The movement is also related to the oxygen dissolved in the soil solution, and to the oxygen in the shoots of the plants. So if you neglect or injure one aspect of these essential and complex movements happening in a plant all the time, you run the risk of affecting all.

TIME OF DAY

The rate of movement of the salts and other nutrients that go up into the plant from the soil solution is evidently governed by the daylight and temperature. A pressure deficit is at work also to make gases (such as carbon dioxide and oxygen) move down from the leaves to lower parts of the plant. These movements, too, are, in general, related to the time of day. It has been found, for example, that a topped palm has the most rapid exudation of its sap in the hours between midnight and dawn, and the least rapid in the hours of the afternoon. The translocation in a case like this involves sugar gradients in the tissues that conduct nutrients up the plant, and then down the phloem cells in a circuit usually governed by processes of osmosis. Some people always pick leafy vegetables in late afternoon to take advantage of the high concentration of food values and nutrients then.

WILTING

If there is plenty of water, the movement of nutrients in the plant is rapid and effective. When it is dry, however, more and more energy is needed to absorb the solutes and to make the systems work. If there is not enough, the plants wilt. And, as we know, that is a condition we hope will never happen to our plants. If it does happen, bubbles may get in and ruin the tissues which should always be damp. This is ruinous, even though the flow of the sap solution can be reestablished when the wilt is not too bad, because a damage to the cells has occurred. The danger of wilt is the main reason I have brought up all this subject of transpiration and translocation in plants, to show that the vital processes and life-support systems in the plants in your flower garden or in your patio will go back to your care in seeing that they are well watered. That water, from the moment its molecules are attracted to the clay surfaces in the soil to the moment it leaves the pores of the leaf in steam form as evaporation, is the life blood, as it were, of your plants. And to go back to my original point: it is like a fertilizer because it is water which provides so many of the essentials in one way or another which make a plant healthy and fertile. (But naturally you do not overdo it, for roots must have oxygen, too, and a plant not

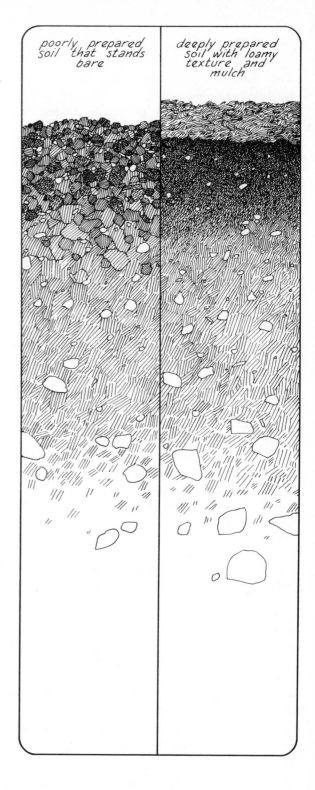

poorly prepared soil that stands bare

deeply prepared soil with loamy texture and mulch

adapted to swamp life cannot endure with its roots in a puddle for too long a time. Amateurs are warned in many connections not to give a lot of a good thing in the false idea that because a little is good, a lot must be a lot better. Explanations like these that tell you what you make happen when you do certain things will, I hope, help you to refrain from overdoing. Or underdoing, either.)

ONE MORE WARNING

A deeply prepared soil, with a loam texture, is a better protection against water deficiency than any other kind. In finely textured clay soil the water is released more slowly than in coarse sandy soils, so though the loss is not so immediately dangerous in times of drought, the supply to relieve your plants is not so rapid as in a sandy soil where the pores are larger and the flow easier. What's more, in a deeply prepared soil, the roots can get down to the lower areas where the supply may be better and compensate for the narrow range of water available during times of stress in the supper soil. And a mulched soil helps to control evaporation.

DUST MULCH

There is, however, the phenomenon of the dust mulch, so-called, when a dry dusty surface acts as a retardant to further loss of water from the soil. This is because there is a double flow of water towards the surface and away from the surface linked to the heating up and cooling off of the soil at different times of day. When water retreats from the soil surface after a period of rapid drying, the total evaporation rate drops—even for a period of days—and water loss is less than under other conditions. It is partly because the length of the column of water from lower and lower supplies keeps increasing that evaporation decreases. In warm weather, as we

often can see, after a rain the surface of the soil dries off very quickly. After this has happened off and on all summer, the net heat loss from the soil is considerable. The upward movement of heat makes the surface very pleasant and crumbly and accounts for the fact that soil is much easier and attractive to work in in the autumn months than in spring when it is cold and wet and very easy to damage by compaction.

❧ FLOWERING AND HOW IT HAPPENS ❧

The final aim of the plant is to make flowers—or rather, seeds—or rather, the embryos in the seeds. Egyptologists say that one reason the peoples of the East made the lotus their sacred flower was that they could see in its embryo a tiny perfectly formed adult flower and that they thereby recognized it as a sign of immortality.

A flower itself is spectacular and attractive to bees and butterflies and all pollinators needed to fertilize the seed and quicken the embryo. Usually the flower has both male and female parts, but there are some with male flowers on one part of the plant and female on another or even on two separate plants. The female part, the pistil, has atop its stem or style a sort of receiving platform called the stigma which is sticky or fuzzy or otherwise usefully coated for catching the male pollen, especially on flowers that are pollinated by the wind. The base of the pistil is a more or less swollen part, the ovary, and in it are the ovule and the egg, or eggs. These cells receive the male cell from the pollen made in the male stamens, which are simpler structures consisting of a filament or stem topped with the anther, the often very beautiful little structure, colored orange or sometimes red, which produces the pollen grains.

It is those pollen grains which are blown by the wind or picked up by birds, wasps, flies, or

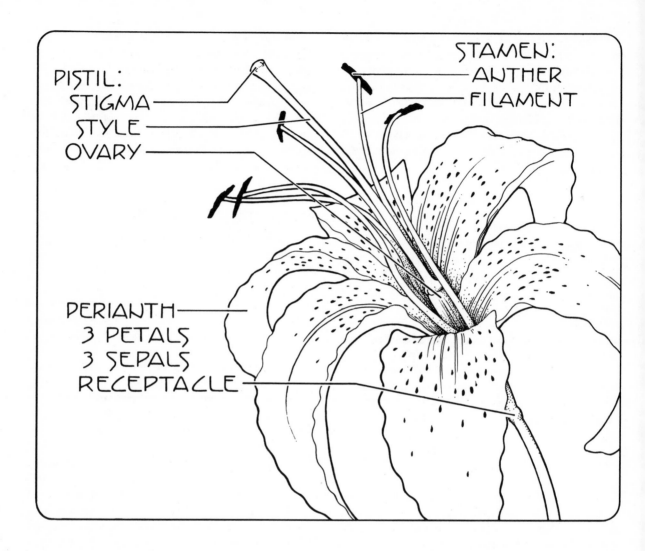

PISTIL:
STIGMA
STYLE
OVARY

STAMEN:
ANTHER
FILAMENT

PERIANTH
3 PETALS
3 SEPALS
RECEPTACLE

other insects as well as the bees and butterflies, as they move from flower to flower and then deposited on the stigmas where the pollen tube begins to grow down so it can put the fertilizing male cell by the receptive female cell. (In gardens drenched with pesticides, of course, there are few if any insects, no pollination, no natural fertilization and then no seeds. I've seen a film of such a condition in a Japanese orchard where every single flower had to be pollinated by hand by conscripted army men.) Luckily there are two sperm cells which come down the pollen tube. One unites with an egg and thus begins the new seed's embryo; the other unites with a structure that begins the growth of the part of the seed where food is stored. Flowering plants are the only ones that have this strange and efficient double-fertilization.

So when you garden for good flowers, you are taking care of the reproductive system which flowers essentially are. The petals and sepals are attractive and protective parts of the flower, and when we say blossom, we usually are referring particularly to the petals. For they are the bright, colorful parts of the flower, spectacular enough to attract the bees or others needed for the fertilization process. And of course the nectar of a flower is the deep attraction, useful to the bees and others. This makes the whole transaction wonderfully symbiotic, where each serves the other organism in a vital way.

Therefore, in gardening with flowers, you are entering into and facilitating the harmonious interdependencies—here on the minute scale of seed fertilization as well on the larger scale of making all parts of your garden harmoniously interdependent and ecologically lively and healthy.

3

Gardening Techniques

Though many plants will grow no matter what you do to them, there are plenty of techniques to learn which will make your part in the process simpler or more effective and less conducive to failures and disappointments. A garden that is well placed and well planned already has a good head start, but if your site and situation are not ideal, there are tricks to use which will greatly compensate for things your garden may lack. Other techniques are just standard practices to keep your plants in fine condition.

A good set of tools is a first need—a good shovel, spading fork, trowels, cultivators and a tiller of some sort if your place is large enough to warrant it. I even like an old kitchen knife to dig out weeds. For a hose, you need a soaking hose for long watering, which is much the best way, and if you want a sprinkler, do not get a rotating one which stirs up a flower garden too much. A wheelbarrow is needed for mixing potting and garden soil, and for bringing compost and other fertilizers and mulches that you will be using. Pruning sheers and clippers are essentials, and probably stakes, rakes and perhaps a fork to pitch and spread mulching hay. If you have moles, get some small windmills called Klippety Klops. For red squirrels you may

need a Hav-a-hart trap. I scare raccoons with a transistor radio, but I am not going to recommend that as a garden tool. Consult your garden center for any of these and for gloves, flats, containers, window boxes and all such conveniences you may want to have, too.

♞ PLANTING TECHNIQUES ♞

Last year I was at a garden club meeting when two women were discussing what should be done to arrange for the two katsura trees we were giving the town for a bicentennial gift. When the question of the actual planting came up, one woman said: "We must have a $50 hole for each of the trees."

It seemed as though everyone in the room knew that the speaker was quoting Amos Pettingill of the White Flower Farm in Litchfield, Connecticut. In his enchanting and helpful catalogues and in his even more helpful book called *The White-Flower-Farm Garden Book* (see Appendix), Pettingill starts right out advising: "Put a $1 plant in a $5 hole, so that the plant's roots can be properly spread, not jammed down *en masse* in a little one." Obviously, by extension, a $10 sapling gets a $50 hole. Actually the katsura trees were a good deal bigger than that, so they warranted a hole of several hundred dollars' proportions.

The whole point is that there is no sense and no excuse for putting a good plant into a hole that is inadequately prepared, too small, undernourished, or carelessly dug. It is possible to dig the hole at the last minute, but much better is to prepare it beforehand and give the fresh, enriched soil mixture a chance to mellow.

When planting a tree or shrub, make sure the hole you dig is big enough for the roots to spread out freely. When the tree is in place, fill the hole half full, tamp down down firmly and then water well. Fill the remainder of the hole, leaving a slight basin to catch water, and mulch. Prune back the top growth so that it balances the root growth.

PREPARING THE HOLE

The hole you dig should be deep enough and wide enough to give all the roots plenty of leeway to spread out quickly into the new soil you prepare. Put the topsoil on one side when you dig, and the subsoil on the other, so that when you return the soil you can fill in around the roots with the topsoil. Do not add chemical fertilizer or potent fresh manure or other high-nitrogen materials like blood meal to the topsoil, but it is quite all right to add some bone meal, compost or mild organic fertilizers like Milorganite thoroughly mixed into the topsoil you put into the bottom of the hole.

HOW TO PLANT

The first rule about planting is that if the tree, shrub or perennial comes bare-rooted, it must never be allowed to have its roots dried out. Keep them wrapped in wet sphagnum moss, or set in a pail of water, or even in mud. Most trees and shrubs can be set at a level slightly deeper than they grew at the nursery, and you can always tell because the soil line shows very clearly on the main stem. Spread the roots evenly and as much as possible for maximum soil contact. See that they do not twist over and around each other in a way that might cause future girdling or strangulation. Fill up the hole half way with topsoil, and tamp it down well. This soil must not be soaking wet, and if the roots have been in mud, it is well to rinse them off before planting. But it is the soil itself which should not be wet because when you tamp it down so that each rootlet is in contact with soil particles (and not just air pockets), you must not tamp on muddy soil which would then compact and you'd have no air pockets at all. (See previous chapter for explanation.) Tamp with your fingers first, then with your foot.

When the hole is half full and firmly tamped,

you can water. A good slow soaking is the best method. Then add the subsoil to the top of the hole and leave a slight basin to catch rain water in the future. The subsoil may be watered again, but it is not necessary to tamp this, and certainly do not do it after watering.

PRECAUTIONS

Each newly planted shrub or tree should be pruned. Cut back enough so that the top growth balances the root growth, and this may mean the removal of half or up to half of the top branches, but preferably not the leader; and a third to a half of several lower branches. (See later section on pruning.) Do not just plant the tree or shrub and forget it; water it well with a slow soak about once a week for the first summer. Both for summer sun which can scald young exposed tissues, and for protection against rabbits and such beasts who will want to eat the bark, wrap the trunk of your new small trees either in burlap or in one of the new wrapping materials available at nurseries. Add a mulch. Stones, pebbles, or organic mulches are possibilities, but keep track of any new residents like mice who might wish to move in under the mulch. In case they do, remove it. Maybe the safest from the start is to choose stone or a pebble mulch.

PLANTING PERENNIALS

The $5 hole for perennials is indeed a good rule of thumb. But as is explained later, in the chapter on perennials, it is often best to prepare a whole new bed, either for newly grown plants or for those you have recently dug up and divided. Certain plants are quite fussy about the depth at which they are planted, because their roots or tubers or rhizomes have special requirements. Peonies, for instance, should be put in with their eyes at an inch and a half below the ground level, and should definitely be mulched the first winter while they are still settling in. You can use hay or some loose material like that, including the loose evergreen boughs which also make such an attractive covering for your plants. Put the mulch material on after the ground has frozen well.

Iris also are fussy. Their rhizomes, which are really stems, should be half above ground, more or less horizontally placed, and firmed in so that the roots which grow down from the rhizomes will be well placed in the earth. Iris are quite tough and survive a careless treatment as long as they are well drained.

⚜IMPROVING DRAINAGE⚜

The best place to have your flower garden, and absolutely the best place to have your iris bed, is on a slope, preferably to the southeast (which I am lucky enough to have). This southeast slope is the best, I believe, because the drainage is in the direction where the morning sun shines on the soil and helps to dry it out. This slope is also protected from the hotter afternoon sun which can dry out the soil too fast and cause wilt in dry spells. (In our climate the wind is from the west and northwest, so that slope also means that the plants are protected from winds, and the wind-break plants cast shadows at the right time of day.)

If you can't arrange for this sort of slope, there is the possibility of drainage tiles put in under your garden, at considerable trouble and expense. A simpler, and often equally effective procedure is to put stones and cinders in the bottom of the hole you dig or the bed you prepare for your plants.

The drain tile, if you do have to resort to that, should be jointed, with tar paper or other suitable material over the joints to prevent entry of soil when the water goes in, and stones and pebbles as well at the open upper end to keep soil out. If you live in a frosty area, put it down three or four feet, and slope it at a rate of about four or five inches per 100 feet and without any dips where silt could collect. There must, of course, be a way to carry off the water at the bottom. And the drain tile must never be put where there are willow, poplar or elm roots because they will invade it. A plastic agricultural tile, which is perforated, is obtainable in all supply stores.

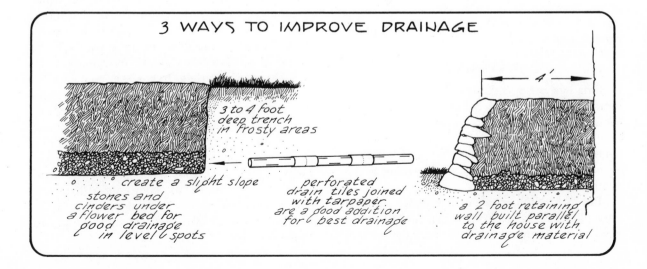

3 WAYS TO IMPROVE DRAINAGE

3 to 4 foot deep trench in frosty areas

create a slight slope

stones and cinders under a flower bed for good drainage in level spots

perforated drain tiles joined with tarpaper are a good addition for best drainage

4'

a 2 foot retaining wall built parallel to the house with drainage material

Another way to achieve good drainage is to make raised beds, and these can be very attractive and useful. A good place to put such a bed is in front of the south or southeast wall of your house. Start with a two or three-foot retaining wall, built parallel to the house, about four feet from it, but do not put in a concrete or other impenetrable bottom, for not only would that defeat the drainage improvement, but also would break the contact between existing soil microorganisms and the new soil you will put in the bed. Cinders can go in the bottom of the new bed, but remember that if you want earthworms to come and go in your garden—as most organic gardeners do—cinders hurt the tender skins of earthworms, and they may stay away. On hot days, excessive evaporation is prevented if there is always a supply of water coming into the bed from below by the capillary action of water drawn up into the topsoil because of the loss through daily evaporation from the surface and the pull on the water column which this causes. A concrete bottom would break that pull.

You have a wide choice of plants to use in raised beds—from dwarf evergreens, small shrubs, bulbs to perennials and annuals. Since the house will provide part shade for the bed, plants that survive in six hours of sunlight per day will do very well. (See chapter on perennials for suggestions.)

WATERING

Small, short sprinklings of plants often do more harm than good because you entice the roots to come to the surface to get the water, and then when the soil dries out again they are stranded there near the hot surface and suffer, or even die. Therefore, a long slow soaking is the proper way to water.

But WARNING: do not overwater some of your plants while watering others which are in need. One example of this situation is the lawn of shallow-rooted grass, watered daily and for rather long periods to keep it green, but so much that specimen trees and bushes in the lawn are oversoaked, and often ruined.

A sprinkler is sometimes the worst way to get the water to your plants. It wets the foliage and in some climates (or at some times of day) it just encourages fungus attack and other troubles. Far better to sink lengths of four-inch drainage tile in at right angles to the soil surface, with the top of the tile level with the surface, and to fill the tile periodically. The water will seep out of this tile (as it seeps in when laid nearly horizontally for drainage purpose). All sorts of substitute funnels have been invented, from plastic bottles to milk cartons. This sort of arrangement is very handy to use when applying compost tea or manure tea to the vicinity of your plants down near the roots.

FERTILIZING

Such teas, made by soaking the compost or manure (dried or raw) in water, combine the two most important additions to your garden: water and fertilizer. Organic gardeners prefer the slow-release, long-lasting fertilizers which are the organic ones as well as the finely ground mineral rocks such as the phosphate and potash rock. The warnings given to those who still use chemical fertilizers are worth everyone's hearing. Do not allow them to come in contact with seeds or with roots. That's the advice given, and it is followed by the advice to put the fertilizer three or four inches away. Though I have grown plants in pure compost—and weeds happily grown by themselves, right on the compost heap—I still think that there is one very good reason for digging in your compost fertilizer at a certain distance from the existing plant. It makes the roots grow and stretch for the goodness, and that strengthens the plant.

I am also a great believer in bone meal. As with blood meal and other organic protein fertilizers, the soil should be warm enough when these are used so that the bacteria which reduce them to usable nitrates are active and not dormant. The quickest bacterial action will take place when the soil is also moist (not soggy) and acid or alkaline enough to suit the bacteria (pH 6.5 to 7.5). The finely ground bone meal is quite quickly available, and if you want a long-term benefit, mix in some more which is coarsely ground, also, so that the release of the nutrients will be slower. Bone meal provides (or used to provide before they souped up their processes of preparation) 4 per cent nitrogen, 21 per cent phosphorus or 30 per cent if steamed, and 1/5 of 1 per cent of potash. The whopping big supply of phosphorus helps to counteract any such adverse or inadvertent lacks as might occur from inadequate humus, acidity, or a clayey soil which locks it up. Your plants might also need phosphorus if there has been too much fresh organic material in the soil causing a shortage of nitrogen and some stunting. I find that bone meal is especially valuable to use when planting bulbs.

In preparing the ground for bulbs it is also a good idea to dig in some peat moss. You can use as much as a bushel for each 50 square feet. Peat moss, though not really fertile, is also good in the soil you use for primroses, and since we plant these flowers on the border of the beds where we have bulbs growing, it serves double purpose. With the soil under the primroses my husband or I sometimes add some dried cow manure. In the spring we avoid fertilizing bulbs, especially with nitrogenous materials because there is no sense in pushing bulbs to make a lot of early growth. After blooming, and on into the fall, it is all right to water the area where tulips and other bulbs grow with manure or compost tea. Some more bone meal at this time does no harm.

RAW VS. MELLOWED ORGANIC MATERIALS

There has been more emphasis on mellowed, well-rotted or dried materials that are used for organic fertilizers than on raw. Both are very good sources of nutrients and soil-conditioners for your flowers, but the mellowed ones are safer. Raw, high-nitrogen materials can injure your plants, but if well incorporated into the soil several weeks before planting, they benefit the soil greatly and will help your plants. Fresh manure, green plants and such things as fish scraps should all be dug in well before planting, especially when the bacteria population is low—either from cold or from previous chemical treatments of soil.

And take heart. Though you can make dire mistakes if you use the wrong amounts of chemical fertilizers, it is almost impossible to use the wrong amounts of organic ones. A little more or less (or even a lot) will not ruin your garden. About the worst that can happen is a stunting of the plants that try to survive on a wad of heavy wet leaves which did not decompose. And almost every gardener will see to it that such a wad gets broken up and worked into the soil before putting little plants or flower seeds in it.

❧PLANTING SEEDS❧

Almost any plant that produces seeds can be grown from seed, even though the requirements for some of them, a few of them, are extraordinary. Germination time of two years is required for certain tree seeds; long cold spells necessary for a dormancy that has to precede germination for some seeds can cause failure if omitted; a few seeds, such as maple seeds for instance, must never be allowed to get dry or they won't be viable; and a few must have light to germinate. In general, however, good soil,

GERMINATION AND RECOMMENDED
SPACING (AT MATURITY) FOR SOME
PERENNIALS AND BIENNIALS

Name	Germination Time (in days)	Spacing Needed (in inches)	Name	Germination Time (in days)	Spacing Needed (in inches)
Alyssum [*Alyssum saxatile*]	21 to 28	24	Gayfeather [*Liatris pycnostachya*]	20	18
Alkanet [*Anchusa italica*]	21 to 28	24	Hibiscus [*H. moscheutos*]	15	18
Anemone [*A. pulsatilla*]	4	35 to 42	Hollyhock [*Althea rosea*]	10	20 to 24
Aster [*A. alpinus*]	14	36	Lupine [*L. polyphyllus*]	20	30 to 35
Avens [*Geum chiloense*]	25	18	Money plant [*Lunaria annua*]	10	24
Bachelor's buttons [*Centaurea montana*]	21 to 28	12	Penstemon [*P. murrayanus grandiflorus*]	10	18
Bellflower [*Campanula lactiflora*]	20	15	Phlox [*P. paniculata*]	25	24
Carnation [*Dianthus caryophyllus*	20	12	Poppy, Iceland [*Papaver nudicaule*	10	24
Columbine [*Aquilegia hybrida*]	30	12 to 18	Primrose [*Primula polyantha*]	25 to 35	12
Coral bells [*Heuchera sanguinea*]	10	18	Sea Lavender [*Limonium latifolia*]	15	30
Coreopsis [*C. grandiflora*]	5	30	Sweet pea, perennial [*Lathyrus latifolius*]	20	24
Daylily [*Hemerocallis*]	15	25 to 30	Sweet William [*Dianthus barbatus*]	5	12
Delphinium [*D. elatum*]	20	24	Veronica, or speedwell [*V. spicata*]	12	18
Foxglove [*Digitalis purpurea*]	20	12	Viola [*V. cornuta*]	10	12

*Petunia Grandiflora 'Malibu,'
Petunia Multiflora 'Coral Satin,'
Ageratum 'Blue Ball,' Zinnia
'Peter Pan Pink' and Zinnia
'Persian Carpet' in shades of
yellow and gold*

Example Impatiens 'Imp' series

Longwood Gardens

Scilla siberica

An exceptional border for simultaneous bloom peaks of different flowers. From background to foreground: Cynoglossum, Red Multiflora Petunia 'Comanche,' Lily, Yellow Calendula 'Kablouna,' Violet grandiflora, Petunia 'Malibu,' edged with red and white bicolor grandiflora Petunia 'Fiesta,' semi-dwarf bedding Zinnia 'Peter Pan Pink,' Marigold 'Double Dwarf French Petite'

enough warmth, some moisture, and a careful patting of the soil around the seeds will mean that they will come up and start new plants for you. As soon as they are up, they have to be protected from the fungus disease, "damping off," especially if grown indoors or in a greenhouse. And though it is moisture which causes this fungus to thrive, plus lack of air circulation, the young plant must never be allowed to dry out. There is an interdependence of closely placed young plants, perhaps through a sharing of water and perhaps through mutual benefits from root exudates, so avoid isolating them. Nevertheless they must not be crowded for long. If the soil is very loose and partially dry, it is possible to pull up the weaker plants in a row or in a flat or peat pot. But my advice is: don't do it. It is better to take a small pair of sharp scissors and snip off the weak and crowding plant at soil level. The remaining little plants will stay strong and grow stronger, especially if they continue their interdependence. Most seed packets tell you what distances you should thin your plants. At first the distance always seems too great. When faced with two- or three-inch plants, it seems almost wasteful to thin them to eight inches apart. But do what the packet says. They will need that space when they mature; and the resources of soil nutrients available to the young plants in an uncrowded space mean that they will grow all that much better.

PLANTING SEEDS INDOORS

There are two absolute necessities for growing good little plants indoors to set out in your garden later—or perhaps route through a cold frame first and then set our in the garden. The first is to get good seeds from a good reliable seedsman (or use the very best of your own home-grown seeds). The second is to have a set-up which will provide the right warmth, moisture, air and light for little plants.

Most of the seeds you will grow for garden flowers or other ornamentals will be more or less fresh seeds, but the point is for them to be viable, or capable of germinating. Some you gather yourself you can keep for several years. The seeds of asters will keep a year or up to 13 years, depending on the variety. Bee balm seeds will remain viable for four to seven years; nasturtiums for five to eight years. If you save the seeds of azaleas, birches, deutzia, hydrangeas, mock orange, potentillas and rhododendrons, for example, you do not need to put them through a cold period, but other plants do need a cold dormancy: maple seeds should get three months of cold, either outdoors or in the refrigerator; barberry seeds need two or three months, bittersweet seeds need three months, as do flowering dogwood, ash, beech, sweetgum, tupelo and most of the members of the *Prunas* group, including cherries. Pine seeds need two months; spruce one to three months and apples one to three months, also. As you undoubtedly have heard, the seeds of hybrid plants do not come true, which means they will not be like the parent from which they were gathered. It is fun, though, with azaleas, for instance, to plant the seed anyway and see what fascinating colors result.

WHERE TO PLANT AND HOW

Almost any container will do if you provide for some drainage and adjust the size to the size of your growing plants, once they are up. The seeds themselves can be planted in a wooden or styrofoam flat, old milk cartons, margarine boxes, plastic or styrofoam cups or old pie tins. Poke holes in the bottom, and use bits of crock or pebbles in the bottom to provide drainage. I find that a little peat moss or sphagnum moss in the bottom is good both for drainage and a back-up supply of moisture if the soil in the container gets dry. Other people use a layer of vermiculite, or even perlite. Since seeds prefer a warm place to germinate—usually between 60° and 80°F., arrange to start them on a small pile of newspapers on a radiator (or on the furnace), over a heating coil buried in the planting soil or even over a heating pad, as a friend of mine does. The heating coil I use buried in styrofoam flats is the kind obtainable from electrical supply companies and nurserymen. When putting it in, be sure that the wires never criss cross. That would be dangerous. The flats I have used have little buttons around which you can loop the wires and keep them apart. Leave the heat on all the time the germination is taking place. Then turn it off at night, for most plants prefer a cooler night temperature than daytime temperature.

It is wise to arrange a glass or clear plastic cover of some sort over the flat once the seeds are in so that you can hold in the moisture and keep the seeds from drying out when they are germinating. If it gets too hot, or if you see the beginnings of the damping-off fungus, set up a fan to cool the area. If you believe it is too moist, use a hair dryer.

The soil mixture should be rich and porous, with enough water-holding material to make a pleasantly moist environment for your seeds and young plants.

One of the most famous mixtures in the world—at least in the English-speaking world, is the John Innes potting mixture. It consists of:

    7 parts good garden loam
    3 parts mellow, ripe compost
    2 parts washed, coarse sand
    1 part leaf mold

The leaf mold and compost help to maintain moisture, and the sand helps to assure pretty good drainage. If the garden loam is not already rich and fine, add a handful of bone meal per bushel.

The depth for planting seeds is just about the width of the seed you are planting. For tiny, tiny seeds, however, all you have to do is sprinkle them on the soil surface, and then press them in. In fact, press in all seeds you plant to make sure that when they begin to grow, they will be in contact with some soil, both for water supply and for nutrients.

Once the seeds are up, see that the little plants are well anchored and well surrounded by soil, not too wet, and not badly crowded. Many people remove the glass or plastic at this time, but you can leave it on a bit longer if you will watch what is happening and snatch it off as soon as trouble seems likely.

TRANSPLANTING

The seeds you start should have been put in the soil not more that eight weeks before the average date of the last killing frost in your area because you don't want the plants to grow tall and spindly before you harden them off to plant outdoors. It is a good idea to transplant them at least once during that period because the process of recovery after transplanting tends to make the young plants stocky and sturdy. A good potting mixture to use for the first transplanting is:

    3 parts loam
    3 parts peat
    2 parts washed sand
    2 parts ripe compost

This mixture will benefit by the addition of a cupful of hoof and horn meal (as recommended by John Innes) or of alfalfa or cottonseed meal if you can't find the hoof and horn meal. All of these are pretty expensive though.

If you suspect that your garden loam has such pests in it as chrysanthemum eelworms, phlox stem eelworms or strawberry mites, you can pasteurize the loam by heating it to 110°F. for 20 minutes. This amount of heat and time is not likely to destroy beneficial bacteria, but remember to cool it off, for many seeds would also be killed at such temperatures as 110° or 115°F.

I have often left potting soil in the oven for longer periods than 20 minutes. I have also planted seeds without pasteurizing the soil at all, and have often had a threat of damping-off and occasionally a real dose of it on my tiny seedlings. When this happens, pick off the fungus you see and dry off the plants at once. Another precaution, mentioned elsewhere, is to sprinkle the top of the flat with fine sand or sterile vermiculite.

Many people now use peat pots for growing seedlings, and even those little pellets which swell up and look like chocolate cupcakes when you put them in water. These pellets, as well as the prepared soil which comes with some of the peat pots when you order them from a nurseryman, usually have some fertilizer in them. I doubt whether it is very often likely to be organic fertilizer. But if you do use prepared pellets, remember two things: the practically pure peat moss is quick to dry out; and it is also just about 100 per cent nutritionless when the first fertilizer is used up. One of my young gardening friends complains that she cannot get good results with these pellets. She may not have added compost tea or a solution of fish emulsion, as she should, or she may not have soaked the cup cake pot or cut through the netting before she put the plant and pot in the earth.

Both the soaking and some degree of breaking up should be done for peat pots as well. When you transfer plants grown in peat pots either to the cold frame or to the garden, the pot must be soaking wet, and you should cut off any rim, and at least crunch the pot in your hands to break the pot, or cut down through it. I know that the ads show the roots happily pushing through the peat, but experience teaches otherwise. If by chance the pot and the soil should dry out, roots will find it impossible to grow through the hardened peat. And there is one more caution: be sure that no part of the peat pot protrudes above the soil line when you

Small clay pots are ideal for starting young plants. They provide good drainage & air circulation, both through the bottom hole and the porous sides. In especially dry environments you can keep the moisture around seedlings high by sinking the pots in a flat filled with peat or sphagnum moss.

plant it. If you do not cut off the rim, or if you let any of the peat stay above ground, it will just act as a wick and dry right out. Then any little roots which touch the peat of the pot will be ruined.

In spite of all these new-fangled ideas and the convenience they bring to gardeners, there is still nothing quite like a good old-fashioned clay flower pot. Its porous sides let out excess moisture, and let in air. And this implies that it almost has a way of breathing as good soil does. If you are going to raise young plants in the dry atmosphere of a house or apartment, however, you can always bury your pots in a flat of damp peat moss or damp sphagnum moss to arrest drying out. (Or you can do this if you are going away for the weekend, along with wrapping the whole pot or flat in a sheet of plastic. I save old cleaners' bags for such purposes.)

LIGHTS

Since plants want to grow to the light, the safest way to grow them and keep them short and strong is to put them under artificial light, right near to the top of the plant. I believe in using Vita-lites, the fluorescent tube lights which have all necessary wave lengths, including the near ultra-violet which plants and all living things need, according to Dr. John Ott, author of *Health and Light.* (See Bibliography.) If you cannot get hold of this kind of light (and try Burpee Seed Co. before you give up), use both white tubes and incandescent bulbs, or the lights with names like Gro-lite plus incandescent bulbs or other boosters. (For details on indoor lights see the book by Raymond Poincelot or one of the others mentioned in the Bibliography.) The point is to give the plants both the kind of light and the intensity needed for good growth, even if you have to rig up four tubes. Always use at least two.

Of course, if you have a greenhouse, all these cautions are not necessary, for you will give your plants the benefit of overhead sunlight. And if you have wide enough south window sills, you can, as generations of indoor gardeners have, raise plants on the window sill. The caution to pay attention to is the one which warns you to see to it that your young plants never get too hot. Give them some cooling air—as long as it is not from a direct draft.

COLD FRAMES

Anyone planning to grow a number of perennials from seeds or to take cuttings to propagate shrubs and trees, would do best to have one or more cold frames. You can care for young plants very well in cold frames, and perennial plants, which improve by being under care for a whole year before being put out in the garden, are especially benefited.

Build them so they face south, with protection on the north, and on the windy side, but not under dripping eaves. Be sure to give them good drainage. You can buy metal-framed, plastic cold frames, but you can also build them yourself with wood and glass. Make the wooden frame no more than six feet wide and 12 feet long, to facilitate working in the cold frame, ventilating it, and controlling any pests

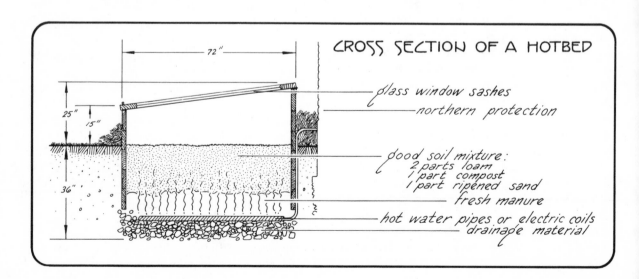

CROSS SECTION OF A HOTBED

72"

25"
15"
36"

glass window sashes
northern protection

good soil mixture:
2 parts loam
1 part compost
1 part ripened sand
fresh manure
hot water pipes or electric coils
drainage material

which might get in. Since the glass top should be on a slant, it is customary to build the back about 25 inches high and the front about 15 inches. Buy windows for the top—two will do it.

Put some drainage material in the bottom, and fill with a good soil mixture. If you wish to use this frame for a hot bed as well, you can either dig a two- or three-foot pit and lay electric heating coils across it, or some hot water pipes if you build up against a house wall, or put in a good thick layer of fresh manure the way everyone used to do before the days of electricity. Even with coils, it helps to put some manure on next, then a soil mixture. For a frame a good proportion is:

> 2 parts loam
> 1 part compost (or peat and leaf mold)
> 1 part sand, ripened in compost heap for a
>   month by leaving a box of sand buried in
>   the pile for that length of time

Protect your plants by lifting the window sashes whenever the temperature nears the 80°F. mark. Actually, if you never do use the frame for a hot bed, only as a cold frame, then you can make the frame longer. But you will still need to air it

carefully. And remember, when you water any little plants in the hot bed or cold frame to use water which is just about the temperature of the air inside. Small plants do not like to be assaulted by a blast of cold water any more than they like a blast of cold air.

With a cold frame you can start perennial seeds during any of several months of the year. You can seed them directly into the frame, and let them grow in that protected place, even over the winter, until it is time to set them out where you want them in the permanent garden.

TRANSPLANTING TO THE GARDEN

The two main rules for transplanting are: first, to see that the ground is well prepared, with richness down where the roots will grow; and second, to reduce shock for the plant as much as you can. When removing young plants from a flat, cut down through the soil between the plants, and move the whole block to the new, richly prepared garden area and to a hole of the correct size. If you use pots—either clay or fiber—turn the pot upside down and tap the edge on something to loosen the root ball. With

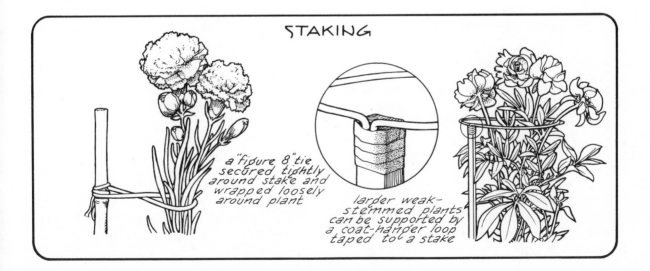

STAKING

a "figure 8" tie secured tightly around stake and wrapped loosely around plant

larger weak-stemmed plants can be supported by a coat-hanger loop taped to a stake

peat pots, as already suggested, wet them, squeeze them and bury the whole pot. One way to make that easier is to cut off the rim that sticks up above the soil line inside the pot. And don't forget to soak the pot before putting it into the ground. There is really no reason why you would ever be putting in bare-root home-grown perennials, but sometimes plants come from the nursery with just wet sphagnum moss around their roots, and of course shrubs and trees that come from long distances are likely to come bare rooted. Plant as soon as possible, never let the roots get dry, and spread the roots over the soft earth in the hole so they can stretch out for nourishment quickly and efficiently. Water the plants when the hole is half full, preferably with a solution of compost tea, manure tea, or fish emulsion if no opossums are around to dig it up. Unless you are putting in a plant that will grow to be a big, spectacular specimen, put perennials in clumps for best display. The clumps may be in groups of six or eight or ten, depending on the size and the tendency of the plant to self-seed or not.

PLANTING FLOWER SEEDS OUTDOORS

Both annual and perennial seeds planted outdoors have certain difficulties to overcome. You plant, in all cool climates, in a season when the weather can get hot very quickly, and then the soil can dry out, or cake, and make it difficult for the little plant to get started. Or, even worse, the plant will have got started all right, but then the sun will hit the shallow roots and tiny shoot and it will die of heat and thirst.

To avoid caking, you can fill the furrow you make for the seeds with vermiculite. Half an inch is plenty, and sprinkle it well before you add the seeds. After covering the seeds to depth appropriate for their size, sprinkle again very thoroughly with a fine mist spray. The vermiculite will hold up to ten times its weight in water, so with this method you not only prevent

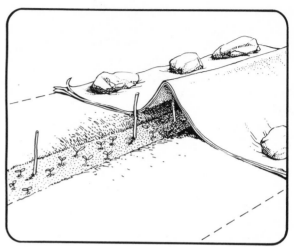

A newspaper tent, as shown here, protects tender young seedlings from the hot, drying rays of the sun.

caking, you also provide a buffer zone to slow down rapid evaporation.

In case more buffering is needed, cover the row with sheets of newspaper or plastic, propped up to an inch or so above the surface so that it won't flap against the seedlings when they come up. The covering can be removed when you see that the plants are up and safe. And as soon as you see the first two true leaves, thin them as recommended. One advantage of the vermiculite is that if you want to transplant the small plants at this point, they come up easily, with little damage to the roots.

❧MULCHING❧

When your new plants are all set in their new place, it is time to think about mulching, for you want to retard water loss, prevent the soil from baking and cracking if your organic matter is low enough to cause that, prevent soil splash on your good plants, and, of course, hold down the weeds. If the soil happens to be either very wet or very dry, hold off for a while until it is of a soft, damp consistency, and wet down any very dry absorbent mulches you may select, such as peat moss. This is a good mulch, frequently used, but it is nutritionless and if it does dry out, it acts as a wick the way a peat pot does, and is a robber of moisture from the soil when it should be protecting the soil and holding in the moisture. Attractive mulches for the summer like cocoa hulls are retentive of moisture, too, and of an equally good color. A good rose mulch for summer is ground corncobs, helping to hold down the disease of black spot. Hay mulches, including alfalfa mulch are not so pretty in the garden, but any legume mulch is a good source of nitrogen, and is well liked by organic gardeners. I like pine needles for a mulch, and am not intimidated by talk about their making the soil acid. If you add some soybean or alfalfa meal, your soil will stay in good shape.

I also believe in a stone mulch, and find that stones put down with some thought as to the design—whether for stepping stones, a pavement area or a pattern edging or encircling —make a very handsome mulch. If you have a plant with a tendency to spread, you can use stone around it (or even shingles) to control its growth, and at the same time control the weeds which may try to invade its area.

Finely shredded mulch—even leaves, grass clippings or finely ground up bark—can be put down in a thin layer around little plants. As they mature, you can keep adding. For larger plants you can put on a thick layer of mulch, and if you want the attractive (and more expensive) mulch to be on top, you can make under-layers of sawdust (and a high-nitrogen meal) or even newspapers. Other under-layer mulches which will need a nitrogen boost are corncobs and straw. The attractive mulches, aside from cocoa hulls and peat, include buckwheat hulls, weathered wood chips, ground bark, leaf mold, shredded seaweed, and, of course, fine well-matured compost. You do not need to worry

about the comparative alkalinity or acidity of the materials you use for mulching because the high percentage of organic matter in a well prepared garden, as well as in the organic mulch itself, will act as a buffer and protect your plants from either variation from neutral (as long as it is not too severe, that is).

A winter mulch, of course, is primarily for the sake of protection, though it also has the virtue of holding down weeds to a certain extent. The best winter mulch there is is snow, but unfortunately we can't rely on an all-winter snow cover in many parts of the country, as we know.

Winter mulch can do more harm than good if it is put on before the ground is well frozen. Aside from increasing heaving, the winter mulch may warm up the soil so much that new growth of tender perennials can get started, and then thoroughly frozen when the next hard frost arrives. The main thing is to have a winter mulch which is loose, with good air circulation and good drainage. It does protect the plant somewhat, but add wind-screening if necessary also. Or move the semi-hardy plants to the cold frame to winter over. All winter mulches should be removed in spring to let the earth warm up, and the new summer mulch postponed until the ground is warm and soft.

STAKING PERENNIALS

If the plant has a tendency to be top heavy, it needs staking. Stakes put in as soon as you put out the plants, in most instances, will be covered by the plants' foliage and hardly show. Use twigs, dark laths, bamboo, green wire or plastic rods, and allow for a height somewhere between six and twelve inches below the mature height of the plants. Put the stakes behind the plants, sunk far enough into the soil to keep them firm.

Tie the plants very loosely with some soft dark or green material, either with a figure-8 loop or with a tight knot to the stake and a very loose loop or knot around the stem, so it has room to grow and to move a very little. Large metal stakes with a circle of wire at the top are used to control peonies, and for sprawling plants which you want to grow upwards, you can make a corset of bamboo to hold them together.

PROPAGATION

DIVISION

See the chapter on perennials for information about propagation and the care of perennials by dividing them into new, smaller plants.

MAKING CUTTINGS

Many trees and shrubs as well as perennials such as phlox, candytuft, carnations and others can be propagated by cuttings—either from growing tips or from the roots. Stem cuttings are perhaps the most usual kind to make, whether hardwood, semi-hardwood, softwood, or cuttings from herbaceous plants. Of these, the hardwood ones are the easiest because all you have to do is take off six or eight inches of the current year's growth from the plant when dormant, cutting just below the node and including two or three nodes in the part cut off. It is best to choose twigs that are between ¼ of an inch and one inch in diameter. Next, the cuttings should grow a callus, and this is done by burying the cut twigs horizontally or upside-down in moist sand, sawdust or peat moss. After the callus forms, they are then inserted in the soil used as rooting medium. The standard for years has been a rooting medium made of:

1 part garden loam
1 part sand
1 part peat moss

This provides some nutrition, and therefore has advantages over pure sand, or pure peat moss, sphagnum moss, vermiculite or perlite, which are also used. If you are taking cuttings of azaleas or rhododendrons, requiring acid soil, a good mixture is sand and peat. Winter cuttings of deciduous hardwoods such as maple, ash, mock orange, and so on are best taken on a cold day when you can leave the twigs to thaw gradually in the sun. (If not, put in the refrigerator to thaw.) This treatment gives them time to harden and be dormant until you put them in the rooting medium in the spring. Cuttings of evergreen trees such as juniper, false cypress or yew, can be taken in any month from September on, when the plants are dormant, and rooted in a protected place like a cold frame, greenhouse, side porch or other place where the temperature can be kept between 45° and 50°F. The usual length of an evergreen cutting is six inches.

Semi-hardwood cuttings, or broadleaf evergreens such as the laurels, rhododendrons, holly, euonymus or andromedas, are taken from wood that is no longer soft, but has not thoroughly matured, usually cut in August or late summer. Cut when it is cool and not dry. Wrap the cuttings at once in wet moss or burlap, or drop into plastic bags with damp moss in them. Keep them moist until inserted in the rooting medium.

Softwood cuttings are tricky because you take the cuttings from very tender parts of the plant where the foliage is only half grown. If the material dries out at all, your results may be nil. Cut on a cool day when the sun is out, put cuttings at once in plastic bags with damp moss, and make the cutting at least four or five inches long, just below a node, and reduce the leaves if they are large and numerous. Never use suckers. The right age for softwood cuttings is when the stem will bend easily and then snap. (If it merely bends, it is too young or too old.)

Whether you believe in using a root-inducing hormone or not, your chances with softwood cuttings are greatly reduced if you do not use one—and all you have to do is dip the stem in

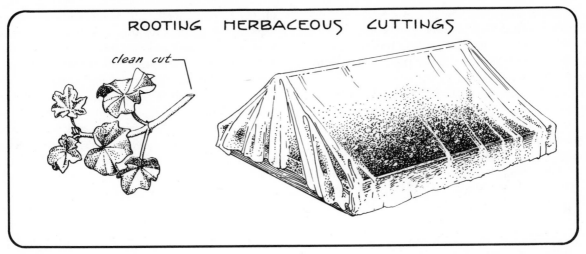

ROOTING HERBACEOUS CUTTINGS

clean cut

To propagate geraniums, phlox, globeflowers, and other herbaceous plants, take good-sized cuttings from healthy plants, and allow them to form calluses along the cut lines. Then insert them in a flat of sand, perlite, or other rooting medium, moisten, and cover with plastic to keep the humidity around them high.

water, shake it, dip it in the powder and insert the stem in the rooting medium. What is in this powder is the substance which a plant itself can produce for new rooting.

The next requirement is bottom heat: about 75° to 80°F. Keep the twigs moist but not wet, warm but not muggy, and properly aired, but not in a draft.

Herbaceous cuttings, such as those I often make with geraniums, are called difficult, because you have to balance the water content of the medium with the atmosphere around the leaves or your stems will rot. It is good to have bottom heat for these cuttings, too, though you can succeed with geraniums, chrysanthemums and coleus, for instance, without it. Use sturdy, well-sized shoots, not leggy ones, and make a very clean cut. Reduce leaves at the top. I sometimes leave the stems of geraniums on the counter or bench for a while to promote callusing. After fixing the cuttings in the flat, I cover it with a sheet of plastic, propped up, and tied not very tight. Keep watch to see that the air does not get hot and sticky inside. Every so

often pull on a cutting to see whether it no longer pulls easily from the soil. That means it has rooted and you can begin to let more air in. The simplest way is to poke holes in the plastic, and to untie the bottom. Finally remove the plastic, and ten days later pinch back the tips to promote good branching.

ROOT CUTTINGS

A good time to take root cuttings is in late winter or early spring, when there is still a high percentage of food in the roots. But many gardeners make the cuttings in the fall, leaving them in, or rather on, a rooting medium of equal parts sand, peat and loam, and covered with a half to an inch of sand, depending on the size of the root, and putting them in the cold frame for the winter. Then they are ready to plant out in the spring. With large roots, take six to eight inch pieces; with small, fine roots, take pieces of two to four inches. The medium with the least rottable material and most sand is the safest. But you have to be sure it stays moist enough.

Shrubs and trees you can propagate by root cuttings include: bittersweet, empress tree, glory bower, golden rain tree, hollies, Indian bean or catalpa, osage orange, smoke tree, sweet shrub, wisteria, yellow wood and others.

Herbaceous plants that are possible for root cuttings are: acanthus, alkanet, baby's breath, bleeding heart, evening primose, globe thistle, globeflower, mullein, oriental poppy, plume poppy, phlox and Stoke's aster.

(For propagation from other types of plants such as bulbs, tubers and rhizomes, see the chapter on those plants.)

LAYERING

Another fairly easy kind of propagation to try, especially for plants you find hard to increase by cuttings, is air-layering. In air-layering you choose a shoot, wound the bark by removing a cylinder off the stem, cutting a notch in it, or by making a slit along the stem. Cover the wound with wet sphagnum moss and wrap plastic over it, tied at each end. Not all trees and shrubs respond well to this method—probably because the moss stays too wet—but some that do succeed include moosewood or striped maple, and some other maples; the silktree, catalpa, clethra, red osier dogwood, cotoneaster, Franklinia, hollies, privet, crabapples, some of the Japanese cherries, Canadian hemlock and some of the viburnums, especially Sargent's. Before the invention of polyethelene film, newspaper or anything else handy like that was used for wrapping the limb used in air layering, which meant the need for watering the moss underneath the paper, but there was less danger of the area's getting too wet. When there is good, strong root formation at the slit, sever the branch to get the new plant. After severing the new plant, keep it in a cool place to accustom it to its new existence.

Probably the original kind of layering was ground layering. With this method you prepare the soil under the low branch of the shrub or tree you wish to propagate by adding peat moss and plenty of sand. Then you pull down the branch to be used, slice into the stem at an acute angle,

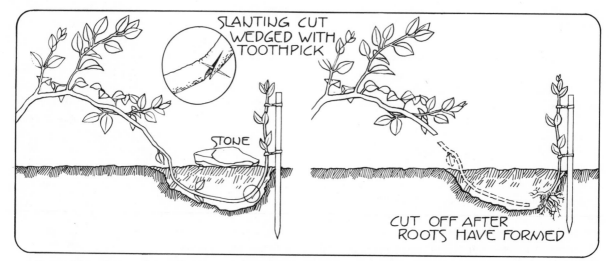

Ground layering, as shown here, is a relatively simple and fool-proof way of propagating shrubs. Allow a good solid set of roots to form before cutting the new plant free of the larger one.

but not deeper than half the width of the stem. Then prop the cut open with a toothpick, dust the cut with rooting hormone if you use that, and push the treated section of the stem down two inches into the prepared soil. Hold the stem down firmly while you cover the treated area with soil. Then either put a good-sized stone or a stout fork of wood over the area and go away for about a year. When you come back the section of the stem so treated will have sprouted many roots. Cut off the new plant and put it in your garden.

PRUNING

Out in nature in a wild area pruning is done by the wind that breaks off branches in a jagged, hit or miss way, or by a rather thorough nibbling back of all twigs and small branches by deer, rabbits or other animals. One good way to get your euonymus pruned and improved is to let the rabbits chew it in the winter. There are many small trees eaten right down to death by rabbits and mice, however, and these should be saved if you want them at the side of the woods or to grow up in the shrub border. For such tender plants the thing to do is to protect your birch seedlings, for instance, with wire cages which the animals cannot chew through. You might be amazed to see the new tiny trees that will establish themselves if you give them that degree of protection.

PRUNING REJUVENATES

The pruning that you do yourself is more systematic and careful. It is a cutting off in well-selected places of the parts of the plant not considered necessary. This may occur when you trim a hedge, but the purpose of pruning is not usually hedge-trimming. It is, rather, a series of cuttings designed to rejuvenate the tree or

shrub—and incidentally to make it more sightly and shapely. In Japanese gardens pruning is also used to cut back both branches and roots to stunt the trees. This is the basis of bonsai tree control.

It may sound odd to say that a tree or shrub is rejuvenated, but the fascinating fact is that the vigor and health of a well-pruned plant are actually renewed. The tree or shrub does take a new lease on life. The reason is that the old, dying and weak branches which sap the strength are taken away. Also excessive, criss-crossing branches are taken out. And branches which are broken, left exposed to fungal attack and beginning to get diseased are cut back to healthy growth and painted over with a protective coating. When so relieved, the remaining tissues perk up and begin to do twice as well. Sometimes you aim to cut off side shoots to make a plant tall and tidy. Some plants can endure having their leader or top branch cut, and the result is that they send out side shoots which make them grow in a lower, thicker form. Plants trimmed for hedges respond this way. It goes without saying that the tools you use to cut the branches must be clean and sharp, the cuts quick and smooth, and that you should use a dressing for the wounds.

WHEN TO PRUNE

The first important time to prune a shrub or tree is when you transplant it. Its roots will already have been pruned and removing some of the branches you cut back on the amount of plant which the reduced root system will need to support. Thus you can give the plant a chance to reestablish itself without too much stress. Most people do not cut back enough of the young plant at this time (or scream when they see the nurseryman do it). But it is a good practice, and will pay in later years when you see the tree or shrub grow into a fine specimen. Gardeners who go in for roses learn how much good the annual pruning will do for their plants. (See section on roses for more details.)

Ornamental flowering shrubs can be pruned and shaped every few years, but it is essential to do it at the right time of year so that you don't upset the blooming periods. Spring-blooming shrubs like forsythias, lilacs, or bridal wreath should not be pruned in early spring; wait until they have bloomed and then prune. If the shrub does not bloom until midseason, you should still wait. But those which are late bloomers, such as shrub altheas, buddleias, and hydrangeas may be pruned early in the spring, and then the blossoms will come on the new wood. Trees that you are training or thinning for air circulation and letting in light should be cut a little each year. Do not put a tree to the stress of major pruning all at once.

When you make a cut, do it somewhat diagonally, without leaving a stub of a branch. Fungus will get into the deteriorating tissues especially if you do not treat the cut surface. The best place to cut a branch stem is just above a bud. And the bud to choose is one which faces out. It is only sensible to avoid pruning in such a way that the new growth points inward and thickens the plant in a pattern contrary to the one you are trying to establish.

The time to prune evergreens is when the new growth is hardening off, and just when the new buds are setting for the next year's growth. In many zones that is in June. They can still be trimmed during July and August if still growing. The amount you take off may be an inch or so, or almost to the base of the new growth. But do not cut into the older growth for it takes too long for the plant to recover. This applies especially to pines and spruces.

With yews, hemlocks and junipers you can prune about a quarter of an inch of the bud, and several new little branches are then likely to come. Large-leaf evergreens such as rhododendron, camellia, the various pieris shrubs and

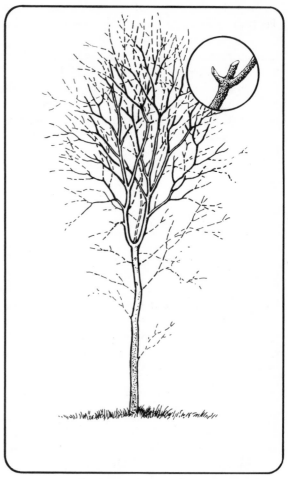

When pruning, make a clean, diagonal cut first above a bud. As shown in the close-up here, prune off the inner stems and leave on the outward-growing ones.

skimmia should be pruned very little, but if you have to do it, to make room for better growth, for instance, do it just after the blooming period. If you use hollies for a screening hedge, you can trim them back judiciously in the spring or very early summer. This is the right time to trim laurel, too.

Fruit trees, especially the dwarf ones now

popular and the bush fruits, should be pruned in the winter or early spring. Many like to prune them in March or April, though it won't harm the plant too much if you prune almost up to blossoming time. The long suckerlike sprouts that shoot out of fruit trees may be removed, however, at any time. You will know which these branches are because they grow straight up from the older limbs and have widely spaced leaves. Take them out, for they are likely to weaken the tree and they certainly warp its shape. You can also attend to broken limbs whenever you see them.

In general, the best times to prune fruit trees are when they are young. Every year you can prune a little to shape the tree, keep excess growth under control, remove the suckers growing from below the graft and the suckerlike branches, and all branches which turn towards the center of the tree. The shape you are aiming at is to have a main central stem, with lateral branches more or less evenly spaced and well distributed around the main stalk. The place where a lateral branch joins the main stem, the crotch, should be strong and well formed. If the angle is too acute, and the crotch is weak, that branch should be removed in favor of the branches which have strong, wide-angled crotches. (This is true of any tree or bush, not only fruit trees.)

Then, when the tree is well shaped, leave it alone until it begins to bear fruit—except for removing broken limbs. Peaches you can trim back annually as much as a foot of terminal growth to encourage fruiting. Pear trees should be pretty well left alone.

Blueberries produce their fruit on the wood of the previous year's growth. Whether you grow these bushes for ornament, for the birds, or for your own blueberry pies, leave them without pruning until they are three years old. The best rule to follow is to prune the weaklings, but leave the strong bushes alone—except for taking off drooping, unsightly branches. If you want larger berries, pinch back a number of the buds. This also helps to guarantee plenty of new growth on the bush for the following year's crop.

If your main aim is to have flowers on your shrubs, the rule-of-thumb to remember is: those blooming in the spring have their flowers on wood of the previous year's growth; those blooming after July usually on new wood of the current year, so prune these in winter or very early spring in hopes of inducing new woody growth.

OTHER TIMES TO PRUNE

Some shrubs lose some of their branches by winter-kill so the plant looks pretty straggly in the spring when the leaves come out on part of the plant, but the rest is dead. This is likely to happen with shrubs such as deutzias, hydrangeas, privets, mock orange, snowberry as well as some of the spireas and dogwoods. And they should be cleaned of the dead wood when you see it. In cold climates some shrubs will die right back and need drastic pruning down to the ground to encourage them to come up fresh from the bottom. This may happen to some of the following: glossy abelia, beauty berry, broom, English holly, evergreen azalea, holly olive, mahonia or Oregon holly-grape, rhododendron, St. John's Wort Goldflower, winter hazel or winter jasmine. Most of these shrubs are usually hardy to Zone 6, if protected, but they can freeze in bad spells. A good pruning will help give them the strength to come back after a hard winter.

Lilacs and some other shrubs look a lot better if you prune off the deadheads after they have bloomed. By preventing the plants from going to seed, you also conserve some of their strength. Others in this group include azaleas, rhododendrons and magnolias as well as the buddleias, sheep and mountain laurels, and the low Danish plant with good autumn coloring very useful for

hedges called stephanandra or cutleaf stephanandra.

Adverse conditions often upset a shrub or tree
and make it advisable to give it a new lease on
life through pruning. You might have inadequate rainfall or excessive rainfall, and a
rising water table—or the equivalent in dry
climates where the lawn sprinkler goes too much
to suit the roots of nearby shrubs. Bad air can do
harm, whether from soot or chemical pollution.
Too dense a crown can shade a bush too much
(and too scanty a one can cause sunscald though
you naturally can't prune to meet that
condition). The trouble might be insects or
disease, especially fire blight, a frequent
bacterial infection of hawthorns, pears and other
fruit trees. Compaction of the soil over the roots
of plants can cause dying limbs; with this
condition a thorough airing of the soil by digging
is also called for. It is obvious that pruning of
plants with these as well as other conditions
causing dead limbs must be quickly done when
there is danger of dead limbs falling on people
who pass by.

HOW TO DO IT

I ride around the countryside and look at
bushes and hedges that have been mathematic-
ally chopped back without any regard to the
natural shape of the shrub and it makes me sad.
It is much better for a specimen shrub to remove
several branches by cutting them at the base and
letting in some air. It is also a good deal easier
than to snip at every single branch. Of course for
dense, squared (or rather, sloped-out) hedges, it's
different. But choose plants like yews or privet
which are suited to that kind of chopping. Plants
like honeysuckles, mock-orange, hydrangeas and
spireas don't need such treatment. Neither do
lilacs, which should only have a little taken out
each year, because these plants will lose their top
bloom if you chop them off. As with other

*To maintain the natural shape of a shrub, prune
off those wild-growing branches near the base,
rather than snipping and chopping all over.*

pruning, cut the branch a little above a bud, or a
little above a leaf joint so the bud there will
develop and bring new growth to the plant.

Make the cut on a slight slant, and not too
near or too far from the outward-pointing bud
which will grow into a new branch. In cutting
off whole branches, again do it on a slight slant,
with the lower part a bit farther from the trunk
than the upper cut, but not far enough to catch
water and cause rot. Leave enough of the bark so
that the wound can heal well after it has been
painted. Do not leave stubs or ragged edges
which can get infections. With big limbs, make
two cuts to prevent tearing the tree when the
branch falls.

SUCKERS

Shoots which come up from the ground
around shrubs like lilacs, or grafted trees like
crabapples and other fruit trees, are called
suckers and are usually removed by careful
gardeners. With shrubs like lilacs they sap the
strength of the shrub, and with grafted fruit trees
they may eventually take over so what you end

up with is the growth from the base stock and not the graft at all. Cut suckers back to the ground. With new young plants, this kind of pruning as well as all other, should be done early. A delay of two or three years might bring ruin to your trees and shrubs (or some of them). Those which are least likely to be injured—in case you want to know—include: sumac, privet, box, forsythia, myrtles and honeysuckles.

DRASTIC PRUNING

Such shrubs, luckily, once you decide to prune, may be sliced right back to within a few inches of the ground, and will come up again, rejuvenated. They will pretty well take care of themselves; and even though you neglect them, so will *Rosa rugosa,* the viburnums, Russian olive and chokeberries. Shrubs which some people like to trim way back every year are the red-stemmed dogwoods (*Cornus stolonifera, C. alba and C. alba siberica*). These they cut back in early spring just before new growth starts because the red color, so attractive with the white snow, is brighter the next winter on younger stems.

OTHER SHRUBS NEED OTHER PRUNING

Remember that all shrubs and small trees do not have the same growth pattern. Some tend to grow up in several sprouts from the base; some from one permanent stem. Those with permanent stems should not be given drastic pruning of that stem. They include the viburnums, smoke trees, and Cornelian cherries. Rotate cutting back of stems in the several-stemmed deutzias, mock orange or spirea, taking out two a year, though you can also cut the remaining stems back about one third.

Shrubs you want to keep compact like cotoneaster and barberries should be pruned when young to get them in shape, and then left alone. Firethorns (pyracantha) need to have their lead shoots cut back about half, preferable just before the spring growth commences.

SMALL FLOWERING TREES

It is best to prune small flowering trees when they are dormant. What you do is cut back any long-growing branches that want to shoot up, especially if the branch seems to want to compete with the leader, or central stalk. Do not touch the leader also cut all branches that rub, and control those that want to go up. Choose a bud or shoot pointing in the direction where it will do most good for the shape or health of the tree, and cut just above it. Trees that should be pruned at this time, this way include Asiatic sweetleaf, crabapples, flowering dogwoods, Franklinia, golden chain tree, golden rain tree, hawthorns, redbuds and Russian olives.

The sudden death of the leaves on one branch, and then the next year the sudden death of all the leaves on fruit trees may indicate that the tree has fireblight. If, however, you prune the tree as soon as there is dry weather after you note its presence, you may be able to save the tree. Aside from the fruit trees and hawthorns, mountain ash trees are also subject to this disease. Some ornamental crabapple trees are more subject than others. (See chapter on outdoor living areas for details.)

Any diseased or dying limb on a tree needs attention and good pruning because once weakened, more troubles come, such as borers, bark beetles and insects which rob the nearby branches of moisture. Then fungi and rot get in. As mentioned above, a weak V crotch may be the very place troubles start.

WARNING: When pruning a grafted tree, you must be sure not to cut off too much of the top growth. If you slash off more than the graft can withstand, the root part of the plant will send up its own shoots, and you will eventually lose the graft part. This can happen with purple-leaved plum, Japanese maples, Koster blue spruce and Schwedler Norway maples as well as others. To avoid this hazard, prune in steps, and never cut more than a quarter of the plant back to graft level.

EASIEST PRUNING

The pleasantest, easiest pruning you can do is that which is incidental to the picking of flowers. I like to pick armfuls of lilacs to bring in to soak in the tub overnight (after hammering the stems to facilitate water uptake) and then to make huge arrangements the next morning. I make them so big that the only place to put them is on the floor. This kind of picking perforce prunes the bush. Later, when I remove the deadheads of the flowers still left on the bush, I pick longish stems, and that adds another bit of pruning. But do not just break off the branches. The word *pick* should not imply that. You use good sharp pruning shears or clippers for this enterprise, just as you would when doing ordinary, systematic pruning.

PINCHING

Some shrubs such as azaleas need to be pruned quite a lot and quite often if you are going to achieve well-rounded plants. This is because they have a tendency to get leggy if left to their own natural growth pattern. Pinch out the tips when the plants are young, and cut to the ground any older branches that shoot up and get too long. For pinching, take off between half and inch and an inch when the shoot is about three inches long. If the growth is young and tender, you can do this with your fingernails. Otherwise use a sharp instrument again, as with other cutting.

Flowers such as chrysanthemums are also pinched. In this way you get a nice bushy plant, and plenty of bloom. Many annuals also benefit from pinching. I always pinch back my petunias, snapdragons and other plants that respond to

this treatment by a new spurt of branching and blossoming activity.

BRINGING FLOWERS INTO THE HOUSE FOR ARRANGEMENTS

When you go to the garden to gather flowers, take the proper equipment with you—a sharp knife and water to put the flowers in. Don't use scissors, for they are likely to injure the cells of the stem, and cut on the slant, with the stem under tepid water if you can figure out how to do it. Otherwise cut the stem a second time, under water. A good carrying device I found at a church fair once was made by soldering two big juice cans on either side of a metal rod with a loop handle. This is simple to make, deep enough and heavy enough to hold the flowers without tipping. For cutting woody stems use shears or pruners. Some people hammer the ends of woody stems, but it is better to slit them with a sharp knife to open the cells which will conduct water into the severed branch. Cut through or just below a node, unless you are also pruning. Then cut again just above a good node which has a bud, so you do not leave a stub to rot.

The time of day to cut flowers is late afternoon when the plant has most sugar made from the day-long photsynthesis. The next best time is to cut flowers in early morning before the sun has had a chance to get to them. Noon is the worst time, or just after noon on a hot day, except that glads should be cut at 2:00 P.M. to delay bud opening. Plants such as pansies, forget-me-nots, clarkia and sweet alyssum do best if you lift the whole plant, wash the roots and make your arrangement with the roots left on.

To make cut flowers and branches last longer, soak them over night in deep water. This treatment doesn't so much add water through the stems as it reduces evaporation. To reduce it further, it is a good idea to use a mist sprayer in the air around the flowers. But do not shut off all air circulation. Keep all utensils very clean, washing them in suds and ammonia. Remove the leaves from the parts of the stems which will be below water in the arrangement, and for flowers like zinnias, the large dahlias, lilacs and mock orange, it is best to remove all leaves, but for pansies and chrysanthemums, for example, that is not necessary.

Some flowers should be submerged when you condition them:begonia, just long enough to get the blossoms wet; yucca, canna lilies, violets, and caladium for a half hour; castor bean for an hour; and most evergreens for a day. With evergreens add a tablespoon of glycerin per quart of water.

Many plants last longer if you split the stems after cutting them: althea, anthurium, artemesia, asters, balsam, and impatiens, beard tongue, butterfly flower or poor man's orchid, candytuft if woody, Christmas rose, clarkia, clematis, crown imperials, daffodils, dracaena, dusty miller, feverfew, flax, globe flower, globe amarath, geraniums, fuchsias, gas plant, heliotrope, herbs hollyhocks, lilies, (cut these above foliage, with short stems), lupine, annual poinsettia, monkshood, morning glories, mountain bluets, nasturtium and leaves, peonies, phlox, plantain lily, primrose, roses, salvia, spider flower, squill, tulips (cut off white part of stem), Virginia bluebells, and wall-flowers as well as all flowers with woody stems.

Conditioning in cold water is the usual procedure, but some flowers do best if started in warm water (between 80° and 100°F.) at first: these include bee balm, foxgloves, flowering tobacco, hollyhocks, primroses, snapdragons and sweet peas. Some flowers such as daffodils should have the sticky juice washed off in warm water; others such as bellflowers, cardinal flower and poppies should have the ends of their stems seared with a match while you count 15. A little vinegar in the water helps to preserve ferns; a little ammonia helps for amaryllis; and some well-washed charcoal is good to keep water clean. After the arrangement is made, change the water every other day or so, cut stems again, preferably under water, and clean away any leaves which can start bacterial action that decays the stems. And, obviously, remove deadheads.

A FEW WORDS ON ROOT PRUNING

There are three main reasons for pruning the roots of shrubs and trees. One is to prepare a tree or shrub for the shock of transplanting. With a smallish plant, cut down straight with a sharp-edged spade all around the bush or tree about 16 to 18 inches from the main stalk (or more if it is a large plant). Then you leave the plant to grow new roots and gain new vigor. You must water the plant well for a month, and fertilize it if needed. Do this at least six weeks before you plan to move the tree or shrub, and if you have time, you can give the plant up to 12 months to readjust after this root-pruning.

A second reason for cutting back roots is to cure a condition called girdling. This means that one of the big underground roots (or sometimes surface roots) is turning back over the other roots and not spreading out and going down into the soil as it should be. Sometimes you can see this rogue root circling round where it should not be. Other times you only know it is girdling because you see that the trunk in a certain section goes straight down instead of slanting out as normal trunks do wherever there are roots. The straight trunk is often a sign that underground girdling is taking place. Take out all girdling roots, because they will strangle the tree and make its leaves turn yellow too early, its growth on that side of the tree will get sparser and sparser, and eventually will make the tree die. We see this happen to sugar maples up here in Vermont once in a while, as we also see cross-over branches in this variety of maple which are lethal, too, because they fill up the inner space of the tree, rub, get diseased and become objectionable and dangerous.

The third reason for root pruning is to stunt the plant for bonsai purposes. (See specialty books on this subject, a few of which are mentioned in the Appendix.)

WEEDING

Though the organic gardener prefers mulching to weeding, there are times when you have to think about weeding, anyway. When the plants are very small, and before you apply any summer mulch, you need to get right there and pull out (or snip out) the weeds which may come in to choke your little new perennials or annuals, or the little shrubs you may decide to grow from seeds.

Since many weeds are truly beneficial— either for good influences from their root exudates or plant aromas, and in certain instances for food for the gardener—it pays to be cautious about your attempts to eliminate them. Good deep-rooted weeds will bring up into the topsoil and into plants' stems fine supplies of nitrogen. When you till them in, weeds will supply the soil with good nutrients, nitrogenous and otherwise, and will supply nutrients of the sort certainly needed by the young plants which will grow in a healthy way to maturity.

People who want to make gardens that are geometrically neat and unchanging will have a tendency to blot out all weeds. I do not think that organic gardeners garden that way. Their technique will be to nurture those weeds which will benefit the garden, and to use mulches to get the others to subside.

In fact, all gardening techniques for the organic gardener are intended to promote growth and not to destroy it. That is one of the clues to successful organic gardening.

INSECTS IN THE GARDEN

I don't really believe in going to a lot of work and trouble about pest control aside from the normal, sensible garden practices which tend to keep pests at a minimum, anyhow. I mean things like giving plants plenty of room and air; seeing to it that they are not too damp, unless they are water plants or bog plants; planting in the sun if that suits them or the shade if that suits them; and are well provided with the nutrients they require. Also, always select disease-resistant varieties and use companion plants. Just as important, as I have said, are practices which create a harmonious environment of living creatures: bees on the flowers; birds in the air and in the trees and bushes, for they are notorious consumers of insects; beneficial bacteria in the soil, for they and the molds and fungi living in the soil provide antibiotics of various sorts; predators other than birds, like the beneficial praying mantises, trichogramma wasps, lady bugs and lacewings which we know consume unwanted pests like aphids (or even the ants who farm and milk aphids for their honeydew).

Berried shrubs and bird houses are good to attract birds; lady bugs can be bought (be sure to get the ones conditioned to be ready to eat aphids), and so can the tiny wasps and the egg cases of praying mantises; sprays can be made from garlic, hot pepper and botanicals such as the plants which have rotenone, pyrethrin and ryania in them; and certain plants can be planted together which have the effect of repelling pests one from another in the practice called companion planting. And then there are the mechanical devices like traps with molasses and bran baits, or like tanglefoot as a gooey substance to put around the trunk of a tree, or like black lights to attract flying insects at night.

BEES AND HONEY PLANTS

Bees are among the invaluable friendly

insects we absolutely rely on because of their role in pollination. An organic gardener who pays attention to the value of these insects will certainly want to include in the garden some of the following trees, shrubs and flowers which are attractive to bees, wasps, butterflies and other helpful insects because of the nectar and pollen that they offer to these creatures.

Trees:

Amur maple, *Acer ginalla*

Autumn olive, *Elaeagnus umbellata*

Bee Bee tree, *Evodia danielli*

Honey Mesquite, *Prosopsis juliflora glandulosa*

Linden, *Tilia americana*

Pea tree, *Caragana arborescens*

Russian olive, *Elaeagnus angustifolia*

Shrubs:

Some of the acacias, *A. berlanderi*, and *A. greggii*

Cotoneaster acutifolia, sometimes called Peking cotoneaster

Elderberry, Honeysuckles, especially Tatarian, *Lonicera tatarica*

Pussy willow, *Salix caprea*, and other willows (helpful to bees when they first come out in the spring)

Raspberry, *Rubus* species, both native and European

Rosa rugosa

Perennials:

Anise hyssop, *Agastache anethiodorum*

Arrow leaf aster, *A. sagittifolius*

New England aster, *A. novae-angliae*

Bee balm, *Monarda didyma*, Butterfly weed, *Asclepias tuberosa*

Catnip, *Nepeta cataria*

Chivirico, *Leonurus sibiricus*

Golden honey plant, *Actinomeris alternifolia*

Globe flower, *Echinops ritro* (blue, small)

Globe thistle, *Echinops spaerocephalus* (tall and hardy)

Perennials [*cont'd*]:

Goldenrod, *Solidago* in species

Hyssop, *Hyssopus officinalis*

Indigo, Wild, *Baptisia australis*

Purple, loosestrife, *Lythrum salicaria*

Milkweed, *Asclepias syriaca*

Marjoram, Wild, Origanum vulgare

Motherwort, *Leonurus cardiaca*

Mountain mint, *Pyncantheumum pilosum*

Persian ground ivy, *Nepeta mussinii* or *N* x *faassenii*

Virginia waterleaf, *Hydrophyllum virginianum* (for shade)

Annuals:

Annual leonurus, very prolific

Blue salvia, *S. farinacea*

Borage, *Borago officinalis*

Dragonhead, *Dracocephalum moldavica*

Mignonette, *Reseda odorata*

Phacelia, *P. tenacetifolia*

Snapdragon, *Antirrhinum majus*

Spider plant, *Cleome spinosa*

Most of the perennials mentioned in this list are rather rank and rampant in growth, so be careful. Keep a close eye on them, and weed them out and thin them when you see that they are beginning to spread. I believe that they are recommended as bee plants for the very reason that they are prolific, and produce many, many flowers for the enticement of bees. A very interesting and useful list of *honey plants* state by state can be found in the *Encyclopedia of Organic Gardening* (Rodale, 1971).

BIRDS IN THE GARDEN

Less prolific are most of the plants recommended to entice birds to come in. Flowers as enticements are not frequently used, though you will find that hummingbirds come frequently to bee balm, cardinal flower, Virginia bluebells, columbines, flowering tobacco, coral bells, phlox, petunias and many others.

Trees:

Apple, *Malus* in species
Arborvitae, *Thuja occidentalis*
Cherry, called European Bird Cherry, *Prunus padus*
Chokecherry, *P. virginiana*
Flowering crabapple, *Malus* in variety
Flowering dogwood and other dogwoods, *Cornus* in variety
Hemlock, *Tsuga canadensis* and others
Hackberry, *Celtis occidentalis*
Hawthorns, *Crataegus* in species
Holly, *Ilex* in species
Highbush, cranberry, *Viburnum trilobum*
Larch, *Larix* in species
Mountain ash, *Sorbus aucuparia* and others
Mulberry, *Morus alba* and others
Pine, *Pinus strobus* and others
Red cedar, *Juniperus virginiana* and *J. scopulorum*
Rose, *Rosa*—the ones with smallish rose hips
Shadblow, *Amelanchier canadensis*
Spruce, *Picea* in species
White birch, *Betula papyrifera*
Yellow birch, *B. lutea*

These trees provide nesting sites, berries, cones, fruits and shelter, for many birds from blue birds who like to nest in apple trees to crossbills who like the cones on pines. Shrubs, too, provide such attractions. Among those you might like to have are:

Bayberry, *Myriea pensylvanica*
Blueberry, *Vaccinium corymbosum*
Blueberry, Lowbush, *V. pensylvanicum*
Boxwood, *Buxus sempervirens*
Butterfly bush, *Buddleia davidii*
Cotoneasters, in species
Elderberry, *Sambucus canadensis*
Firethorn, *Pyracantha coccinea*
Honeysuckle bush, *Lonicera tatarica* and *L. maachi*
Juniper, *Juniperus* in species
Roses, *Rosa* in species

Sumac, *Rhus* in species
Triumph vine, *Campsis radicans*
Viburnums, *Viburnum* in species
Virginia creeper, *Parthenocissus quinquefolia*
Winterberry, *Ilex glabra* and *I. verticillata*

Plant such shrubs as a background to a border, as a hedge along your property line, to fill in corners or as patio or foundation decoration. Supplement such plantings with bird feeders for the winter, suet baskets for the woodpeckers and chickadees, a bird bath for drinking as well as bathing, and put them near trees and shrubs which can serve as shelter when the birds are startled, though not as shelter for cats near the bird bath.

COMPANION PLANTS

There are two basic principles behind the effectiveness of companion plants, or plants which seem to thrive better when planted together. One is that rather mysterious cooperation or interdependence between certain plants which may depend, as stated elsewhere, on aroma, root exudates or even a power to share water below the surface of the ground. The other principle is that of positive action of repelling enemies, both from themselves and from neighboring plants. Janet Gillespie, in her charming book, *Peacock Manure and Marigolds* (see Bibliography), tells about the way her great-aunt took care of her garden, as the title implies. She planted many marigolds along the paths and in many beds, and she used plenty of peacock manure because peacocks were the fowl she happened to have. No one in the family, at the time described in the book, had any idea of the recent scientific discoveries about the root exudates from the marigold family, and especially from *Tagetes minuta*, the small-flowered, tall Mexican marigold which evidently exudes the repellent in greatest potencies. Henry Doubleday

Associates in England, the bio-dynamic garden researchers in Suffolk, have done most of the research, but workers at the Connecticut Agricultural Station at New Haven have also found good results in using marigolds for the control of nematodes or eel worms.

But with or without the scientific evidence, anyone who has grown marigolds can readily observe that they remain pest-free throughout the season—or they do at my place, anyway. And the strong, tangy aroma of some varieties is pretty obvious, too. Therefore, my first advice to gardeners wishing to experiment with companion planting is to put in lavish supplies of marigolds. I like to use them for edging, for spots of color here and there, for pots I can move around to trouble spots, and for green foliage (when I pick off the blossoms which upset a color scheme). As might be expected, the reputation of marigolds has skyrocketed since word got out that they were so useful, and some inexperienced gardeners believe that marigolds will cure all pest troubles. I doubt it, but that doesn't stop me from planting a great many in my garden. Asparagus roots probably have the same faculty of repelling nematodes. And they look lovely and feathery in the flower garden. I have some self-seeded asparagus that grows near the yellow yarrow, and it looks fine.

HERBS

I also use many herbs. At least the principle of the strong scent is at work with herbs, and again we notice that there are few pests which bother them. Some I particularly recommend as both attractive to put in the garden, for a small hedge, for a groundcover, or for specimen plants are:

Bee balm and bergamot — *Monarda Didyma* and *M. fistulosa*. Both rather handsome flowers, and very tangy and pest-free themselves; will grow in part shade.

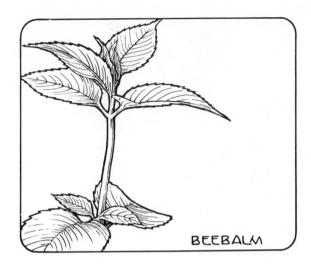

BEEBALM

Caraway — *Carum carvi*. Best in sunny, dry soil; will loosen heavy soil.

Camomile — *Anthemis nobilis* and *Matricaria chamomilla*. Somewhat pungent, with pleasant little daisy-like flowers, useful for edging or any place in the front of the border.

Chives — *Allium schoenoprasum*. This and all other members of the Allium family, especially garlic, are indispensable as pest-control plants. Plant anywhere you can fit them in. Chive flowers are small, globular, and lavender. I think they are very decorative in the garden, and I dry them for winter arrangements by just hanging them up upside-down. (For ornamental alliums see the chapter on bulbs.) Also grow a patch of chives, garlic, onions, scallions, leeks, or ramp which you can raid from time to time to get plants to move to trouble spots. And be sure to grow enough to make sprays.

Geranium — *Pelargonium* in variety. Though discussed in Chapter 8, this flower is so pest-free and so decorative, it is worth mentioning again in this

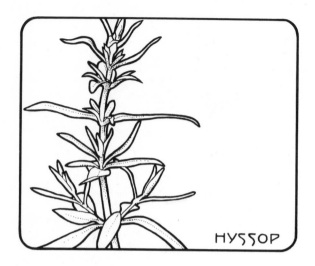

HYSSOP

LAVENDER

connection. Plant where you wish — for example near a tender variety of some flower you want to grow, even though you know it is susceptible to Japanese beetles, for instance.

Hyssop — *Hyssopus officinalis.* This hyssop, as well as the anise hyssop mentioned above, is a dainty, not very conspicuous plant, which will do well when once established. It likes rather limy soil, full sun and good drainage. Make hyssop tea to use on plants with bacterial diseases such as wilts.

Lavender — *Lavandula officinalis.* Though only hardy to Zone 5, it will do well in full sun in any garden soil in warmer zones. Makes an excellent low edging, if trimmed. Natural growth is three feet.

Mint — *Mentha* in species. Useful repellent herbs, but WARNING: they can spread all over the area, and though not too hard to get out, they are a nuisance if intertangled with the roots of some of your prize plants. Underground metal barriers are a precaution you can use. Or grow in pots and put where you want them to be

of benefit, especially to help control an attack of flea beetles.

Parsley — *Petroselinum hortense.* I am not convinced of this plant's repellent powers, but it is so pest-free itself, so handsome a small plant, and so handy to have when you need some salad greens or vitamin C. that I believe in putting it in the flower garden as well as in the vegetable garden. It is a biennial, and I let some go over to the second year and blossom. The flowers are an unattractive, greenish likeness of small or stunted Quenn Anne's lace.

Pot marigold — see annuals.

Pot marjoram — *Origanum vulgare.* A tough, tangy herb. Spreads.

Rosemary — *Rosmarinus officinalis.* My favorite herb. In my zone I have to pot it up and bring it indoors in the winter, but it is hardy to Zone 6.

Rue — *Ruta graveolens.* Needs a moist soil. Might give you a rash.

Sage — *Salvia officinalis.* Perennial, but short-lived.

Southernwood — *Artemisia abrotanum.* This and most of the other members of

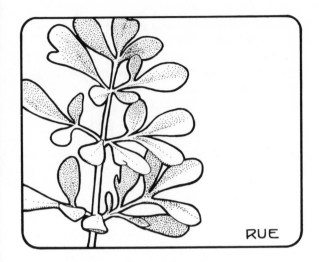

RUE

the artemisia genus are both pest-free and pest-repellent. A trim little plant, good-looking in any garden. (See wormwood also.)

Sweet marjoram — *Origanum majorana hortensis.* My second favorite herb. So I grow it every year. It may not repel much, but is pest-free and a neat little plant.

Sweet woodruff — *Asperula odorata.* Grow it as a groundcover beneath rhododen-

drons and see how healthy they stay. Will grow in part shade.

Tansy — *Tanacetum vulgare.* Another long-used herb for controlling pests. It is pungent, tall, rugged, and is recommended by some gardeners as a handsome addition to the back of the border. Old-fashioned people still plant it at the kitchen door to keep out ants. Grows to three feet or to five feet if the soil suits it.

Thyme — *Thymus* in variety. Low-growing and tangy. Good for terraces and for groundcovers. Watch it if you put it in a flower bed.

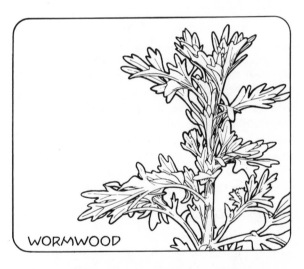

WORMWOOD

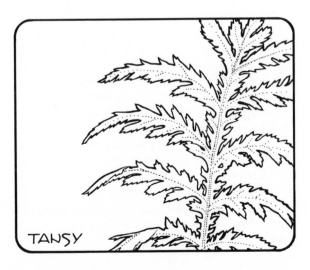

TANSY

Wormwood — *Artemisia absinthium.* This excellent repellent herb will grown from two to four feet tall, in any garden soil, and as most herbs do, it prefers the sun. Like southernwood it has finely divided leaves, silky and hairy. The flowers are very small and inconspicuous, growing in spikes. (There is also a Beach wormwood, *Artemisia stelleriana,* also called Dusty miller, described in the chapter on seaside gardens. It is pest-free.) Tea made of wormwood sprinkled on the soil and tender plants will repel slugs and snails because it is so bitter.

OTHER ANNUALS BESIDES MARIGOLDS

Less tangy than the recommended herbs and marigolds, but famous for its pest-repellent faculty is the nasturtium, a flower almost anyone can be happy to grow. Its cheerful and fragrant flowers, its delicious seeds, and its decorative, salad-green leaves are delightful to have in the garden. We put them around in various beds, planting the seeds wherever there is an appropriate place. I have started them inside, too, but they prefer not to be transplanted. This flower, and the whole plant, can help in the control of white flies and aphids. Grind it up in the blender for a spray, especially in combination with ground-up sage, wormwood and camomile. (See below on sprays.) If white fly persists, combine nasturium and marigolds for control plants, and don't forget to hose down the infected plant—for water is often the best device there is.

Mignonette, or *Reseda odorata*, is a very good plant to put with roses to help envigorate them and protect them. Its effect is doubled if you also add garlic and parsley.

Flowering tobacco, or *Nicotiana alata*, is an annual I grow in several parts of the garden, especially under a porch we sit on in summer evenings sometimes. The nicotine essence is helpful in fending off pest, and if you want to make a spray, some chopped stems, leaves and spent flowers added to a blender nearly full of water will make something to use on plants that are farther away. Speaking of nicotine, you can also get tobacco stems from the florist and make a spray from them and come up with something stronger. It is best to make a hot tea and brew it, not just a blended tea as with many of the other tea plants or compost. (If all else is too hard to get, you can always use a plug of tobacco from the smoke shoppe.)

Datura or angel's trumpet or Jimson weed is another effective (and poisonous) plant. See chapter on annuals.

I have grown tomatoes in flower beds for experimental interest, and I am happy to report that they do indeed have some repellent effect, though not in a warm, windless corner where the aphids got into them. But the tangy plants where they themselves were well-aired and healthy repelled not only insects, but also the woodchuck. For small, incidental invasions, you can also pick off tomato leaves and simply lay them on the pestered plant. I have only begun this experiment, and will be glad to hear from any readers who have had experience in control of rose chafers, ants on peonies, or any other invaders. (I know the ants do not hurt the peonies, but I'm leary of ants as aphid and virus carriers.)

A few other annuals, such as calendula, cosmos and zinnias are all worth using as pest controls. (I also use zinnias as trap plants for Japanese beetles, to keep them out of my corn.)

PERENNIALS FOR PEST CONTROL

Perennials that can suppress bacterial action include some of the plants known to be poisonous such as monkshood and buttercups and others such as columbine and delphinium, all of which may have a bad effect on the bacteria you know are beneficial (including the nitrogen-fixing bacteria on legumes which make nitrogen available to plants). In fact, avoid using those perennials near legumes you want to thrive such as lupines, sweet peas, indigo, any of the clovers or plants you may use as trap plants to distract insects away from your good plants. These last include, for example, the soy beans used to attract Japanese beetles (and even rabbits) away from your good legumes.

Stinging nettle, though often called a weed, is a valuable plant to have growing in some part of the garden where no one will touch it and get stung. If near herbs it doubles their potency and the humus that accumulates underneath these plants, especially if you let them fall and rot into the ground, is almost as good as what accumulates under birch trees or valerian. Nettles are particularly valuable for repelling aphids and plant lice. If the infected plants are too far away from your nettle stand, put on your gloves, harvest some and make a tea in the blender (one cup to one quart of water). Or bury some in a keg for five or six days and get something really ripe and brown.

Valerian is a plant believed to have very good powers of influence. It seems to strengthen many nearby plants, making them resisitant. It can attract earthworms, and again, you can make a spray of the parts of the plant and spread its influence even farther. Then spray other plants, or the ground beneath the plants. The other name for this plant is garden heliotrope.

Geraniums, especially white ones, are believed to distract Japanese beetles from other plants. I have not had definitive experience with them, but I have observed the good condition of the flower garden when geraniums have been combined with other pest-repellent plants.

BOTANICALS FOR DUSTS AND SPRAYS

One of the best-known botanicals, or insect-control sprays is made from the East African pyrethrum. I have a notion that other pyrethrum or painted daisies are beneficial just to grow in the garden. And anyway, I love their big daisy-like flowers. The extracts from pyrethrum are used for flies and aphids, and they are of a low order of toxicity. The others you can buy as powders or sometimes in solution, and you can get pyrethrum, ryania and rotenone, all three in a mixture called Tri-excel,

a powder I use (especially indoors, it so happens) which is mixed with water. You can also get quassia wood chips at the drug store or garden center. Their very bitter taste is hated by insects, especially if you make a spray from a pound of chips soaked in several gallons of water for several days and then simmered for several hours and strained. (For small quantities soak two ounces in one gallon of water.) Its efficacy can be doubled by mixing if with wormwood tea before adding two ounces of soft soap to make a spray that will stick on the plants.

OTHER SPRAYS TO MAKE

Garlic Spray
    3 cloves of garlic
    1 medium-sized onion
    1 teaspoon very hot pepper
    1 quart of water
Blend for a minute or so in a blender, then let it steep for ten minutes before you strain it into your sprayer. A nylon stocking makes an efficient strainer of about the right fineness to get out any fibers that might clog your sprayer. The mixture is very strong and can be diluted with three or four quarts of water before use. Excellent for both sucking and chewing insects.

Rhubarb Spray
    6 rhubarb leaves (which are poisonous)
    2 or 3 quarts of water, or enough to blend
    the leaves
Put through blender, let steep, strain. Use for aphids and June bugs.

Equisetum Spray
    1 cup of chopped horse's tail weed
    1 quart of water
Boil together for 20 minutes, cool and strain.

Stinging Nettle Tea
    1 quart of nettle plants
    water to cover
Leave the plants in the water, well covered, and

with a lid, until the plant material is well rotted. It remains usable for about a month. Dilute with seven parts of water to make a spray for aphids. This tea and equisetum spray combined make a potent and effective combination.

Water and Kerosene
    1 cup of water
    enough kerosene to make a film on top
Use this to drop in Japanese beetles or any other insects you hand pick from your flowers. Hold the cup beneath the beetle when you go to catch it, for Japanese beetles have a way of dropping from their perch when you reach for them.

Salt, or Salt and Water
    2 tablespoons salt
Put it in a saucer, with or without a ¼ cup of water. Then go outdoor and pick up slugs and drop them in. I use tweezers to pick them up. They turn orange and die in a few minutes of osmosis, because the salt draws out their body juices.

Soap and Water
    ½ cup soft soap
    2 quarts water
Mix. Use wherever you see insect pests. Wash off when the invasion is over.

4

Useful Plant Materials
for Planning and Landscaping

It is easy to plan a vegetable garden because you start fresh every year on newly-prepared ground, and vegetables are seldom intended to serve as many purposes as plants in a garden of flowers. What's more, when you use the word *garden* for the vegetable garden, it is very clear what you mean. But when it comes to the other kind—the ornamental one—what does it mean? Is a garden a plot of ground where you grow flowering plants? Or is it the total place you go out into when you leave the house to be with the plants, grass, sun, fresh air, fountain or pool if you have one? We in the United States often say *yard* for such a place, and some people have begun to say *patio*, especially if the yard is small and the garden there is structured and controlled by the walls of the house or fences and hedges.

But the English people use the word *garden* in preference, even when the space they refer to has few plants in it, is a city courtyard with some furniture and potted plants, or is an expanse of lawn at a country place bordered with flower beds and shaded by fruit trees and flowering shrubs. They do not speak of going out into the yard; they go out to the garden.

I wish we used the word that way, too, so that when I say that in comparison with the 50

or so vegetables there are hundreds and hundreds of flowering plants to choose for the garden, the reader would definitely know that I meant the whole area and all its cultivated plants.

When you plan a garden of flowering plants, you also look way ahead to the future because it takes a long time to evolve such a garden—years and even decades. The flowers, even the perennials, are not really permanent, but the trees may last a century, and some of the flowering shrubs, if properly pruned, can last as long.

Maybe you will start with a 50-year-old or 100-year old trees already growing in the garden as focal features to plan around. Or maybe you have to begin with a recently bulldozed lot and plant your own trees, making all the decisions for a fresh start. Maybe instead you are about to refurbish an old run-down garden which needs to have some of its overgrown trees and shrubs eliminated.

The word *landscaping* really means land-shaping, and originally referred to the digging of lakes and making of hills to be accented with groves of trees and all cohered into a fine view from the house. Now the term refers to any kind of alteration of the land in your garden to make it more attractive, whether with lawns, shrubs, trees, flower beds, or as advocated in this book, with plantings or beds of mixed flowers, herbs and other plants valuable for a well-balanced garden population. Such a mixture, to keep the birds coming, for instance, demands plantings of trees and shrubs as well as flowers. And if you want the bees, of course you have to have a succession of plants in flower.

I don't suggest for a minute that you make your garden into a hodge-podge of plant materials. If you are to derive any pleasure from it, the garden must have some order and design to it, and a pleasantly modulated arrangement of heights—both while the plants are growing and maturing and when they have reached their full height. If there is a view, the garden should be arranged so that the view is seen to best advantage, framed by the plants you have, opened for a vista, and with dominant lines leading toward the place where your eye moves up and out to the view. These lines can be established by beds, a path, rows of shrubs, or a striking focal point such as a fountain, statue or specimen low tree which draws your eye to the key place. Where there is a need for privacy, the lines can also be made by hedges and fences, and if you have a terrace or porch or deck to sit on, the overhang that you make for shade can be angled to help frame the view.

UNIFIED DESIGN

Houses at sites where there is no view can have gardens with the total interest right there in the garden space. Some sort of focal point is still needed, and a very handy one to choose is a birdbath or recirculating pool of the kind described in the chapter on water gardens. A balanced pair of bushes near the pool or birdbath, and the lines of the garden beds leading towards it can help accent the focal point and give it importance. There are many other means to use to organize the space in the garden and give it character. Make up your mind that you are going to create a pleasant design, and get started. If you begin with the trees, ask yourself from the beginning whether you are placing them in relation to a unified design, and whether they will seem to pull the whole design together so that when you look out to the garden, you feel its composure and not a jumble of haphazard lines and placements.

SCALE

You have to consider scale. Do the trees you are selecting suit your house and the characteristics of your land? It would be ugly and disastrous to have big overpowering and dense trees with a little informal house, or tiny, pipsqueak trees with a big formal house. Scale is especially important for the plants you select to put at the corners of a house and to mask the foundation. I know people who wince every time they pass a house that has become smotherd by the big evergreens of the forest grown from little trees set in not many years before.

If you snatch up a bargain at the supermarket as though it were a cute little puppy, it may turn into a Great Dane when it grows up. The attractive little plants may have genes that will make them grow to a huge size and become utterly unsuitable. Get good stock, well labeled, and well understood by the person who sells it to you, and that usually means a thoroughly reliable nurseryman.

COLOR

Aside from design and scale there are other considerations to keep in mind when you are making your general plans for garden and yard. One of the most important is color, and this means not only the colors of the flowers you will select to grow, but also of the shrubs, the evergreens, the trees, especially the flowering trees in spring plus a few you can have for later seasons, and the groundcovers and vines, if you decide to have them. There are suggestions throughout for plant materials you can use, and I can't say too strongly that a pleasing variety of carefully modulated colors in the garden will give you year-round satisfaction and something interesting to look at—especially if you include trees and shrubs with berries on them, plants that have good autumn color, or trees and shrubs with unusual or bright colored twigs to brighten up the winter view of the garden.

TEXTURE

Textures are important to think about, too. Try a gradation of plant materials, not sudden juxtapositions. A big coarse-looking tree next to a delicate, finely-textured little shrub looks as ill-placed as a big, shaggy-leaved sunflower would next to a delicate pink bellflower. Even plants of the same general height can look ill-matched. That same little pink bellflower would not go very well with a coarse, informal red bee balm or large, prickly globe thistles. Maybe you don't feel this way about textures, and maybe such mixtures excite you.

OTHER PRINCIPLES

There is an old Chinese adage, said to be a key to the way a master painter teaches his pupil: "First you determine in what way the mountain is superior to the tree. Next you determine in what way the tree is superior to the mountain. Then you play with the brush and ink."

Though a design for a garden will be based on many of the same considerations of dominance and contrast, scale, shape, color, height, line and mass and texture, the garden is of course much more complicated than a flat canvas or paper to work on. For you also have to

determine the nature of the site—whether mostly sunny, shady, up and down hill or flat, dry or moist or in between, and what zone it is in. Your choices of plant material will involve all such aspects so that they may be suitable for the entire climate and ecological realities of your garden. Exposure, direction of slope, and whether or not there is water and existing vegetation to save will all enter in, as well as the multi-purposes you have in mind for the use your family will make of the area. Cost and maintenance must be considered. Maybe you have a season when you want the garden to be at its best, maybe in the spring with the bulbs or the fall with the rich colors of the turning leaves.

The soil will inevitably need to be considered. No matter how diligent you are, if you live on a limestone ledge, there is almost no hope of being able to make and keep your soil acid enough to suit plants like the rhododendrons, including azaleas, and lady's slippers, or many other woodsy wildflowers. You can't grow andromeda, clethra, or leucothoe, or the members of the huckleberry and blueberry family. Some of these are very attractive to birds, but unless your soil is already fairly acid, or you can make it so over a long period and keep up mulching with acid materials, your choices had better be for plants that can grow naturally in your type of soil. Soil of a neutral or slightly acid pH is adequate for many plants, but a few to choose if you have soil a little more acid than that are foxglove, turtlehead, fringed bleeding heart and the fine groundcovers, winterberry and bearberry. Partridgeberry, however, need very acid soil

If you are starting with a recently bulldozed yard, and thin, second-rate topsoil, you may have to be content the first year with only those plants that can survive in poor soil while you build up a good loam. If you are changing over from chemical to organic gardening, the problems are somewhat less acute, and you may

This woodland area is an interesting mixture of heights and shapes because it combines a variety of shrubs, trees, groundcovers, and rock garden plants. It provides shelter for wildlife and makes an excellent windbreak for the lawn in the foreground.

only need to attend to problem areas by reconditioning the land with soil-building legumes such as sweet peas, lupines, indigo or some of the clovers.

In many zones it is essential at the very beginning of your planning to think about windbreaks, and the trees and shrubs most rugged and adaptable for the climate where you live. To be attractive, windbreak plants should grow to good heights, but with a variety of heights so as not to be monotonous, and with a variety of shape, texture, color and growth habit. They should also be attractive as a hedgerow for wildlife, I'd say. Remember that if you put in thorny trees and shrubs like hawthorns and roses, you might get a tangle of weeds where the mess might become rather a problem unless you lay down a very thick mulch. In these days of the aim of easy maintenance, weeding among thorns is not anyone's idea of how to do things easily.

FINAL AIM: A MULTIPURPOSE GARDEN

I certainly do not want to try to dictate how people should feel about their gardens, or the lay-out either. There are dozens of books by landscape architects which show you gardens and foundation plantings made for other people's places and if you want to look at them, they may give you some ideas. If you feel stumped, and don't know how to put your vague feelings and ideas into actual practice, get one of the professional landscape gardeners to help because that is their training, to put such ideas into practical, concrete form. But get one of those who will listen to your special needs and not just force their ideas on you whether you like them or not. Try to get such a professional to understand that tall trees, for you, are not only to mark a line of vision, mark a boundary, frame the house, frame a view (or blot a view) but also are for harboring birds and animals, for providing fruit, for sending roots into the soil to bring up nutrients and recyclable trace elements for the good they will do the whole yard. Try to get your landscape architect to see that when you put a series of shrubs under the trees, they are there not only for the lines of gradation from taller to shorter, but also as cover for the birds, and as providers of berries and fruits as well as flowers. And explain to the professional that with your flowers you want pest-repellent herbs and occasional trap plants as part of the overall design—not just hidden in back here and there, but out front where they take part in the total garden, the health of the total garden, and that such plants have just as much meaning in the design as any other big spectaculars like peonies, glads or phlox.

YOU MUST KNOW YOUR ZONE

Professional landscape gardeners and landscape architects are very good at knowing what plant materials suit what zone, but if you are going to plan you own place without professional help, you need to know something about the plants suitable for the zone where you live. If you are deciding on a ground cover, for example, and think you would like something with yellow flowers during the summer, one of the St. John's worts such as *Hypericum repens* could be expected to do well if you live in a Zone 5, but the taller, handsomer Aaronsbeard, St. John's wort or the one called goldflower would only be suitable in Zones 6 or 7. Though annuals are not fussy as to zone, perennials often are, and the woody shrubs and trees which are forced to be dormant to winter over are the most sensitive of all to the weather, and to the depth of freezing they are subjected to in the ground during the cold winter months. We know that tender plants are killed by frost-bite, and I have seen shrubs that die back and have to be pruned and allowed to come up all over again the next year from the

roots. (It is also interesting to learn that some of the northern fruit trees won't amount to anything if transported to an area in the South where they do not get a dormancy period that they are accustomed to.) Tender trees and shrubs, if kept small enough, can be planted in pots or other containers and moved in and out of the weather as necessary—just as you move tender potted perennials, annuals and house plants. In fact, the new possibilities of containers and the container-grown plants now available at nurseries make landscape problems solvable in many more ways than used to be thought possible.

ZONE MAPS

The zone map will help you to know what will survive where, as discovered by horticulturists working at arboretums all over the country and at research stations of the United States Department of Agriculture. It is convenient that the USDA and the Arnold Arboretum of Harvard University have divided up the country into hardiness zones, and provided maps helpful to work from when you are making selections of plants for your place. The zone map shows where the coldest average temperatures occur. In Zone 4 it averages -10° to -20°F. in winter, and in Zone 5 somewhere around -10° to -5°F. But in Zone 7 you can pretty well rely on its never getting down to zero except in case of catastrophe. Some plants are described in catalogues as not hardy where the temperature falls below 20°F., and that means that you should not attempt to grow them unless you live in Florida, southern Texas, and the southern strip of Arizona, and southern California.

Another important zone consideration for shrubs and fruit trees as well as some other trees with large buds, is the date of the last killing frost after bud-formation. Some buds can be killed then, in the fall; others are merely retarded.

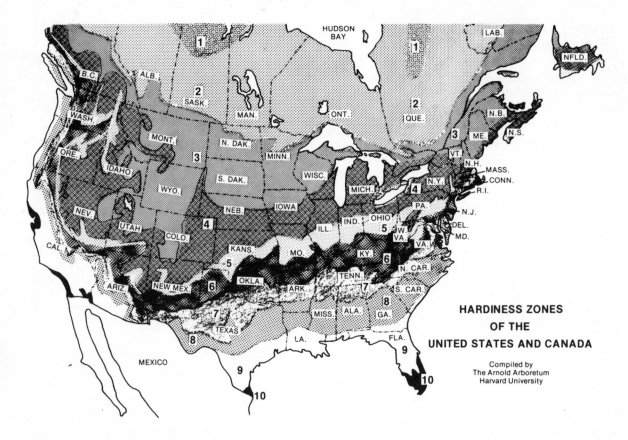

HARDINESS ZONES
OF THE
UNITED STATES AND CANADA

Compiled by
The Arnold Arboretum
Harvard University

Early frosts kill buds, too, and one protection is to keep susceptible trees on the middle of slopes—not way at the bottom or top. The same warm zone in Florida, Texas, California, and Arizona expect their last frost of the winter (if any) in January when the sun is one month on its way back north for spring. In the rest of the deep South, some time in February will usually be the date for the last frost; the date is some time in April in the middle states from eastern New Mexico into western Texas and on up through Kansas, Missouri, Kentucky, Virginia and right up the coast into Maryland, Delaware, New Jersey, Long Island, southern Connecticut and Cape Cod. Where I live in Vermont and in other northern states and in the Rockies, the last date of frost may be May 30th—or even later.

I think the reader would do well to study the Arnold Arboretum map. Note how the zones sweep up the coasts, both east and west because of the influence of the ocean currents, and also note how large bodies of water inland temper the climate, too.

There are interesting and very helpful variations to know about, too. The climate, and maybe even the zone, will vary in different locations on your own property. The average may be the climate that prevails on the west side of your house in a fairly open, flat stretch, and there are certain plants appropriate to grow there. To the south, in a protected corner near white woodwork or cement away from the wind, your zone may very well be actually one or even two zones more southerly than on the west side of the house. To the north of the house, where it is cold and windy, you have weather and

Foxglove (Digitalis)

Phlox

Snapdragon

*Ageratum 'Blue Ball,' Multiflora Petunia 'Coral Satin,' Cynoglossum,
and Snapdragon 'Floral Carpet'*

Triumph Tulip
Longwood Gardens

Example Verbena 'Ideal Florist Mix'

growing conditions like those of a zone farther north. A woody plant you couldn't possible grow on the cold side of the house might do quite well on the south side. But remember how easily some buds get nipped. Susceptible trees like magnolias and some of the fruit trees might better be planted to the north of the house to delay the opening of buds until there is less danger of their becoming nipped by a late frost.

OTHER INDICATORS

In addition to the zone map, some other indicators are good to know about, especially if you live on the edge of a zone and are not sure which zone you are really in and what information about hardiness you ought to rely on. Nature itself is the best teacher, I think, so what is best to rely on is what you learn from looking around you and seeing what grows in your neighborhood.

The chart below gives indicators, plants which will identify the zone for you if you look out the window and see them growing. When you do look out and see dwarf palmettos growing, you know you are way down South in Zone 9 and not in Vermont. Here where I live near the Green Mountains, in Zone 4, if I see privet in someone's hedge, it might be common privet or Amur privet, but to the north or up on the mountains to the east in Zone 3, the hedge would be much more likely to be Amur privet, which is more reliably hardy in that zone.

INDICATOR PLANTS, HARDY IN VARIOUS ZONES

ZONE 2 Arrowwood — *Viburnum dentatum*
Manchu cherry—*Prunus tomentosa*
Rosa rugosa
Siberian dogwood — *Cornus alba siberica*
Siberian peatree — *Caragana arborescens*

ZONE 3 Amur privet — *Ligustrum amurense*
Common lilac — *Syringa vulgaris*

ZONE 3 Staghorn sumac — *Rhus typhina*
Tatarian honeysuckle — *Lonicera tatarica*
Winged euonymus or burning bush — *Euonymus alatus*

ZONE 4 Common privet — *Ligustrum vulgare*
Cornelian cherry — *Cornus mas*
Morrow honeysuckle — *Lonicera morrowii*
Japanese yew — *Taxus cuspidata*
Prairie rose — *Rosa setigera*

ZONE 5 Forsythia — *F. suspensa*
Glossy abelia — *A. Grandiflora*
Japanese andromeda — *Pieris japonica*
Old-fashioned weigela — *W. florida*
Three-spine barberry — *Berberis triacanthophora*

ZONE 6 English yew — *Taxus baccata*
Fortune rhododendron — *R. fortunei*
House hydrangea — *H. macrophylla*
Japanese holly — *Ilex crenata*
Wax myrtle — *Myrica cerifera*

ZONE 7 Box honeysuckle — *Lonicera nitida*
Camellia — *C. japonica*
Cherry-laurel — *Prunus laurocerasus*
Darwin barberry — *Berberis darwinii*

ZONE 8 Chinese trumpetcreeper — *Campsis grandiflora*
Evergreen euonymus — *E. japonicus*
Japanese privet — *Ligustrum japonica*
Musk rose — *Rosa moschata*
Oleander — *Nerium oleander*

ZONE 9 Chinese hibiscus — *H. rosa-sinensis*
Dwarf palmetto — *Sabal minor*
Dwarf fig — *Ficus pumila*
Giant honeysuckle — *Lonicera hildebrandiana*
Sweet viburnum — *Viburnum odoratissimum*

ZONE 10 Bailey acacia — *A. baileyana*
Diamondleaf pittosporum — *P. rhombifolium*
Coral gum — *Eucalyptus torquata*
Fuchsia — *F. hybrida*
Peppertree — *Schinus molle, S. terebinthifolius*

None are mutually exclusive; plants often do well in several zones.

In this part of Vermont forsythias, with a few exceptions do very poorly, though they are supposed to be hardy in Zone 4. In fact, our only guarantee of having forsythia blooms is to cut the branches at Christmas time, bring them in for a few days' soak in a tub, and then force them in a warmish room. In the spring only those parts of the branches under deep snow cover for most of the winter come into bloom. Otherwise the forsythias merely serve as a refuge for chickadees and cardinals who have been startled at the birdfeeder. These bushes were here, put in by the previous owners of our house; with better planning they would have chosen the hardier Korean variety, and would not have planted them in the cold western exposure where they are.

When I drive south from here and begin to see luxuriant forsythia in bloom in the spring, then I know I am in Zone 5.

AND LEARN ABOUT ADVANCING SEASONS

In Dr. Donald Wyman's book about shrubs, *Shrubs and Vines for American Gardens* (see Appendix), he gives a chart showing the time when mountain laurel normally blooms. Of course, as we know from experience, the blooming date may vary as much as a month when conditions are unusual. Dr. Wyman's chart only aims at an average date. For his observation at the Arnold Arboretum near Bostton, the bloom is in mid-June on the average, as it is in Chicago, Rochester, N.Y., and with us in southern Vermont on the few protected slopes where people try to grow it. In New York and Columbus, Ohio mountain laurel blooms usually in early June; in Philadelphia and St. Louis, late May; in the Shenandoah Valley of Virginia in mid-May; in Augusta, Georgia in mid-April. The latest bloom he records is in Seattle, Washington, in late June.

His intention in giving this chart is to indicate to his readers that if you know the advance of spring that it shows and the date of bloom expected in Boston, you can calculate for your own region the date to expect there. This information is also of value in interpreting catalogues, which often seem to assure you of good May bloom, for instance, but you may live where it will be gone by then or perhaps not to be expected until June. To help out, Dr. Wyman provides a few more blooming periods which he calls normal: forsythia, mid-April; spicebush, mid-April, and the early rhododendron, Korean rhododendron, at the same time. Later in April, he expects to see star magnolia, mountain andromeda and some of the crabapples. By mid-May the charming Fothergilla will be in bloom, along with quite a few others such as bridal wreath spirea and a few weeks later, beauty bush and Vanhoutte spirea, the small flowered one. For complete information about all blooming times in his recommended list, see this valuable and helpful handbook on shrubs.

If I move to California, I know the zone variations will be very tricky. In the San Joaquin valley it would be cool enough to grow forsythia as well as the cherries, grapes, fig and walnuts I'd expect to see growing there. And I might be able to grow lilacs, weigelas and peonies. But the hot weather comes early in that valley, I've been told, so flowers like primroses, pansies, heather and stocks could not be expected to do well, and not azaleas, either, if you could manage to get and keep the soil acid enough. If I'd give up the idea of forsythia and settle on fuchsia and tuberous begonias, the northern coastal plain would be the place to go. There, in acid soil, you can also expect to grow fine rhododendrons and azaleas, wonderful stocks and carnations, and I'd hope to have pansies, sweet peas and snapdragons growing all winter. Naturally I couldn't hope to grow such plants if I moved to Palm Springs, but I'd love the grapefruit and roses I could grow there, but in high desert country where the winters can get so cold, I'd have to anticipate losing tropical or subtropical plants like hibiscus or many others from root rot.

FLOWERING TREES

Spring

Pussy willow, *Salix discolor* and *S. gracilistyla*, Z 5 fluffy white, or pink pussies.

Flowering dogwood, *Cornus florida*, Z 4 white and pink.

Cornelian cherry, *Cornus mas*, Z 4 early yellow flowers, before the leaves; edible fruits. To 24 feet.

Flowering crabapples, *Malus floribunda*, Z 4 pink to red, in May.

M. ionensis Plena, Bechtel crab. Z 2 pink, looking and smelling like roses.

M. 'Dorothea', semi-double, deep pink, scab-resistant.

Flowering plum, *Prunus cerasifera pissardi*, or *P. c. 'Atropurpurea'*, Z 4 reddish-purple foliage and pink flowers

Flowering cherry. *Prunus serrulata*, Z 5-6 especially 'Kwanzan,' the Washington cherry tree. White to pink.

Shadbush or shadblow, *Amelanchier candensis*, Z 4 gentle, slender tree, with early white flowers. Later has good fruits for birds.

Star magnolia, *M. stellata*, Z 5 White fragrant April flowers.

Saucer magnolia, *M. soulangiana*, Z 5 White inside, pink-flushed outside, and hardiest of all magnolias.

Carolina silverbell, *Halesia monticola* or *H. carolina*, z 5 grows to 30 feet. Native to the Southeast. Blooms in hundreds of loose clusters in May. No pests.

Golden chain tree, *laburnum wateri* 'Vossii', Clusters of 20 inches, with yellow flowers in late May or early June. Poisonous. Blooms for 2 weeks.

Washington thorn and hawthorns, *Crataegus* phaenopyrum; *C. oxyacantha*, etc. Z 4 White flowers, good fall fruits. Subject to borers. Red double: 'Paul's Scarlet'.

Tree lilac, *Syringa amurensis*, Z 4 Pyramidal to 30 feet, white flowers, not fragrant in June.

New Zealand sophora, *S. tetraptera*, Z 9 Spectacular yellow clusters in May.

Summer

Japanese dogwood, *Cornus kousa*, Z 5 white to pink blooms, lasting several weeks, followed by pink fruits.

Stewartia, *S. pseudo-camellia*, Z 5 flowers like white camellias.

Golden rain tree, *Koelreuteria paniculata*, Z 5-9 About 30 feet. Yellow flowers and yellowish papery pods. No pests. Plant in soil.

Japanese pagoda (or Chinese scholar) tree. *Sophora japonica*, Z 4 To 50 feet. Very satisfactory tree with feathery compound leaves and white pea-like flowers, blooming from the end of July into September. No pests.

Sourwood, *Oxydendrum arboreum*, Z 5 About 25 feet, but sometimes a good bit larger. Flowers in mid-July look like lily-of-the-valley, in clusters. Good dense, lustrous foliage. A native tree, member of the heath family. (But pH 4 to pH 8 is its tolerance.)

Fall

Silk tree, *Albizzia julibrissin*, Z 7 Bright pink, brushlike.

Franklinia, *F. alatamaha*, Z 5 (or *Gordonia alatamaha*) Blooms Sept. and into Oct. With 4-inch cupped white flowers, like single peonies. In cold zones, let it grow as a shrub. Best pH is 5 to 6, and it likes peaty, moist soil.

Smoketree, *Cotinus coggygria*, Z 5 a tree of about 15 feet, with conspicuous fuzzy fruiting panicles in late summer. Flowers are inconspicuous and yellow. Tender north of Washington, D.C. Also a purple variety 'Purpureus.'

Crape myrtle, *Lagerstroemia indica*, Z 7 beautiful showy shrub or small tree with 1½-inch flowers, in pink or purple or white in 5 to 9-inch clusters. Get named varieties, balled and burlaped.

Southern magnolia, *M. grandiflora*, evergreen and with big 8-inch flowers in late summer and early fall.

Floss-silk tree, *Chorisia speciosa*. Yellow flowers in fall.

❧PLANNING MATERIAL❧

Wherever you are going to live, there is a wealth of material to choose from, and a hundred possibilities for making a modern, simple multipurpose garden. Get out the paper and sketch it out, but more important, consult local nurserymen, study catalogues and specialty books and magazines, and go to nurseries and public gardens and arboretums and see for yourself the plants as they grow. Try to see them when they are in bloom, so that you will know what colors you are selecting. For shrubs and trees, try to see mature specimens at arboretums, not just the little plants at the nursery. Plan ahead. Don't just grab up something on impulse when you happen to see it. The secret of good landscaping is to see what changes are needed, to look ahead, and to make an overall plan which delicately balances in a harmonious design the long-term needs of the land and its contours, spaces and inhabitants, and your own feelings, tastes, habits and preferences, including your respect for the total lives that will be led in the garden, and, of course, the needs of the plants that will grow there right away and in the years to come.

TREES

I believe it is wise to plan first for trees, for their shade, for their flowers and fruits which you want for your own enjoyment and for the birds and all other inhabitants you want in the garden. As you think ahead, draw out on paper where the trees should go, allowing for their mature spread and height. Go outdoors frequently to gauge what the trees will look like when they grow tall. And keep testing their fitness for the plan. Are they appropriate to the design? Will one of them or a group be a focal point, and unify or pull the design together? Will they suit your house and the characteristics of your land—not too big for a small house and lot,

or too little and insignificant for a large, formal place?

If your lot is large enough, some tall shade trees suitable to your zone make a fine setting for the flowering trees and shrubs you probably will want to have. Of course there are large flowering trees, too, such as horse chestnuts in the North and tulip trees, North or South and the splendid *Magnolia grandiflora* in the South. I find the European mountain ash, *Sorbus aucuparia*, a very attractive tree with its big, lush clusters of orange or reddish berries in the fall. The flowering ash, *Fraxinus ornus*, will grow to 60 feet, and in warm zones trees like yellowwood, *Cladrastis lutea*, will have pale yellow blooms in June.

Among smaller flowering trees are all the ornamental fruit trees such as crabapples, plums, apricots, Bradford pears and cherries, many of which you can also get as dwarfs, now, even with several varieties on one tree. If I lived in the South, I'd really like to grow a silk tree or two, *Albizzia julibrissin*, as well as the pestless Japanese snowball, *Styrax japonica*, which has been blossoming there each spring ever since Revolutionary days. And if I lived in southern Florida I'd certainly have a tree I think is just about the handsomest tree I've ever seen, the royal poinciana, *Delonix regia*, with its brilliant red flowers in great profusion. In California it would be exciting to have some pepper trees, *Schinus molle*, with their shiny divided leaves, drooping branches and clusters of white flowers, or to fit into a small corner a silk-oak grevillea, *G. robusta*, which has orange flowers in spring. People are now using this tree for a pot plant, but in Australia it grows to 150 feet. Citrus trees, either for pots in the North or outdoors in the South are a delight, with their fragrance, waxy white flowers and fine fruit.

BIRD-ATTRACTING TREES

Mountain ash, hawthorns and many other good trees attract birds. We have a mulberry tree in our yard in Vermont, placed between the vegetable garden and one of the flower borders just where the birds are invited to come in and enjoy the fruits all summer long. I recommend such a tree for everyone in the North or South, either *Morus nigra*, the common or black mulberry or one of the others such as white mulberry, *M. alba*. The fruit is rather insipid, but the birds love it and prefer it so much to the domesticated berries and fruits that they rarely go for anything in the garden besides the soft and succulent fruits of the mulberry tree. It is worth any gardener's knowing that wild fruits and berries are much more to birds' liking than the cultivated cherries, pears, blueberries and other temptations you want them to keep away from. This mulberry tree has under it nothing but a strip of field so it doesn't matter where the berries not eaten by the birds happen to fall to the ground.

I must warn any readers who think of putting a mulberry tree overhanging a terrace, for instance, that the chairs and the paving stones may turn somewhat purple during August. We had a mulberry overhanging the roof and eaves gutters at the old farm where we used to live, so the August run-off of rain from the roof into the cistern meant pale purple water for the rest of the season. We got used to it, of course, but sometimes guests were a little startled when they saw some of the plumbing that was serviced by this water.

OTHER CONSIDERATIONS

There are, therefore, quite a few considerations to keep in mind in choosing trees for your landscaping. Aside from size, type, and placement, shade is obvious, and so are the effects of softening the lines of the house, the boundary of the property, or special areas of the yard. The effect of good trees is always decorative and protective, especially near porches, terraces, and picnic areas. Both flowering and non-flowering trees are desirable for the good housekeeping of

your garden, and the shelter they provide will be welcome to all.

One more point to keep in mind, for the trees you plan to put near shrubs and flowers, and that is the depth of their roots. Shallow rooted trees will rob nourishment much more than deep-rooted trees will. Shallow-rooted include elm, poplar, sycamore, most of the pines, Amur cork and katsura. The deep-rooted and less competitive trees are red maple, moutain ash, pine oak and also red oak and white oak, sweet gum, sweet birch, or white birch, locust, shadblow, the interesting Chinese elms and the Chinese chestnut. Also, in the right zone, you can choose any of the citrus trees or such nut trees as pecan and English walnut if you are concerned about avoiding severe root competition. Obviously any large tree will cast shade and will use up nutrients, so provide both trees and undercover shrubs with what they will need.

SHRUBS

The shrubs you choose, large or small, should be related to the overall design, and serve it as significantly as will the trees and flowers. There is more work to shrubs because they must be pruned to keep them in shape and to rejuvenate them. But if you have a will to take care of them, you can have any shrub that will survive (or whose roots will survive) in your zone. Flowering shrubs are a joy, especially in June when they have such a profusion of bloom. But even more useful for landscaping are evergreens, and I'll especially recommend that you consider dwarf evergreens. Your landscaping will look a good deal better if you choose some tall, medium and little evergreens of different colors to fill corners or as foundation planting. There are some dwarfs which only grow a few inches in ten years, and they are convenient and handsome plants to have. Get a good catalogue and go to a good nursery and pick out evergreens which will make your foundation and incidental planting exciting and lively.

SOME SHRUBS

For Colder Zones

Snowmound spirea *Spiraea nipponica* 'Snowmound'. Low-growing, white flowers in June. Z 4

Bush cherry *Prunus skinneri* 'Baton Rouge'. Pink flowers. Will endure—40°F. *P. skinneri* 'Nakai Chinese' White.

Highbush blueberry *Vaccinium corymbusum*. Needs acid soil; good for birds. Z 3

Rosa rugosa. Very rugged. Any soil. Pink or white flowers. Z 2

Japanese barberry *Berberis thunbergii*. Yellow and red flowers; red berries. Red or purple fall leaves. Z 3

Cornelian cherry *Cornus mas*, a dogwood. April bloom, large, bushy. Small yellow flowers; red edible fruits. Z 4

Memorial rose *Rosa wichuraiana*. Low-growing, very good for banks and for groundcover. Single white roses in mid-July. Z 4-5

Bush cinquefoil *Potentilla fruiticosa*. (50 named varieties) From 3 inch to 6 feet, with all-summer yellow bloom. Silky soft green foliage. Z 2

Kerria (or Globe Flower) *K. japonica*. Old-time favorite with yellow flowers in mid-May. Twigs green all winter.

For Warmer Zones

Glossy abelia *Abelia x grandiflora*. Pink blooms in Aug.; likes part shade. Variety 'Sherwood' is low-growing. Hardy to Z 5

Abelia x 'Edward Goucher'. Lavender blooms in July to Sept. with bronzy foliage in the fall. Hardy to Z 5

Leucothoe *L. catesbaei* (or *L. fontanesiana*). White flowers; lovely shiny foliage, evergreen or semi-evergreen. Z 5. Many varieties, including one with multicolored foliage. Will grow in part shade. Z 5

Evergreen barberry *Berberis darwinii*. Showy yellow or orange flowers in May. Likes shade. Grows 3 feet to 10 feet. Z 8

Cherry-laurel *Prunus caroliniana* (or *Laurocerasus caroliniana*). Blooms in late summer, white florets in racemes. Shiny leaves. Grows to 6 feet to 18 feet but keep pruned as you wish. Z 6-7

Musk rose *Rosa moschata* and var. 'Nastarana'. Fragrant white, tinged pink flower. Other varieties in bright pink and red. Grows to 6 feet. Z 6

Father Hugo's rose *Rosa hugonis*. Yellow flowers, early. Very delicate foliage. Grows 7 feet. Z 5

Sargent hydrangea *H. sargentiana*. Pink and lavender flowers in mid-summer. Z 7

Harlequin glory-bower *Clerodendron trichotomum*. Z 6. Aug. flowers.

PROTECTING SHRUBS

Some of the warmer-zone shrubs can be grown in border zones to the north if you mulch them well or give them winter protection. Others may die up top, but will come up again if pruned to the ground. Ask your nurseryman, but consider some of the excellent rhododendrons and azaleas, if you can keep the soil acid, and some of the beautiful hollies with their fine berries. Another berried shrub is firethorn or pyracantha, also subject to frost damage, and a favorite shrub of mine, Oregon holly grape. Japanese quince is no more reliable than forsythia.

SAFE PLANTS FOR COLD ZONES

In the cold zones you can feel perfectly safe, however, with junipers and many other needle evergreens; with an interesting shrub, ninebark, which has lovely chartreuse foliage in the spring and pinky-red fruits and pods in the fall; daphne, a fragrant little flowering shrub, with pink flowers; and of course the lilacs. High shrubs for the edge of the woods, or for a privacy edging might include Nanking cherry, service-berry or shadblow, Amur maple and perhaps the oddity, Purple-leaved European hazelnut, *Corylus avellana purpurea*, with high purple leaves and spectacular catkins, rather like birch-tree catkins. A hedge-shrub much advertized in recent years is a rather pesty columnar buckthorn *alias* 'Tallhedge,' because it seeds itself all over, or else the birds seed it. But if you can keep the place weeded, buckthorns do grow quickly and are rugged, pestfree shrubs and trees. There are also many viburnums, including the deliciously fragrant one, *V. carlesii*, with a pinkish snowball of flowers in May, and many other fragrant ones, and *V. opulus*, European cranberry, grown here since colonial times. Some varieties have red, some have yellow berries.

We in Vermont are unable to grow the many lovely azaleas that can be grown in other zones, so our landscaping must be confined to other shrubs, with the exception of *R. calendulaceum*, flame azalea and *R. nudiflorum*, Pinxter azalea, a native here and on the protected list of endangered plants, but they can be purchased from nurseries where they are propagated. The flowers are pink and fragrant. Only buy azaleas in your own zone. It is a possibility, if you import deciduous azaleas from zones to the south, to bring in a terrible disease, petal blight or azalea flower spot, which can get loose and go through all the wild members of the rhododendron family, not only the azaleas but the mountain laurels, too. You wouldn't want to be responsible for starting such an epidemic.

And don't forget the small evergreens. A yew to think of is *Taxus brevifolia*, or the very slow-growing *T. cuspidata densa*. (In colder zones get Japanese, not English yews.) Junipers might include *Juniperus communis depressa aurea-spica* or *J. communis compressa*, which only grows one foot in 20 years. For an accent of yellow-green consider a small arborvitae, *Thuja orientalis aurea nana*; and a little golden false cypress, *Chamaecyparis pisifera filifera aurea*. You would be amazed at the numbers of interesting small evergreens that are available (and so rarely used by home gardeners). Go to the national arboretum in Washington, D.C. to see a whole collection of them. Or if you cannot do that, send for the catalogue of Amos Pettingill at the White Flower Farm in Litchfield, Connecticut. Many are available from him. They are suitable for foundation plantings of great interest and variety of color, for groundcovers and banks, for edgings and for accents in your garden design. The availability of these lovely small plants is one thing that makes me satisfied to live in a northern zone.

IN SOUTHERN ZONES

But when I think of what can be grown as flowering trees and flowering shrubs to landscape your property in southern zones, I feel ready to move at a moment's notice.

If you live in the Carolinas, Virginia, Washington, D.C., Maryland or the warmer southeast corners of Pennsylvania and New Jersey, across the Middle South and up the mid-zones of the West Coast states, you can grow hollies, English box, all those lovely azaleas, lavender, skimmia, Hinoki cypress, rosemary, bamboos, magnolias, camellias, the best rhododendrons, especially on the coast, and some of the best cotoneasters. Sweet bay is a possibility, wax myrtle, the handsome pyracantha called Rogers firethorn, which can be trained into all sorts of interesting twiggy shapes to accent its white flowers and red berries, and the large-leaved Chinese photinia, *P. serrulata*, with its six inch heads of white flowers in May and its good red berries in the fall. A cousin, Japanese photinia, *P. glabra*, is somewhat smaller (ten feet instead of thirty feet at maturity) and is very useful in Southeastern states.

And in the warmest zones, just think of the oleanders you can grow, *Nerium oleander*, with the lovely clusters of white, pink or red flowers. And think of the sweet viburnum, flowering senna, princess flower or glory bush; pittosporum, *P. tobira*, with its very fragrant waxy white flowers; the even more fragrant cape-jasmine, *Gardenia jasminoides* (if your soil is rich enough) and other jasmines. Then there are the citrus fruits with their fine blossoms, plumbago, natal plum, with white flowers; imperial veronica, with purple flowers; David's viburnum, with pinkish flowers; and the spreading rock rose, *Cistus* in variety, most of which can be grown up to Zone 7, with protection. And just think of the flower-laden, prolific, bushy vine, the Bougainvillea, you can have to decorate your dooryard or your fence.

In all these zones there are many more shrubs you can discover and use. I've mentioned some of those I'd really like to grow myself. But whatever you choose, aim for a cool, uncrowded pattern for summer and, if you live in a cold zone, an interesting uncluttered winter pattern of bare brances on the deciduous trees and shrubs. In warm zones evergreens lend interest in any season; in cold zones they are valuable for contrast, texture and their cheerful greenness or yellowy chartreuse color the year around but especially in winter. Keep the shape, height, color and texture in mind when you are choosing, as well as the time and color of bloom. You probably will want some sequence of bloom and some variety, but I know one garden, all in white, which is very attractive and peaceful— from its striking, stark yucca blooms to its lush white lilacs and white hydrangeas.

PRIVACY AND HEDGES

American gardeners and home-owners don't care half as much for privacy in their yards as English and European or Japanese people do. As long as the garden for many thousands in this country meant a monocrop lawn to grow and mow, Americans seemed to prefer mowing with the lawn mower as their garden activity. But now with the frequent addition of barbecues and areas of the yard shaped for outdoor cooking and eating, and especially with the proliferation of backyard swimming pools, there is more of an impulse to add screening to the landscape plans. When the pool takes up most of the backyard, as it does in some layouts, screens and hedges are what one needs because there is not room for anything else. Plants to use include the tall arborvitae, hemlock, Cannart juniper, and for deciduous trees, the maples and beeches which can be clipped to hedge shape. Amur maple and Norway maple are possibilities. If you live in Zone 5 or south, don't mind some fruits rolling down at you from its thorny stems, you can use an old-time hedge plant, Osage orange, *Maclura pomifera*. And of course boxwood and privet are good old standards. We in Vermont like hedges of such fragrant and flowerful bushes as lilac, Persian lilac, mock orange, hedge roses and Russian olive. I am partial to the rare and beautiful plant, the large fothegilla, *F. major*, with 20-inch white flowers in mid-May, and wonderful bright autumn foliage. We have long used *Spiraea vanhouttei* and its cousin, bridal wreath, *S. prunifolia*. We think of it as marking not only the time for June brides, but even more so the time when school lets out for the summer.

FINAL STRUCTURAL DECISIONS

Once you have drawn out your plans for trees, shrubs, hedges and boundary plants, and once you have decided where the walls, pools,

GROUNDCOVER PLANTS AND VINES

Name	Hardy to	Comments
Aaronsbeard St. Johnswort *Hypericum calycinum*	Zone 6	Sun or part shade. Light, somewhat sandy soil. Yellow flowers.
Bearberry *Arctostaphylos uva-ursi*	Zone 2	Needs acid soil. Grows 6 to 12 inches. Sun or part shade.
Bearberry cotoneaster *Cotoneaster dammeri*	Zone 5	Small shiny leaves. Grows to 6 to 12 inches. Sun.
Bugle plant *Ajuga reptans*	Zone 4	Very popular groundcover. Spreads easily. Flowers of blue, white, pink. Sun or shade.
Chamaedrys germander *Teucrium chamaedrys*	Zone 5	Grows to 10 inches. Shrubby. Pink or purple flowers. Keep clipped.
Chiloe strawberry *Fragaria chiloensis*	Zone 4 or 5	Parent of cultivated strawberry; native to West Coast. Thick green leaves for groundcover, with runners.
Climbing hydrangea *H. anomala petiolaris*	Zone 4	Actually a vine; will spread horizontally, too.
Creeping cotoneaster *C. adpressa*	Zone 4	Small shiny leaves. Grows to 12 to 24 inches. Likes sun.
Creeping juniper *J. horizontalis* and vars. and other junipers, e.g. Waukegan, Sargent & Shore	Zone 4	These evergreens are good covers especially for banks and other difficult spots. Grow 1 foot or a bit more. Like sun; light soil. They spread. Waukegan turns purple in winter.
Creeping mahonia *M. repens*	Zone 5	Native to West Coast. Spreads by stolons. Soft green foliage. Grows to 12 inches.
Crown vetch *Coronilla varia*		I do not recommend this for anyone; it is rampant.
English Ivy *Hedera helix*	Zone 5	Actually a vine, but an old favorite for groundcovers. Needs light or dense shade. Best not to put under shrubs, but all right under trees.
Fiveleaf akebia *A. quinata*	Zone 4	Really a vine, and best to grow it on a wall. Rosy, waxy flowers. Sun or shade.
Fleece-flowers *Polygonum affine*	Zone 3	Makes a mat, rather coarse, with small red flowers in the fall. Grows to 6 to 9 inches.
Silver fleece vine *P. aubertii*	Zone 4	This vine will grow very rapidly and go where you let it.
Foam-flower *Tiarella cordifolia*	Zone 4	A plant with toothed leaves and spikes of fine, small white flowers. Likes shade and rich acid soil. Blooms April to July.

Name	Hardy to	Comments
Galax *Galax aphylla*	Zone 3	Grows to 3 inches up to 6 . Grows from a rhizome, spreading easily in moist, shady places. The flower stalk is unbranched, with a spike of small white blossoms. May to July. Likes slightly acid soil.
Great prostrate bellflower *Campanula garganica*	Zone 5	This hugs the ground, has gray leaves and blue flowers that bloom from May to Sept. Sun or part shade.
Ground ivy *Nepeta hederacea*	Zone 3	Grows to 3 inches. Rounded leaves and blue flowers. Also called Gill-over-the-ground. Sun or shade. Easily becomes a pest.
Gypsophila, Rosy Creeping *Gypsophyla repens rosea*	Zone 2	Lovely pink variety of Baby's Breath. Full sun. Give lime.
Heath; Spring heath *Erica carnea*	Zone 5	Blooms Jan. to May, if mild enough. Used in rock gardens.
Honeysuckle *Lonicera henryi*	Zone 4	A vine that goes over the ground. There is another called Japanese or Hall's honeysuckle, and I beg you never to get it. It is horribly rampant, invasive and destructive—and advertized in entirely too many catalogues.
Houseleeks, or Hen and chickens *Sempervivum* sp.	Zone 4 or 5	Many kinds. Try several
Leather bergenia *B. crassifolia*	Zone 2	A spectacular plant with large leaves and a spike of pink to purple flowers. Likes moist, shady places and moist walls. Full sun keeps it small. Can grow to 22 inches.
Lily-of-the-valley *Convallaria majalis*	Zone 2	Deliciously fragrant white flowers in May. Foliage large and bright green. Spreads easily. Dense or light shade. Rich soil.
Lily-turf *Liriope spicata*	Zone 4	Grasslike leaves, and whitish, pale lilac flowers. Keep free of grass. These have very small tubers. Divide to propagate.
Memorial rose *Rosa wichuraiana*	Zone 5	Grows to 1 foot. Used for half a century to cover banks and slopes. Small white flowers which come in late summer. Foliage semi-evergreen and glossy. Roots wherever stems touch the ground. Red hips. Average soil. Sun.

Name	Hardy to	Comments
Moss pink *Phlox subulata*	Zone 2	The favorite for rock gardens. Grows to 6 inches.
Pachysandra *P. procumbens;* *P. terminalis*	Zone 4	One of the toughest, most long-lasting, pest-free groundcovers. Shiny leaves; inconspicuous flowers. Spreads.
Periwinkle *Vinca minor*	Zone 4	Very popular, very satisfactory groundcover with dark, small green leaves and blooms that are blue, white, pink or red, according to species. Shade or part shade.
Vinca major	Zone 7	This one is used more in the South than *V. minor*. It is bigger, and its flowers are blue. The variegated variety is often used in window boxes, North or South.
Plantain lily or Funkia *Hosta* species	Zone 2	All species of this plant are good to mass for groundcover use. Their pest-free sturdy growth makes them very good for areas where people do not walk.
Prostrate broom *Cytisus decumbens*	Zone 5	This 8-inch form of broom is excellent for banks and stays in bloom with yellow pea-like flowers from June to Aug. Small leaves. Related to the upright Scotch broom, from which brooms were made in olden times.
Prostrate rosemary *Rosmarinus officinalis*	Zone 8	For those in warm climates this is fine groundcover, e.g. for California gardens. The variety *R. humilis* is a little bit hardier.
Rock Spray *Cotoneaster horizontalis*	Zone 4	Another popular, small-leaved plant, which grows 2 or 3 feet, and is good for banks. Sun or part shade, in good rich soil. Both leaves and red berries last until cold weather.
Roman camomile *Anthemis nobilis*	Zone 4	Finely cut leaves, with daisy-like small flowers. Can be used as grass substitute and can be mowed. Will grow to 12 inches if not mowed.
Salal *Gaultheria shallon*	Zone 5	West Coast plant of great attractiveness, with long evergreen leaves and fine clusters of waxy white flowers in June. Needs acid soil and shade, but will make a lower, matlike growth on poor soil in full sun.

Name	Hardy to	Comments
Scotch heather *Calluna vulgaris*	Zone 5	Where it gets a good start, this plant will go for miles, as it does in Scotland. The varieties come with pink, white and red spikes of flowers, and the leaves will usually be evergreen.
Silky woadwaxen *Genista pilosa*	Zone 5	A legume, with yellow pea-like flowers, that will grow on just about any soil, including under trees if the shade is not too dense. The species *G. tinctoria* is used as a dye plant. This one will grow to 1 foot; *G. tinctoria* to 3 feet. The species *G. sagittalis* is even lower and a little hardier. It is sometimes called Arrow Broom.
Snow-in-summer *Cerastium tomentosum*	Zone 2	I advise against it for it is a pest. Will grow in sun or light shade, with woolly foliage and white flowers. Once in, every little bit of root will send up new plants.
Sweet fern *Comptonia peregrina*	Zone 2	Very popular roadside groundcover in New England, with very fragrant foliage. Grows to several feet under optimum conditions of moisture and peaty soil. Very difficult to transplant, so start with tiny plants or seeds. Is shrubby.
Sweet woodruff *Asperula odorata*	Zone 3	Excellent groundcover, with neat green leaves and good blooms, white in May, June. Pest-free.
Wintercreeper *Euonymus fortunei* varieties	Zone 5	Actually vines, but widely used, sturdy plants. Clip when necessary. Control scale.
Woolly yarrow *Achillea tomentosa*	Zone 2	Fine, evergreen foliage, but gray near the ground. Will grow to 12 inches, but you can keep it cut and in a mat. Small clusters of yellow flowers, May to Sept. Will grow anywhere.
Yellowroot *Xanthorhiza simplicissima* or *X. apiifolia*	Zone 4	Grows to 2 feet, in part shade or dense shade. Often used under trees and shrubs, in rich, humusy soil. Has feathery spikes of purplish flowers in May. Is actually a small deciduous shrub. Increases by underground stolons.

paths and stepping stones are to go, it is time to make some plans for the flower beds. Be sure that you have planned all the necessary areas: for the driveway and entrance, for the outdoor living spaces, the play areas, service areas, and your own work area, with or without a tool house, with or without a greenhouse, but plan a place to keep tools, and of course a good place for at least one compost heap.

I live in an area where it is the custom to use natural growing materials for practically every demarcation of space—except where we perforce also use stones. But if I lived in one of many other areas, I'd certainly consider using a good deal of wood, too—for fences, for casting shade, for demarcating parts of the garden and using the wooden structure for trellises or for backgrounds to plants. Some of the most impressive and prize-winning designs for garden layouts in recent years have been those using wooden dividers and wood-lath overhead structures to cast light shade. The one warning for such

This low stone wall effectively divides shrubby and woodland growth from smaller, perennial plantings, without detracting from the semi-wild, natural landscape.

structures is that they must not drastically cut off the air circulation in the garden, for plants must have air to keep healthy. Low brick and stone walls make very attractive backgrounds for low-growing plants and help to accent the basic shapes of the garden.

There are two other kinds of plants to consider before you begin plans for the flowers and flower beds. They are groundcovers and vines, including the vines which make very good groundcovers. Climbing vines are of course very attractive on fences and houses, if the woodwork or other material of the house is not harmed. They also look well on trees, unless they are the sort that will harm trees such as woodbine, honeysuckle, wild grape or the two demons, poison ivy and wisteria, which can wrap themselves around any young tree, overshade it and ruin it.

GROUNDCOVERS

There are several advantages to groundcovers, and not the least is the way they can fill up a space in the garden for you. They will hold banks, fill places where you can't possibly get a lawn mower, decorate the foundations, the foot of a wall, or climb on a wall, and just make a lovely carpet of plants in any place where you wish to put a great many specimens of one fairly low-growing plant to cover the ground. They are particularly valuable around trees to prevent compaction of the soil over tree roots, and good to use between paving stones on a terrace or patio so the soil can breathe.   The chart shows many of the good possibilities, but if you want to settle for the tried and true, the pestless old favorites, stick to pachysandra, periwinkle, English ivy, the vigorous little carpet bugles or ajugas and the rose used for banks, Memorial rose. Space the plants well when you first put them in and keep them weeded or well mulched until they grow large enough to fill the space and keep the weeds down themselves. One way to help them along is to surround each original clump with shingles, let the groundcover grow out over them, then gently move the shingles out and let the plant spread and its stems take root.

In this way you keep down weeds, and also keep the groundcover plant compact while it is first growing. This is also a method to use—if you do not use stones or bricks—to stop the line of the groundcover plot at a certain place.

5

The Outdoor Living Area

One of the best-loved and most attractive gardens today is the one which encompasses the outdoor living area at the back or side of the house where the family spends a lot of time during the summer. Sometimes there is a swimming pool nearby; sometimes there is only a small decorative pool with or without a fountain or a little waterfall. It may be sunny or shady, softly green or full of colored flowers, up and down hill or on the level, with or without cooking arrangements, lounge chairs or tables where people can play games, sew, read, study or eat their meals, and watch the birds come in to the feeders.

Even without those amenities and in a different location, at the front or by the driveway, an outdoor room can be an entrance hall, well decorated with shrubs and flowers and perhaps a tree or so to make an attractive and inviting place for all who come to the house that way. Sometimes the area is mostly a passageway between a garage and a house, but it still can be a well-planted and pleasant little garden. Sometimes it is mostly a play area for the children, but that too can have interesting flowers, a tree to climb, and good sturdy vines for a sound-barrier and for shade. Many of the plants you can have in any of these spaces can be fragrant, white and showy at night, or soothingly green and soft-colored to suit a mood of relaxation at the end of the day.

ORIGINS

In Spanish, Portuguese and other European cultures from which many of our modern patios actually derive, the outdoor living space was usually a courtyard surrounded by the four wings of the house, and separated from the street by a gate and passageway into the court. Often there were cobblestones or flagstones which came right up to the four walls because of the horse traffic as well as the human traffic and the fact that without stones the place would be a sea of mud in all too many seasons, even in the hot sunny countries near the Mediterranean. The tall walls of the houses cast cool shade in hot weather and in clear, colder weather the court made a pocket of sunshine so that in a good part of the year it was pleasant to be out in the patio.

Window boxes, wall fountains, bins and planters for flowers and for vines were all used, and small trees and shrubs in tubs along with pots of flowers were frequently part of the courtyard decoration. In some places, and especially in areas in from the sea where the weather is colder, there were frequently little greenhouses to stretch the growing seasons and take care of plants in adverse weather. In England such little greenhouses are often seen, and Americans are now beginning to install more and more of these wonderfully helpful structures for growing the plants they want.

OUTDOOR ROOMS ARE USUALLY SMALL SCALE

If you have a big, old-fashioned house, your outdoor living area will probably not be so much a patio as a sizable terrace looking out over the lawn. But if you have a modern, low, one-story or ranch house, the patio area will be proportionate, and low-growing plants characteristic of patio vegetation will be exactly what you will want. Unless your house is on a very pronounced slope or in an already existing woods, the trees you will need to select will not be big elms, ashes and maples, but small Amur maples, flowering crabs, dogwoods, dwarf evergreens, and perhaps some dwarf fruit trees which you may even train to be espaliers against one wall.

Since the location of a patio is always up against one wall, and often two, when there is an ell or the projecting back end of a garage, the feeling of an outside room is already established. I have a friend up the valley who even hangs pictures up on the outside wall under an overhang to establish that living room feeling from the start. Another friend, down the valley, who actually does have four walls around the outdoor living room and therefore calls it an atrium, hangs pots of flowers on two walls, and has fixed up a series of shelves with plants on them on the south-facing wall so you look across to the cheerfulness of plants in all seasons (except the hottest) because there is a wall of glass there in front of the shelves. There are X-shaped paths in the atrium, a pebbled area where there is a table under an umbrella and plenty of comfortable chairs for sitting and snacking or sitting and reading, or playing with the dog. This place has shrubs but not trees.

In two-or three-walled outdoor-living areas you need to have trees to help shade the area and your decisions about these are of first importance. Often the third wall is a trellis covered with a vine. If it happens to be a neighbor's big tall fence or, in the city, the big blank wall of the building next door, it is preferable not to use a vine, but to plant the space in front of the wall or fence in such a way as to mask it and gain some depth with a graduated set of plants. You might have a tree or two at the rear with a gradation of larger to smaller shrubs and then very small shrubs and your flowers in front. There are other tricks to use, and if you are faced with a problem like this, it is best to get a landscape architect to help you solve it.

MAKING PLANS

Whether or not you have professional help in planning your patio, get out the graph paper and pencil, make plans and make a schedule for planting. The plans, I believe, should include making a model of the area and what you want to put in it, and be sure to go out and measure the spaces and mark them some way so you will see for yourself what the sizes and shapes are going to look like once you get them established out there. Figure on the mature size of the plants, and after deciding on the structural items, start with the big plants first—the trees and shrubs. In most climates in the United States, the open side should be to the east or south, not the west because the hot afternoon sun and slanting rays can be very annoying at the end of the day when people want to use the patio.

(This goes for a terrace, too, of course, for there is not very much pleasure in a view if the sun is in your eyes and not much enjoyment of the flowers if you are sweltering in the hot sun; and probably they are sweltering and wilting, too.)

WATER

As usual, I recommend a fountain or pool, and maybe you are fortunate enough to have a swimming pool. One of my neighbors has her swimming pool right there outside the back door so all the children have to do is run out and jump in. Her flowers are in beds under the windows and the trees and shrubs are beyond the pool to cast some shade and make a screen for privacy. If you do put in such large plants, keep them well away from the pool so their roots will not try to invade it, and never even think of putting a willow of any sort or a sycamore in the pool area because their roots will find a way right in. You may already know this if you have an ordinance in your town forbidding such trees as street trees because they always do send their roots right into the drains.

Another friend has put her pool on a higher level, up a small hill so that it is not visible from the patio area. Sometimes you can hear voices up there, but as you look out towards the east, what you see is the restful green lawn, and the flower border around it, not the bright turquoise expanse of the pool bottom. At our place we do not have a swimming pool, but the view downhill from the southeast porch and the terrace below it is toward the lower gardens and encompasses a large concrete birdbath with a pipe leading to it from the house, a Pfitzer juniper above it for shade and shelter for the birds, and a pleasant trickling sound when you turn on the faucet. The birds hear it even if you yourself are too far away to hear. If there were only a little more slope, or the angle from the house were different, or we felt like building it,

I'd gladly put in a recirculating waterfall with a stream leading from it into the birdbath pool.

TREES SUITABLE FOR SMALL PATIOS

It is more important to choose the right trees for the outdoor living area than for any other part of your place. You will be near them, under them and conscious of their shape and color and shade every day you go out. Though very attractive terraces, decks and certain patios have been made around existing big trees, the general proportions of a patio seem to require small trees, and I'd say small flowering trees if you find some you like. I do not hold with the argument that a tree is dirty. It's no dirtier than anyone else; it sheds certain things no longer of use as we all do. And it is just as easy to sweep up after a tree as after a nuisance-dropping creature.

Some trees just seem made for patios. The small Japanese maples have a lovely silhouette, and come in fine colors. The Red Devil maple, with leaves that are reddish in spring, has red flowers and red fruits. Its cousin, *Acer palmatum atropurpureum*, is handsomely red all summer, very hardy and reliable. Other Japanese maples are cut-leaf, for example, "Burgundy Lace" and some have variegated leaves. Go to a nursery and look over the varieties so you can choose the most suitable for your taste. To go with one of these you might choose one or two hornbeam maples, a thickish, many-stemmed tree which will not grow to more than about 30 feet.

A charming tree for spring, especially if you live in the Northeast, and if you can give the young tree some shade, is the shadblow or serviceberry, *Amelanchier laevis*, or *A. canadensis*, which can grow to 60 feet. This is the tree which is easy to spot along the roadsides in the early spring when it flowers before any leaves have appeared on neighboring trees, or on the shade tree either.

I like this tree and grow it, hoping in a way to substitute for the flowering dogwood which we cannot grow here because it is not hardy in our zone—even though the shadblow flowers are much smaller and less showy. Our birds also like to feast on the blue berries which come in June.

Other cheerful early plants are the pussy willows, both the grayish native one, *Salix discolor*,and *S. caprea*,called goat willow, but more appealingly French pussy willow. This is larger and a soft dove gray. *S. gracilistyla*, from Japan, is distinctly pinkish and also quite small. You can use it for gradation, to scale down from the taller to a shorter shrub. (Keep all these willows away from any pool, as warned above.)

Two yellow-flowered small trees to consider if you live in Zones 5, 6 and south are the beautiful Golden Chain Tree and the Golden Rain Tree. The first is a laburnum, *L. watereri*, with clusters of golden yellow flowers that bloom in the spring. It is a legume, of the Pea family, and so is very good for your soil, but do not be tempted to nibble because it is poisonous to eat. The flowers are like a yellow wisteria, and they stay on the tree for two weeks.

The Golden Rain Tree is equally lovely, with big clusters of yellow flowers and handsome pods. Its Latin name is *Koelreuteria paniculata*, and it was discovered in Peru about a hundred years ago or more, where it was seen growing in the Andes and the discoverer said, "A little after 7 o'clock we came under a lowish spreading tree, from which a perfectly clear sky overhead, a smart rain was falling...and we saw cicadas sucking juices of the tender young branches and squirting forth streams of limpid fluids." It reminds one of the days when our ancestors used to believe that not only clouds but also trees could make rain, and they saw it, too, when they saw the drips from the end of young eucalyptus leaves. (You can see it today in many mountainous places where the needles of evergreens literally comb moisture out of the clouds and let it run down the funnels of their needles to increase the "rainfall" in their area under the trees.)

FLOWERING CRABAPPLES AND OTHER SMALL TREES

There are dozens of flowering crabapples you can grow, some of them spectacular, some of them more disease-resistant than others, some of them rather commonplace, and some of them fragrant and enticing. The Dorothea crabapple has flowers which are a lovely pink, double, almost two inches across, and with showy yellow apples later in the season, hanging on into winter and has the advantage of being scab-resistant and the attraction of having fine heavy bloom and plenty of fruits. Learn about others that are resistant before choosing what to plant.

There are plenty of other trees to consider, including, if you live in the city, little-leaf linden, the variety Greenspire, being one of the best. Prune it vigorously when you plant it (and again later—or replace it if it begins to get too big). Shademaster locust, London plane and the pestless Japanese pagoda tree are other big trees which are pollution-tolerant. Among smaller trees for a patio are the dwarf elms, *Ulmus pumila*, and dwarf catalpas, *C. bignonioides nana*. Though a bit tricky to grow in some situations, and though not hardy much beyond Zone 5, there is a fascinating tree, the Franklinia, *F. alatamaha* or *Gordonia alatamaha*, which only grows to 30 feet, and which blooms in the fall with big white single flowers, three inches in diameter. If you want a tree that is incredibly spectacular, see whether you can find and grow the handkerchief tree, or dove tree *Davidia involucrata*, with much bigger white six-inch pendulous wavy blossoms with the two lower petals especially long and mobile. This exotic and beautiful tree from China will grow in England, and evidently does pretty well in the Pacific Northwest, too.

TREES IN TUBS

For trees to grow in tubs, try the Japanese maples discussed above, hop hornbeam and some of the hollies, especially dwarfs such as *Ilex crenata* green island, which though wide, only grows to three feet in ten or 12 years. Another dwarf is *I.c.* Helleri and other is *I.c.* Kingsville, which may only reach four feet in 30 years. Among hollies that are not dwarf and can be very attractive in the patio is the 20-foot Dahoon or Yaupon, *I. cassine*, which has either red or yellow berries and no spines. *I. crenata* is even shorter, about ten feet, but it has black berries and it is not hardy much north of Philadelphia.

WHERE THERE'S WATERING

If you live in a hot climate where you probably will be watering the garden quite a lot, do not try to grow trees that do not like to live where there is constant moisture. Settle, instead, on some alder trees, either speckled alder, *Alnus incana* or Eureopean or black alder, *A. glutinosa*. These, again, are among trees that can grow quite high, with the black alder sometimes reaching 70 feet. But they can be kept shrubby, if you want to train them that way. The speckled alder has oval, dark green leaves and catkin flowers, followed by small cones. It needs a soil with a pH of 5.5 to 6.5, so mulch with peat, oak leaves or sawdust. The leaves of the black alder stay on late into the fall. Even a water tolerant tree like an alder does not want wet roots all the time, however, so let it have time to drain once in a while.

The flowers you grow in an outdoor room should suit your fancy, and be the kind of plants which will fit in with the trees and shrubs there, the kind of soil, and not be so demanding they detract from your outdoor living room enjoyment. I'd suggest that you avoid big beds of petunias, for instance, which take a good deal of time to pick off the deadheads, and settle, instead, for a few handsome pots of petunias or window boxes, which will be much less demanding. I'd also suggest plants with long seasons of bloom. (See the list of these in the chapter on perennials.) Fragrant flowers are of course a boon, and pest-repellent herbs and pungent flowers are all to the good for those who are going to sit outdoors in the outdoor living area of the garden. (See lists of annuals and perennials.)

The colors you choose will partly depend, I should think, on the hours the outdoor living area is most in use. For daytime use, bright yellows and blues, with accents of red or orange make a cheerful setting. For evening use, white, pale primrose yellows, and pale pink are the colors which will make the flowers show up best. Vines are especially decorative to have along the walls of an outdoor living area, perhaps clematis, silver lace vine, or even scarlet runner beans, which have long been favorites of organic gardeners. More subdued vines would include euonymus, the ivies, and bittersweet. WARNING: Do not let bittersweet climb on living trees, or wild grape or Virginia creeper, either. (And don't let poison ivy, but I guess that hardly needs to be mentioned in a flower book.) Beautiful annual vines include the morning glories, and my favorite of these is the 'Heavenly Blue'; or the climbing nasturtiums, in yellow.

SOME CALIFORNIA PATIOS

One lovely California patio I know has a big old live oak tree as the main attraction in the center of the outdoor living area. This is an old tree, there long before there was any thought of having a house nearby. When the owners did decide to build there, they designed the house to sit in proper relationship to this fine tree, and made the patio so that it took advantage of all the best points of the tree.

A big point, for those owners and for anyone

else having an old tree or already-existing tree in the area to be used for the patio, is that there must be a well around the tree and an area of protection for its roots. In the patio I am thinking of there was constructed a 25-inch deep well all around the tree, which stretched out half way to the drip line. It was partly filled with gravel to promote good drainage and to act as a stone mulch around the tree. Around the well, in order to discourage people from walking too close was a two-foot circle of groundcover, lily-turf, *Liriope muscari*, which has rather grasslike foliage but which grows tall enough to discourage people from walking on it. It also endures the shade. There was some talk of changing the groundcover to a rose ground-cover when the children got bigger—preferably to *Rosa wichuraiana*, the Memorial rose, a

The sunken, gravel-filled well and grassy groundcover around this large tree protect its roots and set it off well from the rest of the patio area.

low-growing fragrant white rose often used as a groundcover. Someone had suggested Hall's honeysuckle, *Lonicera japonica*, but that was quickly turned down when the owners heard it was just about the worst pest there is in the plant kingdom.

The patio of a friend of mine in Carmel is a gemlike illustration of what can be done with a small space and some imagination. Her ground-floor apartment has a fairly big glass window and a glass door facing south, and directly beyond the glass and stretching to the high red-wood fence that screens off the street is a charming sunpocket where she grows a dozen or more thriving, low-maintenance plants, both in the ground and in planters and hanging baskets against the fence and attached to the eaves.

When she began this garden seven years ago, she immediately put in plants that would provide some show from the start. There were three hanging baskets of fuchsias, on the deep pink to reddish side. The tree she chose was a

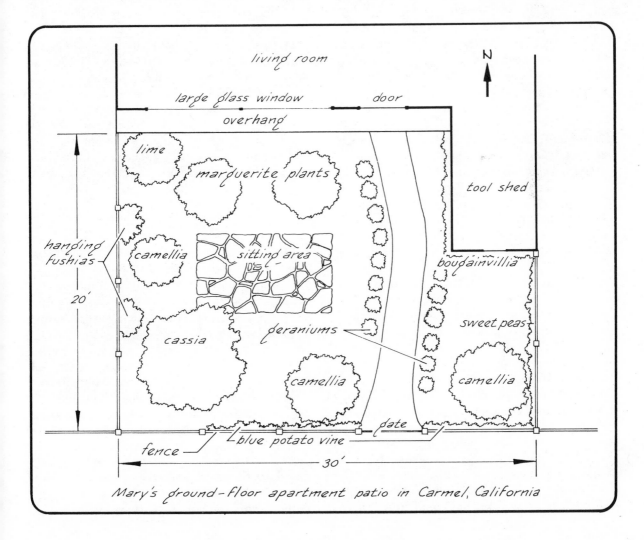

Mary's ground-floor apartment patio in Carmel, California

small cassia tree, called Cassia-bark tree or Chinese cinnamon. Though it can grow to 40 feet in Zone 10, Mary's tree was small and with judicious pruning has not grown out of proportion in the time she has had it. Its Latin name is *Cinnamomum cassia.* What is so attractive about this little tree is that it has nice yellow flowers in bloom most of the year. The first year she grew two blue potato vines on the fence, and in front of them put two big marguerite plants, which also bloom all year. I believe these are Golden Marguerite, *Anthemis tinctoria,* var. Perry's Variety, for they are a delicious bright yellow; and she says, quite a few of her neighbors come practically all year around to pick the yellow flowers for they keep coming and coming and are always in bloom.

The potato vine is also still in fine shape. It produces nothing but small blue or white flowers—no potatoes of any sort, that is—but is a fast grower and is very popular with growers in the Carmel climate, even though it requires a lot of pruning and trimming.

For tub plants Mary decided to use camellias, which did well for several years, and are doing well again, though I must confess that when I saw them just after a rare and disheartening freeze a year or so ago, they were rather pitiful. But they snapped back, and are again blooming, one a rich red, the other pink, though she has moved them out of the patio now because they are so big, and has planted them in the ground on the other side of the building.

Geraniums set along the little path from the door to the fence gate brightened that area of the patio, and just to the south side of the tool shed in the corner, there are excellent San Diego red bougainvilleas. In a vacant space on the west fence where they get a lot of light, Mary put sweet peas, and planted them in October for bloom at Christmas time.

This garden in the early years had a subtle gradation of color from light pink through to dark red, with accents of blue and yellow, but now that the plants have matured and taken on richer tones, Mary has eliminated the pink and much of the red, concentrated on the rich, deep tones of yellow, backed up by some paler yellows, and accented by white and dark as well as light blue. She has also branched out into other kinds of plants. For one, she has a fruit tree, a small lime tree in a huge tub, all set to grow bigger and bigger, and is delighted with its habit of blooming and fruiting at the same time.

The little dabs of sweet alyssum Mary had seven years ago have spread and done so well that they are now practically a groundcover. These are supplemented with white annuals such as white petunias and bellflowers and a striking dark blue lobelia.

When she wants to, there is room to take a chair or two out into this little patio. For the most part, however, people sit inside and look out to enjoy the charm and color of the view throughthe large window right beside it in the living room.

A PATIO ON A BANK

I heard not long ago of an artist with a house in one of those dry canyons in Southern California, so dry that he cuts back most of the flammable bushes and other dry vegetation each year when the August period of danger from fires approaches. This does not bother him at all, for the climate is so favorable and his watering system is so effective that the vegetation is back in good shape again by November. This patio has only one small housewall facing it, but since it is on a slope, the stairs leading down to the lower level and the walls beside the stairs act as the element to define the space and organize it. Against the wall is a fountain where the owner circulates the water and creates a steady spout. Around the area of the faucet are large sempervivums whose rosette shapes make it look

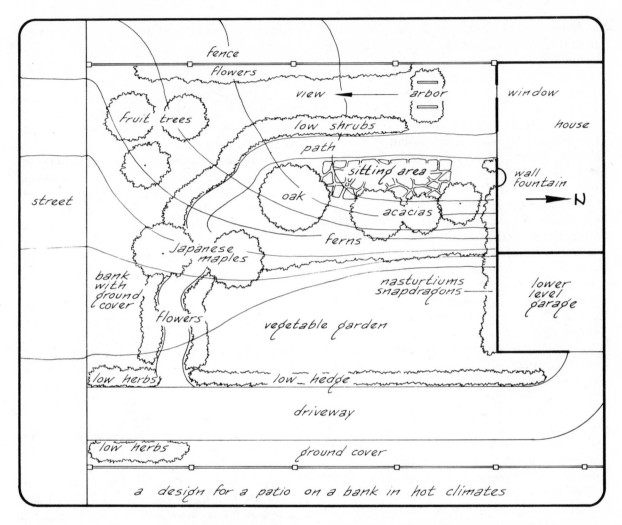

as though the circular head of the background to the faucet had flowers in its hair. Under this hot wall are flowers that like the reflected heat: nasturtiums, snapdragons and ranunculas. Down towards the steps, making shade for other flowers are such trees as an oak, a little redwood, two Japanese maples, several eucalyptus trees and some acacias. Under their shade he grows ferns such as elkhorn, staghorn, leather, Dicksonia and sword fern, though some of them stretch over to grow under an arbor with jasmine

and wisteria growing on it. Among his flowers are clivia, camellias, fuchsias, iris, ice plant, sweet peas and day lilies. For fruit this gardener has avocadoes, guavas, figs and oranges. He also grows herbs. This garden, too, is less a show place for landscape architects than an example of a richly varied, productive and useful garden full of interesting plants, serving many purposes, and being wonderfully in tune with the environment in which it is placed. Everything grows so well that every ascent and descent of the stairs is like walking through a prize greenhouse, with plants tumbling over the stones and filling every cranny.

HANGING PLANTS

In patios like these, potted and hanging plants are often used, and it is important that they have the right culture to survive in the limited environment of the pot. Fuchsias, for instance, are characteristic potted plants though I have seen them growing in the soft, misty moderate, air of southern Ireland in high ledges along the roadside. They are recommended for the organic gardener because they have few pests and are easily grown and easily propagated from slips or cuttings of the softer new growth, taken at almost any time of year, but preferably in the spring, after the plant has had a winter's rest and has recently begun to grow again.

Use a good potting soil, with plenty of humus and good supplies of compost, Fertrell or other organic fertilizer at frequent intervals when they are starting new growth or flowering. They are shallowrooted plants, so be careful about watering during those periods when it's especially harmful for the roots to dry out. One aid is to keep the fuchsias cool, especially during the spring months and especially if you have to keep them indoors during those months. A good temperature for indoors is 50° to 65°F.

After the summer blooming period outdoors, fuchsias need a dormant spell. The rest period best for them is November and December, in a cool place of about 45°F. and in dim light. Give just enough water to keep the wood from drying out and shrinking. By January, you can bring them to the light, kept at 60° to 65°F. and watered just a little bit more. Just as the buds begin to swell, begin pruning. When it is warm, put them outdoors again in your outdoor living area and let them bloom all summer. Some fuchsias do very well in hanging baskets, planted with a layer of sphagnum or green sheet moss as a lining.

Other good plants for hanging baskets include the achimenes, basket begonias, heliotrope, ivy geranium, or Christmas cactus which will bloom then, or at Thanksgiving or perhaps later, and mine the last few years have obliged by a second blooming in March. I also like annuals in hanging baskets and enjoy the ageratum, petunias, annual phlox and nasturtium that all give such a good display. These, too, are all planted in good humusy garden loam, with moss at the bottom. If you are going to hang plants where the dripping water might be bothersome, you can put a little polyethylene in the bottom, with some broken crock over it to help drainage. Don't line the whole basket, because the plants need air on their roots, and a watertight basket would make them waterlogged. Some good foliage plants to include with your flowering plants might include: coleus, English ivy, spider plant, the spiderworts and the related wandering-Jew, as well as the bigleaf periwinkle, a fine rugged plant with bright blue flowers.

It is always pleasant to see the houseplants out on the porch, in the patio or on the terrace. They seem to respond well to the summer air, moisture and sunlight. Croton make a good show, as do the philodendrons, variegated ivies, the peperomias and such easy plants as the thunbergias and ipomeas, or morning glories, which I always used to think of as outdoor vines until I began growing them each winter in my kitchen. My friend who grows such good calomondons and orange trees, puts her whole collection of houseplants out on an eastern terrace, where they get dried off in the morning sun, and not burned and bothered by the hot western sun. Her clivias thrive, as do her Jerusalem cherries, her little heathers, and abutilon or flowering maple. She even brings out her fig and rubber trees.

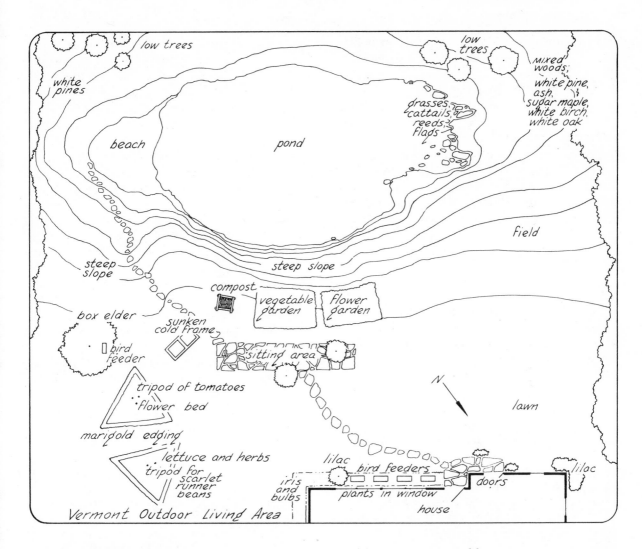

Labels in figure:
low trees — white pines — beach — pond — low trees — mixed woods; white pine, ash, sugar maple, white birch, white oak — grasses, cattails, reeds, flags — field — steep slope — steep slope — compost — vegetable garden — flower garden — box elder — sunken cold frame — bird feeder — sitting area — N — lawn — tripod of tomatoes — flower bed — marigold edging — lettuce and herbs — tripod for scarlet runner beans — lilac — bird feeders — lilac — iris and bulbs — doors — plants in window — house — Vermont Outdoor Living Area

A NORTHEAST OUTDOOR LIVING AREA

Quite a different patio is the outdoor living area of another friend of mine in Vermont. Here, where there are mountain vistas, large or confined, from almost everyone's house, the attempt is usually to open up a view of some sort, not to confine the garden to a small intimate space like those developed in the gardens just described in California. This Vermont friend is primarily an ardent organic vegetable gardener, and his patio is more like a grassy terrace than anything else. It extends from the west and south sides of the house, and overlooks a man-made pond dug out at the foot of the hill, where the family swims, where ducks stop off and where reeds grow and little animals come in for a drink when they are thirsty. Its four walls are the green trees, including white pines, beyond the lawn and the pond. On the brow of the hill are the comfortable chairs, and little tables, inviting one to sit and enjoy the vista to the woods beyond the pool and the suggestion of mountains beyond the woods. There is one shade tree to get under when it is hot, which really is very seldom in this high Vermont location, and there are plantings up against the foundation of the house of irises, spring bulbs, and here and there a small evergreen. From the patio area you look down, surprisingly, on a lush and interesting vegetable garden, in one direction (complete with a small compost heap) and in the other direction to the plants inside the windows of the house and the bird feeders just outside the windows. Traffic goes back and forth through the door leading to the kitchen, and food and cool drinks are easily brought out to the area where the comfortable chairs are.

I described this outdoor living area, even though it does not sound much like the conventional enclosed, three-sided one which is much more characteristic of what many people build today as a patio. But I do it purposely to show that the three walls of nature are just as adequate as any fences of redwood or cypress or any brick or stone walls to convey the feeling of enclosed and inviting space—if you have the acreage to achieve it, that is. I also wanted to show that a mixture of flowers and vegetables, or of flower beds and vegetable gardens, can be so designed and placed as to create a very pleasing effect, even though at first thought that, too, seems rather unconventional. If this neighbor decides to include a hedge of marigolds around his vegetable plot, and to plant feverfew among his edible plants, the effect will be heightened. Recently he let squash and pumpkins grow on his compost heap (pretty well covering it and disguising it.) Maybe another year he will grow morning glories or a clematis. Who knows?

POTTED PLANTS FOR THE
PATIO AND TERRACE

Many people make patio and terrace gardens primarily by using potted plants. Some that are popular and suitable are begonias (especially *B. semperflorens*, and the magnificent hanging basket kinds), geraniums of many kinds, China asters, godetia, lobelias, mignonette (started indoors in cool climates) and also impatiens (also to be started indoors). Very good for trailing plants to spill over a wall or box in which they can be placed are the bellflower, *Campanula fragilis*, the black-eyed Susan vine, *Thunbergia alata*, and the potato vine like the one my friend Mary has, or I think this is hers: *Solanum jasminoides*.

For tub culture people often use the glossy abelia, *A. x grandiflora*, with pleasant pink flowers in the late summer, a good dense plant which will grow to five feet. The variety 'Sherwood' grows only to three feet. Another favorite is *Acanthus spinosus*, the acanthus with big showy leaves; and another is the beautiful Lily of the Nile, *Agapanthus africanus*.

There are lots of others. Consult your nurseryman or garden center. But while you are at it, ask about the ti tree, to grow in a pot or tub, the striking angel's trumpet tree, *Datura arborea*, the coral tree, pineapple guava, and the rose of China. It is one of the attractions of patio gardening to be able to expand your gardening possibilities to lots of new plants by using a method of culture which protects them from the hazards of weather.

PLANTS FOR POTS OR THE GROUND
DEPENDING ON WEATHER

Other very attractive plants for a warm sunny spot in the summer in a patio, for instance on a warm stone wall, or near one, include rosemary, usually in a pot in cold climates (though I have also put mine out in the ground and dug it up again to take back into the house in the fall), and one I wish I could grow, and certainly would if I lived in Florida: barbados cherry, or acerola, *Malpighia glabra*, with pale

Potted plants and trees, together with groundcovers and border plants, dress up this patio. Most potted plants shown here can be brought indoors for winter enjoyment.

pink to rosy red flowers, and excellent high-vitamin C red fruits. It can be grown as a tub tree, but the catch is that it needs evening temperatures of 60°F. and we can never be sure of that sort of temperature up here even in summer.

Or at least grow a banana. That is, if you can have day temperatures of 80°F. and night temperatures of 65°F. The culture for it is to plant it, keep it limed, give it lots of water, weekly feedings of compost, and good rich soil to begin with. Let only one sucker grow at first, but after fruiting you can let another grow up. When the fruit does set, cut off the flowers remaining on the stalk. Do not be surprised if it takes a year and a half for your dwarf banana to bloom and bear fruit. Get the variety *Musa acuminata cavendishii*, which originated in southern China. Some people claim they have got a hundred bananas from a little six-foot tree.

Other unusual fruit trees you can try for patio tubs are the Natal plum, variety 'Fancy', which has fragrant star-shaped white flowers, and red cranberry-flavored fruits. One with equally red fruits, but not edible, is the dwarf pyracantha 'Red Elf', which can be treated as a bonsai and kept small by root-pruning. Christmas peppers are also interesting plants, which keep their fruit on for a long time, and are very pleasing with their yellow or yellow-orange fruits. One man who writes of these refers to his experience of them as "edible fire." I guess I don't want to taste those.

Much pleasanter are the Nagami kumquat plants with sweet flowers in spring and summer and orange fruits good for making preserves. The mistletoe fig, with tiny non-edible fruits, are another possibility as well as Meyers' lemon, Bear's dwarf lime and the little pineapple called *Ananas comosus nanus*. My green-thumb friend would recommend the Calamondin orange tree that she has brought along for 15 years, summering it out on the east side of the house,

and enjoying its winter blossoming and fruiting at the same time when she brings it indoors. A citrus tree with somewhat larger fruits than the little Calamondins is the Owari Satsuma tangerine. And one of the prettiest fruit trees is the dwarf pomegranate, with scarlet flowers and picturesque twiggy branches. This fruit is edible, too, of course.

MORE PLANTS WITH SOMETHING TO EAT ON THEM

Some other pleasantly edible plants to consider for interest and attractiveness in any garden might well include the tree tomato, *Cyphomandra betacea*, which will do a lot better than a banana in coming to fruition, for it begins to bear at seven months and will often go right on bearing every year, if you have luck with it. This tree grows to six or eight feet, but can be root-pruned to keep it smaller, and is quite pleasant to have as a source of fruit (for jam, I think).

Or try some artichokes, in pots in many places, but if you live along a fairly warm seacoast, in the ground, too. They are *Cynara scolymus*, and even if you do not like eating artichokes as a vegetable, the blossoms are very handsome and large and can be used for dried arrangements.

Then there are climbing and alpine strawberries to try, especially if you are looking for somethine unusual to put in hanging baskets. Get 'Superfection' for the climbing one and 'Baron Solemacher' for the alpine. It is best to grow the latter in part shade. An excellent way to grow blueberries, I think, is in tubs, for then you can easily control the acidity of the soil even if you live in a limy area. Use plenty of acid humus, such as acid peat moss, oak leaves and pine needles and keep applying acid mulches so the the micorrhyza will be in constant supply. Have several varieties, so they will cross-fertilize and set fruit, for example 'Collins' for an early one, 'Blueray' for a midseason and 'Coville' for late, or consult your nursery catalogue for two for each period of maturity.

The warm wall of a patio is a splendid place to grow espaliered fruit. If it appeals to you to do that, try pears and, if your climate makes it possible, try peaches. Plant some wild berry bushes to keep the birds away from the fruit.

HERBS AND VEGETABLES

My cousin who lives in a suburban place also grows herbs and a few vegetables in his patio. The herbs he grows in part shade are mint, tarragon, basil, sweet marjoram and garlic, along with a few chives and onions. If you grow some of these in pots, you have them ready to move around to trouble spots in other parts of the garden in case pests arrive. Many people like to plant garlic with their roses, but if you prefer, grow garlic in pots and then move them there when the time of need comes. If your patio is always partly shady, and if you want some other vegetables there, you had best confine yourself to lettuce, parsley, beets, carrots, and cabbage. I love the ornamental cabbages and kales, with reddish, pinkish, and white variegations, which make them extremely ornamental. In fact, too good to eat. Fertilize well, and keep watch for pests. It will help, of course, if you plant plenty of chives, scallions and the *allium* family members mentioned above. As for 'Tiny Tim' or 'Patio' tomatoes, you have good chances of success with them either in the ground or in pots if you put them where they will get very good circulation. A certain amount of shade, though not really good for them, will not mean you'll be unsuccessful; but poor circulation may. For one thing they get aphids, and you will be busy day after day washing off or spraying with garlic spray the bugs that might not be there at all if you only had put you tomatoes where the airs

could blow around them. Rhubarb is an absolutely splendid plant to use for ornamental purposes. I don't know why more people do not use it for foundation planting and in their patios.

FLOWERS THAT BRIGHTEN UP THE PATIO

For easy maintenance and for sheer color there are a few more shrubby plants and herbaceous plants I'd recommend. Certainly azaleas offer a wide range of colors and the possibility of having both deciduous and evergreen bushes, depending on your zone.

Forsythias, flowering quince, other rhododendrons, especially the dwarf ones, hydrangeas, honeysuckles, laurels, small mock oranges, weigelas, a beauty bush or two and the wonderfully fragrant small viburnums will cheer up any patio. I also am very partial to the small shrubby cinquefoils or potentillas. Their cheerful yellow blooms can go on and on during the whole summer, and they are very neat and tidy looking plants. And there are plenty of others.

Read up on them in specialty books, the publications of the plant societies, such as the azalea association, and in the catalogues. Also visit arboretums and nurseries, and remember to select some plants that attract and feed birds.

WARNING: But do not choose plants of any kind for the confined space of most patios unless you are sure that they are not going to spread so rampantly they will become a nuisance. This goes for groundcovers, too. It is a headache to find that the vigorous, aggressive roots of what used to be your favorite groundcover swelling up and tipping your flagstones, or cracking your tiles, or heaving a board of your wooden deck just when Aunt Minnie comes along and heaving her over, too, and breaking her ankle. I have mentioned Hall's honeysuckle; I warn you that that's the kind of thing that will happen if you are foolish enough to fall for the ads and buy that menace. Do not, however, pave a patio solid; all growing plants must have air getting to their roots.

See the chapters on perennials and annuals for many suggestions for small and medium-sized plants suitable for the outdoor living room. See also the section on shady gardens for those that will grow in part shade, and don't forget the charms and possibilities of ageratum, bee balm, bergenia, bleeding heart, candytuft, columbine, coral bells, false dragonhead, ferns, gas plant, gayfeather for the background, the delicate blue of Jacob's ladder, bright yellow leopardsbane, lupines of various colors, meadow rue, plantain lilies that double as groundcover, the dark and handsome monkshood, lots of primroses, the bright yellow native American evening prim-roses, lot of violets, johnny-jump-ups and the short-lived but exquisite Virginia bluebells which bloom in the spring, and make you happy to get out where the garden is. And fill it out with annuals, in the ground and in pots, window boxes and tubs. Even a few wildflowers are appropriate—bloodroot, cardinal flower, dame's rocket or sweet rocket, foamflower, jack-in-the-pulpit and blue lobelias are all attractive, and easy to get from nurseries.

One of the particular pleasures of the outdoor-indoor garden near the house is that of having hanging baskets or pots on pedestals with cascading plants that hang gracefully down. Cascading begonias, fuchsias and petunias most people know about, but have you discovered also the charming small, Japanese cascading chry-santhymums, available in several colors: red, 'Fireball'; pink, 'Daphne'; white, 'Anna', yellow, 'Jane Harte'; orchid, 'Lavender Beauty' and a coppery-bronzy color, 'Hallowe'en'? If you use clay pots or wooden tubs, a good rich potting soil, and gradually move the little plant at the beginning of the season from smaller to larger and larger pots as it grows, you may end up in blooming season with a tremendous cascade of

blooms and the flowers covering nearly every inch of the plant.

It has to be trained, however, by staking it at 12 inches to a 36-inch wire, to which you tie the plant at four-inch intervals. About six inches from the ground bend the wire at a 45° angle so it will begin to grow downwards. Unfortunately cascade chrysanthemums are late-blooming ones, so if you live in a cold climate, you will have to force the plant in order for it to bloom before frost—when you have it outdoors, that is. Begin covering the plant with a blackout cloth in the middle of August at about 4 o'clock in the afternoon, and stop the regular pinching you give to most chrysanthemums. (See perennial chapter.) If you live in a warmer zone, keep right on pinching until the end of September. When the plant is ready to bloom, bend the wire down so that it points towards the earth, and wait for a gorgeous display.

Other annuals you can use besides petunias are sweet alyssum, the reliable blue or white browallia, cape-marigolds, cup flower [Nie-rembergia species), ageratum, especially the cultivars of A. houstonianum which makes fine bushy plants with blue flowers; lobelias, morning glories of the bush type, nasturtiums, and annual phlox, P. drummondi, as well as the more sprawling pinks such as Dianthus latifolius or D. plumarius. And if you have a good sunny place to put them, try sweet peas and a basket of bush sweet peas, for example, 'Bijou'. These are also very satisfactory as window box or pot plants to put on little wooden blocks on a ledge or wall.

Others to try include ivy-leaf geraniums, black-eyed Susan vine, plumbagoes, morning glories, and for the hummingbirds, cardinal climber and cypress vine (both Quamoclit varieties).

All these possibilities for trees, shrubs, flowers and vines and groundcovers for an outdoor-indoor living room will spur you, I hope, to make plans for a place that best suits your style of living and your taste. Luckily plants are not as permanent as concrete foundations or stone fireplaces, and you can easily pull up what you find are inadequate, not to your liking, too fast-growing or too spindly. It hurts to pull up plants, I know. But solace yourself by transferring them immediately to the compost heap and get the satisfaction of recycling them. In other parts of the garden you might let them go; but in the outdoor living area, where you are in intimate contact with them, I see no reason for not experimenting and shifting until you find just what you want. Your aim as an organic gardener to have a balanced population of plants and living things in the garden, will be, I believe, well satisfied when you find the plants for your outdoor living room which balance well with you, too, as a member of the garden.

PART 2

The
Flower Beds

Designing the Flower Beds

Fit the flower beds at angles to emphasize the view, to complement your trees, shrubs and ground covers, and the place where you sit outdoors or look out the window towards the garden. By all means put some of your beds where you can see them from the inside of the house. It is sad to think of gardeners going to lots of work to tend beds so snuggled up to the house that they are never seen except by going outside. Some flowers in the foundation plantings for passers-by and for guests arriving, or for yourself when you come into the yard, are good, but there certainly should be more.

When you look out to the garden, your eye should not be led to zig and zag around in all directions. You should have a restful design and focal points which will bring your eye to rest and act to organize the beds of flowers as well as other spaces and features in the garden. Variations in height, some sort of solidity, and some distinction of shape will lend interest as well as being restful. Sometimes the lines of vision leading to the focal point are in a conventional V-shaped perspective. Sometimes there is an interrupting shape half-way—like a round bed of annuals or herbs, for instance, or a round lily pond with a path leading to it,

splitting to go around it and proceeding on to another section of the garden.

Less formal lay-outs are almost inevitable if your land is hilly or rocky, and the line leading to a distant focal point may be up or down a stone stairway, along a stone wall, or winding up or down to a waterfall or pond. But whatever design you choose, make it feel like you own, make it express what you feel about your relation to the outdoor room that is your garden. If you like curves and swerves, use them. If you are all for the four-square and the neat straight lines, put some in. Though a garden is perforce dominated by the doings of nature and the patterns that nature requires, it is still a place where man asserts his will, too, and your own feelings about the design there as well as the living forms and web of life there are important to discover and express in the garden you make.

CHOOSING FLOWERS

The flowers you choose to grow may fulfill any one of dozens of desires and create one or more of dozens of possible effects. Perhaps your aim is lots of greenery with only a few accents of your favorite colors from season to season.

Perhaps it is to have a fragrant garden to sit out in in the evening, but with plenty of flowers to cut to bring into the house for spring, summer and autumn decoration. Maybe you have enough house plants to keep you busy and not so much interest in cut flowers as in berries and seeds for the birds and other interesting creatures who will come to a well-stocked yard. Maybe you are an experimenter, and want a place where you can have a basic, reliable garden, but plenty of space to try new and difficult species just to see how they will work. Maybe you want flowers that are all useful—for sachets, pot pourris, making jellies, soups, stews and pest-repellents.

Some people say they want an easy garden, with bloom all summer, and the minimum of maintenance. There is in Chapter 8 on perennials a list of flowers that have a long blooming season, and many of them are quite simple to take care of. The style of the ever-blooming flower garden called the herbaceous border, adapted from the English prototype begun in the last century is a style I do not believe is suitable for American gardens of today. If you can be satisfied without full flowering over every inch in all seasons, there are some interesting plants to include in your garden, which will literally give you something to look at in every season.

AROUND THE YEAR

You can begin last fall, as it were, by including Christmas roses, and shrubs like the even earlier witch hazel plants, such as *Hamamelis virginiana* which blooms from Thanksgiving to mid-February, and *H. japonica*, which has yellow flowers in January and on into March. A relative of this witch hazel, *Corylopsis spicata*, will produce flower clusters of yellow blooms in February and March, if you are lucky enough not to have a nipping frost at the wrong moment. The Christmas Rose, which will have been in bloom for most of those winter months, is *Helleborus niger*, hardy to Zone 3, and a great joy to see struggling up out of its mulch to bloom in winter. It is poisonous.

With us, also blooming in winter, but a bit later is the winter aconite, *Eranthis hyemalis*. It pushes aside the snow and sends its soft yellow, but rugged little bloom up into the winter sun as early as late February or early March. Alongside, in the warmth of reflected light from a stone wall, we have the early snowdrops, *Galanthus nivalis*, and I have heard that around Philadelphia you can get these delicate little white flowers to bloom at Christmas time if you give them some sandy soil and a good mulch of manure.

In March we get blooms of the tiny yellow iris, *I. danfordeai*, in a protected southern exposure under a white wall where the microclimate is just about equal to that of 300 miles to the south, or somewhere near Philadelphia instead of southern Vermont. Another little bulb for this season is snowflake, and by a week or so later you can expect meadow saffron, *Tulip kaufmannia*, and the crocuses. They pop up in our front lawn and near the birch trees just a little before the bluebells, *Scilla nonscripta* and *S. sibirica* begin to come out. And soon will come the grape hyacinth, striped squill, the other little irises, while at the same time, farther south, the flowering fruit trees are coming into bloom, and perhaps the anemones. Primroses can be expected to appear in April or May, and in May we love to watch for the coming of all the spring bulbs like narcissi, tulips, and fritillaries, as well as the coming of the crabapples, dogwoods, deutzias, azaleas and eventually the lilacs that go so well with spring bulbs in a well-done lay-out. We used to expect these for Decoration Day, when it was on May 30th, but now with the slight changes we have had in climate, we have them at least a week or ten days before that.

Then comes the riot of late spring and June flowers, too many to mention. But if you are starting a garden, you can expect blooms in June of lily-of-the-valley, peonies, iris, the wonderful roses, rhododendrons, the first daylilies, bellflowers, lupines, poppies and maybe some early lilies. And lots of flowering shrubs.

July brings delphinium, foxglove, coral bells, more poppies, more daylilies, along with the interesting butterfly bush, the chaste tree, German woadwaxen and the nice fragrant buttonbush. This is the great month for perennials, and I believe that there are about 100 which blossom in July—from gladioli to dahlias to shasta daisies to hollyhocks and many more lilies. Plant for July some achillea, called The Pearl, *Achillea ptarmica*, which has small round compact little blooms that go wonderfully with any arrangemet, fresh or dried—a very useful flower to plan for.

In August, along with the wealth of annual flowers and the continuing perennials, you can expect blooms from such trees and shrubs as the Japanese pagoda tree, crape myrtle, sweet pepperbush, mountain camellia, *Stewartia ovata*, tamarisk and the rose of Sharon. The August perennials I particularly like are Stokes' aster, turtlehead, the heleniums, glads, and a fine long-flowering clematis, Scarlet clematis, from Texas.

September begins to look rather fall-like up here in Vermont, but in warmer places it is more like Indian summer all month long. Some wonderful plants come to perfection in this month—from the lovely Franklinia tree, *Gordonia alatamaha*, to the tender blue spirea,

Caryopteris incana and all the asters, the shrub abelia with its profuse white flowers, and an equally tender *Elscholtzia stauntoni*, a native of California which has pinkish flowers, very fragrant. Up here we have to cut it back each year because it gets frost-bite, but south of Delaware it is safe and can be treated as a shrub.

Other more rugged flowers like gayfeather and ironweed come in September, as well as plumbago, and lots of goldenrods and asters. In our garden we have had great displays of the asters called Michaelmas daisies, especially the rich blue one, 'Queen Mary' and a good pink, 'Burr's Pink.' They were in a lower garden where we could see them from every room on the south side of the house, and would be there still except that it came time to do something about the peonies, and we divided them and put the new divisions down there to replace the asters and put phlox in between.

Fall means chrysanthemums, too, and the surprising autumn crocuses, and perhaps some winter daffodil, *Sternbergia lutea*, and a later helenium, *H. hoopesi*, very like a sunflower. Farther south it also means the toadlily, *Tricyrtis hirta*, and perhaps the last blooms on the Strawberry tree, *Arbutus unedo*. Up here it also means the turning of the sugar maples—and we often have the one in front of the house to the west turn a rich yellow, and the one outside my study on the north side turn to a flaming red, to cheer me up as I sit at my typewriter.

So if you plan, you can have a year such as that. And if you like flowers at all, the chances are 99 out of 100 you can be (with some care and good sense) very successful.

7

Bulbs of All Sorts

In my family we generally call all those plants that have bulbous underground parts, and those parts themselves: bulbs. I suppose most people do, too. Some of them are really corms, tubers or rhizomes. A true bulb is the kind that has a dormant, rounded underground stem such as you see on a lily, tulip or narcissus. Sometimes the bulb surrounds the embryo which is next year's plant inside the bulb in a tight layer of food-packed material, as in a tulip bulb or daffodil. Sometimes the bulb is loose and scaly as with lilies. A hyacinth bulb is like one big bud. Daffodils and some lilies send out new little buds. Old or young, all bulbs need special care because next years plant is right there inside them.

A crocus or gladiolus has a corm. This is a solid mass of storage tissue, with several growing tips on top. On the bottom is a sort of plate and the roots grow out from around the edge. Over the summer the plate shrivels and new corms grow on top, with little corms called cormels around the edge.

A tuber is another solid mass of storage tissue but without any base plate. It has eyes or growing points from which both shoots and roots grow. When an old potato tuber is planted, for

instance, it shrinks and disintegrates and the new tubers form on the roots of the new plant that comes up. Dahlias do this, too, and so do tuberous begonias. When you plant their tubers, you should cut them to pieces so each eye or two can sprout. Most perennials which grow this way are called tuberous-rooted.

Then there is the rhizome, such as you see with irises, cannas, Solomon's seal and many others. This is a thickened underground stem, which suggests why rhizomes of iris, for example, are planted horizontally and why some of the rhizone tissue should stay above ground. A rhizome, too, is a storage tissue, and the roots grow from the lower surface, with the stems of the flower stalks and leaves from the upper side. You can divide the rhizome of irises and such plants into pieces, with an eye to a piece, in order to propagate new plants.

In the hot, dry countries where many of our familiar bulbs originated, their storage structures developed over the centuries to help them survive period of enforced dormancy in the dry weather when they no longer had enough moisture to keep up a supply of nutrients. When we went to Greece a few years ago, we saw how essential a bulb is for such plants as the grape

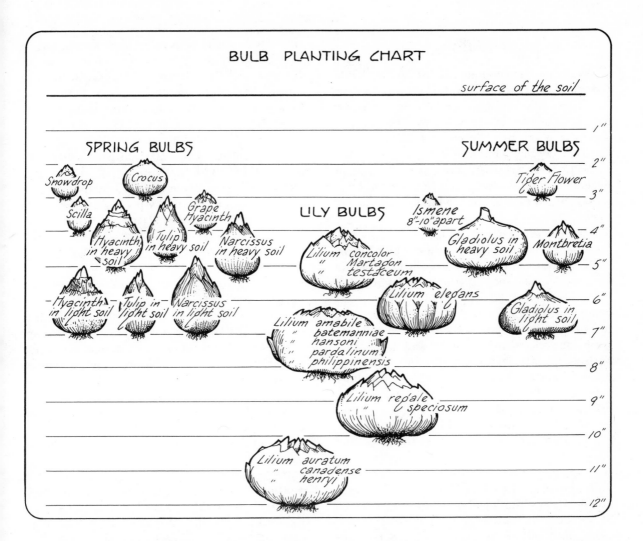

BULB PLANTING CHART

surface of the soil

1"

SPRING BULBS   SUMMER BULBS

2"

Snowdrop   Crocus   Tiger Flower
3"

Scilla   Grape   LILY BULBS   Ismene
              Hyacinth   8"-10"apart
                                                              4"
  Hyacinth   Tulip   Narcissus   Gladiolus in   Montbretia
  in heavy   in heavy soil in heavy soil   Lilium concolor heavy soil
   soil   "   Martagon
                                              "   testaceum   5"

Hyacinth   Tulip in   Narcissus   Lilium elegans
in light soil light soil in light soil   Gladiolus in
                                                              light soil   6"
                          Lilium amabile
                            "   batemanniae   7"
                            "   hansoni
                            "   pardalinum
                            "   philippinensis   8"

                          Lilium regale
                            " speciosum   9"

                                                              10"

            Lilium auratum
              "   canadense   11"
              "   henryi
                                                              12"

hyacinths we saw bursting into bloom on the island of Delos, and how essential a corm is for gladioli we saw near the seacoast of Turkey. In our climates the bulb of these species helps them to live over the winter in the cold period of dormancy. Because the green leaves of the plant make food all summer (or until the leaves die down) it is imperative that you never cut back the foliage until it has withered of its own accord and turned brown. With tulips, of other bulbs that tend to wither prematurely if there is a hot, dry spell, you should provide water and nutrients whenever you get such weather. Though tulips like full sun, it is best to plant bulbs where they can get a little shade and not dry out too fast. Put up sunshades, if needed. Bulbs such as lilies need shade over the lower part of the plant to protect the shallow roots, but plenty of sun up top is good for them. Use a groundcover. I use violets.

❧TULIPS❧

Most of the popular tulips are hybrids, though some of the charming original species native to southern Europe and the Near East are still grown and referred to as "botanicals." Tulips are strong, clear-colored flowers, in almost every shade but blue. They can be tall or short, plain or striped, smooth or ruffled, single or double. Bulb dealers group them in ten or 15 classes, and it pays to know what the commonest mean.

Broken or feathery tulips get that way because they have a virus disease which breaks their natural color and gives them a striped or feathered appearance. In the period soon after tulips were brought to western Europe and caused such a sensation that they sold for vast sums of money, some of them turned up with these fantastic striped patterns and the enthusiasts went wild with delight and put their prices up again. They are still listed in some bulb catalogues, but I wouldn't have one of the diseased things on the place.

This leaves the following groups: Single Early, which are rather short (9 to 16 inches) and often used for forcing indoors after a spell in the cold; Double Early, about the same height and in lovely colors of pink, yellow and cherry-red; Mendel tulips are medium height (16 to 26 inches) large and like an early Darwin; Triumph are similar; and the next class, Cottage, contains all tulips not in other classes. The catalogues, however, give the logical explanation that these cottage tulips are old tulips recently rediscovered in cottage gardens in England. They often have the characteristic of long pointed petals and then, wiry stems. They are old and rugged and can last a long time in a garden provided you can keep the mice away from them.

The next group in the list of classes is Dutch Breeders, usually just called Breeders in this country. Their flowers are oval or cupped, and they run to such colors as brown, purple, red or bronze, blooming about the same time as Cottage and Darwin tulips. Darwin tulips are one of the most commonly grown kinds with long stems up to 32 inches, very strong and in many colors, including black, The red tulip you remember from childhood may very well be a Darwin called 'City of Haarlem', a bright cardinal red with a deep purple base. The Darwin that has stripes is called 'Rembrandt': I suspect it has or has had virus disease,too.

A flamboyant tulip, Parrot, is a class with fringes and big, bold, slashed petals. Then in the official list there are Late Doubles and Species and first crosses. The specie tulips are the botanical tulips, and include little Himalayan varieties such as 'Chrysantha', which is tricolor, and another dainty tulip, *T. clusiana*, which is rose and white with gray-blue leaves. One of my favorites is *T. praestans*, a short scarlet-orange tulip with three or four blossoms on one strong stem. An early hybrid cross is the lily-flowering *T. kaufmannia*, large and creamy with carmine stripes and a yellow center. It is only about 12 inches tall and very early, so it does well and looks handsome and cheerful under trees in the spring. Other hybrids include the *T. greigii* varieties, with an oriental background and often mottled foliage, and the *fosteriana* varieties, usually with an emperor name like 'red Emperor' or 'Yellow Empress'. But there are other colors, too. *Tulipa fosteriana albas* is a big ivory-colored tulip that grows about 18 inches. There is also *Tulipa fosteriana purissima*, which is white, and one called 'Solva', a rose pink and early, as are almost all the botanicals.

CULTURE

There is some difference of opinion about how deep to plant tulip bulbs, whether to plant them twice their depth, six inches, seven inches, or a mammoth 12 inches on the theory that way down there the mice will not get them. But such a depth also can put a terrific strain on the plant as it stretches up to get to the light, so if your soil is so good as to invite moles and mice to come in, I'd suggest you also try other means suggested below to protect your bulbs from the mice. (Moles don't eat bulbs except as a very last resort; but they do make the tunnels for the mice to travel in. What attracts the moles in the first place are probably the earthworms,which come because you a nice , humusy, rich soil.)

The ideal planting time, if your bulbs arrive soon enough, is about four weeks before the ground freezes. You can plant later, but to get good fall root growth, you need to give the bulbs a chance to get established. Perhaps you have already noticed, if you have dug up some old bulbs by mistake in your garden in the fall, that there is a plentiful root system already formed by September. Do not, however, plant in such warm weather that the plants come up and get frozen later.

There are several kinds of gadgets on the market enticing people to dig single holes for bulbs to drop them in and make it all seem like less work. Unfortunately such devices also tempt people not to prepare the soil properly, and so I do not recommend them. It is much better to dig down and remove about six inches of soil where you want a whole group of bulbs to go, to mix in humus, peat moss or compost plus some sand and get all the soil into good condition before you plant. Then cover the bottom of the hole with a sprinkling of bone meal and cover that with sand, to help the drainage and sprinkle on some soil so that the bottom of the bulb will not touch the bone meal. Cover the bulb so that it is at least six inches deep, and deeper if you dare.

I believe you can dare to go deeper if conditions are ideal for the bulb to spend its substance pushing up a long stem. Some like the Darwin tulips have long stems anyway. The point of first importance is to have perfect drainage. Never put tulip bulbs where the soil is heavy with clay and cold and wet. If the layer of sand and the sand and peat moss or humus in the soil are not enough to provide good drainage, add some pebbles in the bottom of the hole underneath the sand and bone meal. It does no good to blame the mice for the disappearance of your tulips if you have put them in a wet, clammy place where they just rot away over the winter.

Another precaution against mice and moles is to prepare the soil well in advance, even up to a week in advance if the weather is good, to give the ground a chance to settle. Of course it is also sensible to arrange barriers of some sort and to keep your plantings away from places where mice make their runways. It helps to clean up trash over the bed where they might make nests and to keep evergreen boughs or other winter mulch off until after there has been a hard frost.

People use different kinds of barriers. Some make a wire mesh cage with holes small enough to let out the roots and keep out the mice, but with enough space in the top to insure safe growth of the shoots. You can put such a cage around a single bulb or around a whole group, if you see to it that the top is both protective and open in the right places. Much easier is to use a tin can the size of a beer can, for example, with both top and bottom cut off, and with the bulb set near enough the bottom so that the roots can grow down without being cramped. Evidently the mice do not fine it inviting to go down into such an arrangement even though tulip bulbs are almost irresistible to them. People also bury moth balls near their bulbs or sprinkle in some flowers of sulfur.

I also recommend doing something about the moles that make the runways for the mice to travel in. Very helpful is the klippety-klop or pinwheel windmill, which can be pushed into the ground so it will vibrate in the wind and thus discourage the moles from coming near.

Evidently they cannot stand the vibration and go elsewhere. I have also tried a spray made of a half cup of castor oil and a quarter of a cup of detergent blended with a cup of water and diluted in a gallon of warm water to sprinkle on the main runways. Moles do not like castor oil. And they do not like castor bean plants either if you want to grow those as a deterrent. To find out which tunnels are the main runways, for several consecutive days stamp on the mole runs you see. The ones that keep bulging up again are the main runs that they like to use every day.

WATERING AND FERTILIZING

Since the tulip plant subsists on its bulb through its first growth and bloom, it is not necessary once it is up and blooming to give it fertilizer until later, nor water unless there is a terribly hot, dry spell. Even then it is more important to give it shade. When the blooming period is over, however, the plant needs both water and nutrients for the much longer period when it is making food and storing it up in the bulb for next year's growth. I never remove the green leaves; I am sure it is much better merely to remove the dead blossom and seed pod and leave the stem to help feed the bulb until all green has gone out of the stem's tissues. It is also a poor practice to braid the leaves, for that cuts off light. Professional gardeners who take care of big municipal displays or big estate gardens have the habit of lifting the whole tulip plant and replanting it in an out-of-the-way sunny place to store up food and die down slowly. Home gardeners rarely do this, and need not. You can take the leaves off when they are thoroughly brown, but I find that if they bother me before that time, it is easy enought to plant something near them to mask them. Anyway, if you have tulips in a bed where other plants grow, it is nearly impossible to fork out the bulbs

without disturbing other plants. WARNING: if for some reason you do decide to dig up tulips, do it before the new root growth gets started in the fall. I know you can lose bulbs if you disturb their roots in that period.

Luckily bulbs, like most garden plants, like a soil that is about neutral or a little acid, with a pH of 6.5 to 7. If you find that your soil is becoming much more acid than that, sprinkle on a small handful of ground dolomitic limestone. Bulbs also like high potash and high phosphate fertilizers after the first year, at a rate of a pound per 20 square feet. Unless you have a climate where there is a long, cool spring, any quick jump to a hot spell after the blooming period can result in the old bulb's cracking and several small ones being formed in its place. Sometimes the next year merely a leaf will appear as the only sign that one of your tulip bulbs is still alive. Then all the fertilizing and watering won't help much unless you dig up the small bulbs, separate them and reset them in a new good, rich soil, with good drainage and other precautions I've already described. Sometimes it pays to plant them even deeper than you have before, because the coolness at a deeper level may deter the bulbs from cracking.

If all these instructions and precautions sound too fussy, and make the growing of tulips sound too difficult, I should add that they are given to help you avoid failures, and to save you some money. Some people have gorgeous tulip gardens each spring because they put in all new bulbs every year, and that can be expensive. Others pay for new bulbs, all right, but get only two or three blooms from the dozen or so they plant. That is both expensive and disheartening. So if you decide to take the trouble to protect your tulips and give them what they need, you can have lots of color and a whole range of shapes and sizes in your spring garden. They will be a delight, and make you happy to see the return of life after the long, dormant winter.

TULIPS IN TUBS AND POTS

Where they can be protected from severe freezing, you can plant tulips in tubs, give them a period of cold, and then grow them so you will have them to bloom where you want them on the terrace or patio in the spring. This method is similar to the long-established habit of forcing bulbs for very early blooming indoors.

The best container for planting bulbs to be forced is called a bulb pan, made of the red clay used in other flower pots, but wide and low, often without a rim around the edge. As with other flower pot planting, you start by putting in and inch of broken crock or stones and pebbles mixed with a little peat moss. With the broken pieces of clay crock you get both drainage and water-absortion in one material. Then put on an inch of mixed sand, loam and peat, and rest your bulbs on that. They are often planted actually touching each other because forced bulbs are rarely used over again and do not need very good root growth or fertilizing for the next year. Then cover the bulbs with good soil up to about a half an inch above the tips, which of course should be pointing upwards.

If you have a cold place or a cold frame to put them in, you can set them there, in a box with a thin layer of peat or sand spread over the bottom and the pot surrounded with either peat or sand to moderate the moisture and keep the pot from drying out. If a heavy freeze comes, put straw or burlap or some other protection around the box to protect the bulbs. Even easier is to bury the pots in the ground, low enough so they will be good and cold, but not frozen, and covered with a mulch of leaves or straw so they can be dug out later. Some people place another slightly larger pot upside down on each planted pot to help protect the new shoot when it begins to grow up. It is also a good idea to insert labels. When the time for forcing comes, bring the pots into the house to a room which can be kept at

about 50°F. If you bring them in at intervals, you can spread the blooming time considerably. Peek in to see that the pot is full of roots, for the bulbs only do well when their roots are well developed before you bring them to the light. Bulbs called prepared tulips can be got from some bulbsmen if you want to begin having bloom early in January. These are the pre-chilled bulbs which are also recommended for Southern and California gardens. Six months at 45°F. has already prepared them for use (see below).

Single Early Tulips that you prepare yourself can be brought in some time in January for flowering from February on 'White Hawk' is a good white one to try, and can be brought in from the cold as early as January first. By January 5th, bring in 'General De Wet', a handsome orange tulip with scarlet veins, and by the middle or end of the month 'Couleur Cardinal', which is red; and 'Pink Beauty'.

Double Early Tulips include the old favorite in white, 'Boule De Neige', which can be brought in by January 15th, as can the rest of the double ones. I have enjoyed 'Electra', cherry; 'Golden Victory'; 'Mr Van Der Hoef', another old favorite in golden yellow; a pink tulip called 'Peach Blosso'; and one with a white margin on a carmine red bloom, 'Willemsoord'.

These same varieties of single and double tulips are often used in outdoor plantings, too. The three other kinds preferred for indoor pots are some of the Triumphs, Darwins and Cottage tulips.

Triumphs you might like would be such vigorous varieties as 'Johanna', salmon pink; 'Red Giant', bright red; 'Apricot Beauty', the white 'Blizzard'; 'Peerless Pink'; 'Sulphur Glory', chrome yellow; or 'Garden Party', white with rose edging. These can be brought in to the warmth any time during the last half of January.

There are quite a few Darwin tulips that do well for forcing. Only two can be brought in early (as early as Christmas day) and these are 'William Copeland', which is mauve, and rosy "Rose Copeland." The others should be brought in about the middle of January. They bloom in March, though the hybrid Darwin tulips will flower in late February, and will be fragrant. Recommended are such varieties as:

Darwins
     'Aristocrat', carmine rose
     'Golden Age', yellow with orange
     'Queen of the Night', dark purple
Among the Darwin Hybrids, suitable for forcing are:
     'Big Chief', old rose
     'Diplomate', scarlet

A few Cottage tulips are used for forcing, including the three white ones, 'Albino', 'Carrara' and 'Maureen', the handsome yellow tulip, 'Mrs. John T. Scheepers', and one called 'Golden Harvest'. The red 'Balalaika' is sometimes classed as a Cottage tulip and sometimes as a Darwin.

Some of the tulips classified as Lily-flowering tulips are very graceful flowers that can be forced: 'Mariette', deep pink; 'Queen of Sheba', brownish red; and 'White Triumphator', white. Of the Parrot tulips which can do pretty well are 'Orange Favorite', 'Red Parrot and a rosy pink one, 'Van Dyck'.

PREPARED OR PRE-CHILLED TULIPS

The prepared tulips mentioned above are ready for delivery in November after their pre-chilling. These can be had from several suppliers, now and include among the Mendel tulips; 'Apricot Beauty' and 'Pink Trophy'. Single Early tulips include 'Bellona', yellow and 'Christmas Gold', canary yellow. The best pre-chilled Triumph tulip is 'Pax', white but there is also 'Orient Express', vermilion and another white one 'Hibernia'. Among the Darwins are 'Gander', deep pink; and 'Paul Richter', scarlet; and among the Darwin Hybrids are 'Beauty of Dover', yellow with a brush of rose; 'Dover', red; 'Gudoshnik', yellow with a brush of peach; 'Jewel of Spring', yellow with rose edge; 'Oxford', orange-red and 'President Kennedy', yellow with rose.

When the prepared tulips arrive, you can plant them immediately in boxes and pots and put them in a cool bright place. If you have a greenhouse, the bench is a good place to put them. The temperature should be between 55° and 65°F., and they can be planted at any time between the first of December and the first of February. They should be stored in a cool place if you postpone planting for any length of time after they arrive. After they get a good start, you can move them into a house with a temperature of 70°F. if you wish. Give them good light so they won't get leggy.

TULIPS FOR OUTDOORS

Many tulip varieties to plant outdoors have proved themselves satisfactory in recent years. Consult the catalogues to find the popular ones of the year.

LITTLE TULIPS

Next to consider for your spring garden are the dainty and lovely Botanical or Specie Tulips, all natives of Asia Minor and Central Asia, and all colorful and cheerful. Most of them are quite short but some have standard sized blossoms so they look big and handsome anyway. The group also includes some that have several blooms on one stem. The first group are the botanicals which usually flower from the end of March through April or into May, including most of the short ones which are very effective as early blooms in the rock garden. From the 25 to 30 species I'll only mention a few, with emphasis on those that I like best.

Tulipa acuminata, the Turkish or Horned tulip, with long, thin, red and yellow, curly petals. Not very pretty. Flowers in May.

Tulipa aucheriana, the Teharan tulip, very short, pink-to-orange, and fragrant.

Tulipa biflora, usually more than two flowers of cream color with yellow and pinkish green coloring. Very early.

Tulipa chrysantha, mostly pure yellow, with alternate red petals on the outer side. About eight inches tall.

Tulipa clusiana, an old favorite, with slender outer petals cherry red and inner ones white with violet base. About nine inches.

Tulipa eichleri, slightly taller, bright red, with pointed petals.

Tulipa dasystemon, or *T. tarda*, dwarf tulip, early-blooming, starlike yellow flowers with white edges and green tints, several on a stem.

Tulipa persica, a late dwarf tulip, with bright fragrant yellow flowers that are bronzy outside.

Tulipa praestans fusilier, a ten-inch beauty, of an exciting orange red with five or six flowers on a stem. Mice love it. So do I.

Tulipa turkestanica, with five to nine creamy flowers with bronze and green flush. About eight inches. Very early flowering.

The best known and most favored botanicals are those that have also been most eagerly hybridized. The Foster tulips, *Tulipa fosteriana*, came from Turkestan, originally as a big crimson bloom with a black base, now called "Red Emperor". These can be planted four inches deep. And it's best to use cages. They happen to be favorites in our family.

Other great favorites among the new hybrids are the *Tulipa kaufmanniana* varieties. These flower in mid-April, are quite short, and have blooms that are the shape of water lilies, often bicolored. The type, from which the others were developed, is called the 'Water Lily tulip, and is a large creamy flower with red stripes and a yellow center. I have them growing under my kitchen windows and by the driveway. Others are: 'Elite', or 'Elite Mixture', with red, cream, and white with a red ring dominating. They are evidently unpredictable seedlings, but all in the open, water-lily shape. 'Gold Coin', deep, yellow, inside and out, red blush interior. 'Heart's Delight', mostly carmine red outside, with cream edges and interior.

Since these water lily tulips all go together so well, I recommend that you save some money and buy collections. With other tulips it is not always wise, because the colors often clash. No such danger with Kaufmanniana Tulips; their shapes, heights and colors all fit each other beautifully.

The next group, *Tulipa greigii* with mottled or striped foliage, would also fit together pretty well. These, too, come in colors of cream, lemon, gold, orange and red. The leaves have mahogany stripes.

One last class of tulips includes the double late ones called Peony-flowered tulips. These are somewhat taller than the early double tulips and have big gorgeous blooms in late May, many of them bicolored. Varieties to consider include:

'Brilliant Fire', vermilion red, 22 inches tall
'Carnival De Nice', lovely white tulip with carmine stripes.
'Eros', old rose, large and showy. About 20 inches tall.
'Orange Triumph', soft orange with brown flush. About 19 inches.

Though not actually a class, a grouping is made by some bulbsmen of Bunch-flowering tulips and Fringed tulips. The several blooms on one stem make the bunched flowers a very attractive variation from the single stem varieties. If you see the names 'Amourette', 'Claudette', 'Georgette', 'Keukenhof' or 'Rose Mist', for instance, you can rely on their being multi-flowered tulips. The color of 'Amourette' is bright red; of 'Claudette' is rosy red with a white edge; of 'Georgette', yellow with red edge; 'Keukenhof', all scarlet and 'Rose Mist', a soft pink. These all have four to six blossoms on a stem.

Fringed tulips include a Cottage tulips called 'New Look', which is a creamy yellow with rose pink at the tops of the petals; 'Blue Heron', lilac; 'Burgundy Lace', bright red; 'Swan Wings', white; 'Rose Wings', rosy pink; and 'Maja', clear yellow. Some of the Parrot tulips also are somewhat fringed.

With such a wealth of possibilities in color, shape, size and foliage tulips offer the gardener the chance to brighten up a spring garden in dozens of different ways. I have grown tulips for years, and I have lost a good many. I have grown them from shallow planting (that is five or six inches) and from deep; in good soil and in soil that was not thoroughly prepared. If I had known enough at the time to follow the advice given in this section on tulips, I would not have had so much difficulty. But I know that any tulips that have come up have been a great pleasure—from the little Himalayan ones we planted by a stone wall on the terrace to the dazzling red *T. praestans* we looked down on from the bedroom windows and the 'Red Emperor' fosterianas to the odd and stylish Parrot tulips I used in the arrangement that won my first blue ribbon at a flower show.

My last warnings are: buy the biggest, best bulbs you can and check each for bruises or signs of rot and send them back if imperfect. Prepare the bed well, with good drainage and plant at the right time. Use plenty of fertilizer and especially bone meal, but no fresh manure. Plant

in full sun, but shade if the foliage withers too soon, too fast. Do not let the pods mature, for the plant needs all its strength to feed the bulbs. If I lived in a warm climate, I'd also dig my tulip bulbs each year after the foliage has turned brown and chill them in the refrigerator at about 40°F. for at least three weeks, or maybe more before replanting them. Protect your bulbs, wherever you live, from the pesky mice. Tulips are wonderful and I hope always to grow them, but some bulbs are easier.

❦ HYACINTHS ❦

One of these is hyacinths. Though these bulbs, like all bulbs, need good drainage, I have had them grow in a part of the garden where tulips were quite fussy, and I suspected it was because the drainage was not too good. They are not so particular about having well-prepared soil, but it is only good gardening sense to provide some pebbles, or sand for drainage, some more sand in the soil, some fertilizer and organic matter, and to see that the bulbs are put in at the right depth.

That means that for hyacinths, the tip should be about three inches below the surface. The size of the bulb will determine how much deeper than that you dig down to prepare the bed. Prepare it deeply because hyacinths have long roots. A good bed underneath the bulbs will keep them from stunting and running out. Provide plenty of bone meal and compost well worked in. As with all bulbs, the foliage must be allowed to die down at its own rate, and not pulled off until completely brown. If your winters are very severe, mulch the hyacinth bulbs after the ground is frozen. It is best to set them about six to eight inches apart, but as they get older and squattier, you may prefer to move them nearer to each other. They do get squattier because after the first year's tall growth, the stems never grow so tall again.

There are also double hyacinths, with delicate inner petals on each floret, and this is the flower type that was most popular and most usual in years gone by. The ones I like which you can still get include:

'Chestnut Flower', soft rose pink, quite pale
'Hollyhock', bright red
'Scarlet Perfection', crimson or scarlet red
'Ben Nevis', white
'Madame Sophie', white
'Dreadnought', blue
'General Kohler', lavender blue

Catalogues often offer hyacinths for bedding at reduced rates, often just by color. These are a good buy, and if you don't mind mixed colors, you can get the bulbs for even less. There are miniature hyacinth bulbs, also called Roman or Dutch Roman. These are *Hyacinthus albulus*, and sometimes go under the name 'Cynthella.' The florets are much farther apart than on *H, orientalis*, which is the common species of hyacinth, and they are much daintier and shorter. They do well in a rock garden, and are also suitable for pots and window boxes. Plant them quite near together. They come in all the same colors as the common hyacinth including bright and dark blue. From some bulbsmen you can get pre-chilled prepared miniature hyacinths to pot up for early forcing as soon as they arrive.

Hyacinths are bulbs that do well in planters and boxes. If you leave them outdoors where the weather is not too severe to freeze them solid in the box, it is best to line the box with layers of newspaper or styrofoam, and place the box in a protected place near the house or in a shed. Where the weather is very cold, bury the box as you would with tulips, and bring it out in the spring to force the plants to grow and bloom. If you live in a city and want to grow hyacinths on a terrace, get prepared, pre-chilled bulbs if possible. They should be planted six inches deep and four inches apart, though for decorative effects, especially the first year you have the bulbs, they can be put closer together. In climates that are not too severe, large hyacinths can also be used in a good rich pocket in a rock garden where the soil is deep enough to put in the bulbs six inches deep. If planted as deep as that, they may last quite a long time and bloom happily year after year.

NARCISSUS

There are lots of classes of narcissi also, and they include the ones that we usually call daffodils and jonquils, though botanically they all belong to the narcissus group, which officially are named, ironically enough, by the American Daffodil Society. The 12 divisions are listed below, but you can send to the Society for the complete list of all available varieties.

I think the flowers of the narcissus group are just about the best there are for an organic gardener. They have no pests to worry you, and no demanding cultural requirements beyond a little bone meal and the humus you put into your soil anyhow. We plant bulbs in every garden, and have a row along the side of the lower lawn, so we can look out in the spring from any window of the house and get a fine view of the bright, spotless flowers as we walk through the rooms. We particularly like the spring season when the life of plants springs up again, and though all the plants express this, the daffodils seem to do it most.

The 12 officially recognized divisions are those used by most good bulbsmen. They are:

I.   Trumpet Narcissus, which people usually call daffodils
II. Large cupped Narcissus, some with yellow cups; some white-petalled, some yellow-petalled
III. Small-cupped Narcissus, same colors as large-cupped

IV.   Doubles
V.   Triandrus, with several flowers on one
      stem
VI.   Cyclamineus Narcissus, rather like
      cyclamens
VII. Jonquilla, which really are jonquils,
      with several flowers on a stem, many
      are fragrant
VIII. Tazetta, which is the one people call
      the narcissus
IX.   Poeticus, also called narcissus, often
      fragrant
X.   Species Narcissus, wild forms and wild
      hybrids
XI.   Split-corona narcissus
XII. All other

CULTURE

Like other bulbs, narcissi need good drainage, some bone meal when first planted, and a rich enough soil to support them for quite a few years. They vary in needs for lifting. Some can be left in the ground for many years, undisturbed, and then they are called naturalized. Suitable for naturalizing are such varieties as 'Carlton', 'Fortune', and 'Trevithian'. My big white daffodils called 'Mount Hood' divide very rapidly, and get so crowded I have to lift and separate these bulbs every two or three years. They are an excellent investment because in ten years I have got as many as a hundred bulbs from an original dozen.

Luckily narcissi and daffodils are not attractive to mice and moles, so you don't have to bother with traps or cages or putting in mint, or castor oil, or other smells they don't like. Since you don't lift daffodil bulbs very often, it is best to sprinkle some fertilizer on the soil during the period when they are storing food in the bulb. Compost tea is a good safe fertilizer to use, especially if the ingredients used to make it were high in phosphorus and potassium. Bone meal and greensand make good additives.

When you first plant them, it is usual to put the bulbs in at a depth of six or seven inches. The time to plant is when there is still a chance for the roots to develop before hard frosts. In the North they can be planted right up through

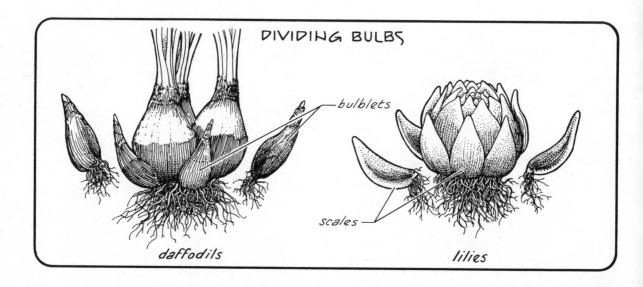

DIVIDING BULBS

bulblets

scales

daffodils

lilies

Scarlet Bedding Salvia, Petunia 'Comanche,' and Cynoglossum 'Dwarf Firmament'

Arabis

Colored-Leaf Geranium

Daisy 'Marguerite'   Longwood Gardens

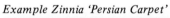

Example Zinnia 'Persian Carpet'

Forget-Me-Nots   Longwood Gardens

November, but in other climates they are sometimes planted as early as September, but avoid letting young sprouts growing up in the fall to get frost-bitten. If your soil is on the moist side, concentrate on the Poeticus group. Good drainage should keep the rest of your bulbs healthy, but if you see poor, stunted specimens, dig them out, for they may have the white maggot of the bulb fly. If you do get an infestation of this pest, lift all the nearby bulbs and soak them for an hour and a half in hot water, kept at 110°F. It is the only pest you might have to worry about, and I never had it. If I did, I think I'd also put a little chlorine bleach in the warm water for control.

In my bulb borders, along the driveway up the slope where we watch the bright spring display from the house, and above and below and beside the little stone walls near the porch and terrace, I mix all sorts of early and late varieties. Some of the mixture has been by design because I like to see the large-cupped and trumpets and doubles near each other, with inter-mixtures of the dainty Triandrus narcissi, including 'Thalia' which is my favorite, but also 'White Marvel' because it has an icy-white perianth with hanging double heads. Another cause for the mixture has been my own curiosity—as with the mixtures of tulips I have grown.

When I have read in a catalogue that there is one Cyclamineus narcissus bigger than all the rest, the 'Peeping Tom' or that I can have an early reflexing one called 'February Gold', I can't resist putting these names on the order blank. Among the jonquils I like to try are the wonderfully fragrant ones such as the double 'Campernelli odorus plenus' and a charming single one, the yellow 'Lintie'. These go well in a mixed garden of spring bulbs with some of the little blue flowers like scilla and grape hyacinths. A really early jonquil is 'Simplex', often blooming in early May. To stretch the season,

plant 'Tittle-tattle', which will bloom late. All these are fragrant, and delightful to pick for the house.

I particularly like to make arrangements on a pin holder in a shallow container, and all the daffodils look very well that way. If the stems curl, you can discipline them with scotch tape, and be sure to control any gummy juice that may run out by cutting the stems under warm water and holding them there in warm water. (And cut above the white part of the stem.) If you mix in tulips, you'll find that their stems bend, but to control that, put a support up the stem.

To have a long season of daffodil bloom, be sure to get varieties that are early, some mid-season, and some late. A few can also be planted in part shade, but they should be moved after several years because a lack of sun during the ripening period tends to make the bulbs run out. Though some people plant their bulbs at different depths, this makes more sense to me with tulips than with daffodils because you leave daffodils in the ground so much longer and they tend to move up or down to the depth that suits them best anyhow.

To keep track of the dividing of the bulbs, notice the green spears as they come up after the first year. A second cluster of these green leaves indicates a new split, and when there is enough space and nutrient in the soil to support it, the chances are that it will send up a blossom the following year. Sometimes you can notice three or four new groups of blades and then flowers, all coming from the same original bulb, if the original was big enough. Finally, when the spears are all crowded together and the flowering begins to diminish, it is time to lift the group and give each newly formed bulblet its own space when you replant. Lift soon after the foliage dies down; do not wait until fall when the roots have all begun to grow vigorously again, for the chances of injuring them are much greater than when the plant is dormant.

If daffodils and narcissi are replanted too shallowly, the flower stems and leaves will be short and not very attractive because the bulb will have been too warm during the food-storing period. As with tulips, be sure to press the bulb well into the soil when you plant. And if the ground is going to heave, mulch with pine boughs to keep the plants in place when they are coming up in the spring. If frost or moles heave the bulbs, replant at the proper depth.

For a fine showing, choose narcissi that will be double as well as single, long-cupped trumpet types as well as short-cupped, and small as well as standard sizes. Some are fragrant; some produce several blooms; all make excellent cut flowers to cheer up the house in the spring. There are many to choose from. Consult the catalogues.

NARCISSI TO FORCE INDOORS

Any of the narcissi in Division X and 'Mistral' in Division XI are good for forcing. Some especially fragrant ones recommended for growing indoors or on a terrace in appropriate climates are the Poetaz 'Cragford', with clusters of white flowers and orange cups; 'Grand Soleil D'or', golden with orange cup; and the old favorite 'Paperwhite', which is white all over. Put these in a dark, cool place for a rooting period of six to eight weeks before bringing them to the light. These bulbs are a bit expensive, but I think it is worth a little extra to see the fresh blooms—and especially to smell them—in the very, very early spring or late winter.

One way to get to know the various classes of narcissi is to grow the various kinds indoors where you can watch them closely and get to know their special virtues. Recommended, for example, are yellow trumpet: 'Golden Harvest', 'King Alfred'; Bi-color trumpets: 'President Lebrun'; white trumpets: 'Mount Hood'; Large-cupped: 'Dick Wellband' and 'Mrs. R. O.

Backhouse' (pink); Double: 'Cheerfulness' and 'White Lion'; Triandrus: 'Thalia', 'Liberty Bells', and 'Silver Chimes'.

CROCUS

This spring bulb comes early, is small and cheerful, and blooms in a variety of blues, lavenders, in white and yellow. In comparsion to tulips and narcissi, crocuses are a good deal less work, and once established can be left in the ground for a long time. Unfortunately, they can be molested by rodents, so it is best to take precautions from the beginning. If you have chipmunks, and you suspect that they are beginning to raid your crocus plantings, peg down some one-inch wire mesh over the places where you have put the bulbs in order to keep the chipmunks from digging them up. (Also see above in section on tulips about mouse and mole-control.) After selecting your colors, figure out how many plants you will need to make a showing in your garden, on your lawn, in your rock garden, or along your driveway.

These bulbs are not fussy about soil, but do like decent drainage, and when you plant them, you need only go down a short ways because crocuses only need to be planted with the tops of their corms 2½ to 3 inches below the surface. A groundcover over them, not necessarily grass, helps to protect their leaves after blooming.

The hardiest are the yellow ones called *Crocus aureus*, but also quite satisfactory for Zone 5 anyway, and in some of Zone 4, are the Scotch crocus, *C. biflorus*; a bright orange one, *C. susianus*; a purple one with white interior, *C. versicolor* as well as the common crocus, *C. vernus* which blooms very early and is usually lilac or white, with or without purple stripes.

If you live farther south, and want to stretch the crocus season, you can add *C. imperati*, white or lilac with three purple stripes, which will come into bloom in the late winter months in Zone 7. In that zone you can also grow *C.*

sieberi, another lilac one which blooms at the same time, and has about the same coloring, but is not fragrant as is *C. imperati*.

Many bulbsmen offer crocuses called 'Ginat', and usually with the color following, such as 'Giant Yellow', 'Giant White' and so on, or pehaps 'Grand Yellow', or 'Grand Lavender'. Other varieties besides these have equally obvious names, including 'Crocus Snowstorm', 'Striped Beauty' (lavender and white) and 'Crocus Purpurea', or 'Purple Beauty'. Once in a while you'll see 'Little Dorrit', amethyst blue; or 'Crocus Remembrance', a soft lavender, or 'Pickwick', another name for the lavender-and-white striped one. No special knowledge is needed for crocuses, however, as you need for choosing tulips and narcissi well.

AUTUMN CROCUS

In addition to spring crocuses, in Zone 6 and some adjacent areas, you can grow rugged, long-lived crocuses that come in the autumn sometimes without leaves, sometimes with; and sometimes pale and dull, sometimes with bright color such as in the bright orange stigmas of the blue *C. speciosus*, a very pleasant crocus to try, even in Zone 5. Other autumn crocuses include: *C. cancellatus*, a fragrant one that blooms in late September; a white one, *C. laevigatus*; *C. medius*, also showy, with scarlet stigmas and deep lavender petals up to two inches long. In Zone 6 this one will come up twice and bloom until Thanksgiving. Even brighter are the petals of *C. pulchellus*. One of the really famous flowers of the world is the Saffron crocus, *C. sativus*, whose petals are either white or lilac, but whose stigmas give the rare and costly saffron-colored powder used in cooking and coloring.

One other flower called Autumn crocus is actually the Colchicum (pronounced with the accent on the first syllable). It is only famous to those who have gout (because their medicine is made from it) and to those who take pleasure in the sudden appearance of these white, rosy-purple or mauve leafless flowers during the fall. Order them in late July or August, plant immediately on arrival, and wait and see. Their leaves will appear the following June, and as with other bulbs, feed and water them as much as you can to give the corms good growth.

Varieties to choose from include: *Colchicum agrippinum*, with several rosy-purple blooms, hardy in Zone 5, and the more common one called autumn crocus or meadow saffron with big four-inch flowers. Its leaves are two inches wide, but those of *C. byzantium* are four inches wide. So are the blossoms. A very rare yellow autumn crocus for those who live in Zone 7 is *C. luteum*. And biggest of all is *C. speciosum*, with six-inch flowers of rosy-purple if grown under ideal conditions. Hybrids of this one and *C. autumnale* are spectacular, especially 'Autumn Queen', deep rich violet and 'Waterlily', a very handsome double lilac, 'The Giant' I do not happen to care for because of its pale purply-mauve color. All these last three grow in bunches, so are especially showy. Order bulbs in July.

For best results, plant autumn crocus an inch or so deeper than spring crocuses, and give them good loam and one or two compost fertilizings when you see that they are in leaf.

CROCUSES FOR POTS

Crocuses to be grown in six-inch bulb pans with 18 corms to the pot, can be planted November 1st, brought in to a 48°F. basement on December 1st, and forced at 50° to 55°F. after January 1st so that they are in bloom in February. If you use later dates for the transfer from the cold to the warmth for some of your pots of crocuses, you can have them to put in a warm corner on the terrace in March or April for early spring pleasure. Among the Dutch crocuses suitable to use for forcing are the white one, 'Jeanne D'Arc', the silvery-lilac 'Pickwick', a deep purple *C. purpureus grandiflorus*, and a warm yellow beauty called 'Yellow Giant'. I like the very interesting species crocuses to use for forcing such as the yellow *C. chrysanthus* 'F. P. Bowles'; the purple, *C. tomasinianus* 'Ruby Giant'; and either of the lavender ones, 'Sieboldi' or *C. chrysanthus* 'Princess Beatrix.'

OTHER SMALL BULBS

In Zones 3 and 4 (as well as farther south), there are quite a few other spring bulbs to adorn your bulb garden. And in the warmer zones there are still others. Many people think at once of the familiar snowdrops and little blue grape hyacinths of spring, but there are others to consider, too.

ANEMONES

Though the most spectacular and bright-colored anemones grow in greenhouses or in warm climates, there are several small native anemones suitable for the border or the woodland garden. One is anemone canadensis, the meadow anemone, hardy to Zone 3, which has white flowers on a long stalk, and goes well under shrubs. In fact, that is exactly where you should put them because they tend to spread rather vigorously, and the competing roots of the bushes will help to control them. This anemone and the American wood anemone as well as the snowdrop anemone all like rich soil and part shade, especially if it is a woodsy place. The Virginia anemone, however, prefers a rocky, drier site. These little inconspicuous flowers along with the delicate wood anemone or windflower and the rue anemone are really most appropriate for the wild garden.

The flowers called Greek windflowers are very handsome flowers to cultivate in the border, *Anemone blanda*, which comes in a vivid blue,

atrocaerulea, and in white, 'Bridesmaid', deep rose, 'Charmer' and in pink, sometimes with white centers to their daisy-like form. These are considered hardy and grow well under shrubs or in other partially shady places preferred by the native anemones. But they need good protection in winter, either from a snow cover or excellent mulch. (For forcing plant six or eight tubers in a six-inch pan and keep in cool dark place indoors—not outdoors—after planting in early November. After six weeks bring them to the light, and force.)

The gorgeous Pasque flowers from Europe, *Anemone pulsatilla*, in blue and reddish purple which bloom in April or earlier and appear on the streets of London offered by flower girls as a sign of spring, do not always do well for us in this country. If you live in the South, try them. Try the beautiful 'Monarch De Caen' strain, with its six-petalled, three-inch flowers in white, blue, rose, scarlet and purple. These are single, as is 'Blue Poppy' and 'The Bride', in white. Double varieties include 'St. Brigid', also in a range of bright colors; 'The Admiral', pink; 'The Governor', scarlet with a white center, and 'His Excellency', scarlet.

An anemone to try if you have a rock garden, or a gravelly soil, is *A. alpina*, alpine anemone from the mountains. This has white flowers, though there is also *A. sulphurea*, which has yellow flowers. The bloom is on an 18-inch stalk, and the plant is considered hardy up to Zone 6. It has a very deep taproot, so is unsuitable for transplanting, but in very well-drained, moist, gravelly soil it may do well from seed.

GRAPE HYACINTH

The grape hyacinth is a sturdy, long-lasting favorite of mine. It is often called by its Latin name, *Muscari*. The commonest variety is *Muscari armeniacum*, Armenian grape hyacinth. I have seen them growing in profusion in

April on a Greek island. 'Heavenly Blue' is the all-time favorite, but you can also grow a lighter blue one, 'Early Giant' which is fragrant, and stretch the season by growing 'Cantab' which comes into bloom a little late. These can be combined with *Muscari botryoides*, which comes in white and pink as well as blue. When they reseed, they come up blue, so if you want to propagate this variety, take offsets, that is, dig the bulbs and divide the new bulblets and replant them all. Grape hyacinths should be planted so that the tops of their bulbs are about 2½ inches below the surface of the soil. If you can put them where they will not interfere with the sprout of a daffodil, they can be put right over deeper-planted bulbs. Extra nourishment will be needed, of course, during the period of green foliage. The tight, blue, rounded, bud-like flowers on the stem give this bulb the name grape.

TROUT LILY

A lovely, delicate wild lily, goes well in the small bulb part of the garden. Many nurseries can now supply the yellow *Erythronium americanum* and also the white variety, *E. albidum*. Plant them two to three inches deep in a cool, moist, partially shady part of the garden. For Zone 5 and the cooler parts of Zone 6 and 7, there is a similar California fawn lily. Put a small stone under each bulb.

SNOWDROPS

Earliest in my garden are snowdrops and winter aconite. The common snowdrop is *Galanthus nivalis*, and often comes out only to be covered again in snow. That doesn't seem to harm it, and it raises its solitary, dainty white bell-shaped flower again as soon as the snow melts. These little bulbs also are planted at two to three inches. They will spread by seed, and

can, if you really want to disturb them, be dug up and propagated by dividing the bulbs and bulblets. From some nurseries you can get the large variety, call Giant snowdrops, *G. elwesii*, but it looks coarse next to the other variety.

WINTER ACONITE

Winter aconite is just about as early as the snowdrop. Called in Latin *Eranthis hyemalis*, it has shiny, six-petaled yellow flowers on very short stems above nice clear green leaves. It, too, withstands snowy weather, and comes right back after being covered by snow. Plant the tubers two inches deep, in a large group for good show, but do not put them in grass as you do some crocuses sometimes. Winter aconites do best where competition with other plants is at a minimum.

GLORY-IN-THE-SNOW

Another early little flower is glory-in-the-snow, *Chionodoxa luciliae*, hardy to Zone 4. It, too, is very short and among the first to bloom in the spring. It has five flowers to each cluster, with bell-shaped florets, blue with a white center. One variety is pink. These flowers like full sun, and do well in some rock gardens. If they like the site, they will increase. Plant two inches deep.

STAR-OF-BETHLEHEM

This is a spring bulb I definitely do not recommend. Though dainty and pleasant, with good, lasting green tubular leaves, it is such a rampant spreader and so persistent that even when you are sure you have rogued it all out, little bits will send up new plants and you have the problem to face all over again. The starlike flowers are striped in green and are poisonous, as are all other parts of this plant. Its Latin name is *Ornithogalum umbellatum*. Hardy to Zone 4.

My neighbor who has a rich, well-composted garden goes frantic every spring because she is again faced with weeding out the irrepressible Stars-of-Bethlehem. But another neighbor who has a dark, neglected, almost hard-pan area under some horsechestnut trees has a few straggly specimens of this little bulb there under the trees which do not seem to bother him a bit. It's just that his soil is so awful the plant won't spread.

SQUILL

But squill, *Scilla* (in species), is a little spring flower I certainly do recommend. The Spanish squill, *Scilla hispanica* (or *S. campanulata*), has long been a favorite. It looks rather like a small hyacinth, and aside from the characteristic squill vivid blue, it also comes in white and in rosy and purplish colors. Better for naturalizing is *S. sibirica*, Siberian Squill, with deep blue, half-inch florets on three-inch spikes. Mine quickly reseed and spread, so before long you can have a carpet of blue if you want it. This variety is the familiar one grown in many spring gardens.

The bluebells you may have seen growing in English spring gardens or that have escaped and gone wild in great numbers along the roadsides are Common blue squill or English bluebell. These are a fragrant variety, about 12 inches tall, with half-inch flowers on a stalk. Bred to have white, pink and red flowers, too. The Latin name is *scilla nonscripta* or *S. nuteus*. *S. Tubergeniana* is white and very early.

A flower called "striped squill" is *Puschkinia libanotica*, which has short five to six inch stalks thick with white bell-shaped flowers. When it is used as a groundcover to go with daffodils, it is very effective. After it is established, it can have as many as ten flowers from one bulb. Quite a few bulbsmen are now carrying this.

SNOWFLAKE

Another of these white flowers, Spring snowflake, also grows about six inches tall, or perhaps a little taller. This one, *Leucojum vernum*, is also very early and has small, rounded, nodding flowers that are almost pure white but tipped with a little bit of green. Plant them two inches deep in good soil, and leave them alone for years. They will appear to greet the first warm days spring after spring.

FRITILLARIES

One of the most charming flowers, and most novel, for the spring garden is the Guinea hen flower, *Fritillaria meleagris*, also called Fritillary and checkered lily. I think the last name is most accurate, and I love its nodding, bell-shaped checkered one-inch flowers when they appear in April. The stems are short and their various colors in the checkered pattern tend to give them protective coloring, so you have to hunt for them in the garden unless you have a thick planting. In our climate in Vermont they last a year or so and then have to be replaced.

A much larger, more gorgeous fritillary is the Crown Imperial, *Fritillaria imperialis*, which stands three feet. I have never grown this flower, but have admired it from afar in the gardens in England, where it has been a great favorite since Shakespeare's day. I now certainly intend to grow them, for I have recently heard that they are excellent repellents for moles and mice. In fact, the best tulip grower in my neighborhood believes that the bulbs and onion-smelling plants of the crown imperials which she spaces about ten feet apart in her tulip beds are what accounts for the fact that she does not ever lose her tulip bulbs. They are rather expensive, but well worth it, I should say. One variety of this beauty is bright red; another yellow. The two-inch, drooping florets surround a green head which is often five or six inches wide. For residents of Zone 5 and 6, these large bulbs of two to three inches across, should be planted away from shrubs and trees in rich soil and in the sun, during the early fall, at a depth of 12 inches, spaced six to 12 inches apart. Fritillaries do not like hot afternoon sun, however.

There are a few other small fritillaries, natives of California and the Northwest, in colors of yellow, pink, purple and white. In the proper climate these are said to be easily cultivated and propagated, usually by offsets from their lily-like bulbs.

ALLIUMS

A charming set of flowering bulbs are those in the onion family, called Alliums. Besides the giant one, *Allium giganteum* which grows to four feet and has round heads of blue or purple flowers five inches across, there are many varieties of four inches to a foot or two that are very decorative.

The lily leek or golden garlic, *Allium moly*, is a dainty yellow flower with florets that dry well, so it is useful for both fresh and dried arrangements. Its romantic name, connecting it with Homer's Odysseus, implies that it used to be regarded as the herb he ate to break the spell of Circe, the enchantress. I like to grow this one, and also *Allium roseum grandiflorum* with soft rose-colored balls of florets. which sometimes have tiny onions on them late in the season the way Egyptian onions do. A bigger one, also much used in arrangements, is Blue Globe onion, *A. caeruleum* or *A. azureum*, which is tall and handsome, often growing to three feet. As most of the others, it flowers in June. A soft pink Allium is *A. oreophilum ostrowskianum*, the Ostrowsky onion, well suited to the rock garden and blooming in May. For June and July bloom you can choose *A. senescens*, with rosy flowers, and its variety *glaucum*, which blooms in August and September.

Another yellow allium, sweet-scented, is *A. luteum*, which will do well in full sun, and a light-textured, well-drained soil. In fact, most alliums prefer this kind of soil. *A. neapolitum*, called daffodil garlic, is a sweet-scented white one and a carmine red one often used in rock gardens is *A. ostrowskianum*. Also used in rock gardens is *A. karataviense*, the Turkestan onion, which has eight-inch stems and pinkish white ball flowers rising from arching leaves.

Well, there are nearly 300 varieties of onions, so I can't go into them all. If you find these round heads and their delicate colors attractive, you have your choice of many sizes and colors, from the florists special *A. neapolitum grandiflorum* with large white flowers to the common chive plants which I use for a border and cut for dried flowers because I like their dainty small lavender heads.

HARDY CYCLAMEN

In addition to the florists' cyclamen there are several varieties of about four or five inches, with delicate small blossoms which can be grown outdoors in some zones. *C. coum* and *C. neapolitanum* are sometimes used in rock gardens, and *C. europaeum* in shady gardens. Given good soil and normal care they will last quite a few years as perennials planted in rich humusy earth. All of these should be planted in late summer under about two inches of soil. Their red flowers are showy, but not large. They are quite tender, and may not be hardy north of Zone 6, though I know of some in Zone 4 and have seen them in Vermont.

HARDY GLOXINIA

This member of the Begonia family is really not a gloxinia in the sense that others belonging to the *Sinningia* group are, including *S. speciosa*, our familiar greenhouse plant. It is *Incarvillea delavayi*, and is used much more in Europe, as a matter of fact, than it is in this country. It is hardy to Zone 6, and can be planted in full sun for best effect. The rose-purple flowers with a yellow tube are about one to two inches in length, and almost as wide. Propagation is by seeds or by division. It is only half-hardy, so lift it in the fall if you live where there are heavy frosts. Bulbs planted in early spring will bloom in late May or June. It likes well-drained, sandy soil, but enrich it with humus.

LITTLE IRISES

Among the loveliest of the early spring flowers are the perfect, fresh blooms of the little hybrids *Iris danfordiae*, a rich yellow bloom that comes before the leaves unfurl; and (*I. pumila*) when it comes up with blue, purple or white flowers. Except in the colder zones *Iris reticulata*, netted iris, is also an early pleasure, so early in my garden it usually gets snowed on several times. Indoor gardeners in colder zones can also grow this dainty iris in pots. (If you do, put and inch and a half of crock in the bottom of the bulb pan, and plant the bulbs in two parts soil, one part sand, and half a part peat moss, with some bonemeal and compost mixed in, and half a part of vermiculite or perlite, as well as a pinch or two of finely ground limestone if the soil is on the acid side.) 'Violet Beauty', 'Royal Blue' and another purple one, 'Wentworth', are handsome flowers. Outdoors plant them three to four inches deep.

SOME OF THE OTHER BULBS I'D GROW IF I LIVED IN CALIFORNIA OR THE SOUTH

BLUE LILY OF THE NILE

This beautiful, tender bulb, *Agapanthus orientalis*, is most suitable for pot culture—and a big pot at that. The soil should be half rich loam including well-rotted compost and half sharp sand. In Zones 9 and 10 it can be grown outdoors in the ground, but gardeners in all the zones often use this lovely blue all-summer bloomer in large decorative pots. It can stand a good deal of feeding, off and on all summer while it blooms. Consider such varieties as *A. africanus*, *A. a. albus*, *A. a. Peter Pan* and a smaller, darker lily of the Nile, *A. mooreanus*. In the fall, dry off your bulbs to store over the winter in a warm 48° to 50°F. cellar, but keep the soil not quite dry. If they need it, divide agapanthus bulbs in the spring.

PERUVIAN LILY (OR PARROT LILY)

Not so tall, and in shades of cream, orange, red or purple are the species of *Alstromeria*, including *aurantica* and *chilensis*. These are half-hardy, so like the lily of the Nile they need to be dug or moved if there is any chance of frost. The tubers can be stored in damp peat moss or sawdust at 45°F. or cooler, and divided at the next planting time. *A. aurantiaca* can usually be wintered successfully in southern gardens. *A. pulchella* is more suited to indoor culture.

ST. BERNARD LILY

A small plant with one-inch lilies suitable for climates where the air is fairly cool, but the winters mild. It propagates by stolons and can also grow in some northern places if lifted in winter.

BABOONROOT

If your soil does not ever freeze, and it is rich and well mulched, then you can grow *Babiana stricta*, the baboon flower, with a blue blossom with a red spot, growing in the freesia-like sprays and appearing in February or March from corms planted four inches deep in October. If you use this flower for a pot plant, dry it out when it goes dormant and the leaves have thoroughly died down, and store the corms at 40° to 50°F.

ALBUCA

A very popular little scilla-like flower widely grown in California now is *Albuca major*, with species *A. minor* and *A. nelsonii.* The showy racemes of white, pale yellow or white with brown stripes bloom well in late spring or early summer and are very good ornamentals, especially the Nelson lily.

CORAL DROPS

Similar are Coral drops, *Bessera elegens,* which are bright red, white-marked flowers, also often grown in California. This elegant little Mexican bulb is very showy and has the virtue of going on blooming even into August and September. If the soil suits it and you give it good bulb culture, you may get six or eight stalks from each bulb and a dozen or so sprays of flowers.

BRODIAEA

Another Western favorite, native to the West is the genus of cormous plants, with funnel shaped clusters of pink or blue or violet, though one, Golden Brodiea, has yellow clusters, and the showiest, Prettyface brodiea, with salmon streak with dark purple. It blooms in late spring, prefers sandy soil, or the rough gravelly soil you have in your rock garden. Full sun and excellent drainage are also needed. Bulbs are available in many nurseries.

MARIPOSA LILY (OR BUTTERFLY TULIP)

Calochortus is a genus that includes nearly 50 species of American origin, native to California and other Western states. These exciting delicate little one- or two-foot lilies will last several years under cultivation if grown in poor, gritty soil with good drainage and full sun. Their white, pink, yellow or purple blooms will persist into summer after beginning during the spring. Other names for them are star tulips, fairy lanterns, and butterfly tulip depending on the group they are in. It is the butterfly tulip which has the alternative name mariposa lily, and which is the showiest and favorite for gardens. I believe that an occasional good gardener is able to grow them in zones as cold as Zone 5 or 4, if the exposure is southerly and the site protected. Mulch well with treatment necessary for some other bulbs in hot areas of the West, these do not require lifting and storing over the hot summer.

RAIN LILY

Cooperia drummondii, and two other species of *Cooperia* are very fragrant, white, pinkish or reddish tiny lilies native to Texas. They bloom in the summer, and are used for naturalizing in Zones 7 and south. If I were to attempt them up north, I'd have to lift them in the fall to store in a cool cellar over the winter.

CRINUM (OR SWAMP LILY)

The Crinum members of the Amaryllis family have rather large bulbs, so they need a lot of room. Sumatra crinum, for instance, though it grows only two to four feet tall needs plenty of room to store up food for its very fragrant, bright red flowers that sometimes come 20 or so to the bulb. In warm climates it is possible to plant the bulbs so they show above ground the way you plant amaryllis. On the edge of their hardiness zone, plant deeper. See that the soil is well enriched, and keep the plant well fertilized with compost tea and extras of bone meal. In Florida people grow Grand Crinum, *C. asiaticum,* which has big leaves, grows to five feet, and blooms all summer with fragrant big white flower clusters. There is also a Florida Crinum,

C. americanum, much smaller, (18 inches to 24 inches) which is rather fussy about its situation. It will not endure temperatures below 25°F., dislikes being moved, and needs very rich soil and water because it came originally from the swamps of Texas or Florida. If you get it to grow, it will bloom most of the summer.

MONTBRETIA

This half-hardy corm, *Crocosmia aurea*, is a member of the Iris family, related to *Tritonia*, and sometimes listed so. It is also called Golden Coppertip, to describe its bright orange-yellow flowers growing in spikes, sometimes even branched spikes. In some lists it is *C. aurea* x *C. crocosmaeflora* or *C. aurea* x *C. pottsii* which is called Montbretia, but whatever name it goes by, if I lived in California or on the Gulf Coast, I am sure I'd have a good time raising these small, bright colored hybrids. Some are orange, some vermilion red, some large and crimson. They need a pH of at least as acid as 6.5. So if your soil is alkaline, settle for gladioli instead.

PERUVIAN DAFFODIL OR ISMENE, ALSO CALLED SPIDER LILY

This lovely lily goes by two Latin names as well as by several common names. It is often listed as *Ismene calathina* but you also see it as *Hymenocallis calathina*. It is wonderfully fragrant and wonderfully graceful and white. The bulbs are usually put in about three or four inches deep, six to twelve inches apart in rich light soil. Plant in the spring and lift in the fall to store in a dry place at about 60°F. The hybrids 'Daphne', 'Festalis' and 'Sulphur Queen' are commonly available and also a new hybrid, 'Calathina Advance', which is fringed and the one I'd grow if I lived in a warm zone. Its trumpet-shaped pure white flowers would be a delight in any protected south-wall place where you could put them.

FAIRY LILY (ZEPHYR LILY)

This is a dainty crocus-like flower I'd like to grow. It blooms in the autumn. *Zephyranthes candida* is white and would be valuable for an edging or in a small group. It is not-hardy in zones colder than Zone 7. Where the ground freezes at all, these bulbs must be lifted and stored over the winter in sphagnum moss, damp sawdust or vermiculite. Dust them first with sulphur to be on the safe side. Other zephyr lilies can be got in pink, copper and bright yellow.

GALTONIA

This is a fine little "spire" lily I wish I could grow. It actually looks rather like a hyacinth. One of its Latin names is *Hyacinthus candicans*, but it is also listed in some catalogues as *Galtonia candicans*. It grows two to four feet, and is rather stiff looking, partly because the pendant florets are small and the stalk quite large. But they are plentiful and scented and a good white, so they do well in several situations—in the border, in the lawn in clumps or wherever you want to put them out in the full sun. It should be planted at least six inches deep. In zones north of Zone 7, the bulbs will have to be lifted preferrably after some heavy waterings. Cut off the tops and store the bulbs in peat moss inside a perforated plastic bag. You can use vermiculite, too. The best temperature is between 40° and 50°F. Divide at planting time in the spring.

TIGER FLOWER

This very popular small bulb from Mexico, *Tigridia pavonia* also called Shell Flower, is used for summer gardens now in Zone 7 and south, in protected parts of Zone 6 gardens, and in gardens to the north where it is necessary to lift the bulbs in the fall and store them in slightly damp soil or peat in a 35° to 50°F. place where the cold and mice cannot get to them. One of my neighbors uses buckwheat hulls for a storage material, but I have never tried that. The foliage must mature after the season as with other bulbs and then be cut off. A good healthy tigridia will bloom during July, August and September. That, of course, is one good reason why this bulb is so popular. Another reason is that the three large petals of the three-to five-inch blossoms are brightly colored in yellows, reds and white, with a distinct red-mottled throat. Put tiger flowers in the sun; plant three to four inches deep in a well-drained place; and watch out for mice.

CALLA LILY

Another Zone 10 flower, *Zantedeschia* (and not to be confused with our native callas) has large, conspicuous flowers that are very spectacular in the warmest regions of Florida and California, but we grow them in the house. They come in white, yellow and pink, or black-throated or spotted. We start calla lilies in pots in March or April and then plant them outdoors after there are no more frosts. At the end of the season we lift them before any fall frosts, dry them off and bring them indoors. I have heard that in the Pacific Northwest a few people have had success growing calla lilies outdoors in well protected places. When you plant calla lilies, leave the growing tip of the rhizome exposed just above the soil surface. After the leaves have begun to die back, withhold water and store the pots on their sides for a while (to prevent any more water getting in). For those who use calla lilies as a pot plant for patios (or indoors) a good time to repot is in September. When you lift the rhizomes, look them all over to see whether there is any root rot. If in doubt, soak the dormant rhizomes in water heated to 122°F. for one hour. The sign of this rot is yellowing leaves and a total loss of the feeder roots. If your trouble is thrips, destroy all infected plants.

SCARBOROUGH LILY

This handsome old-time favorite is the bright red *Vallota speciosa*, so well loved by gardeners during the last century and by some today. Luckily it is still available from good bulbsmen, and will brighten up your garden (if you live in Zone 10) with scarlet blooms in the autumn. The stout stems, five flowers to each, and the three-foot growth habit make this a striking plant. In other zones it can be grown as a pot plant, and should be allowed to rest after its long summer and autumn period of bloom. Keep the roots moist while it is resting, and in May get ready to put it out in full sun again. Some nurseries supply already started plants as well as dormant bulbs. Use it in the patio.

DESERT CANDLE

These big oddities belong to the Lily family, and are striking because they send up huge, tall flower spikes though their leaves are only a foot or so tall. *Eremurus himalaicus* (eight feet tall) is the most common, with a tall stalk having two to three feet of bloom. The flowers are white, but other species are pink or orange. Plant the roots four to six inches below the surface of the ground and surround them with coarse sand and mulch with coal ashes or something similar when the roots reach up to the surface. Because they do this the plants of the desert candle are not well suited to any zones except those where frosts are rare. With good care, they can be grown up to Zone 6—and that means good mulching. Don't disturb desert candles if once they get established. If you want to propagate them, do it from seed.

FALL DAFFODIL

This little plant of the Amaryllis family is from Israel's dry rocky fields. The shiny yellow flowers are about an inch and a half long and the leaves up to a foot long, both coming in autumn. It is hardy in Zone 7, but in cooler climates the bulbs must be lifted after blooming. It thrives in sunny, hot places. In most catalogues it is listed by its Latin name, *Sternbergia lutea*.

FREESIA

The lovely, fragrant greenhouse plant, *Freesia*, in its hybrid forms is familiar to many as a greenhouse plant, but is perfectly suitable to try as an outdoor plant in Zones 9 and 10. The variety 'Charmante' is pink and apricot; 'Flambeau', carmine; 'Buttercup', yellow; 'Maryon', lavender, 'Albatre', white and 'Princess 'Marijke', bronze, yellow and orange. *Freesia refracta* is commonly used for its yellow flowers, though the variety 'Alba', is white; *leichtlinii*, pale yellow with an orange blotch. The trick about growing freesias as pot plants is to pot them between October and January and then to mature them in a really cool place (45° to 55°F.). With luck, they bloom in about ten or twelve weeks after planting. You can dry the bulbs, store them and use them again. They do well in the greenhouse of my garden club, but I have not had luck with them. . .yet.

AMARYLLIS

As many house plant enthusiasts know, this big gorgeous flower is really a *Hippeastrum*, hardy only in Zones 9 or 10. There are several species, but what we all grow are hybrids: 'Mont Blanc', the wonderful, soft white one, now being called Easter Amaryllis; 'Madame Curie',salmon; 'Irene', the delicate pink; or 'Brilliant Star', dark red. What the big bulb prefers is to be planted shallowly, with a third of the bulb above the surface of the peaty soil mixture, and when in pots, in a pot that is not too much bigger than the bulb. If you make your own mixture, use two parts loam, one part leaf mold or peat moss, ¼

part decayed, old manure and the other part bone meal and sand. Be sure to fertilize well after blooming to build up the bulbs for the next year. When the leaves die in August, withhold water, and lay the pots on their sides in a cold place. Do not let the bulbs shrivel, however. Take out the old soil when it is time late in the fall or early winter to repot, and start again with fresh soil. Whether grown in pots or outdoors, always be careful not to break the skin of the leaves or the bulbs because breaks might lead to infection. These six-inch beauties sometimes come two or three to a stalk. My last one came from the bulbsman with the leaves snipped off, but new leaves did grow after the blossoms faded.

❦LILIES❦

Lilies are so beautiful and such a joy when they are successful that it's always worth your while to keep trying until you find the ones which suit your place and your way of gardening. The big bulbs sent to you by the reliable lily dealers are rather expensive to treat as annuals, so use the best methods of cultivation and care, and try to establish some of these outstanding blooms for your garden.

If you do get some of the easier ones to grow, they will go on blooming for years, as a pest-free joy in an organic garden. And they should encourage you to go ahead and try some of the more tricky ones.

CHOOSING LILIES

First send for several catalogues and study them well for their many, many offerings and suggestions. In recent years hybridizing has been so intense and so successful that there are now two or three hundred kinds to choose from. Aim for a succession of bloom and select varieties for June, July, August and even into September. You can have some small, nodding ones and some big upright ones and others in between. Clean, undiseased bulbs are now almost a certainty in this country, though not long ago many imported bulbs were transshipped to the customer in poor condition. The hints I am going to give will help you to read the catalogues and to have some degree of success when your bulbs arrive. The better the bulb, the later it is in arriving, for experienced bulbsmen do not lift them until all their green leaves and stem have died down and stopped feeding the bulbs. This means that if you live in the North as we do, you have to prepare the ground well ahead and mulch it to keep it warm until the bulbs arrive. Buy the biggest bulbs you can get, and that means the most expensive. They are worth it. If the roots are not succulent and fresh and alive when the bulbs arrive, send them back. Also discard or send back bulbs that are bruised or rotten looking anywhere.

CULTURE

Choose a well-drained place for planting lily bulbs and then make the drainage even better. Like tulips, lilies abhor standing in moist, soggy soil. Mix in plenty of humus, and well composted peat moss, oak leaves and garden compost to a depth of two feet. If your bed is made up of rocky subsoil or hardpan clay, you may find it hard to dig down a full two feet. If so, add lots of compost on top. Yearly additions will do much to offset the disadvantages of shallow topsoil. It is better not to use manure, even well rotted manure, because of the danger of fungi and of too much nitrogen. Later, when your bulbs are strong, healthy and well established, a bit of well-rotted manure as side dressing might do. We never use it with lilies. We prefer side dressings of compost.

Most lilies do best if they are in the sun all day, though those such as the lovely recurved *speciosum* lilies and other species from the woodlands prefer part shade. Lilies need either a thick mulch or to be with other plants that can shade the soil around them during the period they are making food to replenish the bulbs for next year's growth. A few lilies are suitable for woodland gardens and rock gardens.

PLANTING LILIES

Dig a deep bed to condition the soil well. Except for Madonna lilies which are planted just an inch under the surface, lily bulbs should be planted with four to six inches of soil on top of them if they are two-inch bulbs, more if larger and a little less if smaller. Lilies usually look well growing in a group, if well aired, so make a hole two feet deep and wide enough to accommodate the group. Mix a rich loam made of two parts good soil, one part compost, one part peat moss, and one part sand. Add a handful of bone meal for each group.

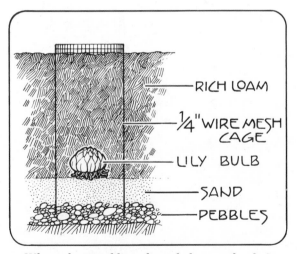

RICH LOAM

¼"WIRE MESH CAGE

LILY BULB

SAND

PEBBLES

When planting lilies, dig a hole to a depth 3 times the size of the bulb, and line it with pebbles and sand. Place the bulb on top of the drainage material, surround it with a cylindrical wire cage for rodent protection, and cover with garden soil.

Now take care of the drainage. Line the hole with sand and pebbles, preferably an inch deep, though half an inch will do if your beds are on a slight slope. When you plant bulbs singly, you can dig smaller holes, deep enough so that there will be soil over them to a depth of three times the size of the bulb. Work in some humus, sludge or composted leaves, a small handful of bone meal, and put pebbles or sand in the bottom of the hole. One of the good things about using sand is that you make a kind of pad there to fend off marauders and help to protect the bulb from damp and rot. If it is a Madonna lily, [*Lilium candidum*] that you are planting shallowly, add some lime.

Be very careful when you do the next job. The roots that come attached to your bulbs are very delicate and should not be broken or bruised, and they should not dry out. Therefore while you fit on wire cages to protect the bulb from mice and other rodents, work quickly and then return the bulb to damp sphagnum moss unless you are going to plant it immediately. The only ones you do not ever have to worry about are the Madonna Lilies, which for some reason mice do not like. See that the bulb has no bad bruises on it, and then roll it in sand or sprinkle it with sand before you put it in the cage or plant it. Some people add some flowers of sulphur dust to the sand, and that is an added protection.

How to Make a Cage— A good way to make the cage for lily bulbs is to get some ¼-inch wire mesh cut in lengths to measure 12 inches by 18 inches. A piece this size can be curved to make a cage five inches in diameter. When stuck in deep enough, it is not necessary to have a bottom piece, and if left projecting slightly above the soil line, no top piece is necessary either. Safest of all is to rest the bottom of this cage on a layer of sand and gravel as deep in the ground as the lily bulb will stand, depending on whether it roots from the stem or from the bulb.

When to Plant— Lilies should be planted in the late fall, in November, though it is possible to keep them in the refrigerator over the winter in slightly damp sphagnum moss if you can't manage to plant them when they arrive from the bulbsman. It is also possible to get bulbs in the spring which have been stored at the nursery in the refrigerator there.

LILIES IN POTS

There are a good many advantages to growing lilies in pots. You can control the soil, the drainage, the watering and fertilizing—as well as the mice—much more easily and they look perfectly marvelous in bloom on the terrace, in the patio, on a balcony or at a doorway. You can even put some in the border part of the day for sun and move them to a place among the shrubs for shade and for a fine effect at tea time. All sorts of containers will do—clay, plastic, or wooden. Allow three bulbs to a 15-inch container, if they are going to grow up to four feet, say; or put in five, if they'll reach only a couple of feet. It helps the bulbs, keeps their roots cool, and makes a nice display if you add a little ground cover planting such as bugleweed (*Ajuga reptans*) or even some petunias or dwarf impatiens, depending on the amount of shade you will be giving them. It is essential to have plenty of good porous humus in the planting mixture, but include also one-third sharp sand to provide free movement of water. Cover the bulbs with three to six inches depending on the size of the bulb, and leave one inch at the top for water.

Pot Culture— Where the weather is moderate, you can winter your pots of lilies outdoors in a sheltered place. If it gets very cold, add a few inches of sawdust or put them under cover where it is dry. Also put them under cover in climates which are very rainy. When the plants begin to grow in the spring, bring them to the sun. Only water sparingly at first, and let the pot get rather dry before the next watering. At ten inches of growth begin to add fish emulsion diluted in water, or add compost tea. Fish emulsion may be safer. Fertilize twice more before the blooms come out. Then gradually decrease water for four weeks, but do not ever let the soil dry out. At this time you have an advantage over lilies grown in the ground, because after the plant begins to die down, you can move it to an out-of-the-way corner to finish off in retirement. Only remove the stem when all green has gone, store over the winter and bring out for the new season in the spring. By removing the top two inches of soil each autumn and providing fresh, well-nourished soil, you can leave the lily bulbs in the pots for several years. Lift and divide when they become overcrowded. (See below for recommended varieties for pots.)

LAST ADVICE

The trickiest thing about lilies, potted or otherwise, is keeping the drainage good, the soil moist but not wet. This, and plenty of air, are the two most important conditions to provide. If you live in a hot, dry climate, you may need to protect the soil with a mulch of pine needles, peat moss or straw around the lilies (or around the lilies plus whatever plant you decide to use as a groundcover). Lift the mulch occasionally to see that the ground beneath it is still moist, and then water with a slow stream if necessary. Do not use a hose because the spray and splatter might invite trouble. Well-composted, or fish-fed plants will, of course, have more resistance than plants grown in poor soil, so your difficulties from disease should be at a minimum. Ten day intervals should be enough for watering. If you do use mulch, put it on first in the fall, to help prevent heaving; and do not use the kind of mulch that packs.

GARDEN CULTURE

Fish emulsion and compost fertilizer are good for lilies planted out in the garden, too, once early in the spring, and once just before they bloom, as well as twice during the maturing period. Avoid high-nitrogen fertilizers because the stalks will get spindly and you will invite disease if you splurge on nitrogen. That is, instead of using blood meal or cottonseed meal, use wood ashes and bone meal to supplement the compost or fish fertilizer. In fact, if your soil has plenty of potash, staking will not be necessary. Where it is very windy and you have to stake; be sure to put the stake into the hole before you plant the bulb.

Also be sure never to poke around or weed in the lily bed in the spring before the shoots have come up. it is very easy to ruin a lily inadvertently if you do. My husband warns me every spring.

NEVER REMOVE LEAVES

After blooming, remove the seed heads, but no leaves or stem. And when cutting lilies for flower arranging, avoid cutting the stem as far down as the leaves, which must stay on the plant to make food. (Since they are large, lilies belong in the part of the arrangement where short stems are best anyhow.) And never mind how the left-over stalks look in the garden. As an organic gardener, you'll come to like their presence because you know what's happening to the plant and you'll respect it. When all the green has gone and you cut back the stalks to ground level, you can sprinkle some sand and sulphur on the cut surface. If you have any suspicions of disease, however, examine the bulbs and throw out any that are bad. A large infestation of botrytis or virus would mean that the whole bed should be moved, and no more lilies grown there for several years. Signs of trouble include badly mottled leaves, warped stalks, blighted buds or the sudden dying of young shoots.

PROPAGATION

Lily bulbs are usually left in the ground all winter, but you may lift them in the fall if you want to remove and replant the little bulblets that form. You can also let a seed pod mature once in a while and plant your own seeds. Some people also reach down in and remove a few scales from lily bulbs, plant those and wait for the bulblets to appear. Be sure to save some of the little bulbils, the black seed-like little structures that grow in the axils of varieties like tiger and sulphur lilies. They germinate easily when planted, and often come up by themselves near your established lilies, as they do just outside my kitchen door. WARNING: Avoid putting tiger lilies, which are subject to a virus, with other lilies which might be harmed. The virus doesn't bother the tiger lilies, but it sickens the others.

PLANNING FOR THREE-MONTH BLOOM OF LILIES

I know few things pleasanter than sitting down with a catalogue from a good lily house to make plans for lilies for the garden. I had a chart all made for this book, but it was decided to leave it out, so I'll recount instead some of the basic information it conveyed.

First I set forth the June-flowering, lilies, telling about the Backhouse hybrids, Bellingham hybrids, Golden Chalice hybrids and Harlequin and Mid-Century hybrids, with suggestions for other varieties to choose for different colors, including such fine upright, easy-to-grow lilies as 'Enchantment' a popular red, 'Hallmark', a good white and the first white lily to bloom, 'Martagon'. One point to make about the Bellingham hybrids is that they are good for

dappled shade, but they do grow better in the West than in the Eastern parts of the country. The short Harlequin hybrids with stems of three to five feet have an amazing 30 flowers on one stem, and their June season of bloom often carries over into July. They do not like full sun, but the slightly taller bright orange 'Hanson' does like lots of sun (but cool feet). And then there is the Madonna lily, *Lilium candidum*, which will grow to five or six feet, and bloom in June, if planted in August, two inches deep in slightly alkaline soil. It will look lovely with the husky Mid-century hybrids, in such appealing varieties as 'Cinnabar', 'Fireflame', 'Paprika' and 'tabasco'. And there are Pastel hybrids in nice pale colors to go with those as well as the reliable disease-resistant Rainbow hybrids, often used for pots, too, so their yellow, orange and red colors will brighten up the patio.

July-flowering lilies are even more spectacular and lovely, beginning with the very hardy Sentinel strain, white with gold throats, which we believe do very well in cold areas, and lasting over from June bloom in some places.

Some very vigorous July lilies are available in the Fiesta strain, in colors from yellow to maroon. They grow to five or six feet, and give them full sun. A four-foot red lily to grow for prolific blooms is 'Fire King' and another easy-to-grow lily, white, is 'George C. Creelman', which has been known to have 30 flowers on a strong stem. If you want very big, tall lilies for special spots, the Centifolium (of the Olympic hybrids) will grow up to seven feet, with white blooms, streaked with brown. And then there are the extremely handsome Dragon varieties, 'Green Dragon', which is white with a chartreuse throat, and the marvelous prize-winner, 'Black Dragon' which is white inside and a softly striped purply brown on the outside. I have grown these with only moderate good luck, but the next time I try I am going to improve the drainage even more (and use good strong cages).

Salvia 'Park's Special Bedding' and Marigolds 'Climax Mix'

Ageratum in foreground and the tree, Mountain ash, behind

Narcissus cyclamineus (a miniature species)   Longwood Gardens

A rock garden path landscaped with groundcovers, shrubs, and evergreens   Longwood Gardens

Hyacinth   Longwood Gardens

Coral Bells (Heuchera)

See the catalogues for the delicious mimosa yellow, shell pink, deep gold and other colors you can get, in pendant varieties and also outward-facing. A lily to think twice about because it gets mosaic is the small white one, 'Duchartress' but I'd recommend 'Connecticut Yankee', developed as a disease-resistant one. It is apricot colored.

Of all lilies, probably the easiest to grow is the Regale lily, white, with wine and brown outside and yellow at the throat. It grows as tall as five or six feet, and when established will produce 18 or 20 flowers on a stem. One of my neighbors specialized in Regale lilies, mostly to give away, it seemed, because they multiplied easily, too. Its cousin, 'Royal Gold', is very similar, but yellow, and equally easy.

In August the exquisite Empress, Imperial and Speciosum lilies come along. I have had best luck with the Speciosum, and even have some 'Red Champion' growing in a spot where they get some shade from a pear tree. In another year I am going to try 'Red Duke', too, which is said to be tall and vigorous. It was new in 1972. Among the Empresses there are the huge ones of China, India and Japan, with the Indian one having ten-inch blooms of crimson, and pink outside. These don't grow too tall, maybe three to six feet, but the Imperial crimson strain may get up to seven feet. Aside from crimson, you can get gold, pink and silver strains, the last considered quite vigorous and hardy. Another hardy August lily is Jamboree, a beautiful crimson with a white edge, disease-resistant, with eight-inch flowers and satisfactory for pots for the patio or terrace. A smaller one, also good for pots, and growing to only 2½ feet, is the Little Rascal strain lily, white with crimson spots, and another red and white one, rather tall and disease-resistant is 'Red Band'. I certainly recommend that if you do decide to grow lilies you will first try the disease-resistant ones. Though most of our lilies now are grown in this country and declared disease-free at the good nurseries, the imported ones can be diseased, and in the old days when most of our lilies were diseased, they got the reputation of being difficult to grow—as indeed they were. (As mentioned above, Tiger lilies do get virus disease, so do not attempt to combine them with other lilies. These originally came from China, and in some areas have actually become naturalized.)

IRISES

There are many species and many varieties of iris, including, of course, the popular bearded iris also called German iris. In addition there are beardless, crested, Juno, Onocyclus, Regelia, Reticulata and Xiphium or the so-called Spanish or English bulbous iris.

They are plants with rhizomes, or underground stems, and their flowers are usually structured so that there are three upper and three lower parts. The upper, upright petals are called "standards" and the three lower or hanging ones are called "falls." In the familiar bearded iris the falls are fuzzy. In the pale lilac, native crested iris (*I. cristata*), a dwarf form described above, the falls have a central crest or ridge. In beardless iris the falls have no crest nor beard. Some are large, some small, and really the only thing to be said against an iris grown on sloping and well-drained land is that its blooming period is so short.

I grow a great many, nevertheless, and they persist year after year because the drainage is good so mine never get borers, which are the bane of gardeners who do not have that good kind of drainage. (Hint: No poisons needed if the drainage is good.)

BEARDED IRIS

This striking, effective flower is a delightful addition to any border, and has been a fascinating subject for hybridizers. Their products have been spectacular developments on the old-time garden favorites of many generations of admirers of the fleur de lis, with other strains introduced from Italy, Poland, Persia and Spain. Since the parentage is so mixed, bearded iris are sometimes not hardy north of Zone 5, nor south of Zone 6. Many are hardy in Zone 4, but in southern zones some irises will run out because they need colder winter dormancies than they can get in warm climates.

In some old gardens I have seen the iris left-overs from the days before the beautiful hybrids arrived. The purple one originally from Germany which gave us the name "German Iris" is still around as an archetypal flower of this group. 'Albicans', the white one, is still frequently met in the South. Another persistent variety is the blue and white 'Florentina', brought over because of the orris powder derived from its roots. In my iris beds I still have one of the antiques, 'Honorabilis', a yellow iris with red markings, which can be used in old-fashioned gardens to great effect. It is not easy to buy these old-timers now.

Some of the tall bearded iris varieties you can include in your color scheme for dark blue or purple are: 'Allegiance', 'Black Swan', 'Edenite', 'Indiglow', 'Sable Night', 'Violet Harmony' or the purple and white variety, 'Dot and Dash'. Blue iris include: 'Blue Sapphire', 'Chivalry', 'Eleanor's Pride', 'Pacific Panorama, and one with white standards and blue falls, 'White Cloth'. All white are: 'Celestial Snow', 'Cliffs of Dover', 'New Snow', 'Piety', 'Snow Goddess' and the blue and white, 'Rococo'. Gold or yellow: 'Millionaire', 'Olympic Torch', 'Orange Parade', 'Rainbow Gold' and 'Wild Ginger'. Consult the catalogues for other suggestions. There are many colors to choose from nowadays, some very novel and beautiful ones.

CULTURE

The time to plant or divide iris is July or August in the North, and considerably later in the South, or after the summer heat has passed its peak. Prepare the soil well with compost but no manure, certainly none where the rhizomes can touch it. It you wish to raise a cover crop and turn it under before planting irises, that will make an excellent preparation. Try clover or rye. Then hold back on the nitrogen.

Make a good, deep bed, preferably on a slope, for the sake of the good drainage. Add drainage material to be on the safe side, and be sure to add it if you have a flat or wettish place you plan to use for irises. When you plant the rhizomes, put them in almost horizontally, with the roots down and the tops of the rhizomes above ground. I go through my iris beds each year, pulling back any debris that might have fallen over the rhizomes, or pushing back any dirt that has crept up over them. They need to be exposed to the sun, so if you mulch, keep it back from the irises. Actually iris do not need mulch. I also pull off any withering leaves I see, and in the fall I cut back the leaves as they die down. Some people like to give their irises a cutting back to a

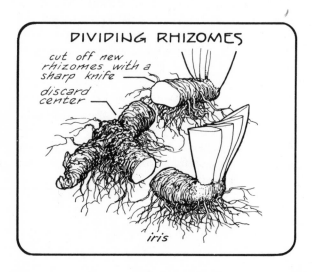

DIVIDING RHIZOMES

cut off new rhizomes with a sharp knife

discard center

iris

fan shape in August. It is pretty, yes; but I do not approve of this because by removing that much of the green leaf, you are just cheating the plant of so much chance to store up food for the next year.

Divide your rhizomes every few years. And each year look them over to see if you can discover any bad spots to cut out.

IRIS ROOT ROT

If soft spots appear, scoop out all the soft parts and then douse the rhizomes in a weak solution of chlorine bleach when you next lift them, and get rid of all rhizomes which are badly infected. This trouble may be in the young or old root, but whatever it is, you can help yourself to avoid it by planting irises on a slope, with good drainage, and always seeing that the rhizomes are free from nearby shading plants. Keep the weeds out, and pull off all dead leaves promptly.

Signs of root rot are watery spots on the leaves near where the bacteria have entered holes, and collapsing leaves. The sure sign is a nasty smell. It is most likely to occur when the plants are too near together, or when the larvae of the iris borer have made the holes.

BORERS

When conditions are not perfect, you may get that borer, especially in old plantings. The young larvae emerge from their eggs early in May, hiding in the leaves at the base, but biting holes. They also get into the buds and flowers and if they attack the rhizomes, the whole plant may collapse. Though it is hard to see this pest, it can be stalled by sprinkling the plant with diatomaceous earth. but as with other borers in squash plants, for instance, a good method is to go after them with a knife and wire and snag them out. You can also pinch the larvae if you can detect where they are. This is easiest when

they are on the leaves, for then you just pinch the whole leaf where they are biting in. In July lift all infected plants, clean them up, cutting away bad places and replant in new soil. Since the eggs overwinter at the base of the plant, another drastic method for getting rid of borer eggs is to pour some kerosene on the plants—just a little—and light a quick fire to burn out the eggs.

Sometimes the best way to treat borers (and rot, too) is to lift, clean, divide and replant your whole iris bed. Use a sharp knife and cut back past all borer holes in the rhizomes, and all rot. Then rest the rhizomes in the sun for three or four days until they dry out well and form calluses over the cut surfaces. Prepare the bed and replant the rhizomes as directed above. A sprinkling of sulphur will also help, and if you have sudden rain, sulphur can be substituted for the sun treatment.

I pass on this information to you as I have gathered it from the experts. I have grown irises for years and have never had borers and only occasionally a bit of rot when the plants were crowded and shaded. And I have not ever used the recommended precaution of dusting the plants several times a summer with a mixture of botanicals such as rotenone and ryania. The secret of my success is very simple: ideal growing conditions on a sunny slope. I lift and divide every four or five years, with plenty left over to give away every time.

GLADIOLUS

This is a favorite tender bulb with many people. Glads grow well in rows in a cutting garden or right in the vegetable garden, but you can also plant corms here and there in a border, or around the patio. Where it is very warm, or where you have a big enough greenhouse, *Gladiolus tristis* can be grown, and as you probably know from florists' gladioli this is the fragrant one. My favorites have been the *G. colvillei*, the small ones, which are much more manageable for flower arranging than the big ones. And I like the delicate colors and bicolor combinations.

CULTURE

Plant glads where they will get full sun, in nice rich porous soil as soon as it is warm in the spring. If I lived in Florida, I'd grow them in winter; and if I lived in northern parts of Canada, I could still grow them in summer. They seem to do well anywhere if given space (six inches apart) and some support (three inches deep and occasionally stakes) and the soil they like. In warmer climates you can keep the corms in the refrigerator for many months, just bringing them out to plant as you want. And in the north some people are able to protect them and grow them as hardy perennials as far north as Zone 5 in Missouri and all the way across to Boston. We always lift ours, dip them in a weak solution of chlorine bleach to control pests, and store the corms when they are thoroughly dry in single layers in a coolish but frost-free place. To winter over in the ground, it is obvious that they must be planted below the frost line. In my Vermont climate the corms I left in for experiment were planted five inches deep, but I lost them. When you lift them, save the new big corm on top and the little cormels around the edge. A good-sized corm is about an inch and a half in diameter. The small cormels need to be soaked before planting to soften the hard shell around them. Plant them nearer together than the bigger corms, lift and replant for two or three years and then they will start to bloom. These should be planted as soon as possible so they can have all summer to make food to supply to the corms. The glads big enough to blossom can be planted at one-week intervals until two to three months before frost. It takes about that long for glads to mature to blooming stage. Small bulbs are a bit more hardy and can be left in the ground more safely; they do not form cormels, so there is no need to dig them up in order to save those for replanting. Some people start corms in pots inside so they get a headstart before being planted out, but I have never done this. It sounds like a good idea if you want to stretch the season.

FEEDING AND CARE

As with other bulbs, a good feeding program is desirable, especially during the time the leaves are making food and sending it down to the corms. Spread compost and a sprinkling of bone meal along the row or around the plant, about four inches from the stem. Good health of your glads can be promoted by well-nourished soil, good air circulation, and the practice of rotating the location of your plantings each year. Thrips are one main threat to glads, and the chlorox dip is a definite help in controlling them if they happen to have gotten to your corms. You can tell they have come if you see small, whitish spots on the leaves which turn brown. They also suck the juices out of buds and they lay eggs in the foliage, and in the flesh of the corms. You

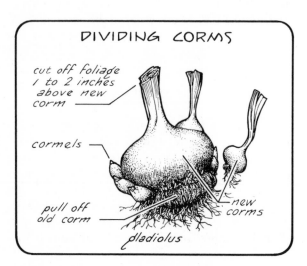

DIVIDING CORMS

cut off foliage 1 to 2 inches above new corm

cormels

pull off old corm

new corms

gladiolus

can see the blister on the corms sometimes. Wash them off during the hot summer months, and use a botanical spray if necessary.

The miniature gladioli come in the same range of colors and bicolors as the high ones. They are often only sold as collections. One of my favorites among the named varieties is 'Atom' and another is 'Peter Pan'. As is true of all continuously hybridized flowers, the names change with the years, so get some good catalogues and pick your choices.

❦DAHLIAS❦

Another well-hybridized and many-formed flower is the dahlia, which you can grow in one or more of 13 forms, in many sizes and in many rich colors, both tall and short, both open and pompon shaped. They are very good for spotting here and there in the beds to provide bloom in late summer when many of the prettiest perennials have finished flowering. This flower used to be called *D. variabilis*, aptly. Now it's called *D. pinnata*.

Class I is the Incurved Cactus Dahlia, a fully double flower with the rays (which are like petals) curving and quill-like.

Class II is the Recurved and Straight Cactus type, also fully double with rays curved or straight.

Class III is the·big, curvy-petaled Peony type.

Class IV is Semi-cactus, again fully double.

Class V is the shape I always think of as dahlia shape, called Formal Decorative, a popular one to grow in many places.

Class VI look like it but the rays are curlier; it's called Informal Decorative.

Class VII. the Ball Dahlia is ball-shaped or slightly flattened.

Class VIII. is the charming Anemone type, with open center and one row of rays.

Class IX is the beautiful, simple Single type.

Class X is the Duplex, with two rows as of ray florets.

Class XI is the Pompon. And its rays are arranged spirally.

Class XII is Collarette, with two ranks of the petal-like structures.

Class XIII is the Miniature Decorative group, or those under three inches, pompons excluded.

I don't know why they bother to call some decorative and some not decorative, for to me all these flowers, whether fresh-cut or dried in an arrangement or out in the garden are very good looking and very useful in making a flower design. Or in other words, are decorative.

CULTURE

In spite of their sub-tropical origin, dahlias can be grown by the organic gardener in all parts of the country with a little care, and with exposure to lots of sun. Since the dahlia tubers grow in clumps, you might think it a good idea to plant these clumps, but it is not a good idea. They should be gently divided, leaving a bud up near the top of the tuber, or up to three buds. A week or so before you get ready to plant, put the tuber clumps in a warm place in a damp medium like wetted peat moss or sphagnum moss, to let the buds develop so you can see them, but not too much because they might get broken at planting time.

The soil preferred by dahlias is a fairly sandy loam, and good drainage below. If you have clay soil, amend it, and put some gravel in the holes for extra drainage. Use besides sand, plenty of compost and plenty of well-rotted manure, sludge or decayed mulch with a half cup of cottonseed meal or other nitrogen supplement and a cup of bone meal and a cup of dried seaweed. As with other bulbous and tuberous

DIVIDING TUBERS

use a sharp knife to cut off part of the crown and one or more dormant eyes

growing bud

dahlias

tuberous begonias

plants, you may need to dig down to 10 or 15 inches and put in a three-inch layer of gravel, cinders or broken clay pots to improve the drainage. When you have made a good rich soil for the dahlia bed, dig it in to a depth of eight inches. Insert stakes every 18 inches in the row for small dahlias, and every three feet for big ones.

To plant the tubers, select a warm day after the soil has warmed up, perhaps as late as late May or early June, and plant them about six inches down in the prepared soil, with the buds pointing up. See that they have about two inches of soil over them. Obviously they should be near enough the stakes to be able to be tied later. If several stalks come from a tuber, cut back all but the most sturdy, and begin to nip the main buds from this one when the stalk is 12 inches tall, and has at least four true leaves. Pinch out both the bud at the top, and the buds just below this.

Keep the small plants well weeded until mid-July and then begin to mulch with a three-inch layer of hay, buckwheat hulls or corncobs, if you do not mind the light color. Nourish the soil well just before applying the mulch, with well-rotted manure, compost, bone meal and a high potassium fertilizer such as greensand. Water well once a week or as needed. Any shortage of water or fertilizer will stunt dahlias and make them unattractive and poor in bloom.

In the fall, the first heavy frost will kill your dahlias if you don't lift them first. Cut them off to within six inches of the ground well before frost, and leave the plants right there for a period of ten days. Then on a warm, sunny day dig up the tubers, being careful to keep your digging fork well away from the tender plants. Dry out in the sun upside down for at least three hours, and drain the stalks if they need it. Store for the winter in a cool, dry place, between 45° and 50°F. in dry sand or peat moss.

During the summer if you see mildew, dust the dahlias with sulphur. If you suspect cutworms, use collars and poke in the soil in the early morning to root them out. If a tiny hornet bites the bark of the stems, find its nest and set fire to it in the evening after dark. For the corn ear worm, find its place of entry and apply mineral oil from a medicine dropper. For other suggestions see *The Organic Way to Plant Protection* by the Editors of Organic Gardening and Farming, Rodale Press.

MIGNON DAHLIAS
OF THE MINIATURE GROUP

Among the smallest of the little dahlias is the ten-inch 'Topmix', which comes in pink, red, white and yellow, all of a rather bright hue. They will flower from June until fall and will make a good edging for gardens of other-sized dahlias or other perennials. Somewhat taller, growing to a foot or a foot and a half are other single-flowering plants which are equally bright colored and prolific. This group of mignons includes 'Irene Van De Zwet', yellow; 'Murillo', pink; 'Nelly Geerlings', scarlet; 'Sneezy', pure white; and 'Wing', flaming red.

The next taller, called the Collarettes to describe the inner row of petals, will grow to two feet. Suggested varieties are 'Bride's Bouquet', pure white, with a white collar around a gold center; 'Clair De Lune', sulphur yellow with creamy collar; 'Florescent', rosy purple 'Geerlings Elite', cardinal red with yellow tips and yellow collar; 'Grand Duc', orange red, golden eye; 'Kaiserwalzer', bright red and a yellow collar, a very neat looking blossom, and very cheerful; 'La Cierva', purple and white; 'Libretta', purple and white also, but more velvety looking; 'Rococo', lilac, with white collar. One other in this group which you might like is an 18-inch single orange beauty, 'G.F. Hemerick'. It goes particularly well with the soft yellow of 'Irene Van Der Zwet'.

POMPON FORM

The neat little round balls of this form are very attractive and very easy to grow because the stems of pompon dahlia are so sturdy you don't even have to stake the plants. They do sprawl, however, so give them more space than you do for some of the other dahlias. For a clean, white pompon try 'Albino'. A nice yellow one is 'Apropos', and a slightly larger one is 'Zonnegoud'. The big lavender-pink three-inch balls of 'Stolze Von Berlin' will please you if you like that color.

CACTUS DAHLIAS

Cactus dahlias are single or double, very showy and grow as large as six inches in diameter. Unlike the pompons they make very good bedding plants. In fact cactus dahlias often make a mound as wide as tall. One lovely cactus dahlia is orange with rosy tones, 'Autumn Leaves'. Another blend is 'Border Princess', with salmon, rose and yellow tints. A darker flower is 'Park Jewel', old rose. And 'Salmon Perfection' is quite a deep salmony red. These are all about 24 inches high. One of 30 inches in height is 'Park Princess', pure pink; and 'Purity' is a good white.

Taller cactus dahlias include: pink ones like 'Appleblossom' and 'Morning Kiss'; salmon-pink, 'Gina Lombaert; red, 'Bacchus', 'Doris Day', 'Perfectos', and 'Royal Sceptre'; the white 'Dentelle De Venice' and the creamy 'Exotica' with pink tips or 'My Love'. Yellow ones include 'Peters Yellow' and 'Dix Jubileum', which is also bronzy.

The favorites for cutting and for their sturdy growth in the garden are the Decorative Dahlias. Among those recommended are:'Arabian Night', maroon, 3½ feet high; 'David Howard', orange, four feet; 'Disneyland', golden yellow, four feet; 'Glory Of Heemstede', handsome primrose yellow, four feet; 'House Of Orange', amber-orange, four feet; and 'New Drakestyn', cerise red, two feet.

One of the loveliest dahlias I've ever seen was half way between a single decorative and a cactus-flowering dahlia, with very graceful gently curving petals and a luscious soft pink color. I am not sure which class it belonged to, but its name was 'Pink Lassie' and it had long stems and delicate small leaves. I wish I were looking at it right now.

BEGONIAS

These warm-climate, amazingly various plants are so hybridized now that the plant specialists have developed begonias, that are small, those that are large and look like roses; others that are spectacular because of their foliage, or those that are plain leaved but blossom handsome. Some are easy to grow, some difficult; some do well outdoors, some only indoors; and some you can grow from seeds if you are careful (seed is incredibly small) but others you'd best get from divided tubers. With all these possibilities any gardener has a choice of plants for shady spots, for a terrace or patio, for an overhanging porch, for a greenhouse and for an edging in the border where the plants get some shade during the day.

VARIETIES

There are fibrous-rooted, rhizomatous and tuberous-rooted begonias, and some that are bulbous or almost so and mostly winter-blooming. The chart shows varieties of each, with a good range of colors and styles to choose from. Maybe there are 6000 varieties, with at least 1000 to choose from for house and patio plants, and dozens for both foliage interest and flower novelty. Their season of bloom runs from a season in the spring, or summer, or both to seasons stretching into the autumn and winter or blooms just in the autumn or winter. *Begonis x lucerna*, a fibrous-rooted one, will bloom nearly all year, as a protected plant, if you give it a rest in the winter. *Begonia nitida*, another fibrous rooted one will bloom that way, too. According to the Royal Horticultural Society's groupings in England, which some catalogues now follow,

Group I is for the bulbous ones; II for Tuberous, III for Rhizomatous (including Rex) and IV for fibrous-rooted begonias.

CULTURE

Though begonias have the reputation of being shade-loving plants, an average of three hours of sunlight a day will be good for many, preferably in the early morning or late afternoon, especially for tuberous begonia plants. They like a moist, but not wet, soil, well drained and very porous. Never let them become scorched in hot, direct sun rays. Move them into the shade or put up curtains or pull down shades to protect them. A good temperature for begonias is 68°F. while they are coming into bloom, but once in bloom, they do better at 59°F.

Tuberous-rooted begonias can be lifted after blooming, and the tubers gently twisted off the plant after it is thoroughly dry. Then store the tubers in a box of dry peat until time to plant again—February or March for late spring or early summer blooming, or in May to June for blooming the following winter.

The foliage and rex group, rhizomatous, should also be given a rest in the winter, when it is best to dry them out, or nearly so. A mist spray will keep them in better condition if you use it fairly often, especially toward the end of the dormant period.

In the fibrous-rooted group you must watch to see when the dormant period is coming after the blooming season, which may be in summer or may be in winter. Patio plants may be dried off right in their pots, and kept over to a second season. Do not, however, expect them to have the quality during the second season they have when they are new and fresh. Probably the best way to keep these begonias going is to plant new seed each year. They will come to bloom in six months if handled well. For potted begonias use two parts sandy loam, one part clean, sharp sand, and ½ part well-rotted cow manure and ½ part well-rotted leaf mold, with some crushed charcoal added to help keep it sweet, and to aid in drainage. To determine the moistness of the soil (and the need for watering potted begonias for patios) pinch some soil in your fingers. If it feels sticky, or sticks to your fingers, do not water yet. If it feels dry and falls right down after you pinch it, water with lukewarm water, which has stood long enough to get rid of any chlorine

Easiest of all to grow are the Wax begonias or Semper-florens, and you can have either single or double. The popular Angel-Wings, grown on every porch and parlor in our Grandmother's day are the most notable of the fibrous types. But for bedding use tuberous begonias and plant them when the soil is warm and partially dried out in the late spring. It is best to mulch the plants so the soil can be kept moist. (Water a little at first after setting out the plants if they need it.) Then in July they start blooming and will keep it up until frost. To get earlier bloom, of course, you start the plants in the house a month or so before planting out time in the house. Do it in March and you may get June bloom. Farther south in Zone 6, you can plant in February for May flowers to set out.

There are some amazingly simple and almost 100 per cent successful instructions for starting tuberous begonia plants indoors. First, on a good March day, find some nice, firm, plump tubers —either from a garden shop or nurseryman or perhaps from one of you own plants. (Remember that once the plant is thoroughly dry, you can twist the tubers off your begonias from the year before to start again.)

Begin them in peat moss, sphagnum moss or vermiculite, in flats or pots, with their concave tops about ½ inch below the surface. Water very sparingly, in bright indirect light, and keep the temperature about 70°F. in the daytime and 60° to 70°F. at night. In a room that is hot and dry, put a piece of paper or polyethylene over the flat, but remove it as soon as growth appears. The roots will be growing anyhow, but the top growth may take a month or six weeks to appear. When the growth reaches two or three inches, it is time to transplant. This time use a potting soil as near to the following as you can manage:

2 parts turfy loam (with the grass roots left in)
3 parts leaf mold or peat moss
1 part coarse washed sand
¼ part dried manure
2 cups bone meal per bushel of the mix

The pH should be about 5.5 to 6. Add acid peat to bring it down to that. If you cannot manage all that, combine equal parts of good topsoil and peat moss or leaf mold. With this mixture, stir in a tablespoon of bone meal into the bottom soil in each pot. Use six to eight-inch pots. Of course, cover the drainage hole with broken crock as you do with other potted plants. Put in an east window when they are planted, and keep them from direct, hot sun. Night temperature of 60° to 65°F. are needed. Leave them there, watering sparingly until all danger of frost is gone outside. Then plant them out in the garden 18 inches apart, and set so that no stem is ever submerged or you might get borers, or other troubles. The site should be shady or part shady. Even on the north side of the house is a possibility if there is a white wall or some reflection of light.

Be careful never to water the foliage of tuberous begonias. And while it is a good idea to use manure tea once a month to encourage good growth, do not let it touch the tubers. If you decide to stake begonias, be sure not to tie their tender stems too tightly. After the first frost, lift the tubers, treat for three minutes in 118°F. hot water, and dry them in the sun for a few hours. After the stem has withered and dried, too, store the tubers in dry peat moss or vermiculite at 50°F. until the process is started again the next winter or early spring. If properly fertilized and carefully handled, begonia tubers will last a long time. But if root rot gets in from the damp in poorly drained soil, you may lose them. Injured roots occur if you cultivate around begonias at any depth to speak of. The roots are much too near the surface to take chances. Take some stem cuttings and propagate the small extra sprouts that come sometimes on the tubers. Pot them up and keep a plastic bag over the pot while they are rooting. If kept alive all summer, small tubers will have formed by fall.

Good grooming of begonias is also necessary Whenever you see wilted leaves and flowers, take them off. This will encourage flowering throughout the summer months, probably for four or five months.

Some people prefer to start new fibrous begonias from seeds instead of from cuttings. This is a popular method of propagation because it provides a lot of plants at little cost, and the plants you get are more likely to be vigorous and sturdier than those you get from cuttings. The seeds you save from your own plants may not come true because of cross-pollination by insects, but you can buy the infinitesimal seeds from many seedsmen if you object to surprises. The process is a bit finicky, but well worth the effort.

There are many methods to use. You can use leaf mold, peat moss, with or without sand, gravel and cinders, underneath for drainage, but be sure that the materials are clean, the potting mixture well firmed down in the container you use and is moist but not wet. Do not cover with more than a sprinkling.

Some fascinating ways to start the seeds have been devised in order to maintain the moist-but-not-wet condition, and the firm, clean medium. You can use bricks—once called "grandmother bricks"—preferably made of clay because it is porous and will maintain the necessary level of moisture without drowning the seeds. Wet the brick, spread on the potting mixture and plant. You can use clay flowerpot saucers, planting the same way and watching to see that the medium does not ever get too wet. If by chance it does, fill a salt shaker with sand and sprinkle the surface, to absorb the extra moisture. This sand should be sterilized by heating it in the oven, and then sifted. Some seed-starters have used a wide-mouthed bottle, laid on a flat side, a good miniature greenhouse for starting seeds on some

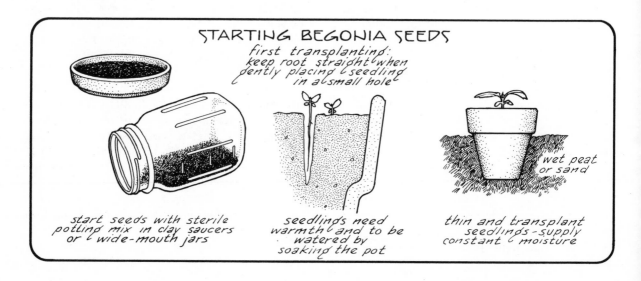

STARTING BEGONIA SEEDS

first transplanting: keep root straight when gently placing seedling in a small hole

start seeds with sterile potting mix in clay saucers or wide-mouth jars

seedlings need warmth and to be watered by soaking the pot

thin and transplant seedlings—supply constant moisture

wet peat or sand

sterile potting mixture laid in the bottle. Others just cover the flat with plastic.

Whichever method you use, be prepared to thin the seedlings while they are small. Use a pair of tweezers to lift them gently out. Keep doing this so they are not crowded. If they become crowded, they will weaken and you'll find that transplanting them is extremely difficult. You are not after quantity but quality, and it is better to have a dozen healthy plants than three dozen weak ones. (And this goes for any plants you grow from seeds.)

Begin transplanting after the seedlings have formed a second pair of leaves. Choose the largest, strongest seedlings, lifting each carefully with two matches. Set the plant in a small hole in the next pot, keeping the root straight. Firm the soil around the seedling very gently, to the previous soil line. Make sure that the little plants are well separated. It is best to water with rainwater, setting the pots in water until the soil is moist, and removing the pots as soon as you see that it is. Bottom heat is needed at this stage, or put the plants in a sunny, but never hot, window with a curtain as shade. A second transplanting is needed when the seedlings look crowded again. They can go into individual pots now, but must be watched to see that the soil never dries out. Set the pots in wetted peat moss or moist sand.

Nowadays several seedsmen sell tiny plastic seed-starting kits for growing finicky or tiny seeds. They are not too expensive and if you can provide bottom heat and the right light, they make propagation by seed a very satisfying way to start begonias. The transplantings will be necessary as with the other methods.

There are many thousands of marvelous begonias to try. Consult the catalogues while you are making up your mind what your choices are going to be.

8

Perennials
[and Some Biennials, Too]

Perennials are of so many kinds, suited to so many situations and types of soil and climate that you can map out a plan for these basic garden plants exactly to meet your needs and desires. If your land is dry and hot, you can start perennials such as golden marguerite, wild indigo, coneflower, rose campion, tawny day-lily, gayfeather, some of the yarrows and some of the pleasant herbs like lavender cotton and meadow sage. If you need plants for moist places, you can establish lily-of-the-valley, astilbe, forget-me-not, foxglove, violets, and supplement them with ferns.

Maybe you need to garden in pots, and will concentrate on some such perennials as lantana, fuchsia, one of the perennial alyssums, plus some tuberous begonias. Perhaps there is a pool or streamside and you'll plan to have marsh marigold, the charming small yellow daisy called leopardsbane or the stately blue or red lobelias and some of the irises.

If you are only home at night, you might choose for your pool the water lily *Victoria regia*, which is very fragrant and expands only after dark. There are other night-blooming flowers, too, such as sweet rocket or dame's rocket, a small, long-blooming plant, actually a biennial, but easy to grow in the perennial border; evening campion, of the pink family and rather weedy; some of the jasmines and the marvelous climbing cactus, night-blooming cereus, for those who live in Zone 10 (or you can grow it in a pot). Certain day lilies bloom at night, one of the tobacco flowers, and several of the sundrops or evening primroses.

THE HERBACEOUS BORDER, YES OR NO

For most of this century a garden of perennials (with or without supplementary annuals) has meant a border garden, long and narrow beside a lawn, or along the sunny side of the house or the driveway. The aim of the English gardeners and landscape designers who invented this kind of garden was to achieve continuous bloom from spring to frost, an interesting variation in heights and a general pattern of tall in back, medium-height plants in the middle, and low plants called edging plants in front. The garden of this sort was usually called an herbacious border, indicating that it did not include any woody plants, and it was intended to have lots of color and plentiful supplies of blooms to cut to take into the house.

144

My advice to today's gardeners is yes, do have this beautiful kind of garden if you have two gardeners to work for you, plenty of resources and equipment for supplying and resupplying the garden with new plants as the old ones run out, and lots of time and patience for planning, replanning and replacing. The two gardeners are needed for the lengthy jobs of soil preparation, weeding, mulching, digging up and dividing, growing seedlings for replacements, and all the planting that needs to be done every year to keep the holes filled and the borders full, properly varied and in continuous bloom.

Almost anyone interested in having a garden of perennials has seen pictures of gorgeous borders at delphinium time, for example, and had a yen for such a border. The trouble is that we all get the idea that perennial means just that: that the plants will stay the way they look in the picture and come up dutifully each year and look just as they had the year before. But that is not the way it happens—especially with delphiniums. They fade away after a few years, or they get crown rot, so you have to grow new ones for replacement. Most gardeners who go in for delphiniums grow new ones every year, to be on the safe side. Other perennials get crowded and overgrown, and keep sending up fresh growth on the outside of the clump and keep dying out in the center. Then it is time to dig up the whole clump and divide it. Perhaps you have room for all the new pieces; perhaps you will need to give some of them away, or make a new garden for them. And some of the handsomest plants for the border like dahlias and gladioli are so tender they have to be dug each fall, cared for and wintered over in a warm, dry place.

If you still want to be very English and you still want to do all that gardening (or have two gardeners do it for you), then go ahead and have a herbaceous border.

Perhaps you prefer the answer of no, as I do. It seems to me that today's customs and life-styles, not to mention new gardening methods and convictions, all point to the desirability of a different kind of garden—even if you do have as much help as two gardeners. My main conviction, as an organic gardener, is that plants of different kinds ought to be grown together, and that it is even rather ostentatious to put masses of all one kind together in a big, splashy, opulent bunches for display. I prefer gardens that combine shrubs, perennials and annuals, with some herbs here and there and even some vegetables if they fit in well.

Herbs you might include are members of the artemisia group, described in the comprehensive list, alliums described in the bulb chapter, and such other pungent, useful repellent plants as members of the sage family, the mints, thymes, marjorams, dark red ornamental basil, and the pestless parsley. Vegetables that are decorative are feathery asparagus, the bold handsome shapes of rhubarb and the ornamental kales and cabbages now available from many seedsmen, Patio or Tiny Tim tomatoes (which many people are growing in pots nowadays), and scarlet runner bean where there is room for it to climb. I have grown most of these in my borders and found them very handsome and satisfactory. Try out what you want, and see what you like best.

The perennials suggested in the list below, though suitable in most instances for big borders or sometimes for rock gardens, are especially chosen for putting in a mixed organic garden. It is a somewhat unusual list for that reason. The standard asters, chrysanthemums, delphiniums, geraniums, peonies, phlox and so on are mentioned, and a few varieties suggested, but you should pore over seed and nursery catalogues, study the many possibilities and their descriptions before making final choices, I predict you'll have many a happy evening if you do.

Some plants are included for the sake of information regarding their pest-repellent qual-

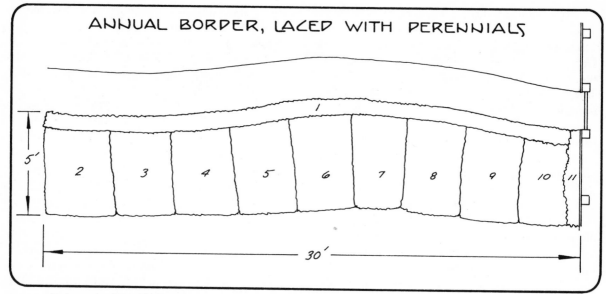

ANNUAL BORDER, LACED WITH PERENNIALS

1) *Ageratum 'Blue Mink'*
2) *Snapdragon 'Little Darling,' 8-12" tall*
3) *Aster 'Pepite Red' or 'Color Carpet,' both 8" tall*
4) *Petunia 'Cherry Blossom,' Lilium 'Cinnabar,' 8-12" tall*
5) *Marigold 'Lemon Drop,' 9" tall*
6) *Petunia 'Red Joy Improved' and Petunia 'Malibu,' L. 'Destiny,' 8" tall*
7) *Zinnia 'Peter Pan Pink,' L. 'Paprika,' 12-14" tall*
8) *Nicotiana 'White Bedder,' L. 'Prosperity,' 12" tall*
9) *Heliotrope 'Marine' (violet), L. 'Burgundy,' 20" tall*
10) *Celosia plumosa 'Golden Triumph,' L. Regale, 2½ ft. tall*
11) *Morning Glory 'Heavenly Blue'*

The season in this bed may be stretched even more by planting blocks of Darwin Hybrid, Kaufmanniana and Greigii tulips in it. These tulips are all early-flowering, so the foliage has usually yellowed sufficiently to be cut off by the time annuals can be set out. Avoid planting midseason and late tulips in an annual bed because the tulip foliage must be left on too long. This interferes with the planting of the annuals, and the drying foliage becomes unsightly.

ities, even if some people regard them more as weeds than as garden plants. Some are included because experience has shown that the plants themselves are pestless. Among these are the repellent angel's trumpet, camomile, catnip, feverfew, and others. The pestless plants which appeal to the organic gardener include other repellent ones, such as the artemesias, pyrethrum daisies, coreopsis, and those mentioned as well as bee balm, daylilies, funkia or plantain lily, lily-of-the-valley, nettles, pachysandra, penstemon, potentialls, the salvias and sages, yarrow and others.

The list mentions flowers that will get out of hand and be a terrible nuisance to you; but also many rugged little plants you might well like to try, whether you have known of them before or not.

I have not included the good clovers you can grow, especially if you are starting a fresh garden in newly plowed land. I do mention lupines and other plants of the pea family, and advise growing some such plants for a year before starting a perennial garden if you actually have just plowed up the land for the first time. Clovers help at any time. Perennial clovers I recommend are red, white clover or shamrock, and alsike, all of which will supply nitrogen to your garden because they have nodules on their roots harboring the beneficial nitrogen-fixing bacteria. (Good annual clovers, by the way, are yellow, crimson and rabbit's foot clover, which is quite a pretty little fuzzy flower.)

Choose your flowers for color, height, soil conditions and suitability for your zone, of course. Other chapters make special recommendations for special conditions such as shade, rock gardens, water gardens and others. What goes well together is basically a matter of personal tastes, for most perennials like a pH of 6.5 to 7.0, which your soil will probably be if you give it plenty of compost. You will obviously put rugged plants together, so as not to have big plants crowding out little ones. But big, deep-rooted plants like phlox will not do much harm to shallow-rooted little ones, especially if, like violets, for instance, the little ones are rugged.

SOIL PREPARATION

A vegetable garden gets ploughed or tilled or dug up, fertilized, cultivated, enriched year after year. If you have a garden purely of annuals you can do more or less the same things. But with perennial flowers and shrubs you have to use a different approach because you can't go tilling right through it and disturbing the plants and their delicate roots.

Therefore a deep, rich preparation of the perennial areas is an absolute necessity if you are to have good blooms and healthy plants. In many situations and for several of the best perennials you will also need to add drainage materials.

Begin your deep digging at least two feet away from any existing small shrubs (or from shrubs you intend to put in), or from their drip line at the tips of the brances if the shrubs are

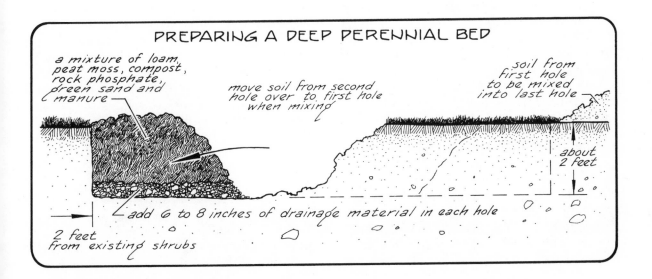

PREPARING A DEEP PERENNIAL BED

a mixture of loam, peat moss, compost, rock phosphate, green sand and manure

move soil from second hole over to first hole when mixing

soil from first hole to be mixed into last hole

about 2 feet

add 6 to 8 inches of drainage material in each hole

2 feet from existing shrubs

bigger. Equip yourself with a good strong spading fork or spade, a cart to move soil and other materials (which include gravel or crushed stone for the bottom of the bed for drainage, peat moss, compost and manure for enriching the soil, and some sand if your soil is very clayey). The standard old way of preparing a bed is some form of trenching, which means you dig out one area, move its soil to the other end of the bed; then dig the next area, mix it with the enrichment materials, spread the drainage material in the bottom of the first hole, and cover that with the new soil. Keep digging anew, using the dug soil to make a fill for the previous section until you come to the end. The last hole is filled with materials mixed in with the soil you dug from the first hole. There are variations on this method, but the principle is the same in each.

Most people in this country with an average soil and no serious hardpan under the top two feet, dig down just about two feet or a little more, but I've known people to go three feet down, and to chop up the hardpan, if that was necessary. Drainage material to be really effective should be at least six inches deep, or even eight inches deep, if you are in any doubt about the natural drainage on your land, and if the area you are going to plant is truly flat. This attention to drainage is especially important if you are going to plant such susceptible plants as irises or delphiniums or lilies. Next make a good mixture of loam, peat moss, compost, with some rock phosphate or bone meal and green sand or granite dust and an addition of well-rotted cow manure, or some other kind of manure. If the space you first dug up was about two or three feet square, use a half-inch layer of manure, and a small handful of the fertilizer powders. The proportion of peat moss to garden soil can be about a third peat moss. This rich a mixture will support your plants through droughts. If you are making narrow beds, one row of digging is

probably enough. For square or wider beds, you may have to go up one side and down the next. It is a lot of work, but it is worth it, and with the slow-release enrichment you put in, your plants will be supported for quite a few years, especially as you will be adding organic mulch to rot down into the beds and make them still richer. A spring dressing of the bed with wood ashes will help neutralize the peat if it is acid peat.

Some people don't trench; they just rototill the bed and add a good layer of compost initially and then topdress each year. Although I prefer trenching, this short cut will work if you have good drainage and your topsoil hasn't been eroded or worn out.

THE RIGHT TIME TO PREPARE THE BED

Every gardener who gets the kind of spring fever which makes one want to dig would rather prepare beds in the spring when that feeling has come. It is all right to prepare a bed in the spring, but it is really much better to do it in the fall. For one thing, the soil is already warm and crumbly, and you do not have the danger of compacting it by getting on it too soon before it dries out and warms up. For another, your compost heaps, after the long, hot summer are in good shape to use, and you will be putting them to work instead of letting them sit there and perhaps leach away good elements during the winter. And for a last reason, a roughened, lumpy soil exposed to the weather all winter will be well conditioned by the freezing and thawing which mellows and prepares the soil as nothing else will. It can always be lightly tilled and smoothed in the spring as needed.

Before you leave the prepared bed, however, give it a good deep hosing to moisten the peat and manure and set in motion the absorption process which should go on all winter from rain and snow. If the bed, even after watering, is still raised above the surrounding area, that is all right. In the seasons to come a slightly raised bed will have better drainage, and the chances are that the aeration will be better also. Instead of actually leveling the bed, let it remain somewhat higher at the back and lower at the front edge, which should be the downhill edge, of course.

PLANTING

Some people prefer to put out their perennial plants in the fall, after the bed is prepared, and in later years to fit in new plants in that season when the soil is soft and crumbly. In moderate or mild climates which will permit a good establishment of roots, this is usually a perfectly good practice. In any climate a late summer planting of bearded iris or oriental poppies is always recommended. But other perennials, in many climates and certainly in cold climates, might better be planted in the spring. In any case, rake and refine the soil once more before you plant.

Whether you buy your plants or raise them yourself from seed, a good practice is to space out your plantings and to plant preferably on a cloudy day—or at least in the evening so the plants will not get too much sun and then wilt. If hot sunny weather continues, shade the tender plants until they get established. Brush, evergreen boughs of leafy branches can be stuck into the ground on the sunny side of the plants, or you can rig up some newspapers to shield them from the heat.

Field-grown plants should be planted about 18 inches apart, but pot grown, or your own little plants from the cold frame where they wintered, can be planted 12 inches apart. (If they get too big the first year, they can be thinned.) Big plants like phlox, delphinium and of course peonies will need to be farther apart—up to two or even three feet for peonies. I believe that a further enrichment of the area right around the roots with more peat moss, sand and compost is very beneficial, and I also believe that perennials planted in the spring do well if they are mulched as soon as the soil seems warm. Usually perennials are set with their crowns at the same level they were at in the field at the nursery, or in the pot or cold frame, but fibrous-rooted kinds like phlox can be put with that line an inch below the surface and peonies should be put with their eyes exactly 1½ inches below ground level, and this means that their stems are just about that much into the soil.

Various needs for particular plants will be indicated in the list below. If you are planning to insert some annuals, for color or pest repellent reasons, for instance, the distances between perennial plants will need to be adjusted, of course. Sometimes it is better to use the annuals as a front border, and not intrude them into the area where you grow perennials at all.

WARNING: Always see that the roots are well spread and in touch with rich soil when you plant perennials; and given water or mild doses of compost tea until they take hold in their new bed.

pH FOR PERENNIALS

Most perennials are satisfied with a neutral or slightly acid soil. A few do not mind at all if the soil is a bit alkaline. These include iris, baby's breath, hollyhocks and windflower. Some of the acid-loving flowers are of especial interest as plants suitable to grow with azaleas, rhododendrons and blueberries. They include plants such as falso indigo, coreopsis, balloon flower and catchfly or moss campion.

BLOOM IN THE GARDEN

The spring garden, aside from the many flowering bulbs, can give you lots of pleasure with its yellow primroses and buttercups, its blue Virginia bluebells and white candytuft and some of the spiderworts, speedwells, violets and blue or red columbines. Then come the roses, delphiniums, more columbines, poppies, peonies and a host of others. Some of these if properly kept picked or snipped off after blooming, and properly nourished with extra doses of manure tea, compost tea or a mild solution of fish emulsion, will bloom again. This cutting back of the deadheads is a good idea in any case, so that the strength of the plant will not be spent in making seeds—unless you plan to gather and plant the seeds, of course. Delphinium will often bloom again; roses will; and the lovely white Carolina phlox called 'Miss Lingard'. Others such as Bouncing Bet, balloon flower, common avens, blanket flower and many of the pinks and the plumy bleeding heart will come again if so coaxed.

If you have a row of phlox and wish to extend its blooming season there are a few ways to do it. One is rather drastic, and involves lifting every third plant or so, and letting it sit on the bare earth for half an hour. Then replant it. Do this when it is just beginning to grow. The drastic treatment will delay the flowering of those lifted plants by about two weeks. The other way to delay bloom is to cut back some of the front shoots after they have begun to grow. Even though the delay is not very marked, the improvement of the blooming shape of the phlox is well worth this effort, for the whole plant looks like a cascade of bloom instead of having all its blossom stiffly located at the top. My best line of phlox is at quite a distance from the windows of the house and the view of those plants is vastly improved by extending the bloom this way.

Another means is to put some of the plants of one species in the sun and some in part or even full shade. If they are sun-loving plants, the shade will delay their bloom (if it doesn't weaken them beyond blooming). Such tricks would only be appropriate for a very special season, I should think, such as the year of a wedding or the visit of a sick grandparent whose only pleasure is the bloom in the garden.

It stands to reason, of course, that you have to pick off the deadheads of any flower if you expect it to go on blooming. The urge of the plant is to reproduce, and it will put all its strength into making seeds if you permit it to. Sometimes a plant will go on blooming and making seeds at the same time. Even so, I believe the plant will be stronger if you take off all the pods you are not especially saving for harvesting the seeds yourself, or to use for dried arrangements as I use the pods of Siberian iris and baptista, for instance.

CARE OF THE GARDEN

The usual weeding and mulching need to be carried on as the plants require. My husband and I usually sprinkle some dried manure around for plants that are busy making food for their roots for winter, especially any that have bulblike or tuberous roots, but we never let the manure get directly to the roots, especially the roots of peonies. Fertilize in late spring and early summer, not in late summer or fall because a late spurt of growth is subject to frost damage. As for mulching, we believe that it is best to remove all winter mulch in the spring, retidy the ground as needed, put on compost, let the soil warm up, and only then to put down whatever summer mulch you are going to use. It should be light and porous, never matting, and just enough to keep weeds down and the soil cool and moist during hot, dry weather. Water your perennials as needed, giving them a long, gentle soak (not a fast overhead sprinkle).

In fall, a thorough clean-up is a good idea. In order to get out all insect eggs and borers or whatever other pests are harboring near the stems of your plants, you really do need to clean out all the summer mulch and add it to the compost heap. Some perennials can be cut right back—phlox and peonies for instance. Others which may have put on new growth in the fall should not be cut but left to winter over as they are. These include oriental poppies, delphinium, primroses, madonna lilies and others.

After the ground has frozen—and only after—it is time to put on the evergreen boughs or other airy winter mulch which will help to keep the ground from thawing and heaving during the winter and very early spring months.

DIVIDING

The big job about perennials is the dividing of the clumps which needs to be done every few years. Perhaps you usually think of dividing just as a method of propagation and increasing the number of plants you have of a certain species. But dividing is also necessary to keep up the health of your plants. As the clump gets bigger and bigger, the feeder roots, which are on the outside of the clump, are less and less able to keep feeding the center part of the clump and it begins to die off. When you lift such a clump, discard the central part, gently pull apart sections of the rim, and replant them in good freshly prepared soil. Hardy asters and chrysanthemums, for instance, will deteriorate quite rapidly unless so treated. Peonies, however, stand up well, do not like to be distrubed, and should not be raised for division for at least seven or eight years. We have some peonies that have flourished in the same place without lifting for fifteen years, and I know of some in the neighborhood that have lasted well for a good deal longer than that. Bearded iris respond well to lifting every five years. I think a bleeding heart likes to stay where it is, but divide it in the fall if you have to.

WHEN TO DIVIDE

Different plants should be lifted at different seasons. Hardy asters and chrysanthemums do better if lifted in very early spring. Iris do best if lifted and divided in late July or August, so that there are still several weeks of warm weather for them to reestablish their roots. Phlox is divided after it has bloomed, in September. This is the right time to divide peonies, too, if you have to. Yarrow, bugbane, monkshood, goldentuft, painted daisies, daylilies and a dozen or so others can be divided in early fall after they have stopped blooming. If you are not sure of the hardiness of a plant, wait until spring. Be sure, of course, to keep the new sets well watered until you are sure that the roots are well established.

RHIZOME PROPAGATION

A few plants with rhizomes can be lifted and divided by cutting the rhizomes into pieces. These include lily-of-the-valley, bloodroot, Siebold primroses, Christmas rose and cannas. Instead of putting the pieces right back into the earth it is advisable to plant them in sand until you are sure that each new piece has rooted. We do not do this with bearded iris, which is also a rhizomatous plant, for it seems to adjust well if put right back into freshly prepared garden soil. Some of the lilies-of-the-valley can be taken indoors to force for winter bloom and then planted out in the spring.

SAVING SEEDS

Another aspect of the care of the perennial is the care of the seed pods if you wish to collect your own seed. If the plants are hybrids, as you probably know, the chances are not very great that the next generation will come true. But with plenty of perennials, the parentage is so attractive that the new offspring will be attractive anyway. Columbines, poppies, coral bells, lupines, forget-me-nots, and plenty of others are all very pleasant to grow from your own seed. Sometimes the pod is such that you can simply watch it until the seeds are dry, and then snip off the pods and store them in an envelope. Others which self-sow themselves readily can simply be helped along by your gathering and scattering the seeds when they are ready, easing them with water and shade if needed. Others which are hard to gather or which will pop and disappear before you have a chance to get at them, can be encased in a small plastic bag and fastened with a rubber band or twist'em so that the seeds will not get away from you.

Plants that are easily propagated by seed include foxglove, bleeding heart, gas plant, baby's breath, evening primrose, balloon flower, sweet rocket, painted daisy, speedwell, turtlehead, as well as those mentioned above and many others. When we wish to use the seeds of the biennials forget-me-nots, we simply pull up the spent plants late in the season and shake them over the spots where we would like to have forget-me-nots grow up the next year. This works pretty well, though in one garden one year we had a veritable groundcover of forget-me-nots the next summer. I was just as glad because it smothered out a nasty weedy grass which had got in there the summer before.

Usually we buy seed. A good time to plant perennial seeds is in the summer, if you can keep track of the tiny seedlings and see that they do not dry out or get too hot (or too muggy). Then put them in the cold frame or give them winter protection so that they will be ready to transplant into the perennial garden in the spring.

Some seeds like delphinium need cool temperatures for germination, somewhere between 49° and 55°F. Others are indifferent, like asters and phlox. A few such as pansies, violas, violets and California bluebells need a temperature somewhere between 55° and 68°F. to germinate. And all those such as columbine, cardinal flower, salvia, and a good many

annuals need really warm temperatures in the range between 68°and 86°F. If the outside temperature is not correct for what you are growing, you can rig up a flat or so in a cool cellar, and give the seedlings some artificial light when they first come up, and then transfer them to the outside later. Most of these seeds germinate best in the dark, or are not fussy about dark or light, but a few such as the cardinal flower and the violas and violets prefer to be in the light, so don't cover them, and let them have light if you start them in the cellar. Do not be surprised if some seeds take a long time to come up. Anemones may take a month or more; candytuft two weeks, as will foxglove, cardinal flower and blue lobelia, poppies, the violas and violets, and the penstemons. Others taking as much as a month include columbine, browallia, perennial buttercups, and the painted daisies.

BIENNIALS FOR THE PERENNIAL BORDER

Certain plants only flower well when they are young, so it is best to have a program of yearly or biennial replacement for delphinium, columbine, foxgloves, sweet william and hollyhocks. Actually some of those are biennials anyway, and can only be expected to bloom for a short time of one or two years. Sow them in June to give them a good start. These are the most popular garden biennials: Canterbury bells, which bloom in June, but earlier in the South; English daisies, which grow in lawns; forget-me-nots—though species such as *Myosotis palustris* is a true perennial; foxgloves, though in some places they self-seed so well you'd hardly know they were not perennial; hollyhocks, same; Iceland poppies, same; pansies, which we treat as annuals and buy at the same time we get ageratum; sweet William, which must be sown early in June; English wallflower, if you can get it to grow; and Siberian wallflower, also to be sown in July and again it is optimistic to expect it

(continued on page 187)

SOME PERENNIALS TO CHOOSE FROM

Name	Description	Comment
Aaron's rod *Thermopsis caroliniana*	Pea family plant, yellow 8 inch racemes; also *T. montana*, shorter; *T. rhombifolia*, for rock gardens.	Blooms in June, July; hardy to Zone 3; has very deep roots; good soil conditioner.
Ageratum, hardy *Eupatorium coelestinum*	Grows to 2 feet, with thin leaves flowers above, blue.	Late bloom, in fall; likes light shade divide in spring.
Alkanet *Anchusa italica*	Try variety 'Dropmore'; blue blue flowers, grows to 4 or 5 feet.	Blooms June, July; refrigerate seed for 72 hours before planting.
A. myosotidiflora Sometimes called Siberian bugloss	Like forget-me-nots; try 'Pride of Dover' and 'Royal Blue'.	Blooms May, June; likes semi-shade; was once a salad herb.
Alyssum Basket of Gold *A. saxatile citrinum* *A. s. compactum* *A. s. flora pleno*	 Pale yellow. Bright yellow. Bright yellow, double.	These alyssums bloom in spring, like well-drained soil, and do very well in a rock garden.
Angel's Trumpet *Datura stramonium*	Spectacular white trumpet flower, 4 inches long, with big prickly seed pod. *D. cornigera*, very fragrant at night. *D. arborea* grows to 20 feet with 10-inch trumpets.	Good pest repellent; all parts poisonous; easy to grow from seed; too easy, gets weedy.
Artemesia group: Dusty miller, mugwort, southernwood, tarragon and wormwood *A. albula* 'Silver King'	 The gray, woolly plant called artemisia; 3 feet.	 Very decorative; spreads.
A. abrotatum *A. annua* *A. absinthium*	Is southern-wood; fine leaves. Sweet wormwood. Common wormwood; white and silky leaves; 4 feet.	Pest-repellent. Very good pest-repellent.
A. vulgaris	Mugwort, with leaves green above, white below; related to *A. lactiflora*, Chinese mugwort, used in acupuncture treatments.	Bloom July to Sept.; rather weedy.
Aster, or Michaelmas daisies	Lovely starlike flowers, many colors, hybridized in England by Ernest Ballard.	Blooms Aug., Sept.; grow in any soil; divide in very early spring, discarding the old center; pinch back to prevent tall growth.
New York aster *A. novi-belgii*	Blue, pink, white, purple 3 to 5 feet.	These have been hybridized, too.

Name	Description	Comment
Farrer aster A. *farreri* A. *frikartii*	Yellow, from China; 1½ feet. These bloom all summer; are hybrids.	Do not grow asters and red pines on the same grounds, because aster is a host to the rust fungus which attacks 2-needled and 3-needled pines. If it comes, destroy the asters to save the pines.
Dwarf asters	Makes a 12-inch mound, lavender, blue, and white.	Blooms Aug., Sept.; good for edging.
Aster alpinus	A hardy, rock garden aster.	Blooms in June; plant seed in sun in early spring.
Astilbe *Astilbe arendsii* and many other hybrids	Plumy, spirea-like flowers in many white, pink, red varieties.	Likes some shade, but will grow in sun, like some damp, but will grow in dry spots.
A. *simplicifolia alba*	From Japan, and feathery white.	This really likes it moist; put near a pool.
A. *simplicifolia rosea*	Pink.	Same; masses of flowers; survives city dirt.
Avens *Geum urbanum* and other varieties	Look rather like single roses, on thin stems; yellow, orange and red.	Blooms May to Oct.; called the blessed herb, herba benedicta or herb bennett; grows to Zone 6.
Baby's breath *Gypsophila paniculata*	Small white, or pink, blossoms giving the gray-green foliage a misty look. The best white one is 'Bristol Fairy'. The double is 'Perfecta'. The large pink is 'Pink 'Pink Fairy'.	Blooms from June on; no special soil needed; but it does like some lime.
G. *repens alba*	This is spreading, and sprawling.	Sprawling plants can be held up by half a dozen encircling stakes; two feet high.
C. *montana*, also called Mountain bluet	Bright blue flowers, silvery leaves.	Blooms all summer; spreads easily.
C. *dealbata*	Beautiful pink and white.	June to Oct. bloom.
Balloon flower *Platycodon grandiflorum*	Neat, crisp blue cup.	Blooms all summer; needs full sun, well-drained; light, sandy soil; very late to come up; so don't weed it out.
P. g. *album* P.g. 'Shell Pink'	White. Pink; plant in semi-shade to preserve the good color.	

Name	Description	Comment
Bee balm *Monarda didyma* also called Bergamot *M. fistulosa* is Wild bergamot *M. media* is Purple bee balm	Red, ragged, pungent member of the mint family; grows 2 to 3 feet. This wild one is lavender. This one is purple, native to Zone 6.	Blooms June to Aug.; hummingbirds love these bee balms; a good variety is 'Cambridge Scarlet'. All but *M. media* are hardy to Zone 3, in average garden soil Bee plant and pest repellent.
Bell flower *Campanula carpatica* *C. c alba* *C. c.* 'China Doll' *C. garganica* *C. lactiflora* *C. persicifolia* *C. porscharskyana* *C. rotundifolia* *C. medium* *C. glomerata superba*	Exquisite blue (or white) 8-inches high; many varieties. Is the white one. Is lavender. For rock gardens, blue. Try 'Pritchard's Variety', with mixed colors, very tall . Try 'Blue Gardenia', which is double; there is a large white one. This variety from Dalmatia is compact, creeping, and light blue, is 12 inches. Will grow in sun or light shade; round leaves. This is the popular Canterbury Bells, but is biennial or annual. The purple version of a big white bellflower. Get 'Royal Purple'; will grow to 18 inches.	All varieties need good drainage and rich soil;bloom all summer. Mostly June blooms bright color; has trailing stems. Will grow to 3 to 6 feet June to Aug. Will grow to 2 feet, and bloom June to Oct. Rabbits eat it to the ground. June to frost; good for rock gardens. For edging or rock garden. See listing in annuals. Hardy to Zone 3, as are most bellflowers. To plant: sow seed, spring to Sept., and cover very lightly; shade the bed at first. Divide mature plants every 2 or 3 years.
Bergenia or Heartleaf bergenia *Bergenia cordifolia*	Large leaves, 6 to 8 inches; pink or rose flowers, in a spike, but there are white and purple varieties, too.	Hardy to Zone 2, a native of Siberia; likes wet soils.
Betony *Stachys lanata* also called Lamb's ear *S. grandiflora* *S. coccinea*	Soft, hairy, grayish foliage and lavender spikes of flowers; will grow 18 to 30 inches. Many rich lavender sprays. A very handsome red variety.	Blooms all summer; average soil, even poor; good for terrace pots.
Bishop's hat *Epimedium grandiflorum*	Small red, violet, white flowers in spring, with distinctive lobed foliage, bronze in autumn; 9 inches.	Often listed as a groundcover; has underground rootstocks; prefers part shade.

Name	Description	Comment
E. versicolor sulphureum	A good yellow, somewhat shorter; wiry stems.	Needs moisture; all are hardy to Zone 3 and will stay green in the warmer zones.
Bleeding heart *Dicentra spectabilis*	Deep pink sprays of drooping heart shaped flowers; will grow 2 to 3 feet.	Blooms May and June; likes sun, but shows up best in part shade; dislikes being moved; plant 2 feet apart.
Fingered bleeding heart *Dicentra exima*	This is more delicate, has ferny leaves.	Blooms all summer, or nearly so; pest-resistant, favorite old-time garden flowers; both these and *D. spectabilis* are very reliable plants to grow.
Bouncing Bet *Saponaria officinalis*	Pale pink flowers, with five petals, blooming in clusters; will grow to 2 or 3 feet, and often blooms at night.	Leaves make froth used as soap; does an almost magic job in restoring old fabrics.
Bugbane *Cimicifuga racemosa* also called Snakeroot	Has plumy spikes of white flowers up to 3 or 4 feet tall, with the whole plant up to 6 feet; handsome big stamens.	Blooms June to Sept.; used in old herb gardens for the sedatives in the roots.
Bugle or bugleweed *Ajuga genevensis*	Small plant, with blue spikes or reddish; can grow to 8 or 10 inches.	Blooms in May, June; average soil; good groundcover.
A. reptans	This is very small, about 4 inches and comes with pink or white flowers, too; some have bronze leaves.	Used as groundcover; the mower will go right over it, if it escapes into the lawn.
Butterfly weed *Aselepias tuberosa*	Very handsome orange flowers about ½ inch in 2-inch umbels; grows to 3 feet, very showy.	Blooms July to Sept.; needs full sun, and will grow in sandy soil or average garden soil.
Camomile (Also see Golden marguerite)	Many varieties, some very fragrant, white or yellow, with deeply cut leaves.	Bloom May to Aug.; used for tea, pest repellent, air sweetener, compost aid.
Anthemis tinctoria	Roman camomile, and can serve as a groundcover and be mowed	
A. sancti johannis	St. John's camomile; big, 2-inch blossoms.	Grows to 1½ feet.

Name	Description	Comment
Corn camomile *A. arvensis agrestis*	Like little white daisies with yellow centers; actually a biennial and very weedy.	Blooms May to Aug.; used for pest-repellent.
Campion, Red *Lychnis diurna* or *L. dioica*	Dense heads of red flowers, though some are pink or white; also called Little Robin, Herb Robert and Robin Hood; there are 7 other attractive varieties.	Somewhat coarse, but reliable perennials, not a bit hard to grow.
Candytuft *Iberis sempervirens*	Low-growing, about 12 inches; masses of white flowers and it blooms for quite a while; try varieties like 'Snowflake', 'Purity', 'Little Gem'.	Starts bloom in May; the foliage stays nice all summer. Use for edging; plant in early spring or late fall, in the sun; thin to 12 inches apart; remove flower heads when young to encourage branching.
Rock candytuft *I. saxatalis*	Very small, 6 inches with tiny round leaves and tiny white flowers; try the variety Autumn Snow' which might bloom twice.	Blooms in April and May; rock garden: hardy to Zone 3.
Canterbury bells (See Bellflower) Cardinal Flower (See Lobelia) Carnation *Dianthus carophyllus*	This is the clove pink, the florists' carnation, which comes in many red, pink, white colors The fragrant gilliflower of old fashioned gardens.	In the garden it blooms in late summer from seeds put in in late spring; full sun; thin to 12 inches apart; cut plants back in late fall and pot them for the winter, in a cold frame if you can; or take cuttings and begin again; suitable for Zones 5 to 9.
Other dianthus varieties: *D. barbatus* *D. deltoides*	Sweet William; Many colors of pink, red, and white. Very low, very hardy; flowers red or pink with a dark red eye, on a 6-inch stem.	Grown as biennial or even annual now. Forms a mat, and can become invading and a pest.
D. plumarius Called Grass pink, Cottage pink, or Scotch pink	Many garden forms, fringed, single, double, rose to purple in color; fragrant; grows 9 to 12 inches; good grayish foliage; try the hardy 'Pink Princess'.	The favorite of colonial gardens.
Catnip *Nepeta cataria* Related catnips: *N. mussini*, Dwarf catnip	Aromatic, minty plant with whitish to purplish small spikes; useful as a 3-foot border plant.	Blooms July to Sept.; is pest-repellent, though attractive to cats. Also is invasive and a pest in itself; I like the dwarf one better.

Name	Description	Comment
Christmas rose *Helleborus niger*	White flowers that bloom in late winter.	Takes two seasons to establish. Do not move or divide. Likes cool, moist shady place. No lime. Plant purchased plants spring or fall.
Chrysanthemums 160 species and 3000 varieties, mostly of *C. morifolium*	You can choose from many colors, different blooming times and from any of the classes: single, semi-double, regular anemone, irregular anemone, pompon, regular or Chinese incurve, irregular or Japanese incurve, reflexed or decorative pompon, decorative or aster-flowered reflex, regular or Chinese reflex, irregular or Japanese reflex, spoon, quill, threads, or spider, plus "azaleamums" and Korean. The popular names also include Cushion, Pompon and Football "mums." Colors range from white to gold to rose to purple. Shapes range from single and daisy-like to small compact, large global, long-petalled and raggedy to hooked or coiled. Grow only the varieties which will mature and bloom in your area before frost comes. And remember that chrysanthemums are short-day plants, so they will not bloom unless the days are short as they are in the fall. (Commercial growers put shading cloths over their plants; you can, too.)	For culture: get top-notch, A-one plants, from very good cuttings in the spring. Pinch out the growing points at 6 inches and again when new growth reaches 6 inches. Feed and water all summer. On a cloudy day in the fall, give an especially good watering and move the plants to the display location in the garden or on the terrace.
Clematis (See Vines) Clove pink (See Carnation)		
Columbine *Aquilegia hubrida*	Most garden columbines are hybrids, with either short or long spurs, in many colors. Try 'Crimson Star', 'Langdon's Rainbow Hybrids', 'Rose Queen' or 'McKana Hybrids'. Beautiful, graceful flowers.	They bloom in early to late June; average soil; some self-seeding; long germination, and they bloom the following year.

Name	Description	Comment
A. chrysantha called Golden Columbine	Long-spurred native of the Rockies, yellow; bushy and very prolific; a white variety is called 'Silver Queen'.	Hardy to Zone 2; no staking needed; average soil.
Long-spurred columbine *A. longissima*	This native of Mexico has the longest spurs of all; is pale yellow, and some have spurs 5 inches long.	Hardy to Zone 3; blooms from July to Oct.
Coneflower *Rudbeckia speciosa*	Too tall, but very showy; can grow to 10 feet; but the variety 'Goldstrum', with deep yellow flowers grows only 2½ feet, so get that for smaller spaces; or try 'Gold Drop', with double flowers, also small	Very easy to grow; good for masses, or for bedding, especially the small ones; you can get seed tapes now for the small ones
var. purpurea or *Echinacea purpurea*	A rather sickly purplish color; very attractive to butterflies Drooping petals.	Thrives in sunny, even windy places. Pest-free, as most coneflowers are.
Coral bells *Heuchera sanguinea*	Nice low-growing rounded leaves, and small red flowers on long stems; also in pink, white and scarlet; florets quite small, so grow in groups; many varieties; try 'Rosamund', pink; 'Queen of Hearts', largest red; 'Snowflake', white or 'White cloud'; for longest bloom, keep cut.	Flowers from late May to Sept.; mulch in winter; plant in spring, water during a drought because roots are shallow; divide in spring; needs good drainage and likes rich soil; excellent for dried arrangements.
Coreopsis (also called Tickseed) *C. lanceolata* and *C. Grandiflora*	Bright yellow daisy-like flowers on strong stems, growing 1 to 3 feet; try varieties 'Goldfink', 'Sunburst', and 'Flore-pleno', the double variety.	Bloom all summer; easy to grow in rich soil and full sun; an old garden favorite, very reliable.
C. auriculata nana	Dwarf, only 6 inches, with orange-yellow flowers that are 2 inches across.	Blooms June to Aug. and does well in rock gardens; is native to the Southeast, but hardy to Zone 4.
Cornflower (See Bachelor's buttons)	One rare yellow one to hunt for is *Centaurea montana citrina*.	
Cowslip (See Primrose)	A bunch of these is called a tisty-tosty.	

Name	Description	Comment
Crown vetch *Coronilla varia*	Pink-lavender pea-like flowers on a creeping legume, spread by long fleshy underground roots.	Widely advertized and a dreadful pest; should be avoided unless you want all your other plants utterly choked out.
Daisy *Chrysanthemum leucanthemum pinnatifidum* Also called Ox-eye daisy	The common field or daisy-chain daisy. White with yellow center, a European native, run wild over here. Gives great charm to meadows.	Blooms in June, July. Not often thought of as a garden flower. Spreads easily by seeds, but I have found it to be a pest.
Other daisies: African daisy is *Arctotis grandis;* Gloriosa daisy is *Rudbeckia speciosa;* Golden daisy is *Doronicum plantagineum*	Grown as an annual, white, pale blue, also hybrids of red and yellow. This is also called Leopardbane. A spring flower, pure yellow, usually about 2½ feet. growing in clumps.	Easy to grow. Does not mind some shade. Divide in late summer. Hardy to Zone 4.
Painted daisy or Pyrethrum *Chrysanthemum coccineum*	Red, but also white and pink. Can grow to 2 or 3 feet. Try varieties 'Crimson Giant', 'Helen', 'Rosary', 'Sensation', 'Victoria'. Some are double.	Plant in full sun, or very light shade. Hardy to Zone 3, and to 2, if protected.
Shasta daisy *Chrysanthemum maximum*	The handsome, cultivated, large white daisy. Try the doubles: 'Esther Read', 'Horace Read' and 'Wirral Supreme'.	Sow in spring. Replace every other year. Hardy to Zone 4.
Swan River daisy *Brachycome iberidifolia*	Treat as an annual, and make successive plantings. Flowers are blue, white or pink. Bushy, 15 inches.	Likes full sun and heat.
Daylily *Hemerocallis fulva*	The common daylily, tawny or dusky burnt-orange, growing 4 or 5 feet. Spreads by underground rootstocks, or rhizomes.	The roadside or ditch lily, brought from China and Europe in the last century. Common in gardens, too. All parts edible.
Lemon daylily *H. flava*	An old yellow favorite, now superceded by new hybrids, especially the very popular lemon-yellow variety. 'Hyperion', which blooms in mid-season, July and Aug.	These and all hybrid daylilies are very easy to grow, are practically pest-free, are adapted to both sun and shade. and are exceptionally beautiful flowers. Divide any time, but in the South during cool months. Easy to grow from seed. Division is needed only every 4 or 5 years, if that.

Name	Description	Comment
Delphinium *D. elatum* and *D. chinensis*	Many hybrid strains are available. Look into the 'Pacific Hybrids', 'Kelway Hybrids', 'Round Table Series' and the 'Wrexham' strains and also 'Blackmore & Langdon' more & Langdon Hybrids'. The colors are blue, pale blue, dark blue, purple, lavender, white, and combinations. The 'Pacfic Hybrids' are very tall, up to 9 feet. The 'Blackmore & Langdon' are quite short, as low as 2 feet, and much bushier, especially if you keep them cut. Plug all cut stems with wax, mud or tape to keep out bugs and water. Never let water sit on the crowns. Spread wood ashes to fend off snails. Dust with sulphur to prevent black spot. If you mulch, try a sterile material like vermiculite. If you get crown rot, start again. There is no cure.	The needs are: plenty of space and air, very good drainage, rich soil and fertilizer. Also great care of the crown and any exposed hollow stalks. Plant seeds in late June; do not crowd seedlings; shade at first; use salt hay on bed the first winter. Plant out in permanent place the next spring. Feed bone meal during the summer.
D. cheilanthum formosum is also called Garland Larkspur	Shorter, not more than 3 or 4 feet. Varieties 'Belladonna', 'Bellamosa'. Especially recommended is the new, small 'Connecticut Yankee'. Plant with roots in plain earth, but with rich mixture and good coarse drainage material underneath. Never crowd, or plant too near a wall or where it is dry and windy. These, like the large delphiniums, do best in the cooler climates. Keep fertilizing, for all are heavy feeders, and also give plenty of water.	The best results are from doing this yearly so you always have replacements. Several transplantings of young plants result in stockier, hardier plants with good husky root systems. Division is possible after the first bloom. Well cut-back plants often flower a second time.
D. grandiflorum, Siberian larkspur or *D. chinensis* in some listings	Bright blue, with 1½ inch florets, hardy to Zone 3. A good bloomer. It also comes in white and lavender.	Best results also come from a layer of coarse drainage material in the planting hole, then a layer of well-rotted manure, then a top layer of soil mixed with compost. Bone meal can be added at this time, as well as later. Use lime, too if your soil is acid.

Name	Description	Comment
Evening primrose *Oenothera fruticosa*	Canary-yellow single blooms, 18-inch plant. Hardy to Zone 4.	Full sun, well-drained soil. Will bloom June to Aug.
Missouri primrose *Oenothera missourensis*	Golden yellow, with 4-inch blossoms. Also called Tufted primrose. Only 12 inches tall.	
False dragonhead *Physotegia virginiana*	Big flower with good spikes. Several varieties *P. grandiflora* 'Bouquet Rose' has a good rose color. 5 feet. *P. v. alba* is pure white and short. 2 feet. 'P. Vivid', is rose-pink and 2 feet also. It appeals to the children because its florets can be pushed to the right or left of the stem and will obediently stay where pushed. Its other name, in fact, is obedient plant.	Will bloom July to Sept. Divide every two years. Some of the pink ones will spread. 'Bouquet Rose' can bloom until after frost.
False Starwort *Boltonia asteroides* *B. latisquama*	Tall, aster-like and flowers in white. Weedy if it self-seeds. Lavender flowers. Others are violet, white and purple.	Blooms in Sept.-Oct. Average soil. Hardy in Zones 4 to 8. Amazingly pestless.
Feverfew *Chrysanthemum parthenium* or *Matricaria chamomilla*	A short-lived perennial, with white flowers or yellow. Varieties include 'Lemon Ball', 'Golden Ball' and 'White Snowball'. This variety is usually more like an annual.	Masses of bloom all summer. Full sun, average soil. Excellent pest repellent. Use in various parts of the garden, and make tincture to rub on skin.
Flax *Linum favum*	Profuse yellow flowers on the variety 'Golden Flax', and blue on the one called 'Heavenly Blue'.	Blooms all summer.
Perennial flax *L. perenne*	Blue flowers, grows to 2 feet.	Blooms June to Aug. Hardy to Zone 4, doesn't mind the dry spots.
Foamflower *Tiarella cordifolia*	White filmy plumes, lobes of leaves deeply cut. Good ground-cover. Will grow 6 to 10 inches. In England it is called False mitrewort.	Hardy to Zone 3, and native to moist woods, so it likes slightly acid soil. Good for border or wild garden.

Name	Description	Comment
Forget-me-not *Myosotis scorpioides* This is called True forget-me-not	The lovely small-flowered blue or sometimes pink or whitish plant that blooms in damp areas. The variety 'Semperflorens' will bloom in July and Aug.	Blooms in April and May. Does especially well near streams, but also in cool climates in borders and fields. Hardy to Zone 3. Likes shade, but will grow in sun in Vermont.
Alpine forget-me-not *M. alpestris* *M. sulvatica*	Listed in many catalogues, but frequently is the above. Smaller with a tufted growth of leaves.	Hardy to Zone 2. Likes some shade. Both forget-me-nots self-sow very easily.
Foxglove *Digitalis ambigua*	Yellow, 30 inches, in graceful spikes. Another yellow is *D. lutea.*	Blooms in June. More truly perennial than others.
D. mertonensis	Strawberry pink, with stalks up to 3 or 4 feet.	Blooms June, July.
D. purpurea	The commonest one, in various colors, up to 4 feet. Usually biennial. Try 'Shirley' and 'Excelsior' hybrids.	Sun or shade; likes moist, rich soil. Protect in winter. Self-seeds.
Fraises des Bois	These are little French strawberries, with white blossoms and edible fruit. Varieties to try: 'Charles V', which has no runners. 8 inches. 'Catherine The Great', larger and the fruits juicier. 'Espalier', has long runners and best grown on a lattice, bears until frost, put in full sun.	They make an excellent and attractive border or edging plant. Average soil, but enrich with dried cow manure and compost. Root some of the nodes for new plants. Also propagate by division.
Fuchsia *F. hybrida*	Common house and hanging-basket plant, with 2000 named varieties in many color combinations in the reds, pinks and purples with and without white. It is capable of blooming in almost any month, but needs a period of rest. Excellent patio plant.	Hardy in Zone 10 for outdoor growing. And I have seen high hedges of fuchsia in County Cork, Ireland. They do well in San Francisco Bay area, too.
Fumitory *Corydalis lutea*	Yellow fumitory has leaves like a maidenhair fern, with soft yellow flowers, in sprays.	Blooms May to Aug. This is the best form. Hardy to Zone 5.

Name	Description	Comment
Funkia *Hosta decorata*	Also called Plantain lily. Large-leaved, shade-loving, decorative plants, with varieties of leaf pattern, green and white. Flowers are usually lavender or bluish, in upright spikes, rising well above the leaves. A fragrant one is 'Honeybells', with grass green leaves, lavender spikes of 3 feet, large 1½-inch florets.	Bloom in Aug., Sept. Hardy to Zone 3. Very useful for shady spots, for groundcovers and in the border. Will grow in the sun, but not well. Average soil. Easy to propagate by division or seeds.
H. lancifolia	Narrow, 6-inch leaves, 2-foot spikes of lavender flowers.	Some have yellow stripes on the leaves.
H. plantaginea	Old-fashioned favorite with fragrant white flowers.	
H. sieboldiana	Has bluish leaves, and short lilac flower spikes.	
H. undulata	Wavy leaves, 5 inches wide. Lavender flowers.	Blooms in July.
Gas plant *Dictamus albus*	Glossy, ash-like leaves. Fragrant white flowers, in June and July. (A match under the flower will make its gas ignite.) Also in pink and purplish varieties, which are more popular than the white.	It takes four years from planting to bloom. Some people get a rash from this plant. Needs light soil and good drainage. Does not like to be transplanted. Smells lemony.
Gayfeather *Liatris scariosa*	Button-like flowers on long stalks up to 4 feet. Purple or rosy-purplish. Native to Eastern states. Butterflies love these.	Average soil. Grows wild in damp meadows. One variety is white.
Kansas gayfeather *L. pycnostachya*	Long leaves, dense spikes.	Blooms July to Oct.
Spike gayfeather *L. spicata*	Usually 3 feet, but can grow to 6 feet. Purple, 15-inch flower clusters. Variety 'Kobold' is more compact, with darker flowers.	Blooms in Sept. Hardy to Zone 3, as are all varieties of gayfeather.

Sedum Species

Ageratum 'Blue Ball,' Petunias 'Coral Satin' and 'Red Joy Improved'

Calendula 'Kablouna' with F. Triploid Marigold, 'Red Seven Star' to the right of it

Grape Hyacinth (Muscari) Longwood Gardens

Dwarf Aster 'Pepite Red' and Ageratum 'Blue Ball'

Gaillardia

Name	Description	Comment
Geranium *Pelargonium hortorum*	Do you want to know the difference between geraniums and pelargoniums? Geraniums, that is cranesbills, have a solid stalk and pelargoniums have a hollow tube behind the flower and a spur joined with the flower stalk. Many varieties and colors, many sizes, single or double, mostly red, pinks, whites and combinations.	The garden flower suitable for pots, window boxes, patios, bedding and house plants. Propagate by making slips each year. Also grow mixed colors from seed.
True geranium *Geranium cinereum*	Large pink flowers, with red stripes. Divided leaves. Short, 6 inches.	Blooms all summer; good for rock gardens.
G. endressii	Taller, 15 inches. Deeply divided leaves. Rosy flowers.	Blooms in July.
G. ibericum	Still taller, 18 inches. Shiny, dark purple flowers, with 7-lobed leaves.	Very handsome border flower.
G. robertianum called Herb Robert	Reddish flowers in clusters.	Blooms all summer; good for wild gardens.
Germander *Teuchrium chamaedrys*	Red or rose or spotted little flowers on a dwarf plant; will grow to 15 inches.	Often used for a very short hedge, for it is like a subshrub. Likes full sun, well-drained garden soil. Evergreen in the South; not in the North. Hardy to Zone 5.
Ginger, Wild *Asarum europaeum* *A. canadense*	Brownish ground-hugging flowers and lovely evergreen 5-inch leaves. This one is taller, with purplish flowers.	Blooms April, May. Shade-loving, hardy to Zone 4. Mix peat into rich loam soil. This one hardy to Zone 2. Both make good evergreen groundcovers.
Globe flower *Trollius europaeus*	Large, globular, butter-cup-like flowers, and dark green, geranium-like leaves. 'T. Byrne's Giant' is lemon yellow, 24 to 30 inches. 'T. Lederbouri' is orange, 30 inches. 'T. Prichard's Giant' is golden yellow and large blooms, 30 inches. A spring favorite for many gardeners.	Will bloom in May and June, and off and on all summer. Likes full sun, moist soil. Has some acrid, poison-qualities that caused it to be named for the malignant troll.

Name	Description	Comment
Siberian globe flower *T. asiaticus*	This one is orange, with 2-inch blooms; grows to 2 feet.	Blooms May to July.
Globe thistle *Echinops exaltatus*	Round, rather prickly flowers, which stay round when the petals are off and the heads dried. They come in greenish to bright blue, but the blue is the desirable one. Get 'Taplow Blue' for the best. The white ones listed are not very attractive.	Excellent for dried arrangements; average soil, in sun or light shade; they spread.
Goldenrod *Solidago* hybrids	The English have hybridized some lovely specimens of this so-called weed. Two good ones are 'Golden Mosa' and 'Leroft', which is more buttercup color than gold.	Average soil; sun. Remember these for seaside and other difficult places. Invasive if not controlled. Host for red pine rust.
Golden glow *Rudbeckia hortensia*	Double yellow flowers in abundance during Aug. Grows to 10 feet, and spreads. 'Golden Globe', a newish variety, does also.	Very popular in the nineteenth century, but not today. Sturdy and long-lived.

Name	Description	Comment
Golden Tuft *Aurinia saxatile* (see *Alyssum saxatile*) Grass, Ornamental. Many species	Ten good perennials are: Blue Fescue-*Festuca ovina glauca.*	
	Blue Wild Rye-*Elymus glaucus.*	To 1 foot. Zone 4.
	Eulalia Grass-*Miscanthus sinensis.*	3 to 5 feet. Zone 5.
	Striped Eulalia-*M. s. variegatus.*	10 feet. Zone 4.
	European Dune Grass-*Elymus arenarius.*	10 feet. Zone 4.
	European Feather Gress-*Stipa pennata.*	8 feet. Zone 5.
	Fountain Grass-*Pennisetum ruppeli* This has purple or rose spikes	3 feet. Zone 5.
	Maiden Grass-*Miscanthus sinensis gracillinus.*	4 feet. Zone 5.
	Pampas Grass-*Cortaderia selloana.* The popular, big one that dries well.	10 feet. Zone 4.
	Plume Grass-*Erianthus ravennae*	8 to 20 feet. Zone 8. (Grow as annual in northern zones.)
	Ribbon Grass-*Phalaris arundinacea picta* or *P. variegata.*	8 to 20 feet. Zone 5.
	Zebra Grass-*Miscanthus sinensis zebrinus.*	4 feet. Zone 3.
		10 feet. Zone 4. Rich soil is best for growing grasses. Some, like Eulalia, will last for two or three decades.

Name	Description	Comment
Groundsel *Senecio aureus*	Golden, with ray flower blooms.	Likes swampy places.
S. cineraria	Silver groundsel, also called Dusty Miller. Yellow ½-inch flowers.	Blooms all summer. Sow in March; set out when warm. Grow in the greenhouse.
S. cruentus	The florists' Cineraria, which comes in purple, blue, cerise, lavender — all with white.	
S. pulcher	Showy groundsel. Purple rays, yellow disk, up to 3 inches. Try 'Desdemona'.	A vigorous, satisfactory perennial.
Harebell *Campanula carpatica* (See Bell flower)		
Heath, Cornish *Erika vagans*	Upstanding, 6 to 12 inches, cerise flowers in whorls, in variety 'Mrs. D. F. Maxwell'; white, 'Lyonesse'; deep pink, 'St. Keverne'.	Blooms June to Oct. Must have acid soil. A long-time favorite up to Zone 5, and perhaps in Zone 4, if protected.
Darley, Heath *E. darleyensis*	Excellent red rock garden heath. Very vigorous.	Blooms in Zone 5 until snow time.
Cross-leaf Heath *E. tetralix*	The hardiest; rosy flowers. Leaves practically evergreen. Grows to 18 inches.	Likes peaty, acid soil.
Spring Heath *Erica carnea*	Very like heather; grows to 1 foot; many choice varieties: 'Sherwood'; 'Sherwood Early Red'; 'Springwood Pink'; 'Springwood White'; 'Vivelli', 6 inches; 'Winter Beauty', rosy pink, also 6 inches, and it spreads.	Flowers in the winter and is hardy to Zone 5. Some of these spread out to 20 or 30 inches. They are said to be tolerant of lime.
Heather *Calluna vulgaris*	Another member of the Heath family, with evergreen foliage and spikes of little white, pink and red flowers. Many varieties to try.	Needs acid soil. And poor soil. If too rich, the plants will not survive. Wild in England, Scotland and on Nantucket. Good for dried arrangements. Bloom from July or early Aug. to Sept. or Oct. In the right soil (sandy peat with good drainage) heathers will make a good groundcover. For best bloom they need sun, though hardy to Zone 4, they need a winter mulch of evergreen boughs.

Name	Description	Comment
Heliotrope, Garden *Valeriana officinalis*	One variety is rose; one is white. Grows to 12 or 18 inches. The flowers are in flat clusters, and are fragrant. Good butterfly plant.	Blooms June to Oct. Hardy to Zone 3. Can spread. Sometimes used to flavor tobacco. Propagate by division or seeds.
Hen and Chickens *Sempervivum tectorum* Also called Houseleeks	Rosettes of 3 to 4 inches, and pink flowers. The variety *calcareum* has bluish leaves, tipped red-brown. Best color in May and June. Dozens of other varieties of *Sempervivums* including: S. *arachnoideum*, the Spiderweb one, red and green, with bright red flowers in July. S. *atroviolaceum*, up to 10 inches. The whole plant is rather lavender. S. *calcareum*, 3-inch plants, red blooms. Leaves have brown tips. S. *monatanum*, likes moist places. S. *minutum*, tiny. S. *triste*, small red leaves.	The very popular rock garden and border plants. Need excellent drainage, sun or part shade. They have many little offsets. Likes rich soil. Spreads well. Most of these are hardy to Zone 5.
Hibiscus (See Mallow) Hollyhock *Althaea rosea*	Tall spikes with mallow-like blooms in red, pink, yellow, white and sometimes lavender. Actually biennials, but they self-sow and keep coming up. Many beautiful varieties are double. English hybrids are excellent. Try 'Pompadour' mixtures, with rich colors like apricot, copper, maroon and purple.	They like sun, and good, deep, rich soil, but I have seen masses of them escaped beside a railroad track. Hollyhocks get the disease of rust, with orange disks all over the leaves. Use sulphur and keep badly infected leaves from dropping and spreading spores.
Honesty *Lunaria annua*	Another flower that, though a biennial, self-sows so readily that it seems to be a perennial. It has a spike of bright purple flowers in spring and 1-inch, flat, round pods with shiny, pearly membrane in the center, used often for dried arrangements.	Average soil; hardy to Zone 4.
Jacob's Ladder *Polemonium coeruleum*	Charming blue flowers, which grow to 12 or 18 inches. Neat pinnate leaves, with up to 20.	Good for the spring garden, the rock garden or the wild flower garden. Will self-sow.

Name	Description	Comment
Jacob's Ladder (cont'd)	leaflets. The variety 'Blue Pearl' is the best color. A white one is called *P. c. album*. *P. reptans* is a light blue, and creeping.	
Johnny-jump-up *Viola tricolor*	The tiny pansy, with three colors: lavender, yellow and white. There are also larger, single-colored violas, very handsome. I let it grow up in my garden wherever it wants to.	Is a short-lived perennial, but self-sows easily. Shakespeare calls it Love-in-Idleness or Heart's-ease. It is the herb which the pixie Puck uses to bewitch young lovers in *A Midsummer Night's Dream*.
V. t. hortensis is the Common pansy	Many colors; many sizes.	Buy them, or have a nurseryman grow them for you from seed.
Kenilworth Ivy *Cymbalaria muralis*	This is a member of the snapdragon family, with ½-inch flowers of lilac blue and a yellow throat. Is trailing.	Hardy to Zone 3. Make cuttings. Use as a pot plant, in baskets or as a groundcover. Will endure alkaline soil, or average soil.
Lamb's Ear *Stachys lanata* (See Betony)		
Lantana *L. camara*	Rather a shrubby plant, with rough leaves and clusters of yellow or red flowers, or in hybrids, pink and white.	Blooms all summer. Hardy in Zones 9 and 10, but excellent in pots or temporary places for the summer in other zones. Good for patios. A beautiful weed in South India, where it tumbles over waste lots, in a riot of color.
L. montevidensis	This is the trailing variety.	Good for hanging baskets.
Larkspur (See Delphinium)		
Lavender Mist *Thalictrum rochebrunianum* (See also Meadow rue)	The best of the meadow rues, growing to 5 or 6 feet, with large masses of lavender-violet flowers.	Blooms from July to early Sept.; hardy to Zone 4; average soil.
Leadwort *Ceratostigma plumbaginoides* (Listed also as *Plumbago larpentae*	Lovely gentian-blue flowers. Bright green, sprawling foliage. Grows to 10 inches, but space 12 inches apart.	Blooms mid-Aug. to Oct.; hardy to Zones 5 and 6, so mulch where it gets cold in winter. Sun or light shade. A good groundcover.
Lemon lily (See Daylily)		

Name	Description	Comment
Leopard's Bane *Doronicum caucasicum*	A charming yellow daisy, which flowers early, 2 inches across. Sometimes the foliage disappears later, but the variety 'Madam Mason' will keep its leaves all summer. This grows to two feet.	Blooms May, June; hardy to Zone 4. Very sturdy, and very easy to grow. Does well in part shade.
D. pardalianches *D. plantagineum*	Can grow to 5 feet. To 4 feet; with many flowers in each clump.	Zone 5 Some flowers of this grow to 3 inches across. Zone 3.
Lily-of-the-valley *Convallaria majalis*	Lovely, fragrant sprays of white flowers; and two tall, neat leaves. Grows to 8 inches. The variety *rosea* has pink flowers; and *fortunei* is larger than the species.	Likes rich, woodsy soil, some shade. Spreads quickly by root-stocks. It has gone wild in our woods, and makes a fine groundcover under the ash trees. Free of pests with us.
Lobelia *L. cardinalis* and *L. fulgens*	This brilliant red cardinal flower is easy to grow from seed. The leaves of *L. fulgens* are dark red, and make a good contrast color in the border. Grows 2 or 3 feet.	Though in the wild the cardinal flower is found near water, it does well in the border. Rich loam.
Loosestrife, purple *Lythrum salicaria*	Rose-purple flowers on 16-inch panicles and 3-foot plants.	Blooms June to Sept. Likes part shade and moisture. Good beside ponds. Does not like to be transplanted. Rather weedy, for it will choke out other plants unless controlled. Some hybrids are more controllable and less weedy.
Lungwort *Pulmonaria augustifolia* (Also called Blue Cowslip)	Blue, lilac, red, or blue and pink flowers, with stalks that uncurl as the flowers come. Grows to 12 inches; some have mottled leaves.	Flowers in March or April. Does well in the shade in average to rich soil. Hardy to Zone 3.
Lupine *Lupinus polyphyllus*	The garden lupine, especially the Russell hybrids, will bloom in pink, yellow, orange, red, blue and purple, also in combinations with white. The big, showy sprays grow to several feet, and they often bloom again if cut. Lupines self-sow	Bloom in June and July. They do best in moist, shady or sunny places, but not where the soil is too rich. Hardy to Zone 3. Spray with soap and water if necessary. They are legumes and provide nitrogen for themselves and nearby plants.

Name	Description	Comment
Lupine (cont'd)	easily, but the color runs to pink, blue and lavender if allowed to do so. I don't mind if they do, and I think they tend to be more sturdy and pest-free plants.	Does well in really poor soil. Blooms all summer.
L. luteus	A 2-foot, fragrant yellow flower.	
Marguerite, Golden *Anthemis tinctoria* (See also camomile)	Handsome, prolific bushy plant of yellow flowers, 2 inches across. Plant grows to 3 feet. Try varieties: 'Kelwayi', dark lemon yellow; 'Moonlight', pale yellow; 'Perry's', bright yellow.	Blooms July, Aug., not a bit fussy as to soil. Needs some sun. Easy to propagate by division or seeds. Pest-free.
Meadowsweet *Filipendula vulgaris*	White or pink feathery plumes, growing to 3 feet. The flowers are like those of spirea, and it is also called *Spiraea ulmaria*. The double is best.	Blooms June, July; hardy to Zone 2; easy to propagate by division or seed; full sun.
Milkwort *Euphorbia epithymoides*	One of a family of 1000 species. This is a bushy, showy 12-inch plant with yellow bracts in May which turn bronze. The foliage is dark green.	Hardy to Zone 4; needs a dry place looks neat and fine all summer.
Monk's Hood *Aconitum napellus*	The common aconite. Grows to 4 feet. With dark blue flowers. The variety *album* has white flowers. *Sparksii* has dark blue flowers, and can grow 6 feet tall. *A. fisheri* is shorter, 2 or 3 feet. and a deep blue. *Spark's* variety is Oxford blue, and will grow to 3 or 4 feet. An earlier bloomer, *A. napellus*, grows to 4 feet. Very good flowers for dried arrangements, and all you have to do is hang them up in a warm, dark place for a week or so.	Blooms Aug. Sept. Thrives in light shade or sun. Needs watering. Is a robust plant. Poisonous, or strongly alkaloid. Long-lived plants which do not like to be moved. Hardy to Zone 2 or 3. Plant 10 inches apart, where there is moist, humusy soil.
Moss Campion *Silene acaulis*	Grows to 2 inches, and is tufted, moss-like, with ½-inch leaves and dainty white flowers in clusters.	Hardy to Zone 5.
S. asterias	Grows in rosettes, with red flowers and stems up to 3 feet.	Blooms June to Sept.; average soil.

Name	Description	Comment
S. maritima	Sea Campion. Grows to 1 foot. Has trailing stems and white flowers about ¾ inch across.	Likes sandy soil.
Mullein *Verbascum nigrum*	Fuzzy leaves, good spikes of flowers, wonderfully hybridized by English gardeners. Try 'Cotswold Gen', 'Pink Domino' which grow to 3 and 4 feet.	Blooms June to Sept.
Verbascum phoeniceum	Mixed colors, with white, pink and salmon. Grows 3 to 6 feet.	Blooms June to Oct. Other mulleins are weeds, but these two varieties are well worth trying. Pestless.
Nettle, Harmless *Labium album* and *Labium purpureum*	Also called Archangels.	Very good for soil-building, for compost-making, and pest-control.
Oriental poppy *Papaver orientale*	Very big, very showy flowers, in many colors. Will grow to 2½ to 3 feet. Do not be surprised if the foliage dies down in Aug. Always plant in the fall.	Likes deep loam, and dislikes transplanting. Plant with crown 3 inches below surface for best results and mulch only the first winter. Blooms in June. In Aug. you can cut down in and make root divisions, which will probably take two years to come into bloom. Put in freshly fertilized new soil (use only well-rotted materials) and keep well watered until established. A salt hay or other mulch will help. Poppies are hardy to Zone 2.
Iceland poppy *P. nudicale*	Smaller flowers about 3 inches, which will grow to 1 or 2 feet. They self-sow and can be grown as biennials. Colors are white, pink, red, yellow, orange. Delicate and prolific.	These need good drainage and a rather light soil.
Pyrethrum or Painted Daisy *Chrysanthemum coccineum* but also called *Pyrethrum coccineum*	Beautiful, 3-inch daisies in red, shades of pink and white. Some are double, often bicolored. 18 to 24 inches.	Will bloom June, July. Full sun, but can take some light shade. Plant spring or fall, 12 to 15 inches apart. (For discussion of insecticidal powers of pyrethrums see discussion of pest control in *Gardening Techniques*.)

Name	Description	Comment
Penstemon or Beard-tongue or Bearlip *P. barbatus*	Lovely stalks of drooping tubular flowers, in pink. The rosy 'Rose Elf' is a fine variety, growing to 18 or 20 inches. 'Prairie Fire' is a bright orange, sometimes only 15 inches tall.	Blooms June to Aug. Full sun, moist place or water well. Hardy to Zone 2 or 3. Pest-free. This one blooms until frost, or June to Sept.
P. heterophyllus	A bright blue variety, from the West. Will grow 15 to 50 inches, depending on the climate and area.	Said to be hardy to Zone 8, but is sold in nurseries in colder zones.
Peony *Paeonia albiflora* or *P. lactiflora*	Spectacular single and double flowers; plants growing to 24 to 36 inches, with strong, lobed foliage and big, 6 to 10-inch flowers. In white, shades of pink and red, and one or two single yellows. Some are fragrant.	Bloom in June, but there are early, mid-season, and late. Hardy to Zone 3. Peonies do not like acid soil or a peat moss mulch.
P. officinalis rubra	This is the good, old-fashioned red peony. The single or Japanese peony also has many varieties, in white, red and gold, pink and gold and clear pinks. See catalogues.	Early.
Tree peony *P. suffruticosa* or *P. moutan*	Only grows to 4 or 5 feet. Large, solitary flowers 6 to 10 inches across. Blossoms rather flat and very showy. Improved by A. P. Saunders of Hamilton College, Clinton, N. Y. and by his daughter Sylvia Saunders. Now send to William Gratwick, Pavilion, N. Y. and ask for the Daphnis hybrids. When established, a tree peony may produce 50 to 100 blooms on one plant, but be glad if you get 20.	Hardy to Zone 5. Difficult to grow, but well worth the effort. These bloom late May and June. Comments: Not truly hardy in Zone 4 or cold parts of 5. Cover with a basket after deep frost, especially the first year. All peonies should be planted with the graft well below ground. One expert will recommend 1½ inches, no more nor less; another 2 or even 3 or 4. They all say: prepare the ground well in advance, making a somewhat sandy loam, with lots of organic matter (1 bushel per 2-foot hole), 5 lbs. of bone meal, some lime, and water it down. The whole point of preparing the bed early is so that it will settle. Plant in a sunny, well-drained place. If drainage is prob-

Name	Description	Comment
Tree Peony (cont'd)		lematical, put gravel in the bottom of the hole. Watch to see whether the plant sinks below the safe level. Peonies with the graft 4 inches below ground level often just will not bloom. Be very wary of pruning tree peonies. Just a little, taking out the dead wood very early in the autumn. Herbaceous peonies and tree peonies do not like being moved; do not like tree roots nearby; do not like grass growing up around them; do not like acid soil. As with trees and shrubs, a plant which will not be moved for years needs very good conditions for long-time growth. This means very well prepared soil, richly provided with long-lasting compost and other nutrients. In hot climates, it also means that some mulch is a good idea. Because the blooms are so heavy. peonies need supports, or circular stakes or chicken wire; trees need their branches propped up at times to hold up the heavy bloom.
Fern-leaved peony *P. tenufolia*	A small red peony, with delicate, fern-like leaves,. Will grow to 18 inches.	Herbaceous peonies should be cut back to the ground in fall. Do not do this to tree peonies. Also give them plenty of space. Peonies are big plants. After they are established, you can add compost fertilizer or water with compost tea every week or so in the summer after the peonies have bloomed. Blooms in May. Another old-fashioned favorite.
Periwinkle *Vinca minor*	Glossy evergreen small plant, a favorite groundcover in our neighborhood. Blue flowers in spring.	Plant 6 inches apart and it will increase rapidly. Prepare soil 6 inches deep. Good loam.

Name	Description	Comment
Big periwinkle *Vinca major*	A larger plant, also used for a groundcover in the South. Flowers are bright blue, coming out in May. Also comes with variegated leaves.	Hardy to Zone. But this is good for window boxes and often used, especially the one with variegated leaves.
Phlox *P. paniculata*	Beautiful, sturdy garden plant, with big, many-flowered heads of pink, red, white and a timid magenta, to which many will revert if you do not keep the deadheads picked off. What's more, if you keep the tops cut side growth will come on for more bloom. Subject to a mildew, but cutting the plants to merely 4 stalks will help to control that. On newly bought always pinch out half the stalks anyway; see catalogues for early, mid-season and late varieties in many colors.	Bloom in August. Full sun, but keep well watered, or moist with mulch. Plant 2 feet or more apart. Plant so the crown is 1 inch below the soil surface. When the clump goes dead in the center, lift and divide. This may need doing every 3 or 4 years. They bloom better after this rejuvenation. Cut front stalks back in June so that all the blooms, in Aug. will not be at the top; only the rear ones. Fertilize well in June. Cut to the ground after frost.
Wild Blue Phlox *Phlox divaricata*	Excellent 8-inch plant with showy blue flowers, often used as a groundcover. The variety 'Laphamii' has lavender flowers. The 'Alba' has white flowers. All are about 12 inches.	Blooms April to June. Moist, woodsy soil and rocks. Good in border and rock garden. Divide in early spring. Take cuttings in late spring.
Moss pink *Phlox subulata*	Prostrate, 6-inch plant, with woody stems and stiff leaves, semi-evergreen. Small clusters of pink, red, white or blue flowers.	Very common in rock gardens. Likes sandy soil. Easy to make cuttings and root them in sand. Plant in spring; take cuttings in the fall.
P. suffruticosa	This is a long-blooming phlox with long, loose heads. The variety to grow is 'Miss Lingard,' which is white and 30 inches tall.	Blooms June to Sept. Good garden soil.
Pink (see carnation) Sea pink (see Statice) Plantain lily (see Funkia) Plumbago *P. larpentae*	28 inches with small blue petalled flowers in clusters.	Blooms all Aug. and Sept. Full sun or part shade. Useful for late-summer bloom.

Name	Description	Comment
Plume poppy *Macleaya cordata*	Huge plant, growing to 6 feet or more, with big sculptured leaves and big plumes of clusters of cream-colored flowers. Good accent in the back of the border or in front of a tall wall. Also a pinkish variety.	Blooms in July and Aug. Can spread. Divide in spring. Full sun, rich soil. Give it lots of room and fertilize with top dressings of compost three times a season.
Poppy mallow *Callirhoe involucrata*	Sprawling, hairy plant with reddish purple flowers, up to 1 or 2 feet.	Likes dry, sunny places, and is hardy to Zone 3. Native to the Middle West.
Potentilla or Cinquefoil *P. aurea verna*	P. alba is 10 inches high, with white flowers in sprays. Trailing potentilla, 3 inches high, with strawberry-like leaves and many yellow flowers.	Hardy to Zone 5. Pest-free. Blooms June to Sept.
A. atrosanguinea	A red potentilla from the Himalayas 18 inches.	Zone 5.
	Variety 'Miss Wilmot', 12 inches, is cerise.	Blooms all summer.
	Variety 'Mons Rouillard', maroon.	Blooms all summer. Very hardy.
Bush cinquefoil *P. fruticosa*	Grows all over the world, with yellow or white flowers. Can grow to 4 feet, but is usually smaller. Reliable, long-blooming and very effective in landscape plantings. Many varieties to try.	Pest-free plants; easy to grow; highly recommended.
Primrose Primula - 400 species	Low-growing, bright-flowered spring and summer favorites. The English primrose, yellow.	Most species like moisture and some shade. Many are apropriate for rock gardens; some for streamsides, but the crown must be dry.
Primula acaulis *Primula auricula*	One-inch Alpine primulas of many colors, with contrasting outer petals and centers. The basal rosette is just about evergreen.	Rather difficult to grow, but a rage in England during the last century. Give special mulches in winter to prevent heaving. Hardy to Zone 3. Can be grown under trees.
Cortusa primrose *P. elatior*	This is the Oxlip primrose, suitable for the border. Yellow, with wrinkled leaves. Some blooms are 1 inch across.	Hardy to Zone 5. Do not disturb when once established.

Name	Description	Comment
P. japonica	This Japanese primrose is commonly grown in moist gardens in the shade, or in part shade. The 1-inch flowers are rose, purple or white.	Not so difficult as some; stalks up to 20 inches.
P. juliae	Popular with European gardeners. Grows only to 3 inches, with rose, red or purplish blooms and wrinkled leaves.	Will stand some dry spells, so a good variety to grow in the South. Hardy to Zone 5.
P. polyantha	The very popular primula, in both English and American gardens, hybrid crosses of *P. elatior, P. veris* and *P. vulgaris.* Many pastel colors; many dwarf forms; with some blooms 1½ inches across.	Bloom in May, hardy to Zone 3. Easiest of all primulas to grow, and not too fussy about having shade.
P. sieboldii	Grows to 9 inches. White, rose or purple flowers, 1½ inches across. Leaves die back in winter.	Stands more sun than even polyantha. Hardy to Zone 4. Quite easy to grow.
P. vulgaris	Called English primrose, and growing to 6 to 9 inches, with flowers of white, yellow, purple, and blue, solitary, on long stems. See catalogues for all the colors and varieties.	Blooms in spring, and is hardy to Zone 5. Used in rock gardens Primulas are easy to divide in early fall. They can be grown from seed in a cold frame in April or May.

Pyrethrum (See Painted Daisy)

Rock cress *Arabis albida*	This is Wall Rock Cress, a 6-inch plant with small ½-inch flowers with whitish leaves. Some are double, some are pink. The double is called 'Flore-Pleno', and blooms longer.	Blooms in April; hardy to Zone 3; will spread to a carpet on good soil.
A. alpina Alpine rock cress	Often confused with *A. albida*, but a finer, daintier variety.	Very good for rock gardens.
A. blepharophylla	This native of California has fragrant, rosy purple flowers on 12-inch stems.	Blooms in May. Hardy to Zone 6.
A. procurrens	This is another 1-foot rock cress with white flowers, but it spreads rapidly by stolons.	Hardy to Zone 4. Like the others, it must be cut back after blooming, or it will get leggy.

Name	Description	Comment
A. rosea	A rose-colored one.	This and the others make a charming display in a mat under dogwoods or quinces in the spring.
Rock rose or Sun rose *Helianthemum nummularium*	Also affectionately called buttercup. Low-growing and almost evergreen. Golden-yellow flowers on 10-inch stems.	Blooms July to Sept. Hardy to Zone 5.
H. n. mutabile	Dwarf and rather shrubby. The white variety is called *H.* 'St. Mary's'. Often used in rock gardens.	Needs full sun, and winter protection. Grows to Zone 5.
Salvia	Salvias are sages. In blue and red and usually fairly hardy and fairly long-blooming. Mint family.	Full sun; average soil.
Salvia argentea	Silver sage, with rosy white flowers. Grows to 2 to 4 feet.	Blooms in June.
S. azurea	Blue sage, with blue flowers. Grows 3 to 4 feet, Biennial.	Blooms Aug., Sept.; hardy to Zone 4.
S. clarea	Clary, or clary sage. Popular herb, with 1-inch whitish-blue flowers. Used to help sore eyes. Biennial, really.	This self-seed, so goes on and on.
S. farinacea	Called Blue Bedder, and to be found in many seed lists. Also called Mealycup Sage. Will grow to 2 feet.	Grows as a perennial in the South. Start seeds in Feb. under a fluorescent lamp.
S. officinalis	The most popular sage, and actually a subshrub, with white, blue or purple flowers, and is called Garden Sage. One variety,'Rubriflora' has red blossoms.	Used in cooking; hardy for a while to Zone 3; woolly leaves.
S. pitcheri	The best blue sage, with 1-inch flowers and 4-foot plants which should be staked.	Blooms late summer to frost; hardy to Zone 5.
S. splendens	Scarlet Sage, and the best for red sage. Used often as both annual and perennial. The blossoms are 1½ across. The best variety is 'St. John's Fire'. Others in	Grows high in warm climates, up to 8 feet. In north only 3 feet before killed by frost.

Name	Description	Comment
S. splendens (cont'd)	pink, salmon or beige are 'Welwyn Hybrids'. All used for bedding plants.	
Sand verbena Abronia fragrans	White flowers on an erect plant, fragrant at night.	Grows where the soil is light and sandy, and in full sun.
A. umbellata	This one is pink, and prostrate. Very good for hanging baskets.	Hardy to Zone 5.
Sandwort Arenaria in 120 species	Pink family plants, low-growing, in mats or tufts. Some true alpines Mostly white, but some in red and purple.	Any light, sandy soil. Propagate by division. Used in rock gardens. And between stepping stones.
Santolina S. chamaecyparissus	This is called Lavender Cotton, and grows to 20 inches. Has a delicate green small-leaved foliage and yellow flowers. Will make a mat. Very aromatic.	Likes light, poor, dry soil. Hardy to Zone 7, so pot up for the winter in colder zones.
S. c. nana	This dwarf variety has silvery foliage, and is very good for edging or for the rockery. Is trimmed to a 6-inch hedge.	
Saxifrage	The name means rock-breaker.	It is suitable for the rock garden; is the seeming rock-breaker.
Saxifraga aizoon or S. paniculata	The leaves grow in rosettes, and the yellow flowers have purple markings. They are ½-inch wide.	Blooms during the summer; hardy to Zone 2.
S. decipiens or S. rosacea	Low plant, 1 foot, with white flowers. Leaves like ivy.	Hardy to Zone 6.
S. sarmentosa	Strawberry saxifrage. Also called Strawberry Geranium. This grows to 2 feet, and is usually a house plant, or used in the patio in summer. Has long runners, with plantlets attached.	Hardy to Zone 7; propagate by planting the plantlets; good for hanging baskets.
S. umbrosa	A favorite plant with the English; called Londonpride Saxifrage, with small white or pink flowers, in a cascade of long leaves.	Hardy to Zone 7.

Name	Description	Comment
S. virginiensis	Virginia Saxifrage, the native Eastern saxifrage, has greenish flowers with no petals.	This is the one for rocky places.
Scabiosa or scabious *Scabiosa caucasia*	This grows to 1½ to 2½ feet, a good garden perennial, and good for cut flowers, with lavender blooms in the summer. Some varieties blue, white.	Blooms in June and on to Sept. if cut. Average soil. Hardy to Zone 2 and 3.
S. lucida	Grows to 1 to 2 feet. has rosy-lilac flowers.	Especially good for rock gardens. Zone 5.
S. ochroleuca	Cream scabious, which grows to 1 to 2½ feet.	Blooms June to Sept.
Sea pink or Sea thrift (see Thrift)		
Shasta Daisy *Chrysanthemum maximum*	A very fine perennial daisy, from a native Pyrenees daisy, redone by Burbank, the great California plant expert and hybridizer. Varieties to try: 'Alaska', large white; 'Lucy', semi-double white; 'Nipponicum', large single, 'Victor', double everblooming if you keep it cut.	Average to rich soil. Plant every two or three years, in case your daisies are short-lived. Mine have been.
Siberian wallflower *Cheiranthus allioni* or *Erysimum asperum*	Golden flowers in loose clusters; or orange; grows to 3 feet.	A lovely plant, rather tricky to grow in this country. Is killed by hot weather but is hardy to Zone 3. Grows wild in some sandy parts of the Middle West. Does well in England.
Snakeroot (See Bugbane)		
Sneezeweed *Helenium autumnale*	Very good fall flower, with many daisy-like, yellow flowers. Also in bronze, gold, red, deep red and red and gold. Recommended varieties: 'Bruno', mahogany; 'Butterpat', pale yellow; 'Chippersfield', orange.	Blooms in Sept. Likes sun and average soil. For neatness' sake, you can cut out all but 3 or 4 stems in early summer. Hardy to Zone 5.
Sneezewort *Achillea ptarmica* The Pearl	This variety, called 'The Pearl', is a superior flower to grow for making flower arrangements.	Blooms all July, Aug.; prefers a dry spot; propagation by cuttings.

Name	Description	Comment
Sneezewort (cont'd)	especially dried arrangements. Its many small, round white blooms light up any arrangement you put them in. Grows to 2 feet or a little more. The best varieties are 'Boule De Neige', 'Angel's Breath', and the double 'Perry's White'.	
Snow-in-summer *Cerastium tomentosum*	Green and white groundcover; white flowers in May, June. Be warned! It is rampant, Grows 3 to 6 inches and spreads very rapidly.	Grows most profusely in dry, sunny places. Some people use it in rock gardens, but they have to control it. Beware!
Southernwood *Artemisia abrotanum* (See Artemisia)		
Speedwell *Veronica alpina alba*	Small white, 6-inch spikes for the rock garden.	Blooms all summer; hardy to Zone 4.
V. chamaedrys	One-foot, compact, almost evergreen. Called germander speedwell. Get 'Crater Lake Blue'.	Blooms in May, June. Hardy to Zone 3. Used for groundcover; it spreads by creeping rootstalks. Control it.
V. incana	Woolly speedwell. Grows to 2 feet. Blue or rose, with leaves to 3 inches and flower spikes to 6 inches. Grayish leaves. Try 'Saraband'.	Blooms in June, July. Attractive foliage, good for edging. Good for sunny, dry places.
V. longifolia or *V. maritima*	The old-fashioned favorite. Small, lilac-blue flowers in spikes. Grows in clumps up to 2 feet wide. Good varieties: 'Blue Champion', 'Sunny Border Blue', 'Icicle', white.	These bloom for 3 months, June through Aug. Good soil, not too dry.
V. l. subsessilis		Rich soil for these.
V. spicata	Spike speedwell. Grows to 1½ feet. Lance-like 2-inch leaves. flowers in blue, pink, purple. Try varieties: 'Nana', dwarf; 'Barcole', deep rose; 'Minuet', pink; 'Blue Champion'.	Blooms June to Sept.; hardy to Zone 3; good drainage and plenty of sun; may need winter protection; divide every three years.
Spider plant (See Saxifrage)		

Name	Description	Comment
Spiderwort *Tradescantia viginiana*	A charming plant with long narrow leaves, and blossoms of blue, pink or white. The blossoms close afternoon, and new ones open the next morning.	Likes rich, woodsy soil. Will bloom July and Aug. Hardy to Zone 3 Self-sows, but also take cuttings in summer or divide in spring. Does best in light shade, with some moisture. Good for wild gardens.
T. flumensis Called Wandering Jew	The prostrate or small trailing plant for pots, patios and house plants. Or groundcover in Zone 9. Green leaves, but the varieties *albo-vitatta* and *variegata* have white markings. Also recommended for window boxes and hanging baskets.	Needs moisture, good light, and not too much sun. The growing tips pushed into the earth will take root. This plus judicious pruning are good ways to rejuvenate the plants.
St. John's Wort *Hypericum fugadaemonum*	Dare-devil or Chase-devil flower, said to cure frights. Blue, but more usually yellow flowers.	Blooms all summer; hardy to Zone 6; likes some sun and average soil.
H. calycinum Aaron's beard St. John's Wort	Grows to 1 or 1½ feet, with bright yellow flowers.	Blooms almost all summer. Not hardy north of New York City, Zone 6.
H. frondosum	Golden flowers; somewhat shrubby.	Blooms July to Aug. Needs some shade and some lime.
Statice or Sea lavender *Limonium latifolium*	A 2½-foot plant, with large feathery mauve flowers on tall stems. Grows in clumps, with perhaps 12 stalks in each. Other varieties in white and red.	Hardy to Zone 3. Though native to marshes and seashores, statice will grow in the border. Outstanding for dried arrangements.
Stinging nettle *Urtica dioica*	Four-foot plant with 5-inch leaves and stalks of small, greenish flowers. Not very pretty, but very useful. Stings when you touch it. Rub on dock leaves to alleviate the sting.	Weedy, grows in any garden soil. Used by organic gardeners as a stimulant in the compost heap, and as a pest repellent. Will grow in shade as well as sun.
Stokes aster *Stokesia laevis*	Lovely large 5-inch asters on 18-inch or shorter stems. The more you cut, the more they come again. Get the variety 'Blue Star', or a white one, 'Silver Moon'.	Blooms July to frost. Full sun; hardy to Zone 5, or 4 if given protection in winter. Likes full sun, sandy loam and very good drainage. Divide every 3 years.

Name	Description	Comment
Stonecrop *Sedum*, many species *S. acre*	Fleshy rock-garden plants, Try: Goldmoss stonecrop Yellow, Zone 3, 2 inches. Variety *aureus* has tips yellow, too.	Blooms May, June. Likes poor soils and drought conditions. Plant spring or fall. Hardy Zones 3 to 8, depending on the species. Many spread rapidly.
S. album	White stonecrop, Zone 3. The variety *murale* is pink, with purplish foliage; popular.	
S. kamschaticum	Dark green scalloped leaves, 3 or 4 inches. Orange-yellow flowers. Variety *floriferum* starts to bloom in May.	Blooms July to Sept. Hardy to Zone 3.
S. maximum atropurpureum	Mahogany plant, with bronzy leaves, rosy flowers, ebony stems. Grows to 2 feet.	This can be grown in the border.
S. rupestra	A very good sedum for rock gardens in Zone 6 and warmer. Leaves are bluish and turn purple for the winter. Pale yellow flowers.	Blooms in July; hardy to Zone 7.
S. sarmentosum	Stringy stonecrop, with pale yellow flowers.	Blooms in July; hardy to Zone 3.
S. spectabile	Showiest sedum. growing to 18 inches, and having fine big 3-inch gray-green leaves and 4-inch clusters of rose-colored flowers.	Hardy to Zone 3; blooms Aug to frost; full sun, light shade.
S. s Dragon's Blood	Reddish bronze leaves, about 1-inch high. Dark red flowers. Widely advertised by nurserymen.	Blooms June on; spreads fairly fast, not remarkably fast.
S. ternatum	Mountain stonecrop, an American native. Has whitish, bluish flowers on 6-inch stalks.	Prefers moist, shady spots. Good for rock gardens. Self-sows.
Sunflower *Helianthus decapetalus multiflorus flora plenus*	The great perennial sunflower, with large sprays of double flowers, bright yellow. Grows to 4 feet.	Blooms July to Sept.
Sunflower, False *Heliopsis helianthoides*	This grows to 5 feet, with a wealth of bloom if grown in good rich soil. Yellow 2½-inch blossoms. Larger on the variety 'Pitcheriana'. And 4 inches on the variety 'Hohlspiegel', which grows to 3 feet.	Blooms July to frost; will grow in poor soil, but are much better plants if grown in rich, deep loam. Hardy to Zone 3.

Name	Description	Comment
H. scabra	The variety 'Gold Greenheart', a double with 3-inch blooms is a great favorite with gardeners who like sunflowers.	Hardy to Zone 2.
H. s incomparabilis	This one is a rich yellow, semi-double variety with a dark center. These two go well together.	Bloom July to frost.
Sun-ray flower *Inula orientalis*	This is a golden sunburst flower, with 3-inch blooms on 2-foot stems. It is very bright and cheery.	Full sun, average soil; hardy to Zone 3.
Inula helenium	This is elecampine, which has escaped to roadsides in the Eastern states. A rather coarse, but also a cheerful flower. 6 feet.	Blooms June to Aug.
Inula royleana	Grows to 6 feet, with 3 or 4-inch orange-yellow flowers. Called Himalayan elecampine.	Blooms June to Sept.
Sun-rose *Helianthemum nummularium*	One-inch flowers on 1-foot plants. Daisy form, in yellow, white and pink, but only having 5 petals. Can be clipped for a groundcover.	Used in rock gardens. Full sun. Hard to transplant them. Like limy soil. Hardy to Zone 5, but protect in winter where cold.
Sweet rocket *Hesperis matronalis*	A lovely 3-foot flower with many florets in a head, whitish, pinkish or purplish and very fragrant. The variety 'Alba' is pure white. The flowers have 4 petals. Also called Dames' Rocket.	Blooms all summer. Average soil. Will self-sow. Likes partial shade.
Sweet William *Dianthus barbatus*	A 2-foot plant with pungently sweet flowers, growing in flat heads. The colors are white, pink, red and various mixtures. Now treated as biennials or by many gardeners as annuals, even. (Because they die out.)	Bloom July to Aug. hardy to Zone 3. Plant in April; add some lime; plant out in June; will grow to 2 feet.
D. deltoides	Only 4 to 15 inches, called Maiden pink, and forms a mat. Also trails.	Blooms May, June. Hardy to Zone 2.

Name	Description	Comment
D. plumarius	Cottage pink or Grass pink. Grows 12 to 18 inches, and flowers of pink, white, red. Used in old-fashioned gardens . Very fragrant. A fine variety is 'Pink Princess', almost coral.	Hardy to Zone 3.
D. winteri	This is a hybrid, and has lemon yellow or apricot, fringed blooms. Longer-lived and very sturdy.	Blooms for weeks in May and June. Hardy to Zone 6, and blooms all summer.

(See also Carnation)

Name	Description	Comment
Sweet woodruff *Asperula odorata*	This old garden favorite, grown often as a groundcover, with clean green leaves up to 12 inches, has white small flowers. The dried foliage is fragrant. Used in May wine.	Blooms May to July; likes some shade. Hardy to Zone 3. Also a good rock garden plant.
Tansy *Tanacetum vulgae*	This European perennial has escaped and gone wild in this country. It grows to 3 feet, has yellow button-like flowers in heads, and is strong-scented. Its leaves and stems are poisonous but the flowers have been used to flavor custards, or the bitter-herb tansie that used to be taken during Lent. Tansy cheese has also been made.	Hardy to Zone 3. Any soil. Blooms in late summer. Use by organic gardeners as a powerful pest-repellent; and to strengthen sprays for insect control.
Thrift *Armeria maritima*	Common Thrift, which grows 6 to 12 inches, with white to rose-colored flowers in round heads. Divides very easily into many new small plants for a groundcover. Try the variety 'Laucheana', crimson.	Very good for rock gardens. Hardy to Zone 3. Blooms May, June.
A. alpina *A. juniperifolia*	Dwarf, tufted species. A 2-inch species, also good for rock gardens.	Needs dry, sandy soil. Full sun. Hardy to Zone 3.

Tickseed (See Coreopsis)

Name	Description	Comment
Treasure Flower *Gazania montana*	Tender daisy-like flowers, growing to 8 to 10 inches. This one is hardiest of several varieties.	Blooms from May to Sept. or June to Sept. Full sun, rich soil. Bright and clear colors make gazanias very attractive to grow. Can be treated as annuals north of Zone 7.
Trumpet flower *Incarvillea delavayi*	The rosette of shiny leaves sends up a cluster of 2-inch rosy purple trumpet flowers on a 1-foot stalk. Very common in English gardens.	Full sun. Good loam soil. Hardy to Zone 6 (Get seeds from Vaughan or Thompson & Morgan).
I. sinensis variabilis	Pink flowers, more shrubby in growth.	Blooms all summer. and will do so from seed sown in the spring. Hardy to Zone 4.
Tufted Pansy *Viola cornuta*	An old garden favorite, with many varieties to choose from. Try 'Catherine Sharp', lavender and purple; 'Floraire', blue; 'John Wallmark', lavender with pale throat. There is also a yellow one, 'Yellow Perfection', 6 to 10 inches.	Bloom from spring to fall. Violas need rich manured soil. They can also be grown as annuals from seed sown indoors in January and set out in April. Hardy to Zone 6 or 5.
Tunic flower *Tunica saxifraga*	This 10-inch flower is a neat, tufted plant, very suitable for the rock garden. There are white, double rose-colored varieties, and look rather like Baby's breath, though the blossoms look a little like pinks.	Blooms July to frost. Hardy to Zone 3. Plant out in spring. Divide any time or take cuttings from non-flowering shoots.
Valerian (See Heliotrope Garden)		
Valerian, Red *Centranthus ruber*	Opposite, gray-green leaves and carmine rose clusters of flowers Called Pretty Betsey in England, where you see it in summer beside the railroad tracks. Fragrant.	Grow in sun or shade. Poor soil keeps it from spreading too much. Self-sows.
Verbena or vervain *Verbena hastata*	This perennial verbena is native to North America, and comes in purple, pink or white flowers growing on spikes.	Blooms in late summer. Does best near water. Most verbenas are annual. (See annuals).
Sand verbena *Abronia umbellata*	Grows to 6 inches, with fragrant pink heads of flowers. Good for hanging baskets. Can also be planted in masses and used for a groundcover.	Drought resistant; good for seashore gardens; likes sandy loam. Start seeds early. Often treated as an annual.

Name	Description	Comment
Veronica (See Speedwell)		
Violet *Viola odorata*	Excellent garden flower, hardy and handsome, often blooming both spring and fall. Try varieties: 'Rosina', rosy pink; 'Royal Robe', deep violet-blue; 'White Czar', large white; 'Parma', is double.	Blooms April, May. Rich loam, sun or shade. Will grow where it is moist. Or almost anywhere, but it does best in part shade.
V. priceana	This is the Confederate violet, blue and white. Native to the Eastern states.	A vigorous and spreading violet. Good for groundcover. Self-sows from the basal, inconspicuous fertile green flower.
Horned violet (See Tufted pansy)		
Virginia Bluebell *Mertensia virginica*	A lovely spring flower, blue with a little pink, growing to 2 feet, or higher in good soil. The buds are pink, and the hummingbirds come as soon as the flowers open.	Blooms in April or May. Sun or shade. Self-sows. Is hardy to Zone 3. The plant dies down in summer.

to do well in the Northern states; mullein, and hound's tongue.

A biennial, as the name implies, takes two years to grow from seed to flower, growing green leaves the first year—like parsley and carrots—and coming into flower, fruit, seeds the second year. Then they usually die. It is the custom to plant biennial seed in the late spring and early summer, the earlier the better, to get well-established plants by winter, though pansies and wallflowers do poorly if too large. In cold climates, keep biennials over the winter in a cold frame. In mild climates they can stay out for the winter, after being transplanted from the flats or nursery bed. Most of the ones growing at my place seed themselves and winter out very well. These include forget-me-nots, foxgloves and hollyhocks, and sometimes sweet William.

HOW TO MEET SPECIAL NEEDS

If you have a damp area, you will need to be careful about which perennials to choose. I'd recommend: astilbe, bee balm, blue flag, cardinal flower, crested iris, ferns, forget-me-not, Joe-pye-weed, a tall handsome purplish flower; lily-of-the-valley, loosestrife, marsh marigold, primroses, especially polyanthus; sneezeweed, swamp milkweed, a smaller cousin of common milkweed; swamp rose-mallow, vinca, violets and yellow flag. Some of those, like the flags, swamp milkweed and marsh marigold will endure quite a lot of water.

If, on the other hand, your soil is poor, dry or sandy, there are flowers suitable for such spots, too. I'd recommend: asters, especially New England aster; butterfly weed, California poppy, camomile, centaurea montana, dianthus, flowering spurge, gaillardia, goldenglow, godetia, lupine, phlox, poppymallow, potentilla, sneezewort, statice, steel globe thistle, tickseed, verbena and yucca.

The shady garden is discussed in another chapter, but among the perennials you can have in shade or part shade are: hardy ageratum, alkanet, astilbe, begonia, bleeding heart, caladium, coleus, columbine, coral bells, lily-of-the-valley, lobelia, periwinkle, plumbago, primroses, torenia, vincas and violets.

THE LONG-BLOOMING GARDEN

Perhaps the most pressing special need for the modern organic gardener is to have a garden full of more or less trouble-free flowers that will bloom a long time and more or less take care of themselves. The following charts give suggestions which will be useful in making choices to fit that need.

PERENNIALS WITH LONG BLOOMING PERIODS

Name	Description and Comment	Blooming Period
Alpine catchfly *Silene alpestris*	White, 6 inches, also a double variety	Blooms all summer
Aster *A. x. fricartii* Wonder of Stafa	1½ to 2 feet, fragrant blue flowers	Blooms July to Nov.
Astilbe hybrids *A. arendsii*	Plumy flowers	June to Aug.
Avens, Chilean *Geum chiloense* Also *G. montamum*	Orange	May to Oct.
Baby's breath *Gypsophila paniculata*	White; keep clipped; best variety is 'Bristol Fairy'	July to Oct.
Balloon flower *Platycodon grandiflora*	Blue, white or pink	June to Sept.
Bee balm *Monarda didyma*	Red, fragrant	June to Aug.
Bell flower *Campanula punctata* and *C. poscharskyana*	Whitish lilac — Trailing form; wall plant	June to Aug. — May to Oct.
Blue Cupid's Dart *Catananche coerulea*	Sow in March indoors; blooms the first year	June to Aug.
Bouncing Bet *Saponaria officinalis*	Pale pink	Blooms all summer, especially at night
Butterfly weed *Asclepias tuberosa*	Beautiful orange much sought after by butterflies especially the Monarch	July to Sept.

Name	Description and Comment	Blooming Period
Camomile *Anthemis nobilis*	Fragrant	May to Oct.
Centaurea *Centaurea dealbata*	Red and white cornflower type	June to Oct.
C. montana *C. montana citrina*	Blue Yellow	May to July April to June
Cinquefoil *Potentilla aurea verna* *P. fruiticosa*	Golden yellow Bush type, many varieties, pest-free	Blooms all summer June to Sept.
Clove pink *Dianthus caryophillis*	Like carnation	June to Nov.
Coneflower *Rudbeckia californica*	Purplish	July to Sept.
Coral bells *Heuchera sanguinea*	Red, pink or white	May or June to Sept.
Coreopsis *C. auriculata nana*	Small creeper	June to Sept.
Cranesbill *Geranium armenium*	Carmine red and reddish Herb Robert	Blooms all summer Also blooms all summer
Cream scabious *Scabiosa ochroleuca*	One to two feet: also Caucasian & Japanes scabiosa	June to Sept.
Eryngium *E. amethystinum* *E. bracteatum*	Thistle like Practically jet black	July to Sept.
Evening Primrose *Oenothera speciosa* *O. missouriana*	Yellow flowers	July to Sept.; blooms all summer
False dragonhead *Physostegia virginiana*	Also called Obedient plant. Lavender spikes	July to Sept.
Feverfew *Chrysanthemum parthenium* *C. matricaria*	Small white daisy Fragrant, like camomile	Blooms all summer Blooms all summer
Flax *Linum perenne and Linum flavum*	Delicate blue flowers Yellow	June to Aug. June to Aug.
Fuchsia hybrids	Hanging plants, etc. *F. riccartonii* is good	Blooms all summer
Funkia *Hosta lancifolia*	Large leaves, lavender flowers, etc.	Varieties bloom July to Sept.
Gaillardia *G. Grandiflora*	Big daisy-like flowers yellow and orange	June to frost

Name	Description and Comment	Blooming Period
Garden helitrope *Valeriana officinalis*	Old-fashioned flower	June to Oct.
Gayfeather *Liatris pycnostachya*	Purple flowers from Kansas	July to Oct.
Globe flower *Trollius americana*	Buttercup family	May to June then on and off all summer
Gloriosa daisy, double *Rudbeckia laciniata hortensia*	Also called Golden Glow	July to Sept.
Golden columbine, *Aquilegia chrysantha*	From the Rocky Mts.	May to July
Golden marguerite *Anthemis tinctoria*	Prolific, sturdy. Several varieties in different yellows	July to Sept. (or longer if warm climate)
Groundsel, or Dusty miller *Senecio cineraria*	Daisy-like, yellow	All summer
Harebell *Campanula carpatica* *C. rotundifolia*	Lovely blue	June to Aug.
Jacob's ladder *Polemonium coeruleum*	Blue and other colors	May to July or June to Aug.
Johnny-jump-up *Viola tricolor*	Tiny pansies and they self-sow	June to Oct.
Lamb's ear *Stachys coccinea*	This is the red one	June to Aug.
Lantana *L. camara*	Red or yellow sage; used for hanging baskets and in warm zones	Can bloom all year
Lobelia *L. fulgens* (red) *L. syphilitica* (blue)	Likes moisture	July to Sept.
Loosestrife *Lythrum salicaria*	Rather weedy, grows in marshes, purple flowers	June to Sept.
Lupine, yellow *L. polyphyllus*	Pea family	June to Sept.
Meadow rue *Thalictrum dipterocarpum*	Try the yellow one, *T. flavum*, large sprays	June to Aug.
Merck dahlia *D. merckii*	From Mexico, bulb plant; grows two feet	July to Sept.
Mullein *Verbascum longifolium*	Several cultivated mulleins, try 'Cotswold Gem'	June to Sept.
Penstemon *P. barbatus* *P. gloxinoides* 'Firebird'	Handsome tubular flowers, hardy to Zone 6	June to Aug. June to frost
Perennial Pea *Lathyrus latifolius*	This spreads, is viny	All summer

Name	Description and Comment	Blooming Period
Plaintain lily (See Funkia)		
Red hot poker *Kniphofia uvaria*	Red, yellow and mixed stalks of bright flowers (Rhizome plant)	July to Sept.
Rose, floribunda	Many colors; many flowers	This is the long-blooming one
Salvia, S. *superba*	Sometimes called Purple Glory sage	June to Sept.
Sea campion *Silene maritima*		Blooms all summer
Shasta daisy *Chrysanthemum maximum*	Many beautiful varieties; try 'Victor'; 'Little Miss Muffet'; a compact dwarf good for edging	"Everblooming"; keep picked
Siberian wallflower *Cheiranthus cheiri* *C. allioni*	Not for the coldest zones; treated as biennial in England	Planted in early spring, will bloom July to Nov.
Silvery cinquefoil *Potentilla* 'Mons Rouillard'	Maroon flowers	June to Aug.
Snakeroot *Cimicifuga racemosa*	White flowers	June to Aug.
Sneezewort *Achillea ptarmica* 'The Pearl'	Small white buttons Excellent for dried arrangements	Blooms all summer
Speedwell *Veronica alpina alba;* *V. spicata*	Flowers in dense clusters	Blooms all summer June to Sept.
Spiderwort *Tradescantia virginiana*	White, blue, violet flowers	Blooms all summer
St. John's wort (Aaron's beard) *Hypericum calycinum*	Three-inch yellow flowers, or other sizes on other varieties ('Sungold', 'Hidcote', etc.)	July to Oct. or all summer
Statice *Statice latifolia*	Also called sea lavender; good for dried flowers	July to Sept.
Stokes aster *Stokesia laevis*	Light blue	June to frost
Stonecrop *Sedum* in variety	Select several varieties; include S. *spectabile* for fall bloom	All season—May to June; June to July; Aug. to frost
Sundrops *Oenothera fruticosa*	Yellow flowers	June to Aug.
Sunflower *Heliopsis scabra*	Try the new hybrid, 'Gold Greenheart'	July to Sept.
Sunray flower *Inula orientalis*	Related to elecampine, often quite big	Aug. to Oct.

Name	Description and Comment	Blooming Period
Sweet rocket *Hesperis matronalis*	Pink, white or purple	Blooms all summer
Tickseed *Coreopsis grandiflora*	Big yellow daisy-like flower	Aug. to Sept.
Transvaal daisy *Gerbera jamesonii* hybrids	Excellent colors	July to Sept. Only for warm zones or greenhouse
Treasure flower *Gazania splendens*	Treated as an annual, but take cuttings in fall to set out the next spring	June to Sept.
Trumpet flower *Incarvillea sinensis variabilis*	This has pink flowers and is rather shrubby	All summer, the first summer
Tunic flower *Tunica saxifraga rosea*	Very hardy, tufty, with flowers like pink baby's breath	July to frost
Verbena *V. hortensis*	Tender perennial. Try the red one, 'Flame'	July until frost
Violet *V. cornuta* *V. gracilis*	Use two varieties	May to Sept. May to Sept.
Yarrow *Achillea millefolium*	Several varieties, some yellow	June to Sept.
Yellow fumitory *Corydalis lutea*	Very small; likes shade; lovely fern-like foliage	May to Sept.

MONTH OF BLOOM

If you are only going to be at home at certain times, or have certain favorite seasons to have flowers in bloom, it helps to know what blooms when.

Most of the earliest flowers are bulbs, beginning to bloom in February such as winter aconite, early Cloth of Gold crocus, the bright blue scillas and the rhizomatous netted iris or the charming little yellow Danford iris. There is the Christmas rose, which might begin in January or December, and the spring heather, also beginning in January.

By April some of the flowers brought into the garden from native habitats such as bloodroot, spring beauties, Dutchman's breeches or marsh marigold, come into bloom. Also the Fringed bleeding heart and the cultivated bleeding heart come along as well as evergreen candytuft, goldentuft alyssum, rockcresses and the charming, fragrant pink Rose daphne. And lots more bulbs.

By May the garden is full of color if you grow bulbs, but there are perennials coming along, too. For instance the good groundcover, carpet bugle, sends up its blue or pink spikes, the columbine begins to bloom, English daisies dot the lawn and the bright yellow leopardbane daisies come out. Others include the first large irises, lupines, the lovely Virginia bluebells, grass pink and sweet William, perhaps in the rock garden, the many primroses and violets. The globeflower begins; the sweet woodruff does, too; and the first tree peonies start to bloom.

June is the month of flowers, too many to

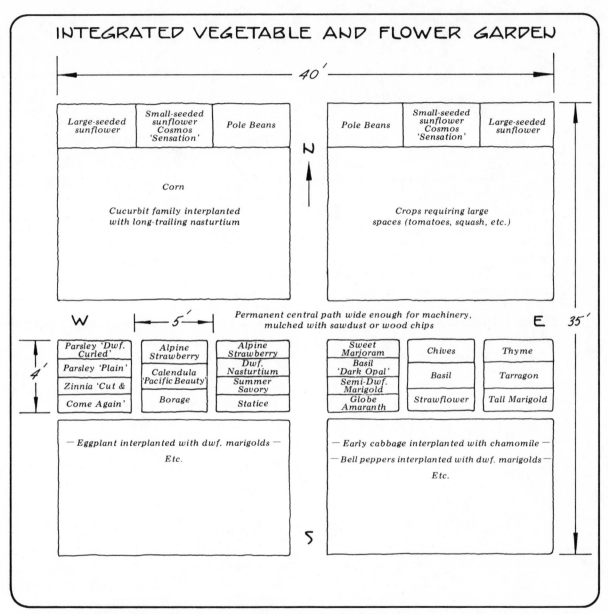

INTEGRATED VEGETABLE AND FLOWER GARDEN

← 40′ →

| Large-seeded sunflower | Small-seeded sunflower Cosmos 'Sensation' | Pole Beans |
| Pole Beans | Small-seeded sunflower Cosmos 'Sensation' | Large-seeded sunflower |

N ↑

Corn

Cucurbit family interplanted with long-trailing nasturtium

Crops requiring large spaces (tomatoes, squash, etc.)

W   ← 5′ →   Permanent central path wide enough for machinery, mulched with sawdust or wood chips   E   35′

Parsley 'Dwf. Curled'	Alpine Strawberry	Alpine Strawberry	Sweet Marjoram	Chives	Thyme
Parsley 'Plain'	Calendula 'Pacific Beauty'	Dwf. Nasturtium	Basil 'Dark Opal'	Basil	Tarragon
Zinnia 'Cut &		Summer Savory	Semi-Dwf. Marigold		
Come Again'	Borage	Statice	Globe Amaranth	Strawflower	Tall Marigold

4′

— Eggplant interplanted with dwf. marigolds —

Etc.

— Early cabbage interplanted with chamomile —
— Bell peppers interplanted with dwf. marigolds —

Etc.

S

The beds along a central path look very attractive and are easy to care for because of all-around access. The plan assumes no fence so that the garden may be entered at any point. If a fence is desired, these beds can be placed along one edge with a wide path on one side.

mention, But some I look forward to every year include the yarrows I like so much, especially *Achillea ptarmica* 'The Pearl' with its fine, buttonlike little white flowers. Larkspurs begin; the baby's breath comes out; the early daylilies start to bloom; and there are all the old favorites such as the bellflowers, bearded iris, peonies, poppies, scabious, campions, purple loosestrife, betony and the first foxgloves and avens. This is the month of rich, opulent flowers, and the flowering shrubs burst into the same kind of bloom to go with the perennials.

In July things tone down a bit, and the warmer, more subdued or bronzy colors of the gaillardias, daylilies and penstemon appear. The nice white Miss Lingard phlox comes along and there are balloon-flowers, Shasta daisies, hollyhocks and the pleasant little yellow camomile of the long warm days.

By August the turtlehead begins, and there are more blanketflowers, or gaillardias, plantain lilies, sneezeweed, plumepoppy, and the hostas come into flower. And of course this month the garden has plenty of annuals to fill out among the sunflowers, coreopsis and false dragonhead.

September brings the wonderful blues of the asters and their cultivated, hybridized varieties called Michaelmas daisies, along with the coneflowers, clump speedwell, helopsis, and the handsome dark blue monkshood. The rosemallow is still in bloom, and Joe-pye-weed and its cousin the greenish-white boneset are still in bloom, too. And chrysanthemums are beginning. And a few flowers are ready to last on until frost, or maybe a bit afterwards.

These include the Japanese anemone, white boltonia, plumbago, Siberian larkspur, most of the chrysanthemums (unless you have forced them somehow with short days or long nights), everblooming sweet-William, the sages, goldenrods and the long-blooming torchlily (a bulb). Then there is the tufted pansy, and some of the long-bloomers which seem to go on and on and on: salvias, Stokes aster, St. John's wort, verbenas and yarrow.

Supplemented by the summer bulbs, and still more annuals, the garden can suit you in every season by a judicious selection of good hardy perennials—especially if you interplant peppermint and other strong herbs to keep them healthy and pestless.

9

Annuals

Annual flowers are the joy of the gardener. Though they are short-lived and can rarely be trusted to seed themselves for another year, they are prolific and almost ardent bloomers, come in all sorts of colors and shapes, in many different heights, and in a range of easy-to-grow species. They are excellent for cut flowers and respond when you pick them with even better flowering than before. Annual flowers of many kinds are available at garden centers, chain stores and roadside stands just when you want to buy some to plant. And you can always grow them from seed yourself.

THEY ARE EASY TO GROW

Some annuals are among the easiest plants in the world to grow—for example, nasturtiums. I just pop the seeds into some fairly rich soil, water them a little, and up they come. Those that come out of a packet always grow, but if you try to grow nasturtiums from seeds just harvested you might have some trouble. I usually plant several varieties outdoors in late May, both in the flower borders where I thin them to five inches apart and in the vegetable garden near the cucumbers where I do not thin them. I have also started nasturtiums indoors just to see them growing and

to get some early blossoms, but they are badly set back when I put them out because nasturtiums really do not like to be transplanted. They take a long time to recover—as all little annuals will if they suffer a set-back of any sort—too hot a sun when small, not enough water just after germinating, or too much, or inadequate fertilizer, air or light. You have noticed, no doubt, that nasturtiums are not sold in the markets. Many of the annuals which are sold you might as well start in flats indoors yourself, such as marigolds, impatiens or annual phlox.

HOW TO PLANT ANNUAL SEEDS INDOORS

Flats are usually all right for planting annuals, if you put some drainage material in the bottom, a cable for bottom heat as needed, and sterilize the soil with a slow, low-heat pasteurization process. (See chapter on gardening techniques.) For those plants mentioned in the list at the end of this chapter which resent transplanting, use peat pots or Jiffy pellets for planting your seeds. Where soaking is indicated on the seed packet, be sure to do this, because you not only save time by softening the seed coat with a good soaking, but the viable little plant that gets started will be stronger and more able to cope with enemies if the seed did not linger, ungerminated, in the damp earth of the flat.

Do not cover the seed with too much soil. If the directions on the packet say ½ of an inch, put on that much. If they say do not cover at all, do not. Simply push the seed down into the potting mixture. To be on the safe side, a potting mixture can be topped with milled sphagnum moss, or fine sand, or with a thin layer of vermiculite or perlite, all of which will cut down the possibility of getting the fungus disease, "damping-off". Very fine seeds can be mixed with sand before you sprinkle them on the flat. In this way you avoid the very thick planting that is hard to avoid with tiny seeds. Use glass or plastic over the flat until germination and bottom heat if indicated. As soon as you see the plants coming, take it off because then air is more important than moisture. The air helps prevent damping-off, and so do vermiculite or milled sphagnum moss mulch. You can always water the flat from below if necessary.

CARE OF SEEDLINGS

Your potting mixture will have been fairly rich, and the nutrients in it will have supported your litte plants well when they first shoot up. But the soil in flats or little peat pots is shallow, and the nutrients soon exhausted, even though you use slow-release fertilizers like compost and rock minerals. To maintain continuous growth keep providing nutrients at least once a week, but it is best to use materials not too high in nitrogen because you do not want your little plants to grow all to green, with big plentiful leaves at the expense of stems, roots and flowers. It is especially important to control the nitrogen level of annuals that are going to be transplanted to the rock garden.

As the time comes near for setting out your plants, begin to introduce them into the outside climate. Start on a warmish afternoon and put them out in a partially shaded place for a short while. Repeat this each day that the weather is favorable, increasing the number of minutes in direct sunlight. If you have a place that can be quickly shaded, you can start them outdoors in the morning, too. But beware of that hot overhead sun at midday. If you have a cold frame, flats of annuals can be acclimatized or hardened by a gradual lifting of the lid so that they get used to the cold air of spring days outside the frame. Plants moved from indoors to a cold frame must be protected from intense overhead sun, also, if the weather is warm.

The principle behind all of these methods is the same: keep your young plants steadily growing in their ability to withstand the kinds of weather they meet in the outdoors in the garden. Continuous growth and continuous hardening equip them for a sturdy mature life, with plenty of bloom and disease-resistant strength. Those plants which will benefit from pinching back should have their lead bud removed. Snapdragons and petunias, for example, are greatly benefited by this practice. See advice, however, in the list at the end of the chapter for some varieties which should not be pinched back.

PLANTING OUT

When the weather has warmed up and the soil is prepared, choose a cloudy day to set out your young annuals in their permanent place. If there are no cloudy days, do your transplanting in the evening. Have the garden soil enriched with compost and bone meal for those plants which need rich soil, or have some stone chips or sand ready for those needing a sparse diet. To reduce the shock effect of transplanting it is a good idea to have some compost tea or mild fish emulsion mixture ready to pour into the hole when you have it dug and before you fit in the young plant. Then spread out the roots very carefully and sprinkle on the garden soil as

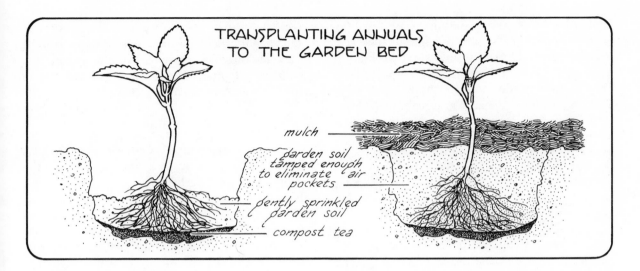

TRANSPLANTING ANNUALS
TO THE GARDEN BED

mulch

garden soil
tamped enough
to eliminate air
pockets

gently sprinkled
garden soil

compost tea

gently as possible, but tamp it down enough so that no air pockets are left around the roots and so that the root hairs can stretch out and easily touch the solution which will nourish the plant.

PROTECTION

If there is a hot sun the first few days your transplants are out, put up a little shade. Shade can be a fold of newspaper, fastened down so it won't blow away; or a hot cap; or some brush stuck into the ground at an angle that will cast a shadow on the young plants. If it is very windy, protection will be needed, too, especially when it is a hot wind.

LATER CARE

Well-started annuals are so strong they hardly need much care for the rest of the season. The most important thing to do is to water the ground around them if it is very hot and dry, though in many instances, a good mulch will hold in just about all the moisture you need. More fertilizer is needed whenever plants seem to have stopped growing. More pinching back if they get spindly. And you always need to keep

the deadheads cut off so that the plants will continue to bloom and not put all their strength instead into making seeds.

As the season ends and your annuals stop blooming, pull them up and put the spent plants on or into the compost heap. Those aromatic pest-repellent plants which still give off aromas even after they stop blooming can of course be left in the garden until frost and fall clean-up. I also make sprays in the blender from some of these aromatic plants, and store the spray essence in the freezer along with the herb butters I make, to preserve good annual herbs before the frosts come to nip them to death.

❧PLANTS STARTED OUTDOORS❧

Some annuals do very well if the seeds are planted right out in the garden where you want them to grow. These include such good edgers as sweet alyssum, baby's breath, bachelor's button, candytuft, cape-marigold and other marigolds if dwarf, annual larkspur, nasturtium, annual phlox and poppies, little portulacas, dwarf sweet peas and the little zinnias. Some of the taller ones which can be planted out in the garden include baby-blue-eyes, garden balsam, blue lace flower, campios, calleopsis or annual tickseed, golden cup, lupine, sunflower, kochia or summer cypress, and tree-mallow. (Some plants that definitely do need to be started early indoors in order to make any season of bloom worth talking about, however, include: ageratum, beard-tongue, butterfly flower, cigar flower, annyal Unwin hybrid dahlias, globe amaranth, lobelias, petunias, pinks, poppy-mallow, scabious, snapdragons, statice, and for good long seasons, wax begonia and wishbone flower.)

The hazards of starting seeds outdoors are two: insufficient water, either for germination or for the tiny seedlings when they first appear; and hot sun. There is less danger of damping-off outdoors because there is usually enough air stirring to prevent the growth of that fungus.

There are on the market now arrangements made of plastic similar to the glass structures used by the English and French for so long called *cloches*. (pronounced to rhyme with bosh.) These are like tiny greenhouses which fit over the row of small plants to protect them. They will keep out the cold, keep in the moisture, and if properly darkened or shaded, will protect the plants from hot sun. Unless it is fairly cool when you use them, they may be more trouble than they are worth because little plants are quite vulnerable to too much heat and moisture all at once, and you might easily get damping-off troubles if it gets muggy under the *cloche*. Thin the plants as directed on the packet. If you can't distinguish your good plants from weeds, grow some indoors a little earlier and get acquainted.

FERTILIZER

It is not important to keep track of the supply of nutrients for annuals started outdoors as for those you plant in flats indoors. The earth itself, especially if you have prepared the bed well, will keep supplying nutrients, and the water table will keep supplying the water to carry them to the neighborhood of the plant's root-hairs. If they dawdle, however, you can always supply a cautious side-dressing of compost or give them a special watering of compost tea.

TEMPERATURE

I believe that temperature is not so important a factor outdoors as it is indoors, where the proper germinating heat is often crucial, and a flat with an electric cable to bring the soil up to that heat almost a necessity. Many annuals germinate best at temperatures in the range of 68° to 80°F. Often the air temperature they prefer is between 70° and 75°F. If they grow too fast—and plants grown under unusual conditions are likely to—reduce the heat to 55° to 60°F., and keep them near to any artificial overhead light you use. In an outdoor hotbed, let in cool air. Outdoors in the garden fast growth and spindliness are not so likely to occur unless you are providing too much nitrogen.

SELF-SEEDERS

We usually grow quite a few of our annuals in the vegetable garden, and in rows that might be called a cutting garden. Since the ground is plowed up or tilled every year in that area, there is not much chance for self-seeders. But in other gardens, what a bonus it is to find that some of the annuals have taken care of replanting themselves, and have sent up new and usually very sturdy little plants for you. Those you might expect to provide you that bonus include: ageratum, if conditions are right, sweet alyssum, baby's breath, bachelor buttons, browallia, California poppies, candytuft, the elegant clarkia, cosmos, four o'clocks if warm enough, hollyhocks, annual larkspur, nicotiana, petunias, spider flower, even some of the marigolds and snapdragons. Sunflowers seem to self-seed, but I have found whole little mounds of sunflower seeds buried together at the edge of a border, which I feel pretty sure were put there not by the plant but by a chipmunk. They had been swiped from a bird-feeder probably, and since we feed the birds (and chipmunks therefore) all year around, we have volunteer sunflower plants coming up in every garden, and sometimes they get started in the lawn besides.

FALL PLANTING

A good time-saver for busy gardeners is to plant some of your annuals during the fall, so they lie dormant over the winter and can come up in the spring when the weather warms up. This strategy is especially valuable for those of us who live in climates where the soil takes a long time to dry off enough to work it in the spring. For using this strategy, however, you must pick those annuals which are not tender perennials treated as annuals. But some of the good old garden favorites are among the list of possibilities.

I'd recommend that you try alyssum, annual phlox, bachelor's buttons, balsam *Impatiens balsamina* candytuft, cosmos, flowering tobacco, larkspur, poppies like Shirley and California poppies, snapdragon, sweet William and other annual members of the pink family, sweet peas and violas. It might even be worth it to try planting some marigolds outdoors in the fall; they might or might not come up the following spring. A friend of mine who practices this kind of early planting simply broadcasts the seeds and immediately covers them with brush and twigs to protect them until the ground is frozen. Then she removes the branches and puts down a very thin, rather porous winter mulch. Once in a while she also plants sweet peas the autumn before, though she usually merely prepares the trench, and trusts the sweet peas to zoom up in early spring as soon as she plants them.

This way of planting is not only a time-saver,

of course. You get earlier blooms, and you also get nice, sturdy plants. The cold-treatment seems to make them very sturdy, as I have noticed often in the snapdragons, johnny-jump-ups, and sometimes petunias that have come up by themselves. If I lived in the warm South or in a warm part of California, I would sow all those annuals in January, plus such others as clarkia, flax, godetia, love-in-a-mist, lupine, pot marigold and sweet sultan. And I'd start tender bulbs, too, such as gold band lilies and glads and tuberous begonias.

SPECIAL EFFECTS, COLOR

Sometimes I use annuals all by themselves in a bed; sometimes I combine them with perennials, or use them to make shade over the roots of bulbs like lilies when they need it in the hot sun. Except for the suitability of the site to the plant, there is nothing that concerns a gardener more in a flower bed than the right color in the right place. Most easy are the white flowers because they go with everything and brighten up any part of the garden where you put them. I like big white African daisies, but I am also partial to edgings of candytuft and low white impatiens. In the middle of a bed, or along under the edge of the porch you can put flowering tobacco. Grow plenty, so that you can feel free to grind up a plant now and again to add to your sprays. Delicate white cosmos, tall white hollyhocks and cascades of white petunias over stone walls or out of hanging baskets on the terrace wall are all very good-looking additions to the garden.

Where a warm color is needed, clumps of calliosis are very useful—and the pleasant yellow of California poppies will spruce a darkish corner. So will marigolds, snapdragons and to fill a tall space, so will sunflowers. Some of the nasturtiums are a bright cheerful yellow, and evening primroses of the annual sort are gentle and delicate. With the yellows a bright touch of orange in other varieties of cosmos, marigold, nasturtium and some of the poppies will supplement orange tassel flower and lantana.

If pink is what you prefer, there are many choices, from pink asters and ageratum, to the sprightly carnations and sweet Williams (really a biennial) the lupines, meadow foam, sweet peas, some of the verbenas and the tall Princes feather. Together or mixed, annuals provide wonderful color.

SPECIAL EFFECTS, ANNUAL VINES

If you want very tall annuals, aside from such big ones as castor bean, cosmos, hollyhock and spider flower, you can grow vines. I usually start some 'Heavenly Blue' morning glories indoors because I like to see them in bloom in the kitchen around the heated, lighted flat in front of the east window. Those get to be too advanced to transplant well, but I start others later to put out after the ground is warm. Other vines to try are balsam vines called balsam-apple and balsam pear, *Momordica balsamina* and *M. charantia*, annuals which can grow to 20 or 30 feet in a season. They both have long yellow flowers, one to four inches, and oval fruits which burst to show their seeds. Balsam-pear has somewhat larger leaves and fruits. These are tender tropical plants which cannot stand cold.

Other annual vines include the popular clockvine, *Thunbergia alata*, with striking small flowers of white to orange and purple throats, which bloom all summer. Like the balsam vines, this vine, too, should be started early indoors in March. There is also the cypress vine, now naturalized in the Middle West, started indoors or outdoors in May, with bright red flowers, in several available varieties, besides one that is white and one that is pinkish. The hybrid variety *Quamoclit sloteri* will bloom with red and white flowers from July to September. *Ipomea*

purpurea, the common morning glory, is a delight, whether the clear bright blue of 'Heavenly Blue' or the striped blue and white of 'Flying Saucers', the pure white of 'Pearly Gates' or the red of 'Scarlet O'Hara' and the lavender of 'Wedding Bells'. I like them all, and enjoy the combinations of colors you can get from growing two or three varieties together on a stone wall or wherever you want them to grow. They open fresh flowers every morning.

Even more useful are climbing nasturtiums, *Tropaeolum peltophorum* with orange flowers and *T. peregrinium*, sometimes called Canary nasturtium, with lovely pale one-inch yellow flowers, a fast climber. There is another with yellow flowers, *T. polyphyllum*, which is a perennial grown as an annual. These handsome plants can be used as pest-repellents as well as for decorative purposes, and of course their leaves, flowers and green seeds are edible.

Other very decorative flowering vines I recommend are the scarlet runner bean and sweet peas. The bean is *Phaseolus coccineus*, and it has the advantage of being a perennial that will live over the winter in Zones 8, 9 and 10. It is a charming vine, with good green leaves, but not so wonderful as sweet peas, *Lathyrus odoratus*, which have been bred for size and for ruffles and for large numbers of bloom on one stem.

The moonflower vine, *Calonyction aculeatum*, is another which is annual in the North, but perennial in the South. It has huge white flowers, six inches across on a long, often six-inch tube. They bloom at night and are fragrant. Some people combine them with other vines so as to have bloom night and day. They go well with 'Scarlet O'Hara' or 'Heavenly Blue' morning glories. They do best if planted indoors in peat pots in March and put out after frost is gone. Another vine to start indoors is the cup-and-saucer vine, *Cobaea scandens*, which is also grown in the South as a perennial. It has bellflower-shaped blossoms, about two inches across, in lilac or purple, on 12-inch stems. It will grow 15 or 20 feet in a single season, but up to 40 feet as a perennial. The blooms will go on and on for six months where the weather is favorable. When you plant the seeds, put them in the earth with the flat sides sideways and thin edges up and down. They seem to grow best this way.

EXTRA POSSIBILITIES

Well-formed, stocky annuals—especially those from the more tender varieties ordinarily started indoors—can be grown outdoors from seeds planted a bit later than you ordinarily plant annual seeds out in the garden. If they stand pinching, keep them pinched back to make them sturdy and stocky. Then in the fall, since they will not have bloomed, pot them up to bring in for winter flowering plants. A great boon to have.

Another boon comes from some of the perennials which you can treat as annuals, such as the forget-me-nots that sow themselves and come up each year as new, seemingly annual plants. Just let them take care of themselves. Then there are the rather new, small delphiniums called 'Connecticut Yankee', which can be sown yearly and used as low-growing plants for the border where they often fit in better than the tall ones and take less care and staking. Some of the penstemons and campanulas are treated as annual, and so is the dusty miller that is a centauria, *Centauria cineraria*. In fact, some of our most common border flowers are really perennials, even though we have always thought of them as annuals. One of those, the four o'clock, which I grew as a child, always surprises me when I remember to think of it as a perennial—so deep is the impression I always had that it was an annual which came up each year as I planted it. Now that I know it is also

called Marvel of Peru, it is more logical to me that a more or less tropical flower can be perennial in its own country, but has to be treated as an annual up here.

ANNUALS ARE USEFUL

Annuals are valuable to organic gardeners because they are practically pestless—or are, in themselves, good pest repellents. The pungent repellents such as marigolds, camomile, fever-few, and nasturtium are good for every garden—even if they are the only annuals in the garden. But I hope all gardeners can find room also for some cosmos, calendula, salvia and soapwort, even if it is a bit weedy and needs to be controlled. Zinnias may get some pests on them, or some mildew, but make garlic sprays and get rid of the invaders if they seriously affect the plants. Also permit the spiders to stay in their big webs, if you are lucky enough to have such helpful scavengers visit your zinnias.

All these annuals are excellent to use as cut flowers. Petunias are long-time favorites and it is essential to keep these flowers picked in order to keep them blooming all summer. I like the smell of marigolds and use them a great deal for indoors arrangements. It is an extra bonus that the branches of marigold that you pick and put in a pin-holder in a shallow container will root very easily, and then you have propagated a new plant to put out again, or pot up for late fall blooming, for a month or so after frost. Potted marigolds are also good to have on hand so you can move them to trouble spots if you see infestations on any of your other flowers. Be sure not to leave the pots in the hot sun without sufficient watering.

Some annuals are very good for drying. Strawflowers only need to be hung in a dark, warm place; and be sure to pick them before they are fully out, for they will continue to open after picking. Others such as zinnias, marigolds,

(*continued on page 217*)

GOOD ANNUALS TO GROW FOR COLOR, STURDINESS AND LONG BLOOM

Name	Description	Comment
African Daisy *Arctotis grandis* (See also Cape Marigold)	Silvery leaves and white petals. Centers almost black. Grows to 24 inches.	Full sun, and a hot, dry place. Start seeds indoors, as late as April.
Ageratum *A. houstonianum*	Usually a fluffy blue flower, though there are pink and white ones, too. Three sizes: 18-inches; 12-inches and dwarf, five inches. Varieties to try: 'Blue Ball Improved', 'Blue Bedder', 'Blue Mink', 'Tall Blue' and 'Fairy Pink' and 'Silver Star'. A good tall one is the 2½-foot 'Mexicanum.	Start seeds indoors Feb. or in March, in sterilized soil. Pinch for sturdy branching and for full bloom, If deadheads are taken off, will bloom all summer. For late fall bloom, start some more seeds outdoors in May, June. It self-seeds, too.
Alyssum; Sweet alyssum *Lobularia maritima or* *Alyssum maritimum*	A one-foot plant which will grow as a perennial in some places. Mounds, with many small flowers; good edger or bedder. Varieties to try: Carpet of Snow', 'Little Gem', 'Royal Carpet', 'Tetra Snowdrift', 'Violet Queen', with colors as suggested. Shearing helps to keep mound shape and to promote good bloom.	Sow outdoors early, and get blooms in a few weeks. Blooms all summer thereafter, especially if you fill out with a second sowing in June. Thin to five inches apart. Pot up, shear and bring in for winter house plant. Pre-chill seeds if they are fresh-gathered. Poor to good soil.
Aster, Annual *Callistephus chinensis* Many varieties including Cactus, Massagno Cactus, Crego or Ostrich Feather, Powder Puff and Singles.	The colors are pinks, reds, lavenders, purples and white, and sizes run from three-foot supergiants to six-inch dwarf and four-inch carpet asters. Wonderful cut flower, lasting a couple of weeks if the room is cool and the water changed.	Blooms from Aug. to frost. New improved varieties are wilt-resistant. 'Dwarf Kerkwell' is a variety to grow indoors in the spring. Sow in Feb. Shallow rooted. Keep well watered.
Baby's Breath *Gypsophila elegans* and *G. muralis*	Delicate white flowers growing to 12 or 18 inches. *G. muralis* is a cushion type.	Plant outdoors in April, for it is quite difficult to transplant satisfactorily. Often self-sows. For longer bloom resow in May, June, July.
Bachelor's button *Centaurea cyanus* also called Cornflower	Perky many-petalled small flowers of blue, pink and white. Grows to 18 inches. Good for growing in the Southwest. Delicate woolly foliage.	Easy annual. Grows in any soil. No pests. Sow late autumn or spring. Resow to prolong the season. They often self-sow. Sun or part shade. Withstands drought.
Balsam (See impatiens)		

Name	Description	Comment
Beard-tongue *Penstemon gloxinioides*	A rather tall penstemon, growing to 24 inches or to 36 if in very fertile soil. Flowers up to two inches in red or pink. Try 'Firebird', 'Garnet' or 'Ruby Red'.	Plant outdoors in spring. Can be potted up and saved for the winter. Also cuttings can be started for another year, so it is actually a perennial treated as an annual.
Begonia, Fibrous-rooted (See Chapter 7)		Plant seeds in Feb.
Bellflower, Annual Canterbury Bells *Campanula ramosissima*	Small, 12-inch plants with blue bell-shaped blooms. *C. drabifolia* is taller, later blooming.	Plant indoors in March. Outdoors they need full sun and rich loam soil. Sometimes self-sow. Slow-growers.
Bells of Ireland *Molucella laevis*	Not very handsome green plant with disk corollas on and around the stem. Tiny white flowers fade away and leave these bells. Then the dried plant is very decorative for dried arrangements.	Sow outdoors in April in full sun, good loam soil.
Browallia *B. americana*	Lovely, prolific blue flower, with small, tubular blossoms. Good for cutting and excellent for pots and hanging baskets. Can also be potted up for winter bloom. Grows to 12 inches. 'Sky Bells' is light blue.	Likes full sun and good rich soil. Sow seed indoors in April, outdoors in May or in July or Aug. for a winter plant. Do not cover seed with soil, and keep at 70°F. Pinch when six inches. Keep fertilizing with fish emulsion or compost tea.
Butterfly flower *Schizanthus pinnatus*	Also called Poor Man's Orchid, with soft, fine foliage and delicate little flowers of violet, rose and brown. Grows one foot, if dwarf; or to two or three feet in rich soil.	Start indoors in April, outdoors in May. It takes six weeks until flower; best to pinch. Easy to grow. Short, but prolific blooming period. Resow if you want to extend it.
California poppy *Eschscholtzia californica*	Orginally golden yellow poppies, now hybridized to come in pale yellow, pink, red, white. Three inches across on 12-inch plants. Varieties to try: 'Canary', 'Carmine King', 'Chrome Queen', 'Fire Flame', 'Mandarin Monarch Art Shades', 'Orange Prince', 'Rosy Queen', 'Toreador'. Good for cutting, even though the petals close at night. Singe stems as soon as cut.	Sow in Sept. or Mar. where the plants are to go. Resents transplanting. Any soil, even hot and sandy. Thin to six inches apart. Full sun. Will bloom all summer if you keep picking off the deadheads. Go easy on rich compost, but peat moss is all right, and watering is, too.

Name	Description	Comment
Calliopsis or Tickseed *Coreopsis tinctoria*	This is the common annual, with yellow, red and brown flowers, two inches across, on 24-inch stems. There are also double and dwarf varieties. Very similar to the perennial coreopsis. Try 'Crimson King'. For a larger, orange one, *C. grandiflora* grows to two feet with three-inch flowers. Behaves like a biennial.	Sow in early spring, or fall. Once started, they self-sow easily. Average soil. For long bloom, sow several times.
Camomile *Matricaria chamomilla*	Another good pest-control plant, growing to 24 inches, with small daisy-like flowers.	Helpful and attractive in any garden. Average soil.
Candytuft *Iberis affinis* *I. amara*	White, with lilac, slightly fragrant. 16 inches. Larger flowers, more fragrant. Grown by florists. Many varieties.	Plant outdoors in April; bloom mid-June to frost. Average soil. Same.
I. umbellata	Called Globe candytuft. Best for home gardeners. Flowers in round clusters, in pink, violet and reddish. Not fragrant.	Same. All should be thinned to about 12 to 16 inches apart because they spread.
Cape marigold *Dimorphotheca annua*	This handsome daisy-like, 12-inch plant with long, pointed petals of white, yellow or orange is a good, sturdy annual. Hybrids are pink and pale yellow.	Plant several times indoors or out.
D. sinuata or *D. aurantica*	White, yellow or orange. Perennial treated as annual.	Especially suited to the Southwest and other hot, dry places. Start indoors in March to assure a long, hot season for it. Can endure poor soil.
Castor bean *Ricinus communis*	Large-leaved, attractive plant to grow both for decorative and pest-repellent reasons. Moles hate it. All parts are poisonous to animals and humans. Some varieties have red leaves.	This can grow to 15 feet, or if you live in the tropics, to 40 feet. Full sun. Start indoors in April or outdoors after frost. Do not overfertilize.
Chinese forget-me-not *Cynoglossum amabile*	A biennial grown as an annual, with many small blue flowers on 18-to 24-inch plants. A related plant, *Anchusa capensis*, is deeper blue with a white throat. This is sometimes called Cape bugloss. Mass for best effect.	Average soil, and they bloom all summer, from June to frost. Start indoors in March and put in a warm, sunny place. Does well in hot, dry places. Sometimes self-sows.

Name	Description	Comment
Chrysanthemum, annual	There are several species: *C. carinatum* is tricolor; *C. coronarium* is tall or dwarf, white or yellow, single or double; *C. segetum* is yellow and the most popular: 'Eastern Star' is pale yellow; 'Evening Star', darker yellow; 'White Star', cream-colored. The blossoms are 2½ inches across; the plants two to three feet high.	Plant in April and pinch back for better bloom. These need sun and very good drainage.
Clarkia *C. elegans*	Lovely colors of salmon, rose, crimson or purple to white. Grows 12 to 36 inches, and does best in the Northwest where it is cool and moist. Single or double.	Plant indoors in April or sow outdoors in fall in good garden soil. Stake if it gets tall. Sun or part shade. Blooms all summer.
Cleome or Spiderflower *C. serrulata* and *C. spinosa*	Big annuals, to three or four feet, with shaggy pink or whitish flower clusters and leafy bracts. Quite showy. Bees come.	Bloom from July to Sept. Sow seeds in April or May where the plants are to grow. Average, even poor soil.
Cockscomb *Celosia cristata* and *C. plumosa*	Crested and plumy cockscombs are attractive velvety red or yellow flowers, good in the garden and for dried arrangements. Try 'Maple Gold', 'Magnifica Crimson' for crested; and 'Fiery Feather', 'Golden Fleece', 'Golden Plume' and 'Scarlet Plume' for the plumy ones.	In average soil these plants grow to one or two feet; if overfertilized with manure tea and rock fertilizers, they grow to four feet. Do not pinch these. They do well in the Southwest. Plant outdoors in April, May. Thin to 12 to 18 inches. Very susceptible to damping-off, especially in the greenhouse. Provide good air circulation. Easy to start indoors in April.
Coleus *C. blumei*	Annual (or perennial) plant with leaves of red, green, yellow or a mixture. Blue or lilac flowers, which you can just cut off if you don't like the color-combination. Will grow to 3 feet. Reddest variety is 'Verschaffeltii'.	Start seed in Feb. or Mar. Set out when warm weather comes, and take cuttings in the fall well before frost. Good edging and pot plant, for foliage interest.
Coneflower *Rudbeckia bicolor*	Also called gloriosa daisy. Yellow with black center, single or double. To two feet. Showy five-inch flowers.	Plant early outdoors, April or early May. Thin to 18 inches apart. Average soil.

Name	Description	Comment
Cornflower (See Bachelor's button)		
Cosmos *C. sulphureus* *C. bipinnatus* and *C. diversifolius*	This group will grow to all heights up to five or six feet. Lovely open flowers, yellow, orange, red, white and lilac. Is pest repellent, and very useful in both borders and the vegetable garden. There are single and double varieties. Tolerates drought and also alkaline soil.	Plant outdoors in April or indoors in March. It sometimes self-sows. You can also try sowing it outdoors in the fall. Blooms July to frost if you use several varieties. .
Creeping zinnia *Sanvitalia procumbens*	Yellow or white flowers, on six-inch or trailing plants. Daisy-like, and there is a double variety, too.	Start indoors in March or outdoors in May or June. Very easy to grow. Likes warm, sunny places like a wall or hot corner. Blooms all summer.
Cup flower *Nierembergia caerulea* *N. frutescens*	One or two-inch flowers of white, blue or violet, cupshaped, on ten to 12-inch stems.	Good for hot areas in the Southwest, for pot plants and for borders. Sow indoors in Feb. and in the fall in the South or Southwest. Not too rich soil. Excellent drainage.
Cupid's Blue Dart *Catananche caerulea*	Though also used in the perennial garden, this 18-inch annual is useful as a yearly replacement, in borders, rock gardens and in pots. It has woolly leaves and blue ray-flowers. There is a white variety, also with two-inch flowers. The leaves grow in a rosette.	Blooms June to Aug. Sow seeds indoors in March and set out after frost. Can be used in dried arrangements.
Dahlia, Annual *D. pinnata*	These grow to 12 or 14 inches with semi-double and double flowers in various colors such as red, rose, yellow and others. Plants bushy, with good green foliage, or bronzy.	Plant early, indoors, or outdoors after frost is gone. Will bloom all summer.
Dianthus (See Pinks)		
Everlasting *Helipterum manglesii* and *H. roseum*	Clusters of small flowers whitish or yellowish. Grows to 18 inches. There is also a big Winged everlasting, *Ammobium alatum*, 36 inches, and with white flowers. Also good to dry.	This also resents transplanting. Put in sun or part shade in average soil. Very good for dried arrangements.

Name	Description	Comment
Farewell-to-Spring *Godetia amoena* and *G. grandiflora*	A lovely somewhat difficult pink or white or crimson flower, 18 to 24 inches tall with sparkling, open and large-petaled flowers.	Likes cool, rich soil, part shade. Plant outdoors in April. Never let it get a setback.
Felicia or Kingfisher daisy *F. bergeriana*	Startlingly blue daisy, eight inches tall, very good for front of border or window boxes.	Blooms July to Oct. Start seeds indoors in March or outdoors in May.
Feverfew *Chrysanthemum parthenium*	Daisy-like, but small. White, pungent. Grows to 12 or up to 30 inches.	Excellent pest repellent. Average soil. Really a perennial. Sun or shade.
Flax, Flowering *Linum grandiflorum*	This flax has red flowers, others have blue. Graceful plants to 24 inches.	Slow growing, but plant outdoors in April. Average soil, sun or part shade. For longer bloom, make several plantings.
Flowering tobacco *Nicotiana alata*	A lovely, prolific, sweet-smelling flower, growing up to 30 inches with trumpet blossoms, white flushed pink or pink. Fragrant at night. Try new variety: 'Nick-Nick' also *N. sanderae*, red, and the one which is open in the day: 'Sensation Daylight'. Black light traps can be put near these plants, which also attract moths of cabbage worms, etc.	Plant indoors in Mar. or outdoors in April or May. Average soil. Sun or part shade. It often self-sows. Will endure acid soil. If you transplant nicotiana, do it on a cloudy day. It can be potted up for more bloom indoors in winter. *N affinis* is most fragrant.
Forget-me-not *Myosotis dissitiflora*	Annual forget-me-nots grow to 12 inches. They come in both blue and pink, and should be spaced about six inches apart.	Sow several times, starting in April, indoors. Will self-sow also.
Four O'clock *Mirabilis jalapa*	This very satisfactory warm-weather annual is a perennial in tropical America, and is also called Marvel of Peru. Its two-inch funnel-shaped flowers are yellow, pink or white. Liked by hummingbirds.	Plant outdoors in May, in light, well-drained soil. Full sun. Will do well in poor or sandy soil. Fleshy roots can be stored over the winter and replanted.

Name	Description	Comment
Gaillardia *G. amblyodon* *G. pulchella*	A brownish-reddish daisy-like flower, two feet tall and very rugged. *G. pulchella* is yellow or purplish.	Plant outdoors in April. Thrives anywhere, even in poor soil.
Globe amaranth *Gomphrena globosa*	An old garden favorite, growing 24 inches high, with salmon, magenta or white blooms rather like clover.	Soak seeds overnight and plant outdoors in May, but you can also start the seeds indoors in March. Good for dried arrangements.
Goldencup or Tulip poppy *Hunnemannia fumariaefolia*	This soft yellow flower has shiny three-inch cups, on two-foot stems, and the variety 'Sunlite' is double. Comes from Mexico.	Plant seed outdoors in May. In South, it can be grown as a perennial. Likes lime.
Goldenwave *Coreopsis drummondii*	Yellow daisy, which grows to two feet. Like perennial, with fine foliage.	Plant outdoors in fall or in April in cold areas.
Groundsel, Purple *Senecio elegans*	An 18-inch plant with purple or rose flowers blending to white, rather like cineraria blooms, but double.	Plant inside in March or outside as early as ground is ready. Put in a cool, moist area.
Harebell phacelia *Phacelia campanularia*	A bright blue California native, which will bloom from July first until frost. Good for window boxes.	Plant April 1 for July 1 bloom. Put in full sun, and add peat moss if in boxes, but soil not too rich.
Heliotrope *Heliotropium curassavicum*	Also called Seaside Heliotrope. Grows to six inches, is creeping, and has spikes of little blue or white blooms all summer and into fall.	Related to tall heliotrope used in pots and hanging baskets, the one that is fragrant.
Hollyhock, Annual *Althaea rosea*	Tall, up to six or seven feet, with rose, pink or white flowers, and big coarse leaves.	Plant outdoors in March or April. In Far South will bloom the year around. Is resistant to drought.
Impatiens *I. balsamina*	Also called Touch-me-not, and a popular garden plant. It comes in white, pink, rose, red, apricot and orange. Grows to two to three feet, usually two. Flowers near stem.	Start in Feb. or March indoors. Needs bottom heat, constant moisture and five to twenty days to come up. Outside it needs at least partial shade, and will grow in almost full shade (but good light). Can be potted for a house plant. Cuttings are easy to root in water almost any time.
Sultan's balsam *I. sultani* This is now called simply Impatience, or Impatiens.	Is also popular. Red, 1½-inch flowers on succulent plants of one to 2½ feet. Other colors now available are pink, pur-	

Name	Description	Comment
Sultan's balsam (cont'd)	ple, salmon and white. Also comes in dwarf sizes. Remarkably persistent bloomers. The new 'Cyclone Hybrids' from Iowa are very sturdy, some with pale green or variegated foliage.	
Kochia (See Summer Cypress)		
Lantana *L. camara*	A shrubby plant grown as a handsome annual for borders, pots, hanging baskets. Yellow, red, orange and lilac flowers in small heads. Prolific. Grows to 12 to 24 inches.	Not really annual; because very slow-growing. They need full sun. Stand heat and drought. Good for Southwest and seaside. In frost-free areas, they thrive all year around. In pots do not use rich soil. For summer bloom take cuttings a year before. Or plant seeds two years before.
Larkspur *Delphinium ajacis* and *D. consolida*	The annual delphinium is a delicate, clear-colored flower in blue, lavender, white or pink spikes, 12 to 24 inches. They also come as doubles.	The seed can be sown fall or spring, in cool weather. Do not like transplanting. Do like rich, deep soil. May need staking. Need cool weather when young.
Lobelia, Edging *L. erinus* and *erinus compacta*	Flowers of violet, blue and white, growing only to four to six inches. Get the very blue one, 'Cambridge Blue'. Or 'Blue Gown'.	Plant indoors in Feb. or March. Transplant when all danger of frost is gone.
Love-in-a-mist *Nigella damascena*	Another blue flower, growing to 18 or 24 inches. It only blooms a short time, is very hardy. Does not like to bloom in very hot weather.	Best to sow in fall. Does not like to be transplanted. Seed pods used for arrangements.
Love-lies-bleeding *Amaranthus caudatus*	Lovely crimson flowers on tall plants of four to six feet. Has a big spike. Related to the houseplant with red, green and yellow variegated leaves, called Joseph's Coat. Also to pigweed, and tumbleweed.	Plant outdoors in May and thin to 18 inches apart. Will grow in poor soil.

Name	Description	Comment
Lupine, Annual *Lupinus hartwegii*	Purple or pink lupines on three foot stems, but smaller than the perennial ones. *L. hirsutus* is blue. *L. luteus* is yellow.	Start in peat pots in March, or plant outdoors in May. Are legumes, good for nitrogen and difficult to move. Full sun or part shade.
Malope *M. trifida*	This has three-inch mallow-like flowers on three-foot stems. Comes in pink, violet or white.	Needs well-drained soil, and full sun. Sow seeds outdoors in April or early May.
Marigold African - *Tagetes erecta* French - *Tagetes patula* Striped - *Tagetes tenuifolia* Mexican - *Tagetes singata* *pumila* or - *Tagetes minuta*	Yellow, gold, orange, henna, deep red flowers, among the very most favored for annual plantings. African are tall; French are more dwarf and bushy; *T. minuta* is famous as the nematode-repellent plant, extensively used by organic gardeners for those and other pests. Some new 1975 varieties: 'Honeycomb', French double, red with gold edges; 'Autumn Haze', orange and deep red; 'Gold Rush', red with gold centers; 'Orange Sherbet', dwarf orange; 'Golden Hawaii', odorless, tall.	Very easy to grow. Sow indoors in March; or outdoors when the soil is mellow. Easy to transplant. Sun or part shade. Will bloom midsummer until frost, or all summer. Excellent for hot, dry areas like the Southwest.
Mignonette *Reseda odorata*	This 15-inch flower is white or reddish, not very pretty but pleasantly fragrant. There is a dwarf variety.	Start in pots indoors in April. Not in flats, for it resents transplanting. Add bone meal; it needs sweet soil. And a cool climate. Part shade is best.
Nasturtium *Tropaeolum majus* and *T. minor*	Tall and dwarf nasturtiums are single or double or semi-double, and sometimes fragrant, and always pest-repellent. Grow in the border, the vegetable garden, in pots and window boxes. Lovely flowers yellow, orange, cherry and creamy lemony pale yellow. Delicious in salads.	Full sun. Good in the Southwest. Sandy and neutral soil is best, but they grow anywhere. Too much manure tea or other nitrogen fertilizer will make them go all to leaf. Plant outdoors in April, using old seeds from the previous summer. Do not transplant.
T. peltophorum *T. peregrinium*	Is the orange climbing nasturtium. Is also a vine, yellow flowers.	
Painted tongue (See Salpiglossis)		

Name	Description	Comment
Periwinkle, Madagascar *Vinca rosea*	This is a rose or white flower growing to 18 inches. It has shiny leaves and is very neat. Can be grown as a perennial in the South.	Plant indoors in Feb. put out in full sun after frost. Is drought-resistant. Relatively pest-free.
Petunias *P. hybrida*	Many varieties of tall, dwarf and trailing petunias. Wonderfully long blooming season, if you keep them picked. Slow to start, and fussy. Colors range from white to dark purple, with rich pinks and reds, plain and ruffled, single and double. Some to try: 'Champagne', creamy ruffled; 'Ricochet', rose and white; 'Viva', dwarf but three-inch flowers;'Blue Skies', very compact and quite rugged;'Red Cascade', 'White Cascade' for hanging baskets. And many others.	Many people buy their petunia plants, but to get specials, you may need to plant them yourself. Beginners often have bad luck starting these from seed because the seeds are so small and are fussy. Mix the seeds with sand and sow over sterilized soil in pots or flats, or sow on top of soil covered with a layer of a sterile medium like perlite. Do not cover the seed. Water from the bottom or with a fine mist spray. To create a beneficial humid environment, cover with glass or plastic and keep out of direct sun until seeds sprout. Keep the soil or perlite moist, but not soggy. Once sprouted, remove the cover and give the seedlings lots of sun or artificial light. Pinch if they begin to get spindly.
Phlox, Annual *P. drummondi*	This 1½-foot plant, with red, white, pink, purple and yellow-buff flowers is very easy to grow and flowers profusely **all summer**. Try 'Tetras', with large flowers; 'Isabellina', which is primrose to buff in color; 'Apricot', a good clear color; 'Twinkles' and 'Globe' mixed are satisfactory, too.	Very easy to grow in any soil, and can be planted outdoors in May or indoors. Put in full sun, and the soil can even be poor sandy. Does well in the Southwest. Plant successively to stretch the season. Not easy to transplant, so grow in pots if not outdoors. Seed takes two weeks to germinate. Can grow this phlox in the South as a winter annual.
Pincushion flower (See Scabious)		
Pinks *Dianthus chinensis*	The annual pink is both single and double, in white, crimson, salmon and deep dark red. It	Sow in a cold frame or other cool place in March. Ten days to germinate and sixteen weeks to

Name	Description	Comment
Pinks (con't)	grows to 12 inches. The variety *heddewigii* is the most available and handsomest. Try 'Marguerite', 'Chabaud' and 'Enfant De Nice'. Also try a new one, 'Cherry Drop', which has two-inch blossoms. Keep pinched at first to encourage bloom.	bloom. Plant outdoors in Sept. or April. Likes rich, moist soil and plenty of sun and warmth when mature.
Poppies Mexican poppy *Argemone grandiflora mexicana*	Yellow or orange flower on two to three-foot stalks.	Plant outdoors in May. Likes the hottest exposures.
Shirley poppy *Papaver roeas*	Orange, red, scarlet, pink, blue. Also called Corn poppy, and famous for growing in Flanders fields. They grow to two or three feet.	Sow in Nov. or March in neutral or sweet soil, not too rich. These plants need plenty of sun and air. Do not pinch back. They self-sow easily.
Poppy mallow *Callirhoe digitata*	Big mallow-like flowers on three-foot stems. Reddish purple to lavender.	Plant early outdoors in average soil. Poor soil is all right.
Portulaca (See Rose moss)		
Pot marigold, or calendula *Calendula officinalis*	A well-loved border plant and bedding annual. Used for color and flavoring in soups, by steeping the petals of the yellow and orange flowers, which are two inches across. Grows to one or two feet.	A good all-year plant in the South. Thrives in Southwest. Very hardy. Plant out in April. Pinch to encourage bloom. Full sun. Average soil.
Rock purslane *Calandrinia grandiflora*	Rose or crimson. Grows to one or two feet. Of Portulaca family.	Does well in very hot dry, sunny, well-drained places. Sow outdoors and thin to six inches, or start in pots and set out when warm. Will only bloom in sunshine.
Rose-of-heaven *Lychnis coeli-rosa*	This member of the campion group grows to 12 inches high and has rosy, red or purplish flowers an inch across. There is a white variety *alba*.	Plant outdoors after frost in full sun in well-drained soil, rich and loamy.

Asters 'Duchesse Mix'

A bed of Aster 'Powderpuffs,' Marigold 'Senator Dirksen,' Celosia plumosa 'Tango,' 'Golden Fleece,' and 'Forest Fire Improved,' and 'Silver Feather,' with Petunia varieties used for edging

Tuberous Begonia

Pansy 'Majestic Giant'   Longwood Gardens

Aster 'Powderpuffs'

Calendula 'Kablouna'

Name	Description	Comment
Rose moss *Portulaca grandiflora*	Fleshy plant which grows to eight inches and has yellow, pink, red, purple and white flowers among its varieties. They are open in the sun, closed at night. Good for dry. barren spots. Will tolerate alkaline soils and drought.	Plant where it is to grow in sandy, warm, sunny place in May, or in April in warmer climates. In 12 weeks, bloom starts and continues until Oct. Very fine seeds, so cover only slightly and thin to six inches apart. Will grow in rather poor soil, and give a great display of color.
Salpiglossis *S. sinuata*	Trumpet-like gold, purple, red or bluish flowers on one to two-foot stalks or in some situations up to three feet. One variety is cream with gold markings. Lovely plants with interesting designs, if you can succeed with them. Germination of some varieties is irregular. 'Hot Jazz', 'Park's Special Bedding', and 'America' are especially recommended.	A bit fussy to grow. Seeds take up to 16 days to germinate at a temperature between 70° and 85°F. in rather light, sandy soil. Thin and transplant in April, and put out in May. Can also be started outdoors in May. Keep fertilizing with compost tea. Full sun. Rich soil. I hope you succeed.
Salvia *Salvia patens* *S. splendens*	The first is blue; the other red. Beautiful bright colors. They grow to 18 inches or three feet and make fine masses of color, but beware of their outshining other flowers in a border.	Full sun. Average soil. Sow indoors in Feb. or March, and plant out after frost.
Scabious, Sweet scabious *Scabiosa atropurpurea*	Lavender, or sometimes rose, blue, white or dull red. Long stems, up to two to three feet, with tufty heads, resembling, they say, pincushions. Hummingbirds come to them.	Start indoors in March or outdoors in April or when the soil is mellow. Full sun. Keep the deadheads cut off and pinch plant if you want it more bushy.
Sea lavender or Statice *Limonium bonduelii*	This is the yellow statice. A dry spray of flowers used by florists and arrangers of dried flowers. Very useful in rock gardens and borders, often at the seashore. Grows to two feet. The lilac or whitish is *L. sinuatum* and the rose-colored one is *L. suworowi*.	Plant indoors in Mar. The seeds come with the sheath still on. It is tedious to pick off, and the seeds will sometimes grow anyway without its removal. Not all seeds viable, and germination takes 7 to 22 days. Transplant outdoors in May or after frost, in good loam. Full sun.

Name	Description	Comment
Snapdragons *Antirrhinum majus*	These handsome, long-blooming flowers now come tall and short and dwarf; salmon, yellow, red, pink, apricot, maroon and white and both rather closed and rather open. Actually perennials, they have been adapted and hybridized to fine, useful annuals.	It is best to buy plants or plant the small seeds indoors in March, or outdoors in April or even the previous Aug. in cold frames. They also self-sow. Pinch back once or twice, and stake if they grow tall. Sun or part shade. Good soil. Will bloom all summer if kept picked.
Spider flower (See *Cleome spinosa*)		
Strawflower *Helichrysum bracteatum*	A very useful annual for dried arrangement makers. Grows to 36 inches and has stiff flowers of yellow , white, pink, rose, maroon and dullish red. Pick in the stage just beyond the bud, for they continue to open after being picked.	Plant indoors in March and put out in May. Or plant oudoors. But they grow slowly. They need rich garden loam. Space six to nine inches.
Summer Cypress *Kochia scoparia* and *K. trichophila*	These rugged, fast-growing annuals get to be about two feet tall very quickly. Some leaves are green, some yellow, some red, and in autumn they all turn reddish purple. *K. trichophila* is rounder and denser, and usually preferred to the other kochia.	Average soil. Plant out where they are to grow, in May. Will endure heat and drought. *K. scoparia* will escape and get weedy in hot areas.
Sunflowers *Helianthus annuus*	This is just about the finest, biggest annual you can grow. It is wonderfully decorative, is a delight to the chickadees and goldfinches who visit it as soon as the seeds turn ripe, and is sometimes a boon to any scarlet runner bean that happens to grow nearby. Gets to be seven feet tall or more, with blooms one foot or more. Plant two or more feet apart. The small-seed varieties are also nice. These grow into 4-to-6-foot plants and branch heavily producing 4-to-8 inch flowers in profusion. 'Color Fashion' and 'Italian Red' are nice.	Plant seeds where they are to grow in April. Average soil but if you want really big ones, fertilize with lots of compost. Difficult to transplant.

Name	Description	Comment
H. annuus 'Primrose Stelia'	This one grows to only two feet. Good for Southwest gardens. Is drought-resistant.	Average soil.
Swan River Daisy *Brachycome iberidifolia*	Small, 12-inch plants with fine blue daisy-like flowers, and also in pink and white.	Plant indoors in April, or outdoors in May. Sow in succession to prolong bloom. (It takes six weeks from planting time until bloom.)
Sweet Peas *Lathyrus odoratus nana*	For many years this was my favorite flower, not only because of its powerfully sweet scent but because of its full, long-blooming crop of flowers, and its need to be the first flower to be planted in the spring. Is a legume, so a good nitrogen supplier. Try 'Burpee's Giant Heat Resistant' and others called 'Giant', including 'Giant Ruffled'.	In early spring (or the fall before,) dig an 18-inch trench (or a little smaller) fill with well-rotted manure and compost to six inches, and plant seeds four inches apart, adding one inch of soil. Soak seeds for 24 hours before planting. Fill trench as plants grow. Support vines.
Dwarf Sweet Pea *Lathyrus odoratus nana*	These grow to about eight inches, on stems that are not truly upright. Space early, mid-season and late varieties so you get prolonged bloom. Try 'Cuthbertson', 'Multiflora', 'Spencer' and 'Little Sweetheart'.	These can be started in three-inch trenches, covered with fine soil and the trench covered with straw or wood chips. Supports not necessary.
Sweet sultan *Centaurea imperialis*	Also called Royal Sweet Sultan. A three-foot plant with solitary flower heads in white, purple or yellow, usually fragrant. Also comes in pink. Flowers up to four inches. *C. moschata* the same, but smaller.	Sow seed in the garden where you want it to grow after frost, but you can also start it in peat pots inside a little earlier. With good rich garden loam this variety, *C. imperialis*, may grow to four feet. Big handsome plant.
Sweet William (See biennials, perennials)		Easy to grow as annual.
Valerian, Annual called Spur valerian *Centranthus macrosiphon*	Rose-colored or white flowers in thick clusters blooming profusely. Grows to 12 inches.	Any soil, even a rather poor, dry one. Plant outdoors in April, or after frost.
Verbena *V. hortensis* or *V. hybrida*	This garden verbena is a very satisfactory annual, with toothed leaves and flower clusters up to	For best results buy plants or start inside in March. Easy to pot up for house plants for the winter.

Name	Description	Comment
Verbena (cont'd)	three inches across. They come in pink, purple, red, white and yellowish. Often used for edging, because they only grow to 12 or 15 inches. Bloom all summer. Used also in rock gardens.	Also easy to root cuttings to keep over for planting out the next spring.
Sand verbena *Abronia umbellata*	This grows to nine inches, and is really prostrate. It is actually a perennial grown as an annual, with rose or purplish fragrant flowers. Very good for hanging baskets and good for dry gardens in the Southwest.	Plant indoors in March and put out after frost in full sun. Remove the husk before planting. Pinch for better growth pattern. Will often root where the branches touch the soil.
Wax begonias (See Begonias in Chapter 7) *Begonia sempervirens*		
Winged everlasting *Ammobium alatum*	This grows to three feet, and is a bushy plant with white composite flowers. Easy to dry for dried arrangements.	Can be planted indoors in April. Then put out 12 inches apart in average soil.
Zinnia *Z. elegans*	Fastest and easiest annual coming in dozens of colors and shapes. I grow half a dozen or more varieties each year. They attract spiders, whose large webs catch many insects. We also have used them for trap plants for Japanese beetles, to keep the beetles away from the corn. Plant datura nearby if you object. There are dwarf zinnias of eight inches or so and big ones of three feet. There are little pompons or cut-and-come-again zinnias and big raggedy ones. The colors are every color except blue. There is even a green zinnia. Some are pastel; some are very bright; some are bicolor. And there are singles and doubles. Try new ones from year to year. Some I have enjoyed include: a big cactus-type called 'Sirocco' which is a good pink.	Plant indoors or out. Transplant any time you wish, even when in bloom. Good garden soil. Sun, but they will bloom with part shade, if not too much. Zinnias can get a mildew which is quite ugly and annoying. It is most likely to happen if the plants are crowded, in the shade, or are just there at the end of a long, rainy or cloudy period towards the end of summer. If you have any weather of this sort, plant your zinnias in full sun, and never water them yourself except right down on the soil. Thin out the plants at once if you see it beginning, and the same goes for leaf spot which occurs under the same conditions. Luckily zinnias get few insect pests. If a borer comes, cut him out. For Japanese beetles, see chapter on pest-control.

Name	Description	Comment
Zinnia(cont'd)	Another big one 'Bonanza', is deep gold, on two-foot plants. 'Torch' is a pretty good orange like this. The Dahlia-type zinnias are compact and good colors, which I like for drying in silica gel. 'Golden State' is a good yellow and 'Crimson Monarch' a fairly good red, though the color fades during drying. For small zinnias I like 'Thumbelina' and the 'Old Mexico' bicolors. 'Cherry Buttons' have a good color for fresh arrangements, especially when combined with 'Peppermint Stick'.	

larkspur, immortelle, and cockscomb are excellent, too.

In the preceding list I have given the most common, most popular annual flowers. I have somewhat slighted the very most common like petunias and marigolds, since I believe all gardeners can find satisfactory selections in seed cataloques and in local garden centers. But I also suggest that you try out new annuals as often as the spirit moves, both those listed here and others. The joy of having some success with an unknown plant is a great one. And even if your experiment doesn't come out too well, there are more seasons to come to try again, or to move on to new possibilities and pleasures.

10

Roses

Unless you have ten green thumbs and are willing to spray nearly every day with things like garlic, pepper, onion, rhubarb, rotenone, sabidilla, pyrethrin and spread diatomaceous earth and more besides, keep away from the new, supersensitive Hybrid Tea Roses. They are beautiful and very fragrant, but so are many of the other rose varieties which have been around for 2000 years or more. With that stretch of time behind them, the old-fashioned roses have built up natural resistance and are less susceptible to the diseases and insects which plague the Hybrid Teas and make many gardeners think they have to use poisonous chemical sprays.

I shall say practically nothing about Hybrid Teas in this chapter and nothing at all about Multiflora roses, often advertized as the Living Fence. It is true that these are rugged little bush roses, which spread out and make a thick thorny barrier, with rose hips on them that are liked by the birds. But there is a danger. They self-seed all over the farmers' fields and pastures and become a horrible nuisance to man and beast in all zones south of the coldest. They are cheap, easy to propagate and widely advertized, but for your own sake and for your neighbors', the word is: don't.

Organic gardeners should consider other kinds of roses—some of which you may not even have heard of before. There are Cabbage roses, Climbers, Cottage, Damask, the Dog Rose, Father Hugo's, the various *floribunda* roses, a new *flora-tea*, Memorial, Moyes, the old favorites called the Musk Rose, Pasture, Roxburgh, Scotch, and the rose which has long been grown by organic gardeners as a source of vitamin C, *Rosa rugosa*. These are all hardier than the modern varieties and require less care than Hybrid Teas and no hard poisons. Nor do you have to be out in your garden every other minute to check for black spot and beetles.

Also look into some of the old Moss roses, Bourbons, and original Tea roses and such natives as Virginia Rose and Carolina. You will be amazed at the hardiness and strength of some of these, particularly *Rosa rugosa* if you have never tried it. The Damask roses, too, are very hardy and thrive in practically any kind of soil.

If you insist on growing modern Hybrid Tea Roses, I can't stop you, but I will warn you that it is difficult for an organic gardener ever to do it successfully.

SANITATION

To grow any roses you have to use the right planting techniques, the right soil preparation, and the simple sanitary measures which will help to keep your plants free from trouble. Do your spring cleaning faithfully (and keep it up whenever necessary). Remove every bit of garden trash and the winter mulch from your roses early in the spring. Let the sun shine on the bare soil for at least a month so that the drying process will kill the fungal spores which may have wintered over in the mulch or soil. All year long, always remove all the rose leaves that fall from the plants to the rose bed. Take them to the compost heap immediately and put them in the middle of the pile so that the heat will kill all spores harbored in the leaves.

Nevertheless, you may still get black spot, mildew, leaf spot, rust or some other rose disease, especially on the more delicate varieties. Then try using rhubarb spray for black spot (see Chapter 3 for the recipe) and the triple-barreled garlic-hot pepper-onion spray (recommended in that chapter also). A good precaution is to plant chives and marigolds with your roses to ward off aphids and mites, for those pests can't stand the smell and exudates of such protective plants. If the bright orange or yellow of the marigold flowers swears with the pinks of your roses, snap off the heads and put them in the compost heap or use the petals for flavoring. (Or grow yellow roses.) It's mostly the root exudate that you have the marigolds for, plus perhaps the odor of the foliage and its pungency—not the flowers. Or for such insects, try the most simple organic method of all: a hose and water. But do it early in the day, and do not let your rose bushes remain damp. Repeat the hosing several days in succession to disrupt the breeding cycle of aphids, and keep it up at intervals until you destroy them all, even if it takes a couple of weeks.

Keep some organic sprays on hand, too. One that is effective and can be made at home is made from rhubarb leaves. These poisonous leaves, strongly tinctured with oxalic acid, are often effective against black spot, a common rose disease and the reason rose-growers practice such strict sanitation in the rose beds. I blend a batch of leaves in the blender with water in the spring when I gather the rhubarb stems to make sauce, and then freeze cubes of the potent essence which can be melted and diluted later as needed.

I also keep the ingredients on hand for the very effective garlic-onion-hot pepper mixture which is diluted to make a good, powerful spray effective for many pests. I vary the proportions from time to time, but a standard mixture is one medium-sized onion, two cloves of garlic and a tablespoon of hot pepper blended with one cup of water. Strain and dilute with 2 gallons of water. The undiluted essence of this spray can be frozen and stored in a plastic bag, too. I put the mash from the strainer around the base of the plants for good measure.

Onion spray unfortified by garlic and hot pepper is a good addition to a tomato essence made by stewing up some tomato leaves and blending them with a little water. Instead of diluting with more water, add some denatured alcohol and use this strong concoction on a cotton swab to dab off and kill aphids and red spider mites.

For rose chafers, keep toads. They will gobble them up by the dozens. If you have a pond, there's no problem. They will come to breed. Those who have no pond are advised to visit a friend when the tiny baby toads have just appeared and to beg for some to take home. Take them just then when they are tiny, for they do not like to be moved later on, and won't stay where you put them.

These old-fashioned methods are more than likely to work with the minor infestations you might get on old-fashioned roses. They may not be so successful with the weaker, susceptible Hybrid Teas, so if you still are set on growing those, good luck!

PLANTING TECHNIQUES

Proper soil preparation, planting techniques and a good fertilizing program all will help you to have healthy plants. For good bloom, choose a site where they will get at least six hours of sun a day, and give them afternoon rather than morning shade. (The sun in the morning helps to dry off any overnight moisture that got on them.) Good sun and afternoon shade also help your roses to maintain good color. Make sure that the rose bushes are not too close to other shrubs, trees or hedges, which are heavy surface feeders, too, and will compete for the nutrients your roses will need to grow healthy and strong. And even though you keep up a good fertilizing program, the other big plants will rob from the roses.

SOIL

Roses aren't finicky about the type of soil they have, though as usual, a good garden loam rich with organic matter is best. But they do make quite a fuss over the soil's drainage capacity. Good drainage is essential because roses can be seriously injured by an excess of water around their roots. If the drainage is not taken care of naturally by a good slope and porous soil, then under-drain the bed with tile drains or with crushed stone or cinders or with both. For tiling, lay a four-inch agricultural tile on the bottom of a two-foot trench, with the sections end to end and the joints covered with strips of tar paper to keep soil out of the tile while the trench is being refilled. There should be a fall of three inches in every 50 linear feet. If you are going to use gravel instead of tile, place a six-inch layer of crushed stone, gravel or cinders at the bottom of the trench you prepare for your bushes. It is best to top a tile with one of those materials, too, to help guide the water into the drainage pipe.

SOIL PREPARATION

Preparation of the soil for planting roses involves digging the bed, making a good mixture, and seeing that it has the proper pH, which should be between 5.5 and 6.5 to keep your roses happy. (If it is too alkaline or acid, they may become chlorotic, with pale leaves from iron deficiency.)

Since rose roots go down at least 20 inches into the soil, the bed must be prepared deeply. Remember that you are planting a shrub which will stay in that same place for years, so provide lots of room and the nice rich soil it will need to get a good start. If your soil is too sandy, add some clay loam, plenty of compost, acid peat moss, and other organic materials, to improve the water-holding capacity as well as to add to the fertility. If, however, the soil is a heavy clay type, add some sand, compost and strawy manure to fertilize the soil and provide for greater aeration. The manure can be fairly fresh if you prepare the bed in the fall for spring planting, but be sure it is well-rotted if you wait until spring to get the bed ready for your new roses.

PREPARING THE BED

I certainly recommend that you prepare the bed the fall before for spring planting. Dig up the bed, add fertilizers and humusy soil conditioners, and let the bed ripen over the winter. If you have to wait until spring, dig up and prepare the bed at least three weeks before you plant so that the fertilizers can work in and the bed has time to settle. If you don't dig up the whole bed, or trench it, you can use the method called double-digging, which is a simpler method for adding enrichment and acid peat moss to the soil because you work in small sections, one at a time. (See Chapter 2 for details.) Be sure to work in a handful of rock phosphate and one of dried seaweed or other material rich in potash when you add the compost and peat moss. If all this is done in the fall, you can also use fresh organic materials which will break down over the winter. Add shredded leaves, barn or chicken house bedding, garden wastes and small amounts of fresh animal manure. But fresh manure must not be used in the spring because it can burn the roots of your roses by the rapid release of nitrogen. Unmellowed materials can also steal the available nitrogen, or rather the bacteria working on the decomposition of those materials can. Ground that settles over the winter has less danger of unexpected air pockets which might cause harm to the roots.

PLANTING

The next step is the actual planting. Ideally you should plant your rose bushes as soon as you get them. This isn't always possible, so keep them in a cool, moist place—even plunging them into a pail of muddy water if they came bare-rooted. They must never dry out; and it is wise to submerge and soak the whole plant if it looks a bit shriveled or cracking.

When you prepare the hole in the prepared bed, dig down at least 18 inches and make the hole wide enough so that it will hold the roots

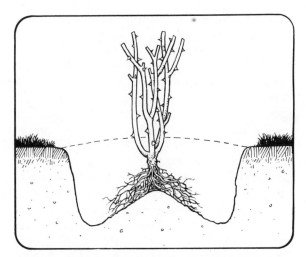

Carefully spread the roots of the rose bush over the mound in the bottom of the hole you've prepared, and make sure the bud or graft union is about 1½ inches below the soil surface when you fill in the hole and tamp it down.

easily without crowding them. Make a little cone-shaped pile of soil in the middle of the hole. Then prune off any dead or badly bruised roots, and spread all the remaining roots of the plant over the mound. Place it so that the bud union or place of the graft of the new part on the old stock is just one to one-and-a-half inches below the surface level of the soil. (If too low the roots will grow from the scion; if too high, the shrub will suffer in the cold.) Now fill the hole half full, tamp it firmly to fill all air pockets, and water thoroughly. When the water subsides, finish filling the hole and tamp it gently again. Now build a mound of soil up around the plant and leave it there until growth begins. Keep up a steady program of fertilizing throughout the life of the bush, using compost and mild manure tea every month or so.

MULCHES

All roses benefit by mulches. And in most climates they need the winter protection which mulches can give, too. Bush roses particularly benefit from summer mulches to keep their roots cool, and to maintain moisture. You can use anything from ground corncobs or peat moss to pine needles, buckwheat hulls and sawdust. Because they are so light in weight and so easy to handle, buckwheat hulls are often used. Also, they can be applied dry, as they are permeable to water, do not cake when wet (as cocoa shells often do) and do not require pre-soaking as peat moss does. Some mulches such as corncobs and sawdust will need additions of nitrogen such as blood meal or cottonseed meal. Be sure both the soil and the mulch are damp when you apply mulch, and put on a good thick layer—at least one to three inches.

WINTER PROTECTION

Before applying a winter mulch, rake up and burn all the old leaves and twigs in the rose bed to prevent them from harboring fungus diseases.

Then rake aside the summer mulch, or carry it to the compost heap. Now build a mound of soil up around the bushes to a height of 10 or 12 inches. This will protect the crown of the plant and keep the wood and buds in the lower part from drying out during winter winds and sunny days.

After the ground has frozen, spread straw or salt hay on as a mulch over the beds—or something similar which will not cake. Maple and elms leaves are especially to be avoided. But do *not* apply the mulch until after the ground has frozen, or you may find that the ground heaves in the spring. (And you don't want to make a place to invite the mice to move in.) Use plenty of this winter mulch, in fact, heap it up over the entire bed until only the tips of the bushes are showing, if that.

Protecting climbers can be done in a number of ways. You may use old cornstalk of evergreen boughs laid up against your trellis, and they both provide good barriers for cold and wind. But again they may invite mice. Don't use burlap without plenty of straw; it stays too moist. One good method is to take down the canes of the climbing roses in October and after removing them from the trellis, lay them on the ground where nature will provide a natural protection of grass as it grows up during the late fall around them. Then mound with earth and after the ground has frozen, you can place mulch over the mound. It is best to hold the canes from wiggling by placing two pieces of strong wood into the earth at right angles as a kind of vise to fasten them down until spring.

PRUNING

There are two types of rose structure, and therefore two kinds of pruning. The hybrid teas, such as 'Peace', 'Charlotte Armstrong' or 'Sutter's Gold', tend to build up their own structure of wood, and then to produce new growth from that wood. Others produce the new growth mostly from the base and tend to grow into large clumps. Orange, coppery and yellow roses, because of their heritage, do better if not pruned much if any. Any climbing hybrids you have should be left to grow as they wish, also, and not pruned.

Since your aims in pruning are to remove diseased, damaged and dead wood, to shape the bush to pleasant proportions and to encourage new growth, there are certain procedures to know about. For hybrid teas, floribundas and grandifloras, after you have removed the dead and weak wood in early spring, take out all the cross-branches, or the ones which want to go toward the center instead of the outside of the bush. This not only improves the looks of the bush, but also airs out the center where bugs and fungi might dwell. (Where very hot, rather than cut right down to the base of the branch, you can leave a stub to grow fresh leaves to help shade the stem from sun scald.) Then the big job is to remove about ⅓ of the length of all new growth for that year. The size of the growth you cut, especially in mild-winter areas, should be no bigger than the average pencil. In cold areas, prune all stems back to wood that is light green or cream colored, whether that reduces it to more than ⅓ off or not. Because you will be putting on winter protection, it is essential not to have any weak, damaged, sickly or susceptible canes or stems under the covering.

Each cut should be made at a 45-degree angle and just above a leaf bud which points outward, with the lower point of the cut on the side of the stem opposite the bud—the cut of course not any lower than the base of the bud because that would interrupt the flow up and down of sap through the cambium to and from the bud, and the new growth from it the following year. It is advisable to paint all cuts, especially if you go down as far as the bud union. Orange shellac or the wound compounds sold at nurseries are good to use. And of course clean up

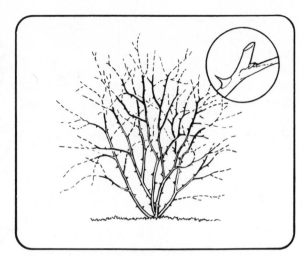

When pruning rose bushes, make cuts at a 45-degree angle, just above a leaf bud which points outward.

all debris, all fallen leaves and twigs which might harbor disease or spores or insect larvae.

If you have hybrid-tea or similar climbers, leave them alone for two or three years, or until the plants are thoroughly established. Take out the dead branches, of course. After two or three years, the climber will have new long canes and side branches, and the blooming will be on those side brances. So obviously you do not want to cut them off, and you will only do so if the cane is weak and unproductive.

You can, however, cut back the blooming lateral branches a few inches or to two or three eyes of those which bloomed that year. The blooms are usually produced on two- or three-year-old wood. When you take off spent blooms, cut back to a stong eye two or three leaves away from the point where the flowering shoot begins.

If you are pruning a large-flowered climber such as 'Paul's Scarlet Climber', only prune after its one blooming period, for roses such as this flower on the last year's wood, which you of course do not want to cut away, Other climbers have more than one blooming period, and can be treated as you do the hybrid tea climbers and others of that type. So can pillar roses and climbing floribundas.

Ramblers, however, must be pruned after the spring or summer blooming period, leaving all new growth, and cutting out the old canes which will not bloom again. Train the new canes to grow as you want them to.

To prune shrub roses, merely shape and trim them, taking out canes which grow crookedly, weak wood, and unproductive branches. Shortening of new long canes will help to encourage strong, productive branches.

VARIETIES

Roses do require a good deal of attention, but they are well worth your efforts if you get the kinds best suited to your resources and climate. There are many types available, but the following are among the most popular, and are ones which you may wish to consider growing in your own garden. Before deciding you might do well to send for their list to the American Rose Society, 4048 Roselea Place, Columbus, Ohio 43214.

THE FLORIBUNDAS

These roses are used particularly in the garden beds and borders where they grow to be hardy, vigorous, good-looking plants. They are the result of a cross between the polyanthas and hybrid teas, and seem to have inherited the best qualities from each.

The varieties do vary a great deal in size, flower form, and color. All Floribundas have beautiful large flowers which bloom for a long period of time and they are all less temperamental than their relatives — the hybrid teas. Pruning Floribundas is simple: just cut the canes back in early spring before the buds begin to swell; they should be cut back a third. In the summer, cut off 4 inches of the stem when you take off each spent cluster.

Floribundas are extremely versatile and can be used in the formal rose garden or as a bush on a small plot of land, in large rock gardens or by the sea. In any environment, the plant is vigorous and very lovely.

If you want to try the Floribundas, I suggest you select from the following varieties: 'Angel Face', rosy lavender; 'Apricot Nectar', apricot; 'Betty Prior', shrimp pink; 'Bon Bon', pink and white bicolor; 'europeana', ruby red; 'Floradora', scarlet orange, a beauty; 'Lilac Charm', lilac; 'Lilli Marlene', dark red; 'Saratoga', pure white; or 'Spartan', salmon orange.

THE GRANDIFLORAS

A cross between the hybrid teas and floribundas, these roses are also used in various garden beds and borders. They are as large and beautiful as hybrid teas, and sometimes more so!

While their flowers are very grand, they are borne in small clusters, differentiating them from the hybrid teas. Like the floribundas, they are easy to take care of and, when you prune the Grandifloras, follow the same procedure as you would with the floribundas.

Some of the best varieties are: 'Aquarius', deep rose; 'Buccaneer', bright yellow; 'Carrousel', vivid dark red; 'Mountain Shasta', pure white; 'Ole', orange red; 'Queen Elizabeth', pink.

THE HYBRID PERPETUALS

Once known as the 'June Roses', these plants are not perpetual bloomers, as their name implies. They do bloom freely during June, however, producing large, beautiful flowers, but with only a few scattered flowers for the rest of the season.

Don't neglect this lovely cross between the Damask rose and the China rose, for there are many excellent varieties which are just as beautiful and more vigorous than the 'modern' roses. The following are recommended: 'American Beauty', cerise red; 'Frau Karl Druschi', pure white; 'General Jacqueminot', dark red; 'George Arends', pink; 'Paul Neyron', deep pink; or 'Ulrich Brunner', scarlet-crimson.

THE HYBRID TEAS

The hybrid teas are very lovely roses, and certainly very popular with today's gardeners. When given good winter protection and proper care, they may bloom as many as four or five months, from June until mid-October.

But the organic gardener must always bear in mind that hybrid teas are very difficult to care for without the help of chemical pesticides. For this reason, I suggest that the serious organic gardener stick to the old-fashioned roses, or try some hybrid crosses.

If you are still determined to grow hybrid teas, however, a few of the more beautiful and successful varieties include: 'American Heritage', yellow tinted pink; 'Christian Dior', cherry red; 'Dainty Bess', rose pink; 'Eclipse', deep yellow; 'El Cid', red-orange; 'First Love', pearly pink; 'Forty-Niner', red-yellow bicolor; 'Helen Traubell', salmon; 'Intermezzo', lavender; 'King's Ransom', golden-yellow; 'Matterhorn', ivory; 'Medallion', apricot-buff; 'Oregold', golden-yellow (1975 All-American); 'Peace', yellow and pink blend; 'Sincera', pure white; 'Snowfire', red and white; and 'Summer Sunshine', pure bright yellow.

THE POLYANTHAS

These roses are the parents of the Floribundas. Don't be fooled if you see modern nurseries selling 'Polyanthas'—they aren't the original plants. Practically no true Polyanthas are grown today, but many hybrids from the species are in existence. See below, however, in the section on Miniature Roses, the little roses sometimes called Polyanthas.

THE FLORA-TEAS

The Flora-teas are the latest contribution to the rose world, from Jackson & Perkins, the famous dealers and nurserymen (See directory). A cross between the floribundas and hybrid teas, these roses have long stems, many blooms, and are compact, easily manageable plants. Jackson & Perkins call this the "Bouquet-Branching Hybrid" and I think that this is quite a good descriptive term for the Flora-teas.

If you want, try this 1975 novelty suggested varieties are: 'Evening Star', pure white; 'Sunfire', deep pink; and 'Viva', red.

THE CLIMBERS

There is only one thing which the Climbers have in common: they are all valuable for walls, trellises, or arbors. Other than that, the Climbers come in all colors, temperaments, and sizes. Some bloom at the height of the season and don't bloom again, while others such as ramblers continue to bloom after the peak is over; some are very hardy, and others are suited to a milder climate. You just have to study a catalogue and determine which Climber is best suited to your area.

A few favorites which you may want to look into and choose from are: Aloha', deep coral pink; 'Blaze', scarlet-red; 'City of York', buff-yellow; 'Golden Showers', golden yellow; 'Jacotte', apricot-orange; or 'White Dawn', pure white.

THE RUGOSA HYBRIDS

A favorite with organic gardeners, the Rugosa Roses are known for their extreme hardiness and ability to thrive in almost any soil.

These are among the few rose species which can thrive by the seashore.

In general, the Rugosa Roses range from six to seven feet high. Their foliage, which is practically disease- and insect-proof, is a dark green color. The texture is thick and wrinkly.

These are the roses I recommend to you. They will give you almost no trouble. With minimal care you will have lovely, vigorous roses. Keep an eye on them so they do not escape and go wild in fields where they are not wanted: 'Agnes', coppery-yellow; 'Blanc Double', 'De Coubert', white; 'Doctor Eckener', coppery-pink; 'Frau Dagmar Hartopp', silvery pink; 'F. J. Grootendorst', red.

THE OLD-FASHIONED ROSES

Old-Fashioned Roses are not seen in very many gardens these days, which I find very disappointing. The different types—Provence, Bourbon, Damask, Noisette, and Moss—are among the most vigorous and hardy of all roses. In addition, they produce the most lovely, delicate, and often fragrant blossoms.

Try the following varieties in your garden. I'm sure that you will get the most exquisite Old-Fashioned Roses imaginable:

Bourbon Roses
'Adam Messerich'	rose-red
'La Reine Victoire'	rose-pink
'Souvenir De La Malmaison'	flesh pink
'Zephrin Drouchin'	bright pink

Damask Roses
'Mme Hardy'	pure white
'Marie Louise'	deep pink

Moss Roses
'Alfred De Dalmas'	blush pink
'Blanche Moreau'	white tinged pink
'Deuil De Paul' 'Fontaine'	maroon red
'Gloire De Mousseaux'	carmine-salmon pink

Noisette Roses
  'Bouquet D'or'   pale yellow
  'Crepescule'   orange-pink fading to
                    apricot-yellow
  'Reve D'or'   buff-yellow

Provence Roses
  'Anais Segalas'   deep pink
  'Konigin Von Dane
    Mark'   flesh pink
  'Unique Blanche'   pure white

SHRUB ROSES
(which I particularly recommend for the organic gardener)

'Austrian Copper'—a five-foot bush with lavish orange-copper blooms in the spring

'Cornelia'—small, coral pink clusters of bloom all summer on an eight-foot bush, or all year in mild climates

'Fruhlingsmorgen'—yellow with pink, single blooms on a very vigorous, six-foot bush; good red hips in fall

'Harison's Yellow'—double yellow, small, prolific blooms on six-foot bushes, which you may have seen around old homesteads, with ferny foliage and thorns

'Nevada'—big, four-inch flowers, creamy and pink come in spring, with some extras later; seven feet

'Prairie Fire'—red clusters on a six-foot bush; stands the cold

'Sparrieshoop'—this one also climbs; has single pink flowers all summer

'Therese Bugnet'—highly recommended for cold climates; has lilac pink double roses in clusters, and only grows to five feet

WARNING: Sometimes gardeners and bird lovers are tempted by the alluring ads for a bush rose with small white flowers known as multiflora rose, and often called a living fence. It has colorful little rose hips that birds do like. It comes from Japan. It has vile thorns. And it is rampant. The birds spread the seeds every-where. In the North, and especially in woodsy sections, the spreading is not always serious, but in warmer areas, the seedling bushes spring up all through the pastures and grain fields and become a terrible pest. So if you have fields—or any consideration for your neighbors—don't get this pest started. Use a more well-behaved rose bush instead. If in doubt, ask your county agent.

Or settle for a native plant which stays under control like *Rosa virginiana*, the Virginia rose, which blooms in mid-June and has good foliage, making a pleasant hedge all summer. It also has fine red fruits in the fall and good red twigs to lend interest in winter.

MINIATURE ROSES

These dainty little roses are becoming more and more popular these days, and it is understandable because they are suited to so many of today's patios and other small gardens. They are easy to manage, too.

Look carefully at your purchases to see whether they are grafted or not; most growers prefer them ungrafted. When you order by mail, you might as well take what you can get, and they will probably come balled. Give them a good soak the minute they arrive, and if there are yellowed leaves, immerse the whole plant for 12 hours and it will undoubtedly come back to health.

Set out these miniatures a little lower than the line indicating where they grew at the nursery, but not so low that any earth touches the lowest branches. Water well, and keep the roots moist because these little roses have very shallow roots, which must not dry out. After the first set of blooms, begin to fertilize, but do it lightly with mellowed compost that is not too high in nitrogen. Prune off all weak growth and any long, leggy branches which distort the trim

MINIATURE ROSES

Red:	'Baby Masquerade', 'Dwarfking', 'Fire Princess', 'Little Buckaroo' and 'Magic Dragon'
Yellow:	'Bit O' Sunshine', 'Gold Coin', 'Little Showoff', 'Rosina', 'Yellow Doll' and others
White:	'Easter Morning', 'Frosty', 'Green Ice', 'Josephine', 'Pixie', 'Simplex' and others.

More modern ones that are easier to find include: 'Perle D'Alconda', with pale pink double flowers; 'Garnet', with double red; 'Yellow Miniature', with a nice bright yellow. Other little roses you can get are 'Cecile Brunner', peach-pink and very prolific Sweetheart rose; and the 15-inch roses sometimes called Polyanthas (though they are probably not the true old Polyanthas). These include 'Carroll Ann', with double-buttercup-shaped pinky-orange flowers, growing in clusters; 'Charlie McCarthy', white; 'Happy', a bright deep red with dark green foliage; and 'Margo Koster', salmon shading to pink and orange. The 'Fairy', or 'Fairy Moss' rose is still a great favorite, with its many soft, pale pink blossoms, which will bloom all summer as a low front edging to any garden. It is also possible to find this rose trained into a little tree rose, splendid for patios and other small gardens. You can also get 'Happy', 'Chrysler Imperial', 'Peace', 'Gold Glow' and the new 'Queen Elizabeth' as three-foot patio tree roses. Get a good catalogue and look them up.

I do not want to close this section without mentioning the sub-zero roses now available, especially hybridized by the expert rose-grower at Stark's Nursery, Dr. Walter D. Brownell. The one named for him is a peach and yellow Hybrid Tea Rose, fragrant, fully double and with quite long stems. And 'Charlotte Brownell' is a lovely yellow to pink rose of the 'Peace' type. Non-organic gardeners in my neighborhood who use pesticides on their roses to control insects say they can succeed with this rose, and also with

shape of the rosebush. If you decide to have miniature roses in pots for the patio or porch, use a container at least five inches deep. Square ones, as with the larger floribundas and others you may wish to put up, are preferable to round pots, for they give just that much more root room.

Old Varieties you may like include:

Pink: 'Baby Bunting', 'Baby Pinocchio', 'Bobolink', 'Candy Pink', 'Fairy Moss', 'Little Chief' and 'Marilyn' some of the other sub-zeroes such as 'Arctic Flame', very red and other red ones, 'Margaret Cahse Smith', 'Red Duchess', 'Handsome Red' and 'Queen O' The Lakes', as well as the pink one, 'Helen Hayes', and the yellow, 'Victory'. One thing that amazes and pleases growers of the sub-zero roses is that they are as resistant to heat as they are to cold, so people find them strong and hardy from coast to coast. I don't grow hybrid tea roses because my convictions persuade me to grow other kinds, but were I to start, I think these sub-zero roses are the ones I might try.

Verbena 'Ideal Florist Mix,' Cynoglossum 'Dwarf Firmament,' and Zinnia 'Peter Pan Pink'

Hyacinth　　　　　Longwood Gardens

Bougainvillea　　　　　Longwood Gardens

Petunias 'Happiness' (rose pink), 'Fiesta' (red and white bicolor), and 'Sugar Plum' (pink-veined plum); with Marigolds 'Double Dwarf French Petite'

Cineraria   Longwood Gardens

Fibrous-rooted Begonia, Double-flowered and bronze-leaved

PART 3

Special Gardens

11

Rock Gardens

Among the easy-maintenance gardens are rock gardens— even though they are often very tricky to build and to water. Actually there are two kinds of rock gardens: the one for the specialist, which concentrates on alpine plants native to mountains watered by melting glaciers and snow; and another for plants that do well in association with rocks, though not necessarily from alpine mountain habitats. This second kind might be on a sunny slope, in a shady glen or in a raised bed that you make with rocks.

Once you get your rocks in place, either on a bank or wall or in some other arrangement that uses rocks, and once you perfect the drainage and watering system for your rock garden plants, and then get your planting and initial weeding and mulching done, there is very little other work to do aside from the small chores of snipping off deadheads or clipping back little shrubby plants that want to go rampant.

Start with the easy plants which are not too fussy about their kind of soil, whether it is alkaline, acid or neutral and not too fussy about the amount of water they get or the temperature of the soil around their roots. Then, as you get to know your plants, and the needs of more demanding plants, adjust your soil or drainage,

and try some of those and take your chances on the lovely, spectacular but delicate alpines that have been the delight of so many gardeners for so many years.

ORIGINS

When you build a rock garden, plan to retain the simplicity which has been a part of rock gardening since the concept started, back in Shakespeare's day. As Englishmen began traveling on the Continent, they brought back to England samples of the lovely alpine flowers which grow on the mountains so freely and profusely. It is from the cultivation of these wild flowers that alpine rock gardening, as we know it today, originated. English gardeners soon realized that in order for the plants to survive in England, the rugged, rock-chip mountain soil had to be recreated. This native mountain soil is thin, very stony, and mixed in with bits of moss and other humusy scraps. There are rocks everywhere on the mountains, essential both for good drainage and to hold some of the moisture which alpine plants also need. These plants simply cannot endure with their roots sticking into the middle of a stagnant pool of water, and they cannot survive if the hot sun beats down on the soil around their roots and burns them. The rock chips everywhere on the high mountain sides act as a stone mulch, and a rock gardener is well advised to use the same sort of material around his alpine plants.

The origin for the other kind of rock garden is the woodland or streamside habitat for native plants which you introduce into your yard where you have or bring in rocks and stones. Many of the plants customarily used are native to the United States, but some beauties which adapt well come from the Mediterranean, other parts of Europe, and from the East. These often have a wider range of tolerance than the alpine plants, and so are much less fussy as to pH of the soil, drainage and maintenance of the exactly right degree of moisture and coolness. They are also less likely to winterkill, for they do not derive from a situation where there has been for aeons a constant protective snow cover in the winter. Some of these less fussy plants are especially adapted to wall gardens and look very handsome trailing down over the rocks. In California and other warm (and rather damp) places you can have absolutely gorgeous displays of fuchsias draped down a wall. Even the lowly sedum can look graceful as it cascades over the stones in a wall. Quite a few ordinary perennials are suitable to use, too.

In more recent years there have been many imitations of ancient courtyard gardens, patios, gardens on ledges and around pool and other adaptations of the old uses of stone and rock and the new concepts of outdoor garden living rooms. Even stone barbecue areas can serve.

STYLE AND STRUCTURE

The whole point about a rock garden is to have it simple and naturalistic. It exists for the plants, not the rocks. And there is no point in making it look like a section in a geology museum, a set of dentures, or a grotesque place with nooks and crannies for plastic dwarfs or pink flamingoes.

If you want to make it fancy, put in a recirculating stream, waterfall and pool, such as one of those described in Chapter 12, and add some waterside plants to your rock garden or alpine plants. In fact, even the underground irrigation system described below may be enough to satisfy your desires for extras. But whatever it is you do to your rock garden, both for your own aesthetic pleasure and for the welfare of your plants, keep the place as near to the natural habitat as you can. Most experienced rock gardeners advise you to go out into the countryside and study the way nature has spread out or piled up the rocks, the way they relate to outcroppings of underground rocks, and the way plants establish themselves in relation to rocks. Then get out the pencil and paper that you will need to plan your own rock garden. If it is only a wall you are going to plant, study pictures or existing wall gardens. For either kind you may be able to observe outstanding examples at botanical gardens or show places.

CONSTRUCTION OF A WALL GARDEN

Say you have a slope, and want to hold it back with a wall, or build some steps up it with a low wall on each side. In either case, a wall about three feet high is a good height to start with.

Dig out the area, square it down, gather your stones and prepare your soil and drainage materials. Also consider underground irrigation if you are going to grow alpines. The stones you use should be native, if possible, or porous tufa rocks if you bring them in from the outside. If you have an old stone wall, or know of one where you can get stones, these old rough oblong stones will have the added attraction of some weathering, and small accumulations of humus on them. Do not use old, worn stones, however.

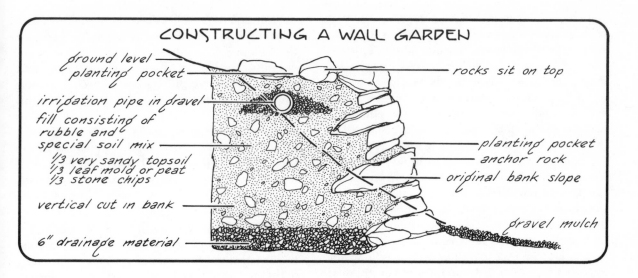

CONSTRUCTING A WALL GARDEN

ground level
planting pocket
rocks sit on top
irrigation pipe in gravel
fill consisting of rubble and special soil mix
⅓ very sandy topsoil
⅓ leaf mold or peat
⅓ stone chips
planting pocket
anchor rock
original bank slope
vertical cut in bank
6" drainage material
gravel mulch

It would be much better to buy new, quarried stones, because old smooth ones that have been rounded by time are too difficult to fit together. They also have a tendency to come loose after a couple of years, which not only will prevent good drainage, but may topple your wall as well. And don't go all out for a collection of different granite, limestone, quartz and other stones. You will only give yourself additional problems. If you have to bring in rocks from the outside, get as porous ones as you can. These will hold more water and release it as the plants require. If you have a solid base, that is fine. If you only have a soft, wobbly base, put in a solid concrete one to hold the wall.

After digging out the area, fill the bottom with six inches of good drainage material like gravel, pebbles, cinders and broken brick, then add finer gravel and sand and let it shake down. Hose it to help it along. Next build up the bank, inserting stones here and there, and an irrigation pipe set in gravel near the top. When ready to build the wall, remember three or four main principles.

First, put all stones in at an angle, sloping down as well as in. This helps to catch water and to send it into the area of the plants' roots. Second leave good little pockets between the stones for the new plants. Some people put the plants in as they go along building up the wall. This is precarious, but if you are very skillful, go ahead and do it that way. Successful spreading of roots is more likely if you do. The third principle is that of protecting lower plants from overhang. Do not let any overhanging stones keep the rain off the plants and roots below. And of course a fourth principle is to see to it that each stone is set firmly into the ground by putting it at least one-third under the surface, and by tamping thoroughly.

If you also see to it that each stone as you progress upwards is put in a little farther back so that the front edge of each successive stone is farther back in the soil than the one which preceded it, you will meet the requirements of most of these principles.

A rock garden on a natural slope (with or without natural out-croppings of rock already there) can provide several different kinds of habitat and make it possible for you to grow flowers from several different kinds of places. Though again you will need soil that is not too rich, and plenty of sun, you can have a variety of soils and places that are shady, moist or dry, and with or without running water above ground. You still need good drainage except for definitely marsh-loving plants by a pond.

If you plan to include any of the more difficult rock garden plants, and your climate is one where droughts occur, you may also need to introduce an underground irrigation system.

The main things to keep in mind when you make a rock garden by scattering rocks on a slope are to place the rocks so that they look as though naturally deposited there, and, where rocks are grouped close together, to place them as you do in a wall, with the face running both in and down, for the sake of catching the rain water and directing it towards the roots of your plants.

If you possibly can, you should include a little stream, with a waterfall or so, and a pool or two. Even if there is no natural brook for you to use, there are very simple and relatively inexpensive ways to construct such an addition by using today's plastic and electric gadgets.

A fine sunny slope with clumps and cascades of sun-loving flowers among the rocks makes a fine show. Perhaps even more beautiful is a slope with trees and shrubs, groundcovers in the shade, and shade-loving flowers in the woodsy parts and along the waterway. With a pool or so in the sun, you can also add sun-loving waterside plants. Some of the spectacular gardens of the world have been built with this kind of layout. Some are in botanical gardens for all to see. Once established and once the first weedings and mulchings are done, a rock garden pretty nearly takes care of itself.

SOIL TO USE

On a slope or when you build a wall, it is important to have the right soil mixture, and to have it ready to put in as you build. With a wall,

the soil behind and between the stones acts as a sort of mortar and fills all the interstices between the stones. A good mixture is composed of one-third very sandy topsoil, one-third leaf mold or peat, and one-third stone chips or gravel. Work the soil into the first course of rocks, and into the spaces between them. Pack the soil in very tightly, because you don't want the rocks to shift around. Make sure you do not let any of the fill project higher than the backs of the first rocks for this would destroy the tilt all the way up. When it is all packed in, spread a half-inch layer thick on the top of the stones.

Now plant. It is possible to do this in the spring, but if you are putting in alpine plants, most of them are dormant. in the late summer, so that is a good time to do it. With a new garden like this you have a chance to put in a lot of miniatures, alpines, prostrate little shrubs, low groundcovers, and even very small trees you may always have wanted to have. Study which ones will increase, which will stay more or less as they are, and make your decisions. It is best, I think, to use potted, nursery-grown plants when you start a rock garden, for they are more likely to take hold quickly, and with a delicate structure like a wall, you would rather have everything succeed at once if you possibly can. With potted plants, the time of year is not so crucial, either.

More important is the condition of the soil. It should be moist, not wet; and it should be crumbly, not sticky. Wait for a day when it is in the correct moist, crumbly condition. Wet soil. as you know, will just cake around the roots and cut off air. In an open garden you still have some chance of getting in and opening up the soil for air. In a wall, how can you do that?

Be sure to firm the soil around the roots, however, as best you can. This may mean that you will really have to ram it down in, to get rid of any big air pockets in the soil. If possible, put in at least three or four of each variety so the plants will not look lonesome and ineffective beside the comparatively big stones. But big spreaders like alyssum, and annual phlox or some of the stonecrops will fill up the spaces soon enough and even tumble over the stones. Where there are little nooks, put in the littlest plants. Each plant, after its roots are well in, will need at least a ½-inch layer of soil. If you are planting and building at the same time this is not difficult to arrange, but if you are planting afterwards, you may find some lack of space and have to rearrange your plans. If this happens often enough, you may find yourself converted to the method of planting and building at the same time after all.

RAISED BED

In gardens where there is no slope, or no natural outcropping to start plantings for a rock garden, you can start on level ground and make a raised bed. The procedure is just about the same as that used for building a wall, except that you have four sides. It should also be lower, for you will not have the extensive soil bank in back of the stones to supply the ground water to keep the soil moist. In a rock garden built on a natural bank, the water table may be much more available, and the way you conditioned the soil inside the bank will make it more retentive of rain water than it would otherwise have been.

Fill the raised bed, however, with good drainage at the bottom, and then use plenty of largish stones along with the gravelly soil mixture while filling the center of the raised bed. It is more satisfactory to build up the four walls and plant them at the same time if you can. Since a raised bed will be considerably lower than the constructed wall, it is not hazardous to do it this way, and you do have the advantage of being able to spread out the roots without the crowding they sometimes get if you plant your

flowers in a finished wall. A rock garden on a slope also has this advantage.

SOIL FOR TRUE ALPINES

Flowers that come from the Alps and other high mountain slopes need conditions similar to moraine soils. Actually a moraine is the mixture of materials left by a retreating glacier, and it is mostly stones and gravel. With time, some humus accumulates and then the first colonizers like little artemisias and little saxifrages begin to appear. To imitate this sort of natural habitat on your own slope, you want to dig out all clay—if you soil is clayey—and make a new mixture of sand, grit, a little peat or other unrich humus, and, of course, arrange for excellent drainage. The weathered cinders, ashes, clinkers, broken brick and even broken pottery that you put in for underground drainage means that the roots of your plants will not only get the benefit of the water that runs through, but also of the air that comes along afterwards, which is equally beneficial, especially when it is warm. The proportions for alpine campanulas, gentians and saxifrages, and all the others, can be one-third unwashed river sand (or builder's sand if you cannot get the nutritious river sand—don't use beach sand; it's too salty and smooth) one-third sphagnum moss and one-third good friable loam. If in doubt, cut down on the loam, and if you cannot get sphagnum moss some peat will do. On the mountains these plants are sustained by inorganic materials dissolved in the soil solution that adheres to the rocks and pebbles. You can actually see your flowers rot if you give them manure or any other rich fertilizer, or even if you give them too much good loam. In the man-made garden, some yearly top dressings of compost are all right, especially if you mix it with grit of some sort, preferrably broken-up sandstone. Again, see that this top dressing is not too rich in nitrogen. If it is, your plants will go all to green leaf and refuse to flower.

THE PATTERN OF FLOW

Imagine a mountainside with snows above always melting and always sending down lots of water in a more or less continuous flow. Because the ground is rocky and porous, much of that flow is underground, and the plants growing on the mountainside have their roots down in the spaces where the water goes by. As it rushes over the stones and chips and gravel, it picks up bits of mineral, inorganic nutrients, and the roots of the plants thrive on that nutritious soil-solution. Though other tiny bits of humus get stuck and cling to the rocks and gravel, much of it is washed down, and the fine clay is washed down, too.

All of this is why, when you build a rock garden for alpines, you want to have at least five pails of drainage material for every pail of soil mixture.

LIMING

There is a temptation to lime the soil for rock gardens, especially if you need to break up clay. Better to lay down a plastic or to dig out the clay and take it away than use lime. Lime-loving plants can usually get along pretty well without the lime, and the ones which prefer granite soils instead of limestone will just be killed by additions of lime. In the chart which follows some of each are indicated. Of course, if you can prepare a special place for just lime-loving plants, it is perfectly all right to lime that area, and your plants will like it. Use dolomitic limestone if possible.

POSSIBILITIES FOR PLANTS

A rock garden can have wildflowers as well as cultivated or imported plants, ferns, grasses and reeds, flowering trees and shrubs, either as background and to grow tall for shade, or as miniatures to spread out among the rocks as prostrate plants and shrubby groundcovers. Some suggestions follow below, but for much broader coverage see the excellent book by the old Swiss pioneer in rock gardening, Henry Correvon, whose book, *Rock Garden and Alpine Plants* (Macmillan, 1930) is full of suggestions, anecdotes, personal experiences and discoveries, and pages of specific comments on the plants you can try to grow. Another good book, by an American, is that of H. Lincoln Foster, (no relation) *Rock Gardening, A Guide to Growing Alpines and Other Wildflowers in the American Garden* (Houghton Mifflin, 1968). You might prefer to read them both at once, or the Foster before the Correvon, because Foster gives a list of the common names to help you with the main lists, which are according to Latin names in both books. There is also the two-volume classic by a man much admired by Correvon, *The English Rock-Garden* by Reginald Farrer, a name you can recognize in quite a few Latin plant names. A useful how-to book, especially for Northwestern gardeners is the Sunset Book by George Schenk, published in 1964: *How to Plan, Establish and Maintain Rock Gardens*, with hints about construction for anyone. For Easterners there is the pamphlet put out by the Brooklyn Botanical Garden, *Rock Gardens*, as one of their very helpful series. A catalogue by such a place as Alpenglow, 13328 King George Hwy., Surrey, British Columbia, V3T 2T6, is a boon for those seeking suggestions about flowers and small shrubs and dwarf, slow-growing conifers—even though the descriptions make it sound as though everything were equally easy to grow. The Rock Garden, Rte 2, Litchfield, Maine, 04350 is another good source; and so are Lounsberry Gardens, Box 135, Oakford, Illinois, 62673, and Mincemoyer Nursery, on Country Line Rd., Jackson, New Jersey, 08527, where you can get ferns and wildflowers as well as insect-repelling plants and organic gardening aids. A place that states they have nursery-grown wildflowers (the only kind I'd feel comfortable about getting) is Wick's Wildgardens, Box 115, Conshohocken State Rd., Gladwyne, Pennsylvania, 19035. Their catalogue is only two pages long, but you can get a 64-page catalogue which includes unusual alpines or rock garden plants and native perennials at The Wild Garden, Box 487, Bothell, Washington, 98011. Seeds, of course, are available at all the big seed houses.

The lists that follow are to whet your interest and open some of the treasures you can have. Plan to get enough plants of enough varieties so that the final effect will not look spotty and haphazard. Of course, you can propagate and increase some of your flowers and take cuttings of some of your dwarf shrubs. But if you plant a wall, it is not going to be very easy to keep changing things around, planting and replanting at will. A few rock garden plants like some of the pinks, are active self-seeders, so there will be plenty of them. Also have some specimen plants, a solitary beauty here and there for interest, and include some of the fragrant plants, the starred ones in the list, and enough honey plants such as alyssum, penstemon, daphne and others.

I haven't grown alpines, but I do use rocks as background walls for many of my spring bulbs, some with ivy or with morning glories or roses climbing on them, and I do benefit from the good drainage in a bed at the top of one wall by the terrace. Of the rock gardens I am acquainted with, my favorites are those which have good color in the spring, plenty of cheery spring bulbs, and enough interesting cultivated and wild plants to keep one returning over and over to see the treasures there, whether in a shady corner, or out in the sun on a warm slope.

In the list which follows there are plants which have been tried out in various kinds of rock gardens. Because some of them are really very sensitive to the soil pH, the preference has often been indicated. Aside from the listing here, there are also a good many notations in the lists in the chapter, *Perennials*, among which are suitable plants such as: alpine aster, dwarf aster, alyssum 'Basket of Gold', alpine pink, moss pink, betony, carnation, Cheddar pink, many of the bellflowers, baby's breath, bishop's hat, coral bells, fringed bleeding heart, rock candytuft, funkia or plantain lily, leadwort, lily-of-the-valley and other groundcovers, many of the rock cresses, salvias, true geraniums, wild phlox and blue phlox, lady's mantle, saxifrage, scabious, the potentillas, many of the primroses, including the auriculas in an alpine garden, thrift, vinca and wild ginger, both the latter as good groundcovers.

FLOWERS FOR THE ROCK GARDEN

Name	Soil Preference	Height	Color	Comments
Alpine Anemone *Anemone alpina*	Alkaline	18 inches	White flowers; fern-like foliage green	Variety *sulphurea* has yellow flowers.
Baby's Breath *Gypsophila paniculata*	Alkaline	3 inches	Small white flowers.	Can be as many as 1000 flowers in single-branched panicle in July.
Beardtongue *Penstemon barbatus*	None	3 feet to 6 feet	Red flowers; linear dark green leaves.	Many species of *Penstemon* excellent in the rock garden; try *P. acaulis; P. montanus; P. nitidus.*
Bellflower *Aubreita deltoida*	Alkaline	3 inches to 6 inches	Flowers red to purple.	Flowers from April to June; excellent for edging in the rock garden; not full sun; good on wall.
Bunchberry *Cornus canadensis*	Acid	9 inches	Evergreen leaves; yellow flowers.	Blooms May and June; good ground cover if given enough moisture; berries are edible—can be used for puddings, etc.
*Columbine, Alpinerock *Aquilegia betolonii*	None	1 inch	Violet-blue flowers; small grey-green leaves.	This columbine is well suited to the rock garden. Try also: *A. alpine; A. canadensis; A. flabellata.*
Coral Bells *Heuchera sanguinea*		1 foot to 2 feet	Red to pink flowers.	Excellent for edgings in the rock garden.
Edelweiss *Leontopodium alpinum*		6 inches	Yellow flowers; white, woolly leaves.	Blooms July and Aug.; one of the most popular of all the alpine flowers.
*Garland Flower *Daphne cneorum*	Alkaline	6 inches		Thrives in a rich soil: blooms in May and June; will need some protection in winter; try also: *D. alpina; D. odora.*
Geranium *Geraniaceae*, the *Geraniaceae* species	Alkaline	4 inches to 2 feet	Most flowers are in varying shades of pink.	Good for the rock garden as they bloom for long periods during the early summer. Try *G. dalmaticum; G. macrorrizum; G. subcaulescens.*
Hardy Cyclamen *C. europaeum* and others.	Alkaline	3 inches to 4 inches	Pink, white and red flowers.	There are a number of hardy cyclamens but the ones best in the rock garden are *C. europaeum; C. coum;* and *C. neopolitan.* The *europaeum* bloom from Aug. to Sept., while the *coum* are in flower from Jan. to April, so there is a wide range of flowering. Not rel-

*Fragrant

Plant	Soil	Height	Flowers/Foliage	Description
*Grape Hyacinth *Muscari botryoides*		1 foot	Blue-purple flowers.	iably hardy north of New York City, though one neighbor of mine grows them here in Vermont. Very fragrant small bulb flowers which bloom in late April or early May; one of my favorites because of the delicious scent.
Heather *Erika*, the *Erika* species	Acid	18 inches to 18 feet	White, rose, deep pink, crimson, and blood-red flowers; grey-green foliage.	Any species of Erica is good to use in the rock garden—as accents or with azaleas. A sure bet. *E. odorata* and *E. australis* are very fragrant.
*Iris, Dwarf (Crested) *Iris cristata*	Alkaline	3 inches to 4 inches	Pale lilac flowers.	Creep fairly rapidly along the ground; the flowers bloom in May and June; very small, and delicate.
Lady's-Slipper, Yellow *Cypripedium pubescens*	Alkaline	22 inches	Yellow and brown flowers.	This is the only Lady's-slipper which I can recommend for the rock garden, as the others demand a soil of a very low pH and a very special fungus population. They are lovely plants, and I suggest that you use only this species.
*Lewisia Tweedy *Lewisia tweedyi*	Acid	4 inches	Salmon-pink flowers; evergreen foliage.	One of the most beautiful of the *Lewisa*; species; try any of the *Lewisa*; they do well in rock gardens; *L. spinosum* is fragrant.
*Madwort *Alyssum*, the *Alyssum* species	Alkaline	3 inches to 1 foot	Yellow flowers; foliage varies from greyish to evergreen.	Most of the species of *Alyssum* are quite good in the rock garden; Try *A. saxatile*; *A. spinoseum roseum*.
*Partridgeberry *Mitchella repens*	Acid	groundcover	Pinkish-white flowers set against evergreen leaves with white veins.	Excellent groundcover for dwarf shrubs or acid-soil plants wanting a shady or semi-shady environment for their roots.
Periwinkle *Vinca minor*	Alkaline	groundcover	Lilac-blue flowers and rich, dark foliage.	Popular groundcover because it is such a healthy plant; pretty, too.
*Pasqueflower *Anemone pulsatilla*	Alkaline	1 foot	Large, two-inch, bluish, or purple flowers. Also white, pink and red varieties.	Popular rock garden flower, due to its lovely bell-shaped flowers. Purple petals yield a green dye, not permanent, which is used to dye Easter eggs.

FLOWERS FOR THE ROCK GARDEN (cont'd)

Name	Soil Preference	Height	Color	Comments
Persian Candytuft *Aethionema grandiflorum*	Alkaline	6 inches to 8 inches	Rose-colored blossoms against bluish foliage.	This is a good border plant. It loves sunshine and sandy soil. Has a spicy aroma.
Phlox *Phlox*, the *Phlox* species	Acid	5 inches to 4 feet	White, deep pink, lavender and purple flowers.	There are too many fine species *Phlox* to list them all here, but you might want to try some of these: *P. nivalis; P. stolonifera; P. speciosa; P. divaricata.*
*Pinks *Dianthus*, the *Dianthus* species	Alkaline	2 inches to 3 feet	Flowers come in almost every color.	*Dianthus* are particularly good in the rock garden because their flowering season is so long. From spring to autumn, you can have various types of *Dianthus* in bloom.
Primrose *Primulo*, the *Primula* species	Alkaline	3 inches to 4 feet	White, rose, lilac, violet, orange, pink, purple, etc. flowers.	You could devote your entire rock garden to the cultivation of *Primulas*...instead, try these varieties: *P. apennina; P. hirsuta; P. tyrolensis; P. clusiana; P. mistassinica; P. vulgaris.*
*Rockjasmine *Andromeda chamaejasme*	Alkaline	3 inches	White to pink flowers.	A good rock garden plant, and a very lovely little Alpine. Needs constant moisture.
Saxifrage *Saxifraga*, the *Saxifraga* species	Alkaline	1 inch to 3 feet	Colors range from white, yellow, and reds to purple.	There are nearly 300 species of *Saxifraga*, most of which are good in the garden. I suggest that you try: *S. aizoon; S. longifolia; S. caespi tosa; S. grisebachii; S. burseriana.*
Sempervivum *Sempervivum*, the *sempervivum* species	Alkaline	4 inches to 1 foot	Greenish, yellow and red flowers; outstanding foliage.	No rock garden is complete without "Hens-and-chickens". There are hundreds of species, but I suggest you try: *S. arachnoideum; S. ciliata; S. tectorum.*
St. John's Wort *Hypericum reptans*	Alkaline	ground-cover		Does well in the rock garden as ground cover. There are other varieties of St. John's Wort but I don't recommend them as they contain a heat-resistant

Name	Soil	Height	Flower	Notes
Violets *Viola*, the *Viola* species	Acid	2 inches to 12 inches	White, yellow, blue, purple, and rose flowers.	principle which causes photo-sensitization, and are potentially poisonous. These are one of my favorite flowers—and there are quite a few which you may want to try in your rock garden. Among them are: *V. cornuta*; *V. odorata*; *V. papilionaceae*; *V. pubescens*; *V. tricolor*.
Waterlily Tulip *Tulipa kaufmannia* Many other bulbs are suitable for rock gardens. See chapter on bulbs.	Slightly acid pH 6-6.5	5 inches to 10 inches	White with light yellow, and red streaks.	One of the earliest bloomers. This is a very good ornamental flower, in addition to being a great rock garden plant—and a universal favorite.
Wood Sorrel *Oxalis montana*	Alkaline	6 inches	White flowers, veined pink.	Bloom from May to Aug. I find this one of the most beautiful of plants—very delicate. *O. magellanica* is particularly fragrant.
Yarrow *Achillea tomentosa*	None; not rich	8 inches	Yellow, with grey-green foliage.	Blooms July, Aug.; full sun,

12

Water Gardens

Whatever form it is in, water is—after flowers, of course,—the one best feature you can have in the garden. It is entrancing to look at, a joy to hear, and the flowers you can grow in water and near it are among the most beautiful there are. I don't know anyone who doesn't love water lilies, and the irises and flags swaying gracefully beside a stream or pond are a close runner-up.

POOLS

The reflections in the pool can double your pleasure. Or your distress, if you permit the pool to be placed where what you see reflected is the back of you neighbor's tool shed, your own laundry wheel or garbage cans, or the dull, dreary face of an apartment building's blank wall. I love to visit my neighbor's pool where, instead, I can watch the reflections of gently moving foliage and ornamental grass, clouds, blooms and buds, and on summer afternoons the darting of dragonflies and swallows that pass over the pool hunting for insects.

If your garden, like the one where I visit this pool, is designed as an outdoor room for relaxation, water makes it twice as restful—or maybe more so. After you relax in the hot sun, a pool large enough to get into adds the extra pleasure of cooling you off. All pools and running water can cool the air somewhat, and the sound of water, as we know, gives the psychological effect of cooling, too. My garden gives me an intensified experience of the revolving seasons as I see in miniature and close by, thegreat sweeping cycles of the year. Water gardens intensify that feeling even more, and make the changes seem more poignant and more present.

WHAT KIND TO CHOOSE

If you can arrange for running water, do so. Where there is a slope, it is easy enough to foresee how pleasant a waterfall, and a small stream leading to a pool below would be. If you are so lucky as already to have a stream coming down a slope, it is even easier to imagine damming up the brook at some point and creating a pool. But even on flat land, you can introduce a mound of some sort, construct a waterfall down it, and a little stream leading to a pool in which you can have a circulating pump that will carry the water back up to the waterfall. In a way, this situation is the luckiest

A very pleasing series of little waterfalls created by lining part of a brook bottom with plastic and damming it with rocks and flat tiles.

for you can choose exactly where and what kind of pool to have.

I certainly recommend that all gardeners use recirculating water for their gardens. You save water that way, in the first place; but you also save yourself the bother of finding a proper drainage system, proper treatment of the soil so it won't waterlog and get swampy below the pool, and the nuisance of having just one more thing to get out of order—in case, for instance, the roots of nearby shrubs decide to invade the drain. Most important of all, you can maintain a temperature of the water suitable to plants and fish, without its being chilled unduly.

The great advances today in waterproof plastic materials such as PVC, polyvinyl chloride, have made it possible to have pools and even streams with plastic bottoms, so you don't even have to go to the bother and expense of concrete structures any more. They have to be replaced, yes; but so do most concrete pools, too, when they begin to crack and leak. Obviously it is easier to pull out and replace a plastic pool bottom than a concrete one. And it is no more trouble to put the masking stones around a plastic pool than a concrete one. And no more trouble to put masking sand over plastic than over concrete. A recirculating pool, where the rainfall is enough to replace the water lost through evaporation, can go on and on. When evaporation exceeds the new rain supply, tap water can be used to fill the pool again, as long as it is added in small enough amounts to keep the temperature from dropping so quickly it upsets the pool balance and disturbs the plants and the fish you will have in your pool to help maintain that balance.

Some other advantages of a plastic pool over a concrete one are that you don't have to go through the big operation of pouring the concrete all at one time to avoid cracks, or the bother of having to keep filling and draining the pool for weeks until the alkalines are washed away. Since it is best to grow your water lilies and other water plants in tubs or boxes or baskets, you won't have a soil bottom to the pool, and only need a sandy bottom of some attractive natural color.

SIZE

Though it is possible to grow a water lily in a space as small as a sunken barrel, a larger place is needed for most water lilies, especially if you plan to grow the kind you can leave in the water all winter. Where the weather will make the pool freeze over you will need a depth of three feet. Unfortunately the ready-made plastic or fiberglass pools you can buy usually are not that

deep, so inspect the dimensions carefully before you buy. There are little waterlilies, the Chinese waterlilies, which you can grow in shallow water, as shallow as six inches; but the bigger ones are much more attractive. If you want the biggest, most spectacular lilies of all, use tropicals in big three-foot boxes at least a foot deep, and, if you live in the north, treat them as annuals, and get new ones each year. (A warm greenhouse could carry them over if the night temperature is 70°F. or warmer.)

The overall size of a pool is of course up to individual choice, but the thing to remember is that a really successful still water pool must have a large enough surface area in relation to the total capacity so that there are no drastic temperature fluctuations. Neither your plants nor your fish could stand that. This means that a square pool would best be seven feet on each side, or a rectangular pool, ten feet by five. In figuring a free form, oval, kidney-shaped or dumbell-shaped pool allow for 50 square feet. Of course, there are pools smaller than this, but the experts predict that smaller pools will be more difficult to balance, and more subject to the fluctuations of temperature which disturb that balance.

WHAT BALANCE MEANS

A decision about the shape and size of your pool is actually determined by the condition referred to as "green water." All pools have it at some time or other, but the degree and duration does depend on the design of the pool.

It is caused by algae, either the free-swimming minute green kinds or the filamentous kinds which grow in threads. One of these, blanket-weed, which grows rather furrily, can be an awful nuisance if not controlled. It is a menace; the others are not, and the fish rather enjoy that green pea-soup water, or so it seems. All these algae get into your pool from spores in

A free-form, plastic lined pool before and after filling it with water and landscaping around it.

the air, and all thrive under conditions of light and warmth in the presence of carbon dioxide and mineral nutrients. New pools with fresh soil in the planting boxes and minerals in the water are bound to get algal growth in them.

If you go into a panic and change the water, you just start up a new cycle, and do not solve your problem at all. Leave the pool alone, and let the growth subside of it own accord. I have

been told that the disappearance of the algae and the arrival of clear water can come as rapidly as overnight. It is the clearwater pool which is called a balanced pool.

It does not imply any static condition, for an alive environment is never static. What it means is that the predator patterns, and the rhythms of growing and decaying, are healthy, normal and clear. The clarity indicates that the population explosion of algae has consumed the excess mineral salts, has met the competition of oxygenating plants, which also consume salts, and the shading foliage of the water lilies and other floating plants which have cut down the optimum conditions of warmth and sunlight. On the morning that all is clear there simply are not enough algae left to rise up and make the water green any more.

Nevertheless, if your pool is not the right shape, you may have green water conditions persist for an inordinately long time. A saucer-shaped pool is much more likely to heat up in the day from the sunlight than is a square-bottomed pool, which will hold nearly twice as much water. (A saucer pool cools off at night to make fluctuations which are not good for the fish.) Vertical sides, however, are not advisable because of the soil-stabilization problems, so you had best design your pool to have sloping sides about 20° from the vertical, and while making that slope, put in a shelf near the top on which you can rest the plants which prefer not to be in deep water. Pools with this shape will not hold quite twice as much water as a saucer-shaped bowl, but in a circular pool ten feet across, it has been estimated a sloped pool with a marginal shelf will hold 612 gallons as compared to 380 gallons in the saucer-shaped one, and that is a healthy difference. Another advantage to a 20° slope is that the really good tubs often come with that slope, too so they just fit.

DEPTH

A pool as shallow as 15 inches is inadequate. If you are tempted to buy a ready-made fiberglass pool, for instance, be sure that you get one deeper than that or you will run into trouble. The reliable, well-established water-garden firms will provide you with something that will work. Avoid cheap substitutes.

Depths needed:
18 inches, if the area is 100 square feet
24 inches, if larger than that up to 300 square feet
30 inches, if 300 square feet
36 inches, if 1000 square feet or larger

There are exceptions, but those figures give you a guide for choosing what to do. Get expert advice if you possibly can. The companies which specialize in water lilies are always ready to help. These estimates may be rather generous, but it is better to be on the safe side. The shallow depth needed by arrowhead or little calla lilies, for instance, you can achieve by making a shelf, which is usually adequate if the shelf is nine inches down from the surface of the water. It need not extend all the way around the pool because you probably will not use enough plants for shallow water to warrant it. A complete perimeter of such plants would spoil the design of the pool and make it look as though it had a tonsure haircut.

MADE PONDS

Several of my friends have put in what we usually call farm ponds, dug out in moist places where the water settles and makes it difficult to do any gardening except for swamp plants. One of my colleagues at the college where I used to teach had such a place and scooped it out, expecting it to fill up the next year and be beautiful. It didn't. And it took several additions of fine clay to the bottom before the leakage stopped. But now it is well set, half-surrounded by osiers, a few willows, tall Joe-pye-weed and some bird-attracting bushes like high-bush cranberry and two Russian olives. The grass slopes down to the water's edge on the other side opposite the high vegetation, and it makes a pleasant approach and a pleasant sight when you drive by on the road leading up to the house. All the toads in the neighborhood come there to breed, and it is great fun to chase baby toads by the pond in season. (The owner catches some for his biology project; I like to get some to take home for insect control for my own garden.) This is a naturalized water garden, in keeping with the other gardens at this place, and with no effort to introduce the formal, exotic water lilies used by others whose aim is a standard lily pond.

Another farm pond, quite a lot larger, was built by one of my neighbors mostly for the sake of her five sons and daughter, to give them a place to play and swim and fish during the summer. This pond was stocked with trout, and for plants just the reeds and the field grasses, buttercups and daisies which grew up naturally. It worked well, and was a joy to all the family until some child in the neighborhood who didn't know any better dumped a bowl of goldfish in, and the population explosion was awful. Also in the favorable environment the new generations kept being bigger and bigger—finally as big as carp. So be warned.

A POOL AS A FOCAL POINT

In one village in my Vermont town, as in so many New England mill towns, the big house of the most affluent citizen is at the top of the hill, and its grounds are well laid out and well landscaped, with several gardens including a formal one which can be viewed from the house. This big house is now a museum, but the formal garden is still visible, with its long path from the steps below the north porch leading to an oblong pool with a statue in it, which in the old days held the fountain. The edging plants are still there: arrowheads, hostas, and a clump or so of ornamental grass. The fountain is still, and the lilies are gone, but there used to be hardy water lilies in the pool and an occasional showy tropical lily to brighten things up. This kind of decorative small water garden as part of a larger garden laid out in formal squares is not very popular today, though that kind of pool, and the statue-fountain are both very appropriate for a city garden, it seems to me, where the space is confined, the view closer to the house, and the sound near enough so you can hear it. Wall fountains are especially pleasant in city gardens, and reminiscent of courtyard gardens in European cities.

A JAPANESE GARDEN

Aside from the European tradition so influential in the ways people use water in their gardens, there is now a very strong and fascinating Japanese tradition which makes for lovely, restful and interesting gardens. (And one of the marvels of this tradition is that you can have such a garden with no water at all—by using sand that is raked to imitate water, and stones placed so they look as though they were in a lake or river setting.)

One I liked was an exquisite small example which lived up to the usual Japanese aim of reproducing in miniature a favorite landscape. It not only had a little mountain, with its stream of water and a waterfall; it also had a small lake with stones in it simulating islands. The largest was actually an island, with enough soil by the stone to have a small pine tree growing. Another had a bonsai pine tree in a pot, so carefully placed that you didn't even realize it was a pot. The water lapped at these stones in the gentlest possible way, almost silently. There were three peninsulas reaching out into the lake, one large and two smaller, each with its miniature trees, and there were stepping stones between one of the smaller ones to the island with the small pine. At first I thought there should have been a bridge there like those I knew in Japanese gardens as a child, but the garden was really more special and individual without a bridge. The water grasses you could look down on as you went along the stepping stones were near enough to appreciate.

The Japanese garden here effectively uses sand and rocks to imitate water settings.

The iris leaves hinted that the bloom in early summer must be lovely. I know now that a Japanese garden expresses a theme in the most harmonious, thoughtful way the owner can make it. As an inspiration for meditation in a garden such as this the stepping stones pulled the design and meaning together as an essential part of the whole. Many Japanese gardens have no flowers. But where the climate is suitable, a flowering dogwood or a few azalea plants can be worked into a design, as long as they fit into a overall intention or the story, as it were, of the garden.

I have seen larger and smaller Japanese gardens than this. One spread over a whole block in a small New York city, complete with a large tea house, many interesting specimens of trees and a winding river, with many aquatic plants growing beside it, and in the still water stretches of the stream. A small one was just a tiny little garden outside a downstairs bedroom window, backed by a bamboo fence, and containing sand, stones, and some tall grasses. A very restful place to start calmly for the day.

MOVING WATER

A small pool in the yard for growing water lilies and aquatic plants can stand by itself; but I believe that a fountain in the middle or to one side is both attractive and useful. It lends interest for sight and sound, and it helps keep the water oxygenated for the fish. If you have ever seen fish gasping for oxygen on a sultry summer day of very low pressure before a storm, you know how they need it. (And if you do see them gasping that way, you'd better get out the hose and agitate the water quickly, to let air in.) Fish like moving water; water lilies do not; so a fountain is a good compromise. Water lilies need warmer water than most fish, so use recirculating water that will retain some of the heat of the sun.

Or have a waterfall and a small stream instead of a fountain, but be sure to have the outlet for the falling water immediately below its point of entry into the pool so that it is pumped back to recirculate before it has a chance to upset or perhaps cool the lilies.

One very pleasant thing to do is to combine a water garden and a rock garden along a stream. A lift of two or three feet is enough to get quite a good effect, and is ample to get oxygen into a pool of 100 square feet. The whole arrangement can be lined with plastic and have the rocks put over it. (Never try to combine rocks and concrete, for the bond is never adequate and you'll have leakage and trouble right along.) Most good water garden supply houses now carry all the equipment you will need—pumps, filters, recirculating pumps, fountain heads, and even fiberglass rocks down which the water can fall. They also carry appropriate fishes and snails, clams and salamanders which scavenge out any undesirable pests that might come to your pool. Creatures of this sort are good to have whether you have still or moving water. You can buy tadpoles, too, and remind yourself (if you lived in the country as a child) of the lazy summer days when you used to hunt frogs and tadpoles. That's what they remind me of, anyway.

LIGHTS

One fine addition the the effectiveness of your pool is to have some lights. A light beside the pool can be very appealing, but even more attractive are submersible lights which will shine up through the water and show off your water plants to wonderful advantage. These too are available from good dealers. (See directory for suggestions.)

OXYGENATING PLANTS

In addition to water lilies and other decorative plants, you will need those which provide oxygen for the water through their respiration. They grow underwater and include such plants as anacharis, with dark green foliage; milfoil, with small grass-like leaves; cabomba, with glossy leaves which spread out like a fan; ludwigia, with green and pink leaves; *Sagittaria sinensis* with strong dark leaves; and villisneria, which has long, finger-like leaves. These are all relatively inexpensive plants, and well worth your investment for the fish who eat up the insects for you, for the snails who keep the algae under control, for the tadpoles who scour out decayed matter, and for the water itself, to keep it healthy and clear and well-oxygenated.

FERNS

Before discussing the water lilies and other plants to have in a water garden, I'd like to mention some ferns which are always attractively green and cool-looking near pools, streams and ponds.

Some which tolerate full sun are the hay-scented fern, interrupted fern, lady fern, ostrich fern, sensitive fern and Virginia chain fern. Those preferring shade include American maidenhair fern, berry bladder fern, Christmas fern, common polypody, crested wood fern, ebony spleenwort, Goldie's fern, New York fern, the lovely royal fern and spinulose wood fern. Some of these, like the dainty little ebony spleenwort and the Christmas fern as well as the common polypody look lovely and do well if put with rocks.

WATER LILIES

These are the magnificent flowers that grow in tubs or pots—or of course in the soil of natural ponds—in the deeper water. The hardy ones are *Nymphaeae* and are usually divided into the two categories of night bloomers and day bloomers. Among the day bloomers you can get, for example, such handsome white flowers as 'Alice Tricker', 'Isabelle Pring', and 'Mrs.George H.

Pring', propagated as you might imagine by the hybridist George H. Pring. For yellow lilies try 'Aviator Pring', 'St. Louis' or 'St. Louis Gold', which is a slightly darker yellow. Pink water lilies include 'Cleveland', 'Independence', both deep pink, a lighter one, 'Peach Blow', a bright pink, 'Mrs. C. W. Ward', and one that is almost crimson, 'Patricia'. There are even red water lilies, such as 'Evelyn Randig', which veers towards magenta; 'Red Star', rosy red; and 'Rio Rita', pinkish red. As might be expected from the name 'American Beauty' is just that color of bright red, the color of the rose of that name.

Some people like the bluish-purplish-lavender water lilies, but I am not much taken by these. If you do like them, there is a lilac one 'August Koch'; one that is more purple, 'Director Moore'; and really dark purple ones, much better looking, such as 'Midnight', 'Panama-Pacific', and 'Royal Purple'. The blue are more attractive: 'Bob Trickett', 'Col Lindbergh', 'Henry Shaw', 'Shirley Ann' and a large one 'Mrs. Edwards Whitaker'.

All those water lilies are tropicals, which means that you can grow them well in the warmer zones, but that they will have to be taken up or replaced in colder zones.

HARDY WATER LILIES

The hardy lilies, *Nymphaea gracilis* in variety, will survive, however, in colder zones, especially if they are stored well down under the ice in winter, and given good hay or straw protection so their roots never freeze. One method is to drain the pool for winter and fill it with leaves over the mulch.

The old standard white water lily you probably know well is represented in many collections as 'Marliac White'. Other white ones are 'Gladstone', a very double one called 'Gonnere', 'Hermine' with pointed petals and a little one, 'White Pygmy'. The good yellow ones include 'Chromatella' and 'Sunrise'. Red ones are 'Attraction', 'Conqueror', with white sepals; 'Gloriosa', with very large fragrant flowers; and 'Sultan' which is very similar but more cherry red. A few water lilies have changeable colors; 'Aurora', from rosy yellow to deep red; 'Comanche', apricot to bronze; 'Paul Hariot', yellow to pinkish to orangish; 'Robinsoni', vermilion to orange yellow towards the center.

NIGHT BLOOMING WATER LILIES

Most exotic of all are the tropical water lilies which bloom in the night. Most visible and most effective are the white ones, 'Juno' and 'Missouri'. Both are large, flat and of a fine, clear white. Fairly showy also are the pink ones, 'Mrs. George C. Hitchcock' and 'Sturtevant', which does particularly well in hot climates. Red ones, if you have the light to enjoy them, include 'Devonshire', which is quite a bright red; 'Emily Grant Hutchins', a really beautiful rather rosy-colored water lily; 'Frank Trelease', dark red; and 'H. C. Haarstick', with coppery foliage and red blooms.

SOMETHING ELSE

I doubt whether any readers of this book will be growing this plant, but you might as well hear about it before I go on to speak of culture for water lilies. This is the plant called *Victoria cruziana* with leaves six feet across. I have heard that there is a water garden near Santa Barbara where the monsters grow, and that the 15-inch flowers bloom white one evening, pink the next and smell like pineapples. That we ought to see—and smell.

LOTUS

Then there is also the lotus, the ancient sacred flower of the Nile, which the Egyptians reverenced, I have been told, because they

observed that this flower magically contained a tiny replica of itself within its seed. Actually quite a few plants do this, but evidently the Egyptians first saw it in the lotus. There are several kinds you can order from water garden nurserymen. The Egyptian lotus itself is called *Nelumbium speciosum*, with a pink flower and a subtle fragrance—hardy to Zone 5. Another, *Nelumbium lutea*, is the yellow American lotus which has flowers up to nine inches across, and sometimes listed as American Chinquapin. Then there is a cream-colored one, *N. flavescens*, and the red-striped one, *N. album striatum*. There is also a rose lotus, a double one said to be rare, which has deep pink global flowers.

CULTURE OF WATER LILIES

It is always best to plant water lilies in containers. Then, even in a pond, you can move them around, control the planting medium and the fertilizing program, and handle them more easily for winter protection than if they simply grow in the bottom of a pond. In a concrete or plastic pool, it is advisable to put them in tubs or boxes, preferably large enough to hold a bushel of potting soil. The depth of the water over the upper surface of the tub should be nine to 12 inches, and the water lilies will do best if spaced three to five feet apart. They also do best if the tub is placed on two stones for support, and not directly on the bottom of the pool. In contrast, it is perfectly all right to place the pots of oxygenating plants right on the bottom.

As an exception, a small artificial pool or tub of water may be filled with six inches of soil at the bottom over which there are six to nine inches of water. Then the root of the water lily may be pressed down into the soil. This method of pressing the root down may also be used in natural ponds. In larger artificial pools, where you use the one-bushel tubs, boxes or plastic baskets, plant the roots in the upper layer of the

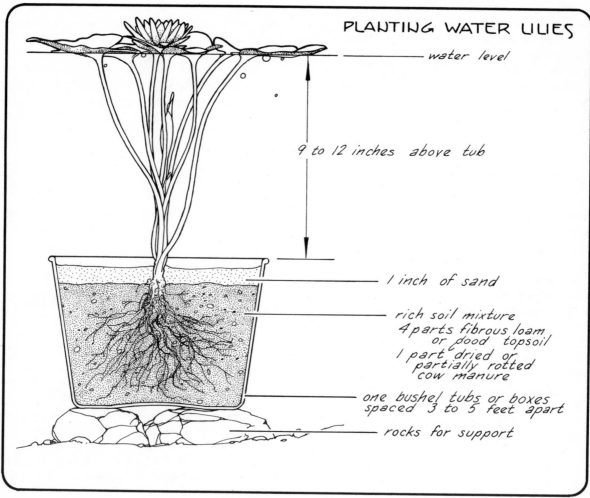

PLANTING WATER LILIES

- water level

9 to 12 inches above tub

1 inch of sand

rich soil mixture
4 parts fibrous loam
    or good topsoil
1 part dried or
    partially rotted
    cow manure

one bushel tubs or boxes
spaced 3 to 5 feet apart

rocks for support

rich soil in the tubs. The soil mixture should be made of four parts fibrous loam or good top soil and one part dried or partially rotted cow manure. Do not use leaf mold, muck, peat moss or sand, or perlite, because perlite escapes and floats, and the others are injurious.

There are good reasons why you do not want mud, pond sediments and silt in your pool. The scum you may or may not be able to see on the tiny particles is made up of algae, fungi and bacteria which are attached to the silt in lacy, complex patterns. There are literally countless bacteria attached to sediment particles with nutrients adsorbed to their surfaces. What happens is that these bacteria mineralize the organic matter thus creating the nutrients for algal growth, and you can get green pea-soup water in serious proportions. Nitrates and phosphates build up. Studies at Lake Tahoe in California have shown that 80 per cent of the nitrates released through mineralization originate on particles that have sunk way down below the area where algae thrive and photosynthesize. This deep level, in a big lake like that one, can reach down 300 feet. Where it is darker and deeper, of course, the algae do not thrive.

After planting the root, just at a level where the top will be at the top of the soil, a one-inch layer of sand, gravel or pebbles may be added. This helps to keep the water clear and to keep the fish from roiling up the soul and making the pool muddy—as they certainly will if you cover the whole bottom of the pool with soil. If the tubs or baskets leak soil, line them with old sheets.

Tropical lilies do best in water of about 70°F., and with four to six inches over them. Hardy water lilies need more water, and do well in cooler water. Lotus tubers need warm water, also, and need to be planted in a horizontal position two inches below the surface of the soil. When first planted give them four to six inches of water over the soil surface, but after they are established, increase the depth to eight inches or a little more. These, too, and all pots and tubs in the pool need the one-inch layer of sand.

In the winter, take up the tropical lilies, as suggested above, and protect the hardy water lilies. If you plan to leave fish in the pool instead of draining it, cover it with tightly fitting shutters or boards and put the leaves on top of them, at least 15 inches deep, and something on top of the leaves to keep them from blowing— chicken wire, boughs or corn stalks. Storing the boxes in a cool, moist basement, with plenty of moss or wet burlap around them is another protection you can give.

FLOATING AND MARGINAL PLANTS

One of the advantages of water lilies in a pool is that their large leaves cast shadows and thus hold down the algal growth. Floating and marginal plants help to do that, too. Some that are recommended for this purpose are salvinia, S. braziliensis, with soft velvety green floating leaves; shell flower, Pistia stratiotes, with a rosette of green leaves, recommended for any areas you have that get some shade; water fern, Ceratopteris thalictroides, with the curious habit of more little plants at the edge of their leaves and likely to get out of control. Water garden nurseries also list water hyacinths, the plant that has gone rampant all through the canals and waterways of Florida. Luckily there is a law forbidding these plants to be transported across state lines, so only the people who live in the same state as the nursery selling them are able to get hold of them in case they are tempted. I certainly am not. Duckweed is another floating plant I am not tempted by.

Marginal plants to put on the shelves are those which do not need or like the deep water suitable for water lilies. Arrowhead has long been used for pools, both giant and double. Cattails are also useful and attractive natives, and very handy to have if you make dried arrangements. Forget-me-nots of the aquatic variety add a good spot of color, and there is a little calla lily that will do well on a marginal shelf. The beautiful red cardinal flower is native to wet places, and often obtainable from water garden nurseries. So are marsh marigold, the yellow flowers of spring, various irises and flags, water arum, water plantain and water cress, which you can pluck at will to put in the salad. I have grown this cress in a pool that was still much of the time, but it does best in running water. These are all fairly hardy plants.

For warmer climates there are many tropicals you can grow. Aside from the butterfly lilies, the blue flowering temple plant, a water-loving dracaena and papyrus, both large and dwarf, there are the feathery parrot feather, West Indian spider lily, umbrella palms, and several species of taro.

WATERSIDE PLANTS

Not exactly in the pool, but near it there are any number of waterside plants to grow. These are also appropriate for the banks of natural streams and ponds, and for the edges of any dampish areas you may have at your place. Though one of my favorites, *Iris laevigata*, with its clear violet-blue flowers in late spring, is appropriate either in the margin or at the waterside, other irises are very fine as waterside plants, too. The big yellow *I pseudacorus* is one. And the Siberian irises are others. *I. sibirica* 'Perry's Blue' is a fine example. This one likes less water over its roots than the water iris, *I. laevigata*. Cotton grass, bog bean and the summer-blooming *Pontederia cordata* with its blue flowers can stand water over the soil they are planted in, but other waterside plants such as astilbe, meadow sweet, *Filipendula ulmaria variegata*, various funkias, purple loosestrife, and the primulas of the candelabra type cannot. Ferns, as mentioned above, do well too. And very spectacular are the big handsome spathes of *Lysichitum americanum*, which has a yellow hood, and *L. camtschatcense*, which has a white hood.

Farther out from the pool or up the bank you have any number of opportunities for background plants; small conifers, flowering shrubs like azaleas and potentillas, or dwarf trees—as long as their roots do not intrude and disturb the other plants.

HEALTH OF THE POOL AND THE FISH

The worst thing for your fish is to let vegetation such as old leaves, rotten bits of twigs, spent flower heads and any other sort of decaying vegetable matter get into the pool, or stay there for any length of time if it does fall in. Fungus diseases can be carried to them that can be fatal. Such detritus is bad for your ornamental plants, too. So that is one of the main reasons you do not want to have trees overhanging your water garden, or bushes too near it. Keep a scoop or a net handy so that you can clean the surface of the water as you would a swimming pool. And if bits of decaying matter come down from the waterfall or from a stream, get those bits out as fast as you can, also. The insects are usually snapped up and eaten by the fish, and this goes for mosquitoes, too, as you probably know. But uneaten bugs or other animal organic matter which you see should be removed as well. Be sure your pool is well supplied with scavengers and oxygenating plants.

If you see that your plants are having difficulty, wash them with a good strong stream of water as a first aid. Aphids, for example, will probably promptly disappear if given that treatment.

Your plants sooner or later will need some more fertilizer, in fact, people who use chemical fertilizers are likely to insert a pellet into each tub every two weeks. Organic gardeners can make their own pellets out of dried blood and diatomaceous earth, bone meal and potash rock. It is also advisable to add some extra dried cow manure at the bottom of the tub when you plant your lilies and marginals.

BIRDS

If you want the birds to come to your pool, it is best not to have an active fountain, which is likely to frighten them. They do like the dripping sound of water, however, and even a small plastic pool or a pan painted sand color with a hose running to it, will attract birds. This can be surrounded by stones, and rigged up so that one side is lower than the other to keep the water slowly running. With a little careful management this kind of make-shift can be planted with some moisture-loving plants such as forget-me-nots or iris. Both for the birds and for your lily pool it is best to use water that has had a chance to get rid of the chlorine. In small amounts it can be left in buckets in the sun. With a whole pool, it is best to let the water give off its chlorine for a week or two before planting.

Larger ponds will attract ducks, and perhaps geese and even swans. If you have such luck, grow some marginal plants they will like. Water garden people sometimes talk about marginal plants as though they were merely decorative (perhaps because they do not fill the function of shading the water as pad lilies do), but the function of bird feed, to my way of thinking, is a good and honorable one.

Burreeds are among the favorites of water birds. You may, if you live in the Northeast, be familiar with the common giant variety, *Sparganium eurycarpum*, because of the striking bur-like seed heads, in balls along the stem. (You might also attract crane, snipe and perhaps a muskrat with this plant.) Eelgrass is another favorite of the ducks, especially brants, and baldpates, and pintails and scoters on the Pacific coast. Bulrushes, wild rice, sweet flag, and out in the water arrowhead and the particular favorite of water birds: pondweeds, the *Potamogeton* varieties, especially *P. pectinatus*, sago pondweed. (For a good, thorough discussion of what the birds and small animal like to eat, see the book *American Wildlife and Plants*, by Martin, Zim and Nelson. It will give you hints about the feeding habits of water birds and the upland birds as well.) (See Appendix.)

13

Seaside Gardens

In recent years when I've stayed at the seashore, I've been much too busy sunning and bathing and exploring the sands and dunes to care what kind of garden there was; but if I lived all year around at the seaside, I'd certainly care. And from memories of Dorothy Perkins and Rugosa Roses along the fences and in dooryards on Cape Cod, I know that there are some plants you can expect to do wonderfully well in sandy soil and salty air. There are even plants which will do well where there is salt spray, and I understand they get nutrients out of the spray to help nourish themselves and make up for the scarcity of nutrients in the sandy soils.

PLANT BEACH GRASS

Attention to manure and humus and a consistent program of adding them to the soil will help to build up a sandy soil. Of course drainage is good already, and the organic matter you add will readily create a soil that plants can thrive in. If you have to start with nothing more than a sand dune, you will need to anchor down the sand as well as build it up. Plant beach grass, *Ammophila breviligulata*, and let it spread, and for interest add such others as Broom sedge, *Andropogon virginicus*, Sea oats, *Uniola panic-*

ulata, Weeping lovegrass, *Eragrostis curvula*, or if you live on the West coast European beach grass, *Ammophila arenaria*. Plant them up to eight inches deep and fertilize well in spring and early summer, with a thorough watering at the same time. Where there is a lot of off-sea wind, put up a fence, too.

PLANT WINDBREAKS

Also start planting windbreaks for higher, more permanent protection for the seaside garden you are going to have. Trees such as American holly, Scotch Austrain and mugho pines, white and scrub oaks, a rugged maple like Norway maple, and perhaps fillers like Colorado spruce or the fast-growing white poplar.

SHRUBS

Shrubs which can also be used for fillers include the beautiful grayish bayberry, with its fragrant gray berries which the birds like so well (and also the candlemakers); the picturesque beach plum, now becoming available in many nurseries; lilacs, highbush blueberries where you can make the soil acid with oak leaves and peat; and the wonderful roses lile *Rosa rugosa* and the ramblers. To stabilize dunes there is nothing like the Memorial rose, *R. wichuriana*, which is a very reliable groundcover for sandy places. As you may have noticed in seaside, sandy places, Scotch broom is also a handsome year-round plant to enjoy—with neat green foliage and charming pea-like blooms in May. You can also grow at the seaside such shrubs as barberry, privet, the cotoneaster called Rock spray, red osier dogwood, sumac, and the Clethra called Summersweet.

PERENNIALS AND ANNUALS

For color and cheerfulness you will also want to have flowers as well as shrubs and trees. The flowers which have the word *"sea"* (or in Latin, *"maritiums- a. -um"*) attached to them already give you a hint of things to grow: sea pink or thrift, *Armeria maritima*, will do well; and so will sea-holly, *Eryngium maritimum;* sea bindweed, *Calystegia soldanella*, with big pink flowers; sea-poppy, *Glaucium flavum;* and sea-lavender, *Limonium latifolium*. There are also Sea dahlia, *Coreopsis maritima;* Sea goldenrod, *Solidago sempervirens* and sea hollyhock, *Hibiscus moscheutos*. In addition, try Aaron's rod, *Thermopsis caroliniana*, with flowers like lupine, and the other lupine-like plant, Blue false lupine, which is *Baptista australis*, as well as Golden aster, *Chrysopsis falcata* and some of the common annuals like cosmos, nasturtiums, petunias and zinnias.

CARE OF PLANTS

Some of the plants listed above do well near inlets and other places that are marshy. Some will survive where it is drier. Where the soil is dry and sandy, it is best to keep building it up so that it will hold moisture and give your plants a better chance to survive. Watering helps, of course, but water-holding humus and other organic materials are best. Not only incorporate all kinds of organic materials that are porous, but also mulch with organic materials, too. Even hay as a mulch is good, and any sheet composting you can manage, with green plants as well as dry—with fresh kitchen wastes as well as composted. And use seaweed. There it is on the sea shore, especially in rocky places, so gather it up and bring it in to the garden, both for a mulch and for incorporating into the soil. If you can shred it, all the better, for then the small bits and pieces will decompose and release their goodness to the soil more quickly than the large festooning pieces will. It is advisable to wash off the salt before you use seaweed. It is also very helpful to seaside soil to plant green manure crops whenever you can and to plow them or till them in. Let all pine needles, leaves and other detritus from your trees and shrubs fall to the land and fertilize it. Sandy soil will take just about all the organic treatment you can give it.

SEASHORE FERTILIZERS

People who live near the sea are particularly fortunate in being near several other sources of fertilizers. For calcium and phosphorous there are the oyster and clam shells you can get. Rich, well-endowed mud from mud flats is available. All sorts of fish scraps can be got at the fish wharf or fish market, including the scales of fish, their innards, and the shells of shellfish. The fish scraps are so high in nutrients that it is dangerous to put them fresh into the vicinity of your plants. Compost those scraps along with your green matter, and you will find that you have a rich, nutritious, fine black home-made fertilizer as a result.

Seaweed, as you probably know, is an excellent fertilizer. Shred it for good results; or use it as a mulch, and let it decay gradually into the soil. Since, unlike fibrous plants, it does not

A carefully planned seaside garden that sets off the wide sweep of the ocean beyond. The natural stone wall acts as a windbreak for the shrubs, wildflowers, and perennials growing in front of it.

have any cellulose, it mixes down into the soil quite quickly. It is rich in sea minerals which your plants are well nourished by.

DESIGN FOR A SEASIDE GARDEN

Since views are very important at the seaside, presuming you have a view of the ocean, or of an estuary, keep a vista open when you design your garden, even though you have to flank it with windbreak plants. If a small stonewall can be introduced, perhaps in a graceful curve to each side of the vista opening, you can grow small and colorful plants in front of the protection of the wall which you might not be able to nurse along if exposed to the sea breezes that can trickle through the stoutest windbreak. Where stone can be got hold of fairly easily, this is a feature to be considered. And though they are not very common in seaside gardens, I'd certainly recommend that here, as in other gardens, you do your best to include some water, either in the form of a pool, or a recirculating waterfall, stream and pool, or a

fountain. With all that ocean out there it may seem a bit too much to add more water, but the source of fresh water for the birds, and for your own enjoyment can be just as great at a seaside place as back in the woods on some mountainside, or in a highly-paved suburban place.

WILDFLOWERS AT THE SEASIDE

The informal effect appropriate for a seaside garden is enhanced by using wildflowers. In many places there will already be plants you can preserve, but anyone who has wrestled with a tangle of wild roses or sumac is not in much of a mood to save any of it. But you will find useful bayberries, clethra, marsh elder, and perhaps the pleasant gray woolly beach wormwood which is known as dusty miller. Where I used to summer as a child I took a great deal of interest in the wildflowers, though not the garden ones. I remember a good deal of beach pea, seaside goldenrod, and something we called woolly hudsonia, with yellow flowers in early summer and grayish leaves. On our way to the post office my sister and I used to pass large stands of gorse, which also had yellow blooms.

If you have a marshy place and are in need of a groundcover, I can think of nothing pleasanter than having cranberries, though a carpet of bearberries would be very attractive, too. Both need acid soil. We only passed by cultivated fields of cranberries or bogs, as we called them, and we thought longingly of the Thanksgiving feasts they would end up at.

One of the spinsters up the road from one house where we stayed had a meadow garden behind a wild rose hedge. She encouraged such flowering field flowers as blue chicory, Queen Anne's lace, and black-eyed Susans. If she had thought of it, she might also have introduced some butterfly weed, with wonderful orange flowers and just as attractive to butterflies as the name implies. Later in the summer this field had golden asters and its lavish bloom was followed by the purple wild aster we called blazing star.

On the way to this seaside town when we drove down from a Boston suburb, we used to stop at places near Plymouth. There in the spring we saw birdsfoot violets, wild geraniums, yellow stargrass, and back in the woodsy places, wild lily-of-the-valley, little checkerberry plants and the flower you just can't transplant, pink lady's slippers, growing in profusion on the pine needles along the edge of the woods. One family we stopped to see had a brook, and I remember trout lilies, jewelweed, turtlehead, bee balm and both red and blue lobelia—the red one being what I now call cardinal flower. Where it is

moist and sandy you are also likely to see (or used to see) silverweed and golden hedgehyssop, as well as goose tansy, sea pinks and sometimes rose mallow or sea hollyhock.

Down by the inlets and salt marshes we became acquainted with the teeming life of the estuaries, the eelgrass and smooth cordgrass, which are very tolerant to the salt in the brackish water, also the glassworts and sea lavender, the marsh goldenrod and spearscale. All those plants decaying, especially the salt hay from the grasses, contribute to the strange but beguiling smell of the salt flats—beguiling, that is, to people who have spent exciting hours at the seashore in their youth. Somewhat farther inland are the other handsome grasses, panic grass and the lovely purple-plumed *Phragmites communis* familar to those who travel along New Jersey flats where it covers acres and acres. And then come the comparatively upland plants like the bayberries, wood sage, groundsel, and eventually the small red maples and red cedars. All of these can be grown in a seaside garden if you have the right degree of wetness, and if you want them to come into your garden.

My family didn't happen to. They preferred bachelor's buttons, cosmos, portulacas, nasturtiums and other familiar annuals which could be planted and brought to bloom in the fairly short summers we went to the sea. For a much more ambitious seacoast gardener see the book by Thalassa Cruso, *Making Things Grow Outdoors*, where she tells of her efforts in what she calls the "country garden."

14

Shady Gardens

Sometimes a homeowner is fated to have a shady garden because of the way the land lies or because there are shadows from a neighbor's house, tall shrubs or tall trees, and of course there is always the shady site of one's own house. Perhaps you have a shady place because you refuse to cut down the trees that are there, or have purposely planted them for your own reasons—for shading a terrace or patio for protection or privacy, or for cover for the birds and other wildlife you like to have in the yard. Some people just love woodsy areas and make a garden that is designed from the first to be a shady garden, as my friend and mentor did when she built her new house. In fact, she and her husband had the lot for quite a while ahead of time, and simply let the brush and small trees grow up until they had the kind of vegetation, screening and habitat areas they wanted. Then they built, placing the house not only in relation to the sun and slope, but also in relation to the fine stand of young white pines which had developed. The garden now is a gem of shade-loving plants at the edge of the woods and under the high branches of the white pines. (All low branches were trimmed off.)

The rewards of such a garden are wonderful. You get more birds to come in than in other gardens, especially if you provide water that they can hear—either a trickling brook, or some other moving water, or just a hanging pail with a nail hole in the bottom, plugged with a stick that doesn't quite fit, so that there is a drip-drip-drip into a pan or water or birdbath below. The dappled shade is endlessly interesting, and there are secluded places to walk and find the surprising flowers that will bloom away from the full sun. The Japanese, my friend has told me, call the making of a garden in such a place: "building a wood for bird call."

THREE KINDS OF SHADE

There are at least three main kinds of shade to take into consideration. Under thick woods with trees having dense foliage, as on the north side of the house, you have full shade. If your house has one side that faces northwest or northeast, not strictly north, you may have a fairly light bright area, but without sun except during late June. If the house is white, it might provide just the kind of light preferred by the fussier begonias, for instance.

A second kind of shade, light shade or part shade as it is sometimes called in the seedsmen's catalogues, is characteristic of deciduous woods, where there is good air circulation, but no continuous sun.

A third kind, which I call half-shade or half-sun because it means both but is also sometimes called part shade, or semi-shade, is characteristic of what you get on the unshaded east side of a house, and also on the west side. Take an hour count and if you get six hours of sun, that counts as half-shade, even though the exact twelve hours of sun only occurs at the equinoctial days in March and September. There is a difference, of course, between the plants that would favor being on the east or west sides of your house. Those that are most subject to troubles from being damp do better on the east side because then they get the morning sun to dry them off quickly. Those that are particularly tender about hot afternoon sunshine also do best on the east side where they are in the shade during the afternoon. Rugged, unfussy plants like petunias thrive on either side, as well as in full sun, of course.

WOODLAND SHADE

In a normal woods garden with the varieties of vegetation you have in a natural place, you probably would get some of each of these kinds of shade, and the transitions may be very abrupt. Where you would put a plant that can endure dense shade such as a small maple, sweet fern or one of the anemones or oxalies, you would not use forget-me-not, but right next to the shady spot might be some half-shade where the forget-me-not would do very well. In the denser shade you might also put a stand of early bulbs such as Spanish squill, some ferns, some andromeda, some of the laurels and yews, and perhaps impatiens and chrysanthemums, though those two flowers do well in part shade and part sun. Also for half-shade where the forget-me-nots will grow, you can plant many flowers such as loosestrife, Virginia bluebells, bee balm,

bouncing Bet and the annuals (or biennials) ageratum, foxglove, sweet alyssum, honesty and salpiglossis or painted tongue. Shrubs for semi-shade include dwarf high-bush cranberry, winged euonymus, azaleas, rhododendron, blueberries and many others.

GARDEN DESIGN

Before selecting your materials, however, think of your design, and if the shade comes from trees, think of the competition from tree roots or the roots of big shrubs, too, for that matter. A garden at the edge of the woods is very effective. And since the lines of the shrubs and small trees in the woods are rather fuzzy and blurred, the lines of the garden look very handsome if they are distinct, sharp and pronounced. A shady walk, mulched with ground bark or some other dark woodsy material would make a good demarcation by a very low yew hedge, or a garden itself. On the other side, where the lawn or ground cover comes up to the garden, a clear demarcation by a very low hew hedge, or a border flower such as evergreen candytuft can be used. My friend uses a line of red bricks on their sides, so that the demarcation is distinct in the change of color from green to red to the brown of the pine-needle and ground-bark mulch in the background, under the shade-loving flowers and small foliage plants. A straight line for a woodside garden is all right, if you want it that way, but my preference would be for curved lines and some irregularities in the layout. Maybe you are fortunate enough to have some rocks, or a stream, or maybe you could introduce one.

PLANTS IN THE SHADE NEED SPACE

The spacing of plants growing in the shade must be quite wide. Since they do not get the sun very much, their food-making processes, their

The gentle curves of the path and bordering daffodils and groundcovers repeat the sweeping lines of the woodland beyond, in this garden at the edge of the woods.

photosynthesis, can be rather restricted. They need all the nutrients they can get, and if there is competition with big roots, they need space to compensate. They also need space for air circulation. Since shaded plants do not have the benefit of making their own food in normal sunlight, they will need lots of high-humus, high-nutrient additions in their soil as well as a minimum of competition from nearby plants. Weed at once. Add plenty of manure, compost, leaf mold, and keep an organic mulch over the area which will continuously decay and keep providing more and more nutrients. For acid-loving plants keep adding pine needles, ground bark, rotted sawdust, or wood chips, even up to three inches. The mulch also, of course, has the extra benefit of being a weed-control and conserver of moisture. It is not too often to apply fertilizer to a woods garden every other week. Use compost tea, manure tea, a solution of fish emulsion or Fertrell or other organic fertilizer. A well-spaced, well-mulched woodside garden offers a rare and beautiful garden sight. The plants are so well placed and so visible in their separate stands that you can really get a good look at them, much better than the view you get in a garden where many blooms, much closer together, are all at once to be seen and taken in.

WHAT TO PLANT

The passing of the seasons will offer a series of lovely sights. In the spring you can have the spring bulbs, trilliums, primroses, jack-in-the-pulpits, wild ginger, and many others. If there is not enough sun for the leaves of your bulb plants to make food for storage for next year's growth, you can very carefully lift them and transplant them into a sunny place for the summer and replant them in the fall. You can also treat your bulbs as annuals and replace them with new bulbs every year, but that is rather expensive and a waste.

The small bulbs are not so much in need of building up food, of course, as the larger bulbs such as tulips and daffodils. Among the small bulbs I recommend winter aconite, the first to appear with us, in a corner under some lilacs. Nearby and coming out almost as early are the little snowdrops. They both bloom so early that the foliage of the lilacs does not shade them from the sun, so even before their own foliage dies down—which is within a fairly short time—they have plenty of chance to make food.

Other small bulbs to consider are the lovely *scillas* or squills, which come in a brilliant blue and also in pink and white. Then there are the dainty trout-lilies; glory-of-the-snow, *Chion-*

odoxa luciliae; grape hyacinths; the little snowflakes, *Leucojum vernum*, and many of the crocuses.

Many varieties of daffodil, narcissus, and tulips do well in part shade, especially among the tulips the so-called species tulips like *Tulipa clusiana* and *T. kaufmannia* (mainly because they are small, but also perhaps because they are not hybrids). Suggestions about particular varieties of bulbs can be found in the chapter, *Bulbs of All Sorts*.

Along with the bulbs you can have Virginia bluebells and the spring wild flowers. And then as the spring goes on, flowering trees and shrubs like flowering or Kousa dogwood, some of the azaleas, barberries and viburnums, and for flowers, more primroses, leopardbane, bishop's hat, and lily-of-the-valley. During the summer you can enjoy bleeding heart, day lilies, balloon-flower, astilbe, and later on monkshood, meadow rue, false dragonhead, meadowsweet funkia or plantain lily, asters and many others. Annuals to put in the shade luckily include such good edgers as ageratum, alyssum, periwinkle and pansy. And for the middle area, impatiens and nicotiana, which are taller. If you have luck growing cardinal flower, these brilliant red beauties will brighten up a shady place very cheerfully.

Some of the irises, the small ones, do quite well in shade. You can have an early dwarf blue one, *Iris reticulata*, and in half-shade it is easy to grow *Iris cristata*, *I. pumila*, *I. gracilipes* and *I. verna*. And of course the begonias, both tuberous and wax, much prefer shade though some sun will not hurt them at all, contrary to popular belief in many quarters. (What they can't stand is direct, hot, intense mid-day and afternoon sun.)

Remember that house plants like to spend the summer outdoors in the shade. Fuchsias will do very well. To these you might add any ferns you have. Permanent ferns that are excellent in shady places include the delicate maidenhair, the evergreen Christmas fern and such big, handsome specimens as the cinnamon, interrupted and ostrich ferns.

GROW YOUR OWN FROM SEED

Under ordinary circumstances annual plants grown under fairly rugged cold frame and outdoor circumstances by nurserymen are a good buy, and often are less likely to be leggy than the ones you grow yourself. Nevertheless, I believe it is a good idea to grow your own plants yourself if you can. Then you are the one who sees to their early culture, their hardening off, their initial habits of adapting to their environment. For plants to go into a shade garden this can be even more important than for plants going into the sun.

Some of the annuals to grow might well include the ageratum, *A. houstonianum*, and 'Blue Bedder' is a good one to try. Sow indoors in March, and expect germination in from five to ten days. Barely cover the seed, and take off the cover of glass or plastic when you see the seedlings appear. This all-summer bloomer can be planted in frost-free areas as early as January. This flower, like many mentioned below, will do well if it gets six hours of sunlight, but a little more or less will be all right if that is all that the situation allows.

Annual asters can also be tried. They will germinate in seven to 14 days, and can be planted indoors in April. Again barely cover the seed. These take all summer to come to bloom, but they do make a fine display when their season arrives. Even so, the perennial asters are even more satisfactory.

Balloon flowers, *Platycodon grandiflorum*, another satisfactory perennial can be sown indoors in February or March, where it will probably germinate in seven to 15 days. Since it resents transplanting, it is best to start this summer bloomer in peat pots.

A fine plant for part shade is the Blue torenia, *T. fournieri*, which needs a long season to come to bloom, so plant it in February. It only takes five days to germinate and will do best in rich, moist soil both indoors and out. Once established, it will bloom all summer.

Others needing not more than six hours of sun include flowering tobacco, *Nicotiana alata*, which is a very graceful plant with fragrant white and slightly colored, or pink and purplish trumpets. One variety has almost green trumpets. Its very fine seeds take about 14 days to germinate, and can be started in April. Give them plenty of space outdoors, but a group is more effective than single specimens.

Pansies, which of course are really biennials, are good to use, though their season is even shorter in the shade than in the sun. I always buy mine, and try to plan to have some other plant to replace them when they go by. More satisfactory are those flowers which will go on blooming once you get them in.

In the shady garden I described above this role is filled by the begonias my friend grows from seed. She starts the seed early in prepared peat pot trays, keeps them moist and covered until the seedlings appear, and then gradually hardens them off in the door of her garage when the weather permits. For these tender, shade-loving little plants she has rigged up a series of curtains which can be lowered when the afternoon sun gets too warm. Then when the time comes to set them out in the garden, she puts her begonia plants in a part of the garden that is open to the northwest. In our long Vermont summer days, they get just enough sun in this location to make them thrive and bloom all summer. It is also the part of the garden which faces the driveway, so the sight of the perky little pink blossoms is a pleasure to all who drive in.

Now as never before impatiens, also called patience, and one variety called balsam, are plants of great popularity. Though they do best, and grow most hardy if sown outdoors—or if they self-sow, it is possible to grow them in peat pots indoors. Their germination period is supposed to be in seven to ten days, but I have known them to take nearly 15 days. And at that, it was not until some bottom heat had been applied that the plants finally came up. Impatiens is not too particular as to soil, but they do crave lots of moisture. If you do not keep watering this flower, it will quickly wilt. It is a fine flower to grow, (See chapter on Annuals for suggestions about other things to do with it.)

Primroses are lovely, modest additions to a shady garden. Though the variety, *Primula polyantha,* consists of hybrids that do not come true from saved seed, it is fun to grow them to see what you'll get (and you can always throw out the ones that don't suit you). A fine variety with red or rosy flowers, rather dwarf, is the Julia Primrose, which blooms early, as early as April or May. Before planting, primrose seeds need chilling, and if you know that the seedsman has not done this, put them in the refrigerator for a month or six weeks. Then plant in a warm room and wait three to four weeks for germination. You can omit the refrigerator treatment by starting them outdoors in a cold frame in November.

POSSIBLE WILDFLOWERS, PREFERRING NEUTRAL SOIL

Because some wildflowers are so fussy about having acid soil, it is perhaps best to concentrate on growing only the fairly common ones which do well in more or less neutral soil. Get them from a reliable nursery—unless you happen to have them growing on your own land.

Alumroot, American and Colorado columbine, bishop's cap, black snakeroot, bloodroot, blueblee (*Campanula rotundifolia*), Canada violets and other violets, Dutchman's breeches

and its relative squirrel corn, foam flower, wild lily-of-the-valley and wild lupine, liverwort, may-apple, rue anemone, Solomon's seal and false Solomon's seal, spring beauty, and as already mentioned, trillium and trout lily.

POSSIBLE SHRUBS

Though definitely preferring acid soil, the azaleas are such gorgeous plants to grow that if you can manage it, it would certainly be good to include such beauties as flame azalea, pinxter flower, rhodora and swamp azaleas. Other shrubs are the chokeberries, several dogwoods, elderberry, inkberry, leucothoe, nannyberry, and sweet pepperbush. Though also needing acid soil, if you live in the right zone, you might be able to include the excellent small rhododendrons (or the large ones) and some mountain laurel.

Beware of introducing the awful disease petal blight to your area. It comes from the South, so if you have to get plants from a southern nursery, ask for bare root plants, with all the buds removed. You might, nevertheless, introduce the beginnings of this pest into your area, and then you might be responsible for the infestation of all the mountain laurels, for example, in your state. Better than to do this would be to deal with a nursery north of the infested area.

GROUNDCOVERS FOR SHADE

If you have less time to spend on a shady garden than it takes to care for perennials and annuals, you can alway use groundcovers. They will more or less take care of themselves as soon as they have been established and are thick enough to no longer need weeding.

A satisfactory and good looking groundcover is plumbago or blue leadwort, *Ceratostigma larpentae*, with good green foliage and blue flowers in August and September. As with most other groundcovers, it is not only attractive but useful, since it helps to hold banks and prevent soil erosion. Others good for that use include bugleweed or carpet bugle, *Ajuga reptans*, periwinkle, sweet woodruff, pachysandra, English ivy, lily-of-the-valley, the euonymus species such as wintercreeper and its relatives, and the lovely *phlox divaricata*, sometimes called blue phlox, with its dainty lavender flowers in the spring. Some of the very low and prostrate evergreens are also valuable. (See Chapter 11 on rock gardens for suggestions.)

CITY GARDENS IN THE SHADE

If there is any air pollution in your city, you are somewhat restricted, of course, as to the plants that will do well for you. Among the needle-leaved evergreens, for instance, only the yews are recommended. Some of the broad-leaved evergreens, however, will survive: the species of *Euonymus fortunei*, Japanese andromeda and Japanese holly, and the holly called inkberry, as well as leucothoe, creeping mahonia and some of the azaleas and rhododendrons.

Deciduous shrubs you can use include five-leaved akebia and the ever-faithful privets. But try also mock-orange, hydrangea, sweet pepperbush and weigela, which may do all right if you do not live next to a sulphur-belching factory or power plant.

The groundcovers, luckily, are fairly impervious, especially funkia, bugleweed, pachysandra, periwinkle, a few of the sedums, and epimedium, bishop's hat. Plants like Virginia bluebell, which you can use for a groundcover or in mass plantings for spring show, or violets, whose leaves last longer, will also withstand city conditions. Ferns to use include evergreen Christmas fern and polypody, also the hay-scented fern and two big ones, cinnamon fern and interrupted fern, both handsome fillers for any corner.

Bulbs are all right to use, too, especially the smaller ones. Scilla and grape hyacinths are possibilities, and also lily-of-the-valley and the small iris, *Iris cristata*. I have seen the leaves of large bearded iris thrive in planters on a shady city roof, but I must say that the blooming of those plants was rather scanty. The vines were more successful, both English and Boston ivy and silver lace vine. Others to try are Virginia creeper, virgin's bower or Virginia clematis, and Japanese wisteria. Some sun will encourage blooming.

Don't bother with annuals except for impatiens, flowering tobacco and wishbone flower (*Torenia fournieri*). Use potted plants such as fuchsias, wax begonia and caladiums instead. And also in weather which will not damage your plants, you can move out philodendron, wandering Jew, rubber plants and monsteras without doing them too much harm. Wash the leaves, however, if they get sooty.

Most of the rugged city plants will take care of their insect troubles themselves. For the euonymus, however, you may want to treat it with a miscible oil spray in the spring to control scale insects. If any appear later, try swabbing them off with alcohol on a piece of cotton. If aphids appear, use soap and water or a mild spray of Tri-excel. Pick up all slugs and snails and drop them into a dish of salt or cup of very salty water.

WHERE THERE IS WATER

For areas in and around a pool in the shade you can grow the sword-leaved, prettily striped plant sweet flag, *Acorus calamus;* water plantain, *Alisma plantago-aquatica*, marsh marigold, bogbean, yellow pond lily and other water lilies, pickerel weed, arrowhead, and the handsome water arum or wild calla. Ferns go well near water, and other wildflowers like cohosh or bugbane, *Cimicifuga racemosa*, spiked loosestrife, spiderwort and Joe-pye-weed. Keep them under control, for the nice moist conditions may induce them to spread. (See Chapter 12 on water gardens also.)

EVERYONE CAN HAVE A GARDEN

These and other plants are all suitable for shady places or half-shady, so no one need sulk and say it is impossible to have a garden because geraniums and petunias won't do well in one's yard. Grow other plants. Nature, luckily, has blanketed the world with green plants, and since many of them perforce grow in the shade under tall shrubs, vines and trees, many of them are available for cultivated gardens. Just learn what they are and go to work to make yourself a garden that is suitable for your place. And experiment. You may find that your place will support plants not always considered shade-tolerant, even though they may turn out to be half size or sparsely blooming. Maybe you will find you like them in those conditions.

15

Wildflower Gardens

Now that we have the federal Endangered Species Act of 1973, and will have nationwide lists of the plants which are presently endangered or threatened of extinction before long, there has grown up a whole new attitude in this country about bringing native plants into the garden to make a wildflower garden. About 30 states have already prepared lists of endangered wildflowers, ferns and other plants, and in some states the fine for picking or pulling up such rarities runs as high as $15 per blossom (or maybe higher). There has been entirely too much vandalism of wild plants, and both thoughtless pickers and greedy commercial exploiters of plants have been responsible.

If people would be content to use the commoner, more rugged wildflowers we see growing along the roadsides, or if people who feel they are so special they must have special rarities in their gardens only knew what really very special conditions these plants required and how unlikely one is to be able to provide them, then the problem of the wildflower garden would be less serious than it is today.

The trouble with so much of the moving of wild plants is that people either do not know or completely disregard the widely various soil and habitat requirements of the flowers or shrubs

they want to move into their gardens. In many instances the unfamiliar, unsuitable habitat of the garden will kill the plants in time. Endangered species should not be moved from their habitats at all. If you really believe you want to do something about these plants, go to the wild place where they grow and propagate them there, by layering or making cuttings or gathering seeds and planting them. Some of these operations can be done at home, and then the new plants returned to the natural habitat. Help from an expert botanist or consulting a skilled wildflower propagator is advisable.

SOIL FOR WOODLAND PLANTS

Acid-loving woods plants need at least 25 per cent humus, with a continual mulch of tannin-bearing leaves such as oak and pine needles. Peat moss, if imported from Canada or Europe, is likely to be acid, but domestic peat is likely to be alkaline, so be sure to get the imported kind for use in building up the humus content, and to help lower the pH of the soil. Add dusting sulfur to lower the pH especially if your wildflowers have inadvertently been watered with water of a high alkalinity. If there is lime in or under your soil, you will have to use pots or plastic-lined beds, for the water table will be limy and the earthworms will add limy castings when they come up to feed on the rich humus. My advice would be to grow other plants.

Test your soil before consulting with the nursery where you plan to get your plants, and inquire about what wild plants would probably do best in the kind of soil you will be starting out with. Also consult about the program of soil improvement you will have to keep up to suit the wild plants. Conversations about such topics will help you to decide how reliable the firm is.

One day I was visiting a wildflower nursery and watching the packing of pink lady slippers (notoriously difficult to grow under cultivation). They were to be shipped to California. I made a remark about how little chance they had to survive out there in most zones and waited for an answer. The packer answered all right, but he merely said: "Well, if these die, they will just order some more. We get lots of repeat orders from California." I silently groaned. Though I did see many plants growing under lath at that nursery, and know they might have been propagating some species, I am pretty sure about where the plants came from in the first place.

As compared to ordinary gardening with perennials and annual flowers, wildflower gardening requires more study of habits, habitats and capacities of the flowers you want to bring in from the wild, and more exact awareness in your own garden of the soil, moisture, degrees of shade and microclimates which you can provide to meet the exact need of the wild plant. It is more than likely that the needs are very special—or the plant would have become a cultivated plant long ago. Aside from consideration of soil, moisture, exposure, and the associated microorganisms which the plants need for their nutrients and hormones, there is another need plants have to maintain association with neighboring mosses, grasses and other plants normally living in the same habitat. With alpines, even the rock chips on the ground can determine whether the plant can live in a certain place or not. Such special conditions are sometimes very hard to maintain. Remember that the deep duff soil of a forest has a humus content of nearly 100 per cent, as compared to garden soils of ten to 15 per cent when good. The moisture-holding capacity of 100 per cent humus is obviously much higher than ordinary soils. Also, in a forest, the wild flowers under a canopy of trees are usually fairly widely spaced. To give them plenty of room you may have to modify your shady places considerably. You may have to clear out many of the shrubs that grow there to make a proper habitat for woods flowers.

The function of the fungi for acid-loving plants such as the lady slippers and the heathers, as well as most of the rhododendrons, is, among other things, to provide hormones. According to scientists who have studied the mycorrhizal associations between the roots of acid-loving plants and fungi, the plants themselves are not able to provide the hormones for themselves, so they have to rely on the fungi that grow up into their roots between the cells. It is also believed that the fungi provide proteins which the plants have difficulty in providing for themselves. In exchange, in this symbiotic relationship, the plants provide carbohydrates for the fungi.

There are many, many flowering plants that grow wild in woodlands, and I direct you to the lovely books devoted entirely to these flowers for a more complete discussion than I have room for here. See the Appendix for some that I recommend. The following woodland wildflowers are among my favorites.

TRAILING ARBUTUS

I know of an enthusiastic propagator, Mrs. Tom Siler, a garden club member in North

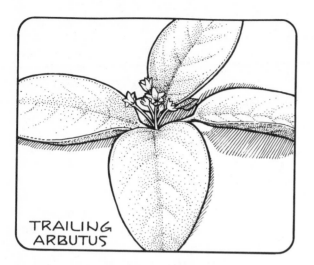

TRAILING ARBUTUS

Carolina, who goes to the mountains in early May to search for the small arbutus pod, which is, she says, "about the size and color of a healthy pea. It turns red later, and then black, as it ripens, and contains hundreds of minute black seeds."

When she gets the seeds home, what this propagator then does is to scatter the tiny seeds on a three-inch layer of mixed peat and sand in a flat, hardly covering them at all, but pressing them firmly into the mixture with the back of a tablespoon. To water, she uses city water that has stood overnight to get rid of some of the chlorine and to bring it to room temperature. In her first effort the germination took 33 days, and then the very tiny seedlings appeared. After ten weeks under gro-lights, she transplanted the little arbutuses into clay pots with some broken crock and chips of stone for drainage and good rich soil from her own woods with the right pH of 4.5. When they were in the pots, she moved them from a position of six inches below the lights down to 13 inches below. Once a month she fertilized the 105 pots she was able to get started with a weak solution of compost tea. The following March about half her plants had grown to be vigorous and healthy. Ten died and

of the remainder she noted that those which were weakest were the ones she left longest in the peat and sand before transplanting.

Those that survived were moved outside with the vigorous plants, to be hardened off before being planted out in their native habitat. This last transplanting to the ground in the woods was done in the fall, and she left them there to make it on their own. (I hope she used some sort of protective cage to fend off mice. And I hope she gets out each spring now ahead of the ants to collect seeds and propagate again.)

WILD BLUEBERRY

You can kill a wild blueberry plant by injudicious moving. The mycorrhizal or root needs of this plant are such that the plant has a root-relationship to the soil fungi which has to be satisfied if the plant is to survive. One way to insure it is to propagate the blueberries right where you find them growing. If you think you can bring them in from the wild, insure that you provide a highly acid soil, and bring in enough woods soil to provide the needed fungi. This plant, as well as many other woodland plants, must be protected from high winds, too much direct hot sunlight, and periods of drought. Wind and weather hazards are important to think of along with all the others.

JACK-IN-THE-PULPIT

There are other less demanding plants, of course, which can be propagated quite easily. You can gather the seeds or make a root division of jack-in-the-pulpit, and plant the resulting new plants in a partly shady portion of your garden. The soil requirements are much less exacting, and you can go on year after year, increasing the number of your plants until you have a fine showing. It is also possible to buy plants of this flower at nurseries, and if you do, try to deal

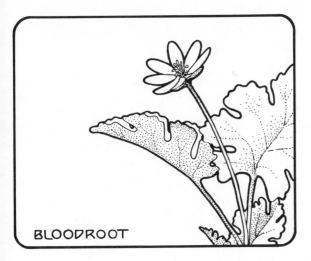

BLOODROOT

with a nursery which is actively engaged in propagating. Once established you can expect some natural propagation from seed, and it is a joy to watch where they will grow up in the shady part of the garden.

BLOODROOT

Another plant which spreads itself around when once established is bloodroot. I love to see its clean, white star-shaped flowers in early spring and to discover where it has spread to in some odd corner under shrubs or in rich humus by a rock. Root division is easy once you have well-rooted plants, and to sow the seeds, gather them when fresh and sow at once. Wait a year for them to appear. Best success will result from sowing them in half humus and half sand, with a one-inch cover of sphagnum moss.

DOG-TOOTH VIOLET

This plant, *Erythronium americanum*, and many of the other erythronium are available from bulb houses now. They are easy to get and not too hard to grow in the right soil, if you can wait five years for the bloom. One is called Trout

lily, and is a pleasant wild plant to grow. The bulb wants to keeping going on down deeper and deeper, so put a small stone under it to stop it.

CYPRIPEDIUM PUBESCENS

The only orchid I can recommend for a wildflower garden is the yellow lady's slipper, which is not so fussy about its soil and exposure. I have in my garden a clump of these lovely flowers, given us ten or 12 years ago by people who had had it over 20 years. It is practically pestless—unlike many other orchids—and many nurseries carry it. If you insist on orchids, this is the one to order. Do not attempt the pink ones. Given some shade, good drainage and a soil not so rich it will attract the wrong fungi, yellow lady's slippers might do pretty well for you.

Hepaticas, windflowers, clintonia, foamflower, wild geranium and some of the trilliums all need acid soil with a pH kept to about five with pine needles, rotting wood and oak leaves. Watering which is often crucial, should be with rainwater or otherwise de-chlorinated and de-alkalinized water.

FOR MORE NEUTRAL SOILS

If your soil is between pH 6 and pH 7, you are getting to a condition good for many ferns and for false Solomon's seal, bloodroot, alum root or coral beels, the dicentras like Dutchman's breeches and squirrel corn, and for one of my favorites for blue in the garden in spring, Virginia bluebells, *Mertensia virginica*. Add no lime to the soil, but keep it in condition with humus, manure, compost and decomposed leaves.

REALLY ALKALINE SOIL

Plants native to limy regions, some native to the seaside and to regions of the West which have alkaline soils can be grown in ordinary garden soils if you give them enough finely ground, dolomitic limestone, to raise the pH to seven or up to eight. Grass-of-parnassus likes limy areas, and some that like sandy places besides include Adam's needle, wild indigo, bird's foot violet and beach pea. Over pH 8, only certain western desert plants such as cacti, some yuccas and the succulents and desert shrubs will survive. Where the pH is that high, flowering shrubs are the best sources of flowers, though some of the desert wildflowers that come and go in a few days are very handsome.

ALWAYS PROPAGATE

All over the country now, there are people engaged in definite programs of propagation of wildflowers. One extensive program is the effort by members of garden clubs in every state to provide the state highway departments with wildflower seeds to scatter along the margins of the roads in order to improve the roadside planting with native wildflowers. One friend of mine up near Burlington, Vermont has offered to ride in the truck with the highway workers during the summer to point out which flowers already growing on the roadsides have not yet gone to seed themselves and should not be cut. In this way she will be protecting those species and providing for them to propagate themselves by going to seed naturally. Other women engaged in this project gather seeds of the appropriate species after tying small plastic bags over the pods while they are ripening and thus protecting the seeds so they can be gathered before the birds get them or before the pods pop and the seeds are scattered. The highway departments have all cooperated and said they'd be glad to scatter the seeds along the roads as their crews went along. In many cases the officials were very glad to learn of native materials which would reduce maintenance costs. It is obvious that low-growing native materials that do not need to be mowed are bound to reduce such costs.

COMMON BLUE VIOLET

VIOLETS

Very useful and attractive plants for a wildflower garden, for a groundcover and for certain roadsides are the violets. One that is best to use where the soil is moist and fairly acid is the primrose violet, *Viola primulifolia*, with white and purple flowers and leaves that do not look like violet leaves at all. A less fussy and prolific violet is the one called dooryard violet, *V. papilionacea*, with light purple flowers, native to cool woods from northern Vermont and New Hampshire and down to West Virginia. From the same range comes the Canada violet, with white flowers and good leafy stems, with the leaves heart-shaped as you'd expect a violet to have. Somewhat similar is the handsome longspur violet, a soft lavender color, which will grow in neutral soil if is woodsy and cool. These violets can be supplemented by some of the rarer yellow violets and commoner cultivated Confederate violets, to make a good display and, if wanted, a good groundcover.

FERNS

Ferns are also appropriate for moist woodsy

places and some other habitats, including roadsides where the maintenance is minimal. The daintiest of all is the maidenhair fern, with a delicate palm-shaped flat spread of leaves. It does well in shady places, or as a filler alongside a porch if there are trees nearby. Its Latin name is *Adiantum pedatum*, and it is carried by most of the wildflower nurseries in the East. Another which will thrive in moist, stony places is a fern of about the same height of a foot or so, the male fern, *Dryopteris felix-mas*. Slightly taller is the lady fern, *Athyrium felix-femina*, which spreads very easily. The familiar Christmas fern, *Polystichum acrostichoides*, grows to foot or a foot and a half, but the leaves often lie down so they do not seem so tall. I have bought Christmas ferns to put under some bushes where they got little or no attention and were in the most undistinguished soil, but they have thrived. Even more satisfactory is the evergreen woodfern, *Dryopteris marginalis*, which makes a good, thick dark planting. It likes part shade and a moist humusy soil, and if the soil is rocky, so much the better. (This fern is also called marginal woodfern in some catalogues.) Notice the new growth each fall around the base of the blades; do not cut this off for it is next year's fern.

There are many other ferns to consider, but settle for the ones that are not rare, and not too fussy. Some of the rarest are also the fussiest. One common fern you should know about is the sensitive fern which grows in marshy places and along roadsides in ditches. It is good for such places, even in the sun. It spreads rapidly, and might spread faster than you wished. But better to grow this fern, I'd say, than a rarity which grows naturally only in limestone pockets on hillsides and in places that nevertheless can stay moist. I know of one little fern demanding such growing conditions, and yet advertized by at least one nurseryman. I also know that it is rare enough so that environmentalists have tried to save an area from highway construction where

there was a single station of this rarity. (For the last five years it has remained saved.)

OTHER GROUNDCOVERS

If you can really keep your soil as acid as pH 4 to pH 5, there is a splendid groundcover to use, the bearberry, *Arctostaphylos uva-ursi*. It is an evergreen plant, hardy to Zone 2, with small white or pinkish flowers like blueberry blossoms, and good shiny red berries not more than half an inch in diameter. It forms a fine thick mat, and will do well in sun or part shade, but it likes poor, sandy soil best. Plant it in sandy soil and also sprinkle more sand on it so that the sand will wash down in and fill all the cracks. If rains flush the sand away, add more. Use acid peat moss and leaf mold of oak leaves to keep the soil acid.

Common thrift or sea pink, *Armeria maritima* is another good groundcover for sandy places. It grows about six inches high, with white and pink flowers in 12-inch stalks from mid-May to mid-June. Once you get a few plants going, you can divide and divide until you have a hundred or two hundred. This plant is good for rock gardens and edging, also.

A very good groundcover which is handsome and serviceable is wild ginger, *Asarum canadense*, which needs woodsy soil and shade. (No relation to the Chinese Ginger used in cooking.) The variety *A. virginicum* is evergreen, and so is *A. european*. Make the soil rich with humus, compost and leaf mold. The large, clean healthy leaves hide, small reddish-brown flowers in May, but stay neat and healthy all summer.

St. John's worts are good rugged plants to recommend to any highway department, though they often frighten gardeners because they can be very nuisancy and rampant. One called Blue Ridge St. John's wort, does not root so easily as many of the others, and therefore is quite safe to introduce as a groundcover. It has yellow blossoms and very small leaves which stay on the plant in Zones 5 and south right over the winter. This is called *Hypericum buckleyi*.

A much more delicate groundcover is wild Sweet William, *Phlox divaricata*, which has lovely little blossoms that come out in May. The blue or mauve clusters of flowers on 12- or 18-inch plants blooms well in either sun or shade. It likes moist, neutral, well-fertilized soil. A woods area is most satisfactory for this groundcover because it does get a bit lanky after a while.

WILDFLOWERS FOR WET PLACES

In places which can be kept truly wet, you can grow such delicate and interesting flowers as climbing aconite, *Aconitum uncinatum* and marsh marigold, *Caltha palustris*. The first blooms in late summer, with blue flowers, and the other in spring, with bright yellow flowers. A flower well worth propagating is the bluish-purple bottle gentian, which likes moist humusy soil. Its seeds are very tiny and should be grown on milled sphagnum moss.

More rugged flowers include turtlehead, *Chelone glabra*, which is white and *C. obliqua*,

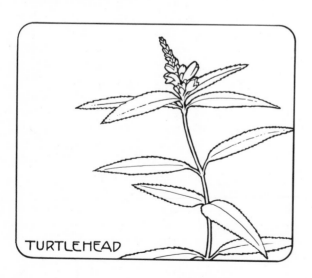

TURTLEHEAD

which is pink. Both like fairly acid soil, but the white can stand it nearly to neutral, if there is plenty of water and some shade when the weather is hottest. These members of the snapdragon family bloom in late summer, and the flowers do look like turtles' heads. Where you have plenty of room, try the swamp rose mallow, *Hibiscus palustris*, which can grow up to six or eight feet. The flowers come in pink, white or purplish. And then there is the cardinal flower, which will also grow in drier spots. It is fairly easy to propagate from seed, but to keep the old plant going, the stalk should be cut before it goes to seed. Several nurseries now sell seeds of the cardinal flower, *Lobelia cardinalis*, whose bright red flowers come out in late summer.

Other flowers you can try include spiderwort, *Tradescantia virginiana;* tall meadow rue, *Thalictrum polygamum;* false hellebore, *Veratrum viride;* and spatterdock or yellow pond lily, *Nuphar advena*, the rapidly spreading native suitable for large ponds. (For other waterlilies, see chapter on water gardens.)

WILDFLOWERS FOR DRY, SUNNY PLACES

Flowers that thrive in dry, sunny places, in my belief, are those which are most suitable for the organic gardener to grow as wildflower specimens. There are many bright, cheery daisies, black-eyed Susans, sunflowers and bee balms or bergamots which are not fussy about the acidity or alkalinity of the soil, and which will provide lots of color with very little care needed. Other plants for sunny places include the daisy-like *Heliopsis helianthoides* or *H. scabra*, which are not quite as big as sunflowers, but are just as yellow and handsome. Nurseries carry seeds of some of the cultivars now, and I particularly recommend the one with a soft greenish center called 'Gold greenheart'.

If you like coral bells in the perennial garden, you'll also like the ones that grow wild in several states. Those which are also called alum root, *Heuchera americana*, or *H. sanguinea* have good thick green, heart-shaped leaves and slender spikes of white, pink or red little bells. These heucheras make a very good groundcover, and the flowers are in bloom a long time. Many are hardy up to Vermont, and in states farther south it is worth trying *Heuchera villosa*, with white flowers and the habit of blooming all summer. (Apply to North Carolina nurseries.)

One of my favorite sights in June is to see a field overrun with lupines. Their pastel spikes and many pease-blossom florets always make a fine show. There are many kinds—as you can tell if you look at the five columns of lupine sources listed in Mattoon's *Plant Buyer's Guide*, published by the Massachusetts Horticultural Society. They run all the way from the cream-colored western lupine, *Lupinus argenteus* to the eight-foot tree lupine, *L. arboreus*, with fragrant yellow blossoms, and native to California, as many of the lupines are. The common wild lupine of the east is *L. perennis* and can be found in open sunny woods. The soil it prefers is poor, sandy and rather acid.

I'd also recommend for the sunny garden some of the evening primroses, such as the Ozark sundrop, *Oenothera missouriensis*. This has big showy yellow flowers, up to five inches across, and will bloom from June to September. Others with smaller flowers include *O. perennis*, native to the Eastern states, and a rosy-flowered one from the Midwest, *O. rosea*. These all grow to about two feet.

And then there are the many asters. For suggestions, see the chapter on perennials. I see no reason why you should not introduce some of the spectacular English hybrids called Michaelmas daisies (pronounced mikklemus). There is no reason to be purist about a wildflower section of your garden, especially if you are an organic gardener. And there is no reason to be a purist about growing asters and daisies and black-eyed Susans, just because you see them growing along the road and hear other people refer to these handsome flowers as weeds.

As with other parts of the garden, or other kinds of gardens, the point is not to outsmart and overcompete with other gardeners to grow the rarest at any cost. It is to provide the unity and grace of your garden by keeping it well-balanced and healthy, and to nurture there just what is suitable and shows itself happy to be there. So if you decide on wildflowers and consult other books for more definite information, please keep in mind that though other gardeners may want to defy nature and go in for the rare and endangered, the organic gardener characteristically does not.

16

Old-Fashioned Gardens

If you are lucky enough to live in an old house, or if you live in a part of the country where an old-fashioned garden is appropriate, you have quite a wide choice of the kind of garden to put in. It might be a colonial garden, or a Spanish courtyard, or an imitation of one of the old English styles of garden, or it might be a mixed garden but restricted to just those plants used in the early days in America. In this era of bicentennial celebrations there is quite a lot of interest in installing the kind of garden typical of 1776. Some people, thinking of an old-fashioned garden, foresee an herbaceous perennial border, bright with cultivated plants favored towards the end of the last century, but for this kind of garden see the discussion, warnings and descriptions in the chapter on perennials.

ADVANTAGES

Aside from the sentimental or nostalgic values in making an old-fashioned garden, there are other advantages which are fairly obvious. For one thing, the old garden favorites are those that have been tried out over and over during long periods and found to be hardy and suitable for gardens. For another thing these flowers are not too demanding. Busy colonial housewives had not much time to fuss over delicate flowers—especially if they also had the chores of taking care of the vegetable gardens and the chickens besides. And a third good reason for valuing an old-fashioned garden is that it was usually a compact, well-balanced mixture of plants used for different purposes, quite in accord with the principles of the organic gardener. There were plants for medical, culinary and cosmetic purposes, plants for dyes, and for the sheer pleasure of having something bright and familiar in the yard and to bring in to decorate the house. The designs of old-time gardens were real space-savers, whether for the use of space in back of the house as kitchen gardens or in front as an ornamental garden.

As modern organic gardeners have found (or rediscovered) these mixtures of plants often prove to be companionate and combined so as to be beneficial to each other when planted together either as pest repellents one for the other or as helpful to each other because of protective or nutritive root exudates or because of emanations of some sort from the plants above ground. Today, for example, we plant peppermint, feverfew and camomile as strong-scented repellents. In olden times (and now again) such plants were kept in the garden for making

Foreground: Lamium ('Skullcap' – a creeping groundcover),
Forget-Me-Not (Myosotis alpestris – the true biennial form);
Left: Primula polyanthus (Barnhaven mix)

A series of free-form pools
form this lovely water garden

Ajuga genevensis, a rather rampant groundcover

Egyptian lotus

A delicate woodland arrangement including Christmas fern, Epimedium sulphureum, Primula polyanthus (Barnhaven mix), European wild ginger, and Phlox dwaricata

A New York terrace garden

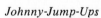

Johnny-Jump-Ups

A rock and water garden highlighted by a pink azalea and yellow sweet alyssum

soothing teas and poultices. But they were there and did their duty. Today we import ladybugs and buy the egg cases of praying mantises to step up the population of beneficial insects in our yards. In olden times it was routine to have bee hives, dovecotes, and often fountains, hare warrens and pheasant grounds as well as the flowers which attract butterflies and bees. The chickens they kept loose in their yards are among the best insect controls there are.

DECIDING WHAT TO HAVE

If you want to have an old-fashioned garden, you will have to choose whether you want something authentic, with all its oddities, or a garden that gives the aura of oldness by featuring some of the old roses for instance and some pinks or gilliflowers for the atmosphere they give. Maybe a few such flowers and some espaliered old-fashioned apple trees would be sufficient. Probably few people today would want to follow the practice in some old gardens of broadcast planting, where many kinds of seeds were thrown onto the ground and allowed to come up any way with a result that can look rather messy unless you succeed in getting a riot of color from one season to the next.

Before deciding, it might be advantageous to visit gardens at Williamsburg, Virginia or Sturbridge or Stockbridge, Massachusetts (or at least look at the books which give illustrations of those gardens, published at Williamsburg and Sturbridge). Then you can see how the old-timers combined flowers, fruits and herbs in simple, effective designs. For colonial and 18th century gardens you need to hunt up a reconstituted example; for 19th century herbaceous border gardens to look at just inquire from local people and garden club members; they are all around, still going now. Nevertheless, I call these, also, old-fashioned in comparison to the efficiency and low-maintenance gardens needed by people of today, when 98 per cent of us now do our own gardening work. If it is a space problem you have, not a labor problem, the compact colonial garden may well offer a pleasant alternative for you.

GARDEN ORIGINS: MEDIAEVAL

Most gardening in this part of the world stems from the mediaeval monastery garden. There the monks grew both herbs for medicines, dyes and flavorings and also flowers for the altar to the Virgin. Since they were mostly sworn to poverty, these monks usually had a kitchen garden, too, to raise cabbages and turnips, and some apple and pear trees to produce enough vegetables and fruits to carry them over the winter. They were great plant specialists, studying and practicing grafting, improvement of the species, and the properties of all the plants they grew for medical and other useful purposes. Many had shrubs and vines growing in their cloisters, and almost all featured lilies and roses. The monks learned to force flowers and fruits, and they often, especially the Benedictines, expected soldiers and other wayfarers who were sick or injured to come to the door for herbal treatment. It was a Carthusian monk, Otto Brunfels, who wrote the first German herbal, or book about plants. There were no individual gardens until a later period, but the flowers grown by monks for the altar included many of those we still know today. Besides roses and lilies, there were many blue flowers cultivated, because blue is the Virgin's color; and many whose names we still hear: Our Lady's Smock, Our Lady's Thistle, Our Lady's Slipper and Our Lady's Tears—which is probably the flower we today call lily-of-the-valley. Costmary and Rosemary carry a relic in their name of the old flower homage paid by the monks, as do also marigolds (or Mary-golds).

Few people today, however, are concerned

about recreating a monastery garden, or in picking all their snowdrops to strew over a place holy to the Virgin Mary on Candlemas Day. Though many of the readers of this book will, I trust, hold to the idea of a mixed garden, they will take more interest, perhaps, in the gardens of the next period of the early Renaissance, which were frankly ornamental in several ways and derived from the walled gardens actually started for lords and ladies in the chivalry tradition of the late mediaeval period. You can still see representations of those walled gardens in tapestries and old manuscripts, with a lamb or a unicorn for the lords and ladies to play with and some fruit trees and roses to sit by and a few tall trees for shade.

Of most interest are the gardens of the time of Shakespeare and Queen Elizabeth I, which is also the time of the coming of the early settlers to this country. By this time it was no longer considered somewhat blasphemous for anybody but monks to take an interest in the things of nature for their own sake (instead of as symbols of God's bounty) and dozens of people were studying plants, writing herbals and gardening books, and diligently starting gardens of their own. One early gardener was William Turner, an Englishman who began a garden near London at Kew, which has now grown and grown and become the huge royal botanical garden of England, and is still a wonderful reminder of the great steps forward in gardening at that period. It would be exciting to anyone to attempt a recreation of Turner's first beginning of such a garden. Or perhaps even more exciting to recreate the garden of an even more famous early gardener, John Gerard, who grew hundreds of native and imported plants in his garden right in London. This gardener was evidently more passionately interested in living plants than all his predecessors put together. For 20 years he supervised the gardens of Lord Burleigh and then wrote an herbal for him, a big compendium of information about the medicinal and alchemical properties of all the plants he knew. Though our interest has waned in all the alchemical talk, the book is valuable in showing what plants were actually known and grown in the early 17th century.

The more popular book for practicing gardeners was the book of advice (in rhyming couplets) written by Thomas Tusser, *Five Hundred Points of Good Husbandry*. This was published somewhat earlier, and went into 13 editions between 1573 and 1598. Tusser writes about skirrets, cabbages, beets, carrots, beans and asparagus, as householders would expect, but he also gives pointers on growing primroses, marigolds, violets, tansy and sage, and describes herbs for strewing on the floor to scent the house, such as lavender, pennyroyal, mints, roses and violets. For potted plants and window boxes he recommends daffydownlilies (daffodils), flower de luce (iris), Queen's gilliflowers, sweetbrier, lark's foot, heart's ease, paggles, sweet William, sops-in-wine, holyoaks. Here in this list is a good start for anyone wanting to begin to make an old-time garden, but the question is which of today's flowers do these fine old names refer to? Some I guess, as indicated; some I happen to know, such as heart's ease for Johnny-jump-ups and others are still current. Holyoaks are hollyhocks; sops-in-wine refers to sweet John, a variety of sweet William; Queen's gilliflower is probably the best and biggest carnation; and lark's foot must certainly be larkspur. What skirret is I am not sure, but I have read that it is a corruption of *Sium sisarum*, an aromatic herb with white flowers in umbels, rather like a parsley flower, and with edible roots. Paggles still stumps me, but I like the sound of the name.

By 1603 the first seed catalogues came out, and how-to books were produced of many sorts—often so entangled with astrological and other abstruse systems of sympathetic magic that it is hard to find any clear facts in them. Yet the

One of the formal gardens so popular in late 17th and 18th century England.

concept of a flower garden was growing and some writers even talked about soil, what it is, and what various plants need from it. One of them named Hugh Plat actually described the compost he made from "cow dung and horse dung well rotted in fine earth and claret wine lees." Another writer suggests how to rid your garden of moles: "Put Garlick, Onion, or Leeks into the mouths of the holes, and they will come out quickly as amazed."

These writers often referred to flower gardens as Gardens of Pleasure, one of the best names ever used for an outdoor living space full of pleasant plants, and a name I think ought to be revived. Sometimes the Garden of Pleasure was described as being "for solace," and to set bee hives in, therefore it was bordered with lavender (a favorite of bees) and rosemary, March violets, gillyflowers (which are pinks) and daisies, lily-of-the-valley, narcissus, hyacinth, tulips (which cost vast sums, up to about $35 a bulb, in those days) and peonies, bellflowers called Canterbury bells and a good many other sweet-smelling herbs.

My favorite of these old books is called *Paridisi in Sole Paradisus Terrestris*, by John Parkinson, with the first three words of that title a punning Latin version of his own name: park-in-sun. This is a real garden book, three-quarters devoted to flowers with hundreds of woodcuts of such favorites of the time as crown imperials (the big handsome fritillary) lilies, crocuses, primroses, iris, hyacinths and the new, very popular tulips, which had just been brought from Turkey via Venice. Parkinson had learned about the needs of both English and foreign flowers and writes about them.

Soon more emphasis was given to landscaping, garden design and aesthetic considerations, especially as gardens became more and more formal. According to the next 17th century writers, the Garden of Pleasure should be seen from a spot that forms a lovely picture from the best room in the house. It should also be "so situated to be protected from cold winds so as to seem to be in a perpetual spring, except in extreme weather"— a situation more probable, of course, in England than here in this country. The human side is stressed, too, when the writers suggest that people should walk out to get the healthful effect of breathing sweet odors, and to enjoy the piquant experience of seeing fresh, ripe fruit against a warm garden wall. The paths, they sensibly say, should be of stones so the people can walk in all weathers and keep their shoes clean. And there should be a pleasure-house, preferably on a mount. As good patriots they commend the 'York and Lancaster' rose, to symbolize and commemorate in one red-and-white rose, the resolution of the old feud between the red roses and the white, or the two feuding English ducal houses. This rose is still available from specialists.

During the late 17th and 18th centuries formal gardens got bigger and bigger and more and more elaborate, but cottage gardens went on just about as they had been when established in Shakespeare's day (when the cottage tulips were first grown in them). An old-fashioned garden today might well be patterned on the style and plantings of the cottage gardens of that period. And it is quite certain that the English gardens and colonial gardens in this country were similar. The American cottage housewives who tended these gardens while their husbands were at work kept right on growing the same culinary and medicinal plants in this country as they had at home in their English cottage gardens. As the name implies, the garden was small, usually walled or hedged and laid out in small beds, near the house in a back yard.

LAYOUT

A common layout for such a garden was in a square with cross walks that turn it into four square beds. To reproduce such a garden today the owner might well plant flowers in one square, herbs for the kitchen in another, vegetables in another and in the fourth medicinal, cosmetic and dye-plant flowers and herbs. One bed would have old favorites like cornflower, iris, peonies and hollyhocks, with spring bulbs such as crocus and spring primroses. If the housewives grew sweet-smelling flowers, they called it a tussie-mussie garden, or one for flowers that you use in making a bouquet, nosegay or tussie mussie. This garden often had lemon verbena, heliotrop, lavender violets, marjoram, rosemary and mignonette. The dye-plant garden contained woad, *Isatis tinctoria;* lady's bedstraw, *Galium verum;* wild senna, *Cassia marilandica* and indigo, *Baptisia tinctoria.* For an evergreen sub-shrub to edge the beds they often used rue, *Ruta graveolens,* a very pleasant little plant because it turns so green so early in the spring, and easy because it will grow in almost any kind of soil. Along with such plants the early American settlers liked to put tansy, chicory, purslane, sweet clover and dandelion, for they brought seeds and plants of all of these, never suspecting that they would spread as they have until we think of them as weeds.

Another plant characteristic of old gardens was angelica, which unfortunately also can be a pest. (*Angelica archangelica* is its pretty Latin name.) Where the ground is moist this plant will grow to six or seven feet. One plant is enough. It was used for making candy or little decorations for cakes. Smaller and more manageable are borage, *Borago officianlis* and hyssop, *H. officinalis* (with the second name indicating it was used for medicine). Thyme, *Thymus* in variety, was used as a fumigant and that is just what its name means. (It had been burned by the Greeks to mask the smell of burning flesh at their sacrifices.) This is a well-known group of plants, and the wild thyme on Mount Hymettus

has flowers from which the bees make the best-known thyme-honey in the world. There are 50 varieties to choose from, but you may wish to avoid those which will remind you of the smell of a wet cat. Get lemon thyme, which was often used in colonial gardens, but now we can also get orange, anise and various other spice-smelling thymes, too.

Lemon verbena, *Lippia citriodora* or *Aloysia citriodora,* was brought over in the late 18th century, a more tender plant which in the North must be cut back and kept just moist in a cold cellar over the early part of the winter, and then brought to the warmth in February to revive on a sunny windowsill, and then set back out in the garden in the spring. The other, easier method used for saving lemon verbena is to make a lot of slips from its branches and start them in wet sand mixed with vermiculite in the fall. The leaves cut off before setting the stems in sand for rooting can be your main crop of lemon verbena for drying. These slips can be potted up in average soil as soon as they root and moved gradually to the sunlight.

Other plants often propagated by colonial gardeners are heliotrope and mignonette. This little flower, *Reseda odorata,* was long a favorite in Europe, and was so popular in London during the latter part of the eighteenth century that it was in nearly every windowbox in the city. Another city favorite, lavender, *Lavandula vera,* is still an urban flower in England, and is now lavishly used in the little garden behind St. Paul's in London, where its pale bluish flowers seem to thrive in the foggy air. For centuries it has been used to sweeten the air where clothes are stored.

A more medicinal plant, and a very common one in the old gardens is calendula, often called pot marigold, *Calendula officinalis.* I think modern gardeners might well begin to use it as the old-timers did: for possets, broths and other drinks to comfort the heart and spirits. Custards, syrups and jams made from these and other flowers were used to convey that comfort, as well as to please the palate, one assumes. When saffron was in short supply, calendula was also used for coloring, as well as marigolds and safflower. Saffron was used too in soup, as well as violets, daisies, borage flowers, gillyflowers, rosebuds and English cowslips. The town with the lovely name of Saffron Walden got that name because it was where there were huge fields of this plant growing in mediaeval times. It is said that half the food they ate contained this flower for flavoring. But the old-timers were not fussy. They also put away barrels of marigold petals to color and flavor their soups. Those who could grow them and preserve them also put primroses in soups, the spring buds of elder and violet leaves, and they made syrups out of roses, violets, broom, mints including peppermint, flowers of rosemary, balm, mallows, elder, and of course orange where the weather was warm enough to grow orange trees. The clove gillyflower was the greatest favorite.

Once in a while the housewives made cordials as well as syrups and powders, and also lotions and ointments. Any of these were sweetened according to what was growing in the garden: iris, nasturtiums, peonies, poppies, violets, lilies, bachelor's button and also the flowers of such herbs as thyme, camomile and of course lavender. If the ointment was for wounds, it also contained St. John's wort, believed to be of great power for healing. And a really nippy cordial could be turned out by the cottage gardeners by using some ginger and saffron dissolved in wine and sunned for two or three weeks.

SOME NEW BUT REALLY OLD PRINCIPLES

One old garden writer of the early 18th century, with the incredible name of Batty Langley, brought out a book called *New Principles of Gardening*, in which he went all out for newfangled ideas such as including a hayrick in the garden (not bad for the mulcher or compost maker) or a woodpile (also useful unless it turns into a nesting place for woodchucks) or a few basins and fountains (good for any garden, as already stated). He also said the "new principles" should lead one to put up aviaries, rabbit warrens, deer paddocks, bee hives (all ecologically sound, of course) and also should lead one to go in for a few decorations like ruins, arbors, amphitheatres and a gazebo, or perhaps a pleached arbor, some statues and a tree house. Zany as this sounds, Batty Langley does move up to the idea of the multi-purpose garden as advocated in this book. He suggests a varied habitat, with places designed to invite and keep the birds, bees and animals in the garden so they will be good for the garden. He also advises the person who makes a garden to have inviting seats, fountains and shade—or to make, that is, the kind of outdoor living area that we think of as a garden today.

EARLY AMERICAN COLONIAL GARDENS

In the rural settlements the trend was to have gardens that were predominantly functional, quite near the house to be seen and enjoyed, and also near to the animals' pens, the orchard and the vegetable plot. The herbs mixed in with vegetables and flowers were all for useful purposes and also to look at. The roses used everywhere, no matter how often the petals were used for sachets, pot pourris, medicines, rose-waters and dyes, also were and are wonderful to look at. Violets which they grew are pretty in a room as well as fragrant and useful for candies.

In a surviving old garden in Connecticut where the layout is still evident, the flower garden was in the front yard, observable from the front rooms of the house, and to guests who arrived by the front door. The slope in this

Connecticut garden is to the south, a very gentle slope, and very near to it, in a raised bed, is the place where the colonists grew the early vegetables which needed the warmth of the slope in spring: peas, lettuce, radishes, onions and carrots—all started early. In this Connecticut garden, as so often in English gardens, there was a walled space, where plants can be protected from a northwest prevailing wind, whether by stone wall or wooden fence, a device often used in colonial gardens for protection. Sometimes in these gardens the annual flowers were held back until the early vegetables were over. Then they were planted in where the vegetables had been. Hedges at the front of colonial gardens were rare; in fact, in some town there were laws against any but the lowest hedge at the front line of the property.

Gardens in Boston or Albany, New York were more staid and formal, in keeping with their urban surroundings. In early periods these gardens had no shrubs, and started only with flowers until the shrubs became available in the 19th century. Flower lists for old colonial gardens include such flowers as bluebells, crown imperial and other 18th century favorites such as oriental poppies, bellflower, foxgloves, sweet William, larkspur, feverfew, white lupine, bergamot, honesty (a biennial) gypsophyla and double buttercup, sweet peas, rose campion, snapdragons and bachelor's buttons as well as the herbs. In the next century new additions of woody vines and shrubs begin to be added. Wisteria was planted, and also Scotch viburnum, snowberry, trumpet honeysuckle, Virgin's bower, balloon vine and others. These gardeners were also busy introducing bleeding heart, which came from China in 1846, and often planted thereafter. Other plants brought in during this period include spireas, deutsias, the lovely yellow Fortune's rose, named for one of the plant explorers; forsythia, named for another,

and the exquisite Father Hugo's rose, named for still another.

Southern urban formal gardens began to have local materials, such as the beautiful southern magnolias. And in the North local flowering dogwoods were soon introduced. Some enthusiastic gardeners brought in native plants like trillium, jack-in-the-pulpit, dog-tooth violet and bloodroot. The bulbs planted in 19th century gardens included yellow crocus, winter aconite, the early irises and the plant they called butter-and-eggs plant which is really our daffodil. Other native plants used in gardens included the handsome big purply-pink Joe-pye-weed, which blooms in late summer, and its cousin boneset, with a greenish white flower, both very useful and handsome as plants for dried arrangements, but used in those days primarily for medicines. These late-season flowers were often combined with other late flowers such as monk's-hood and gentian (probably the bottle gentian because fringed gentian is resistant to moving). All of the dandelions they had in their gardens were the result of those that had carefully been brought over from Europe as garden specialties.

In the mild climate broom was introduced and in a few places also gorse. In the South sweet shrub, *Calycanthus floridus*, was a great favorite. And in several zones so were flowering currant, elder, dog rose, garden heliotrope and the smaller flowers, nasturtiums, sage, southernwood and thyme.

Tansy, as already mentioned, was even then a multi-purpose herb. It was rubbed over raw meat that had to sit around, in order to fend off flies. It was used with eggs to make a custard, or tansie, and was sometimes fried, chopped and flavored with ginger, nutmeg and cinnamon. A very healthy mixture, so they said, was tansy along with feverfew, parsley and violet mixed into an omelet—and it obviously is quite high in vitamin C. A standard mixture made from tansy leaves and rum was called tansy bitters. And the last vital use of it was for wrapping a corpse; its shape and scent have been known to last 200 years. Today country people, as already mentioned, plant tansy at the door to discourage ants from coming in that way. In addition tansy has pleasant, fern-like green leaves and neat button-like flowers in a head. It is excellent to dry for dried arrangements because it turns out a good yellow, and it is easy to handle. Eaten in any quantities more than a few tastes or so it is poisonous.

In garden design, there was very little change from the coming of the Pilgrims until the middle of the 19th century. The four-square shape did not vary much, though city gardens usually had a focal point like an arbor or summer house, a sundial or a bit of topiary or trimmed plant to look like a rooster, for instance. Sometimes the beds were raised, and as in continental parterre gardens, the design was more often derived from the walks laid out to shape the beds, not from the groups of plants. Almost all beds had a short hedge-like edging, small boxwood in the South and moss pink or germander and of course lavender also.

The need for protection from animals, snakes, fires, Indians or other creatures that might sneak up on the house unawares had not yet led to the lawns so prevalent today to protect us. The old-timers, however, did not have any bushes up near to their houses, and did have fences for privacy and to keep out the animals and Indians. Only where the ideas of the landscape architects of large English estates took hold of large landholders here did the fences come down and the walls get leveled. The new style, when it reached these landowners, influenced them to make their acres look like rolling rural countryside, with pastures, cows and sheep, trees and meadows stretching out and nothing to spoil the view. The flowers were cleared out of such gardens, and the well-cropped grass became the dominant feature, and the parent of the modern lawn. Though this style never spread far in this country, places like Mount Vernon do show some of the influence. There it is combined, however, with the old style of gardens near the house, and a vista opening to a natural view beyond.

Flower gardens of the early 19th century had balsams, single and double, in red, white, purple and pink. They also had several colors of bachelor's buttons, globe amaranth, and the many sweet Williams, primroses, and cowslips and hollyhocks everywhere. But there were no petunias, no zinnias, no African marigold and for hedges, no yews. Much less popular then than now were snapdragons, larkspurs or delphiniums and heavenly blue morning glories, though they did grow other morning glories in red, white, purple and a dark blue.

Some of the imported plants were sent to England to the enthusiastic, almost fanatical plant collectors there, and then sent on to this country. From Japan came winterberry as early as 1597, as we know because it was listed in the garden of John Gerard in London. Flowers that found their way to England about the same time include wind flower, varieties of bellflower from southern Europe, candytuft, celandine poppy, used with milk for warts and the itch, and the European columbine. From America there was a remarkable stream of imports to England, including the cardinal flower; but the imports from the Orient were the most extensive and important. The common tawny lily, *Hemerocallis fulva*, was known to both John Gerard and Parkinson who wrote the garden book. New were crocuses, daffodils, the oxeye daisy (our common daisy) and datura or angel's trumpet.

The iris known in colonial times was *Iris germanica*, our bearded iris, but of course not bred to any such degree as nowadays by the developers in the Northwest. The delphinium,

An English cottage garden with its small, neat beds of herbs, flowers, and vegetables, surrounded by paths which are in turn bordered by hedges.

also not yet developed, was a small larkspur, used to make ink. The common white lily, *Lilium candidum*, had a use as a face lotion, but people also attempted to grow the native spotted lily, *Lilium canadense*, now so rare and still so beautiful. Lupine, especially white and blue ones were grown, and aside from the common French marigolds a small Mexican one was known, *Tagetes erecta*.

A familiar sight in a colonial garden was the cultivated mullein, which was used for emollients. And soon there were peonies and poppies, too. Various kinds of crowsfoot and Dame's rocket, *Hesperia matrionalis*, came from western and central Asia, with both purple and white flowers. Scabious was brought from Southern Europe. Parkinson called it a flower of fields and woods, and where it has escaped in my neighborhood, it certainly is a flower of the fields, for in June near where I live there are several fields which are more lavender than green for a week or so when the scabious is in bloom.

Rose campion was a common flower, *Lychnis chalcedonica*, a flower which is coming back into favor today. Strawflower and everlasting were old-time favorites, and, as soon as they arrived from western South America, so were the sunflowers. There were crazes for new introductions like toadflax, Jimson weed or datura, tomato, and the *Valerian officinalis* used by the ratcatchers. (Cats go for it, too.) Wallflowers and yarrow were available in colonial times and Yucca was evidently moved to gardens at an early day.

PLANTING HABITS

One noticeable difference between an old-fashioned and a modern garden is the manner of planting. At least in today's gardens we tend to plant things in rows; and in our flower gardens in clumps or plots. The colonial gardener, on the other hand, tended to broadcast seed over the garden, and let things come up together. We know that in nature things are not put into chapters and categorized as they are in books. Perhaps the only categorizing the cottage gardener did was to separate her penennials and annuals, in a rather unsystematic way, if at all. As the housewife and gardener learned about plant habits, she probably had sense enough to keep the heavy-rooted, big plants away from the tiny, delicate-rooted ones. And she probably learned to put a little lime around her peonies if her soil was acid.

Then, too, there was the question of quantity. For flowers she wanted in abundance, like clove gillyflowers, marigolds, and borage for flavoring were undoubtedly put into plots as well as broadcast. This was evidently the practice also for some plants commonly grown for medicinal uses, such as elecampine, bugloss, feverfew to help in case of any kind of fever, and everlasting for using against moths that get into woolen clothing. A few poisonous plants were grown to be used in very small quantities to dull pain, and this is not so odd as it sounds when you think of the still current uses of foxglove or digitalis and belladonna in one to ten drop doses. When you try to imagine these rather hit-or-miss gardens resulting from broadcast planting, remember that in general the colonists had many little beds in the garden, not the big long ones that resulted for the late-19th century herbaceous borders and familiar today. As the Elizabethan gardener Parkinson says, "the Garden of Pleasure is wholly formable in every part with squares, trayles, and knots to be still maintained in their due form and beautie." Knots were gardens with very short hedges marking an interweaving geometrical design, often for herbs with the hedge material also an herb, or small boxwood. The small beds pleased the old gardeners, and Parkinson also suggest they be used in a kitchen garden "to facilitate the taking up of roots and salads."

Another authority of the early period, Leonard Meager, wrote a book which went into many editions. He set out to discuss the ordering of the Garden of Pleasure, with its variety of knots and "wilderness work," as well as all the best ways of raising flowers, including directions for arbors, hedges and other useful things to know in order to delight.

His advice for an old-time garden is first to build a wall or outside fence; then a border; then a walk; then some more quarter-borders; and finally beds and knots with a few plats—by which he means areas of grass. His specific recommendations for the knots were Dutch or French box, *Buxus sempervirens* perhaps the variety *suffruticosa*, a dwarf box; hyssop, germander, thrift, and pot marjoram. For plants to be used, if cut often, he adds pinks, double violets, and "Grass cut oft, Periwinkle cut oft, and Lavender-cotton, Herb of Grace, Rosemary and Sage." Then, as now, box is considered the best plant for making low hedges. And Meager is right; it must be pruned oft to keep it in shape and rejuvenated.

If possible, the gardener was advised also to harvest broom-buds, elder-buds to pickle with leeks and artichokes for winter. Flowers for pickles familiar in old gardens included clove gilliflowers, cowslips, bugloss flowers, arch-angel flowers and burage. Many of the potherb and pickle flowers and plants are familiar today, even though the spelling is odd. Nep, for instance, must mean *Nepeta cataria* or catnip or perhaps the useful *N. grandiflora*, Caucasian nepeta, which will bloom all summer with blue flowers. Sive is surely chives and succory chicory. Colworts, I am afraid, means coltsfoot, *Tussilago farfara*, used as a cough medicine, and cheerful as one of the first flowers of spring, but you'll be sorry if you put it in your garden because it spreads everywhere and even the tiniest scrap of root you do not get out will send up another plant to pester you. Shelot must be shallot, and arch-angel must be angelica.

As I have been doing throughout this book, Meager, too, gives you warnings about some plants. Of Italian starwort he says "apt to run in a garden (and thereby gives the hint that this may well be Star-of Bethlehem, which I warned you about in the chapter on bulbs). Of double sopewort, *Saponaria ocymoides* probably, he says "a busie runner in a garden."

For plants to grow in containers, Meager suggests various "Bulbo's and Tubero's" such as anemones, crown imperial and also the smaller fritillaries, Flowerdeluces, hyacinths, Indian Juca, Kings-spear, Lilies, Molies, Martagons, Munks-hoods, Star-flowers, tulips in many varieties, Bulbo's violets, and he also suggests in another place crocus, saffron flowers, colchecons, grape-flowers, hollowroot flower, crissmass flower, ranunculo, sow-bread, spider-wort and winter wolfe-bane. He thinks of those flowers as also "fit to furnish a garden".

Again some of these names can be deduced from the way they sound, or from the translation. Indian Juca must be yucca which had just been sent to England at Meager's time. Ranunculo is one of the buttercups, and I believe grape-flowers mean grape hyacinths. Crissmas flower is certainly the Christmas rose and Bears-ear must be the spectacularly lovely Alpine primroses which became such a craze later in the century, *Primula auricula* (Latin for ear of, at least). Molies strike me as being *Allium moly*, the lovely and interesting ornamental members of the onion family. Bulbo's violets I believe to be nothing but violet with bulbous seed pods down near the soil surface, and I assume that colchecon is autumn crocus.

With suggestions such as these you can have fun figuring them out, have fun looking up where some of the less familiar plants can be found, and then the final pleasure of mapping out and planting an old-fashioned garden of your own. Whether it is planted in a broadcast fashion or in little beds, the garden will yield you plants just like the ones grown in olden times and will offer uses, too, if you care to follow through on the ideas of the old-time garden.

Lady's bedstraw, *Galium verum*, can be used to make cheese as a rennet to curdle the milk. The handsome leaves of beets are good for salads, and also to provide a dye. Bloodroot is also a dye plant, and so are the leaves of the lily-of-the-valley and the flowers of day lilies and goldenrod. Bouncing bet or soapwort can be used to cleanse fine fabrics or to polish the pewter. You can make your own rouge from bugloss, *Anchusa officinalis*. The good plant camomile (whose name derives from a term for apple fragrance) is now both cultivated and wild. The catnip you grow, if not all reserved for the cats, can be used for fragrance and pep-up in the bath water or fried into tansies or little fritters. When your coffee or Sanka needs fortifying, add ground, dried chicory root, and try, if you can, to distinguish between *Cichorium intybus* (chicory) and *Cichorium endiva* (endive). According to the Elizabethan garden writer, Parkinson, "they are both of one kindred; and although they differ a little the one from the other, yet they agree both in this, that they are eaten eyther grenne or whited, of many." (By many, I think he means.) He thought that both grew only in gardens, and like most plantsmen of his day he could not foresee the time when the blue flowers of chicory would be a familiar weed along our roads.

It is startling to discover that the way to have an authentic 17th century American garden is to mix together plants which we would now call flowers, culinary herbs, dye plants, medicinal plants, vegetables and weeds. The botanists know now that many, or nearly all the plants we call weeds, were imported by the colonists because they wanted to have them in their gardens for salads, or medicines and other household uses, or for the beauty they were familiar with in the land they came from. And it is equally startling to recognize that these old gardeners grew poisonous plants on purpose, to numb themselves when in pain. One writer on the period notes that the colonists ate an amazing amount of sugar that came in to the colonies by the shipload from the Barbados. Evidently they had a lot of toothaches. We have now lost the skills we would need to dose ourselves with foxglove or monks-hood or something like angel's trumpet on our gums, and we know so much about allergies we certainly wouldn't wish to run the risk of internal rashes.

The decorative reasons for growing such flowers are quite enough for us—unless we recall that today's gardens also serve the purposes of supporting the ecosystems of the yard, its bird and other populations, and the soil itself and its millions of micro-inhabitants. So whether you decide on an old-fashioned or new-fangled garden, your aim as an organic flower gardener will be multi-purpose, too, and this book (if it has done the job it set out to do) will have shown you some of the ways and means to do that. And whether you are just beginning gardening or switching over from conventional flower gardening to organic gardening, you will find you are getting a new, absorbing interest in gardening which you never suspected could happen, and that each day's effort and experiment are giving you ever-widening horizons.

Appendix

✿HORTICULTURAL SOCIETIES✿

American Begonia Society, Inc. 139 North Ledoux Rd., Beverly Hills, CA 90211

American Bonsai Society, 953 South Shore Dr., Lake Waukomis, Parksville, MO 64151

American Daffodil Society, 89 Chichester Rd., New Canaan, CT 06840

American Fern Society Biological Science Group, University of Connecticut, Storrs, CT 06268

American Horticultual Society, Mt. Vernon, VA 22121

American Iris Society, 2315 Tower Grove Ave., St. Louis, MO 63110

Connecticut Horticultural Society, 199 Griswold Road, Wethersfield, CT 06109

Directory of American Horticulture, Mt. Vernon, VA American Horticultural Society, 1974.

The Herb Society of America, 300 Massachusetts Ave., Boston, MA 02115

The Indoor Light Gardening Society of America, Inc. 423 Powers Dr., Bay Village, OH 44140

The International Geranium Society, 11960 Pascal Ave., Colton, CA 92324

The Massachusetts Horticultural Society, 300 Massachusetts Ave., Boston, MA

Minnesota State Horticultural Society, St. Paul Campus, University of Minnesota, St. Paul, MN

New Hampshire Horticultural Society, State Office Annex, Concord, NH 03300

Pennsylvania Horticultural Society, 325 Walnut St., Philadelphia, PA 19106

The Director, Royal Botanical Gardens Box 399, Hamilton, Ont.

Vermont State Horticultural Society, University of Vermont, Burlington, VT 05401

✿ARBORETUMS✿

Alexandra Botanic Garden and Hunnewell Arboretum, Wellesley College, Wellesley, MA 02101

Arnold Arboretum, The Arborway, Jamaica, Plains, MA 02130

Arbury Arboretum, Washington La. and Ardleigh St., Germantown, PA 19152

Arboretum of the Barnes Foundation, 300 Latches La., Merion Sta., PA 19066

Bartlett Arboretum of the State of Connecticut 151 Brookdale Rd., Stamford, CT 06903

Barton-Pell Mansion, Shore Rd., Pelham Bay Park, Bronx, NY 10464

Boston Public Gardens, Boston, MA

Brooklyn Botanic Gardens, 1000 Washington Ave., Brooklyn, NY

Cedar Brook Park, Plainfield, NJ 07061

Connecticut Arboretum at Connecticut College P. O. Box 1511, New London, CT 06320

Coover Arboretum, Route 3, Dillsburg, PA 17019 Especially known for its wildflowers, holly, oak, rhododendron, etc.

Thomas C. Desmond Arboretum, Rte. 1, Newburgh, NY 12550

Duke Gardens Foundation, Rte. 206 South, Somerville, NJ 08876

Ellis School Arboretum, Newtown Square, PA 19073
Especially nice for its shade and flower trees.
Fay Highland Botanical Plantation, 371 Deering Hall,
University of Maine, Orono, ME 04473
George Landis Arboretum, Esperance, NY 12066
Longwood Gardens, Kennett Square, PA 19348
Morris Arboretum, University of Pennsylvania.
Address: Route 422, Chestnut Hill, PA. Mail:
9414 Meadowbrook Avenue, Philadelphia, PA
19118
Norfolk Botanical Gardens, Airport Road, Norfolk VA
23518
Old Westbury Gardens, P.O. Box 265, Old Westbury,
NY 11568
Readers' Digest Gardens, Pleasantville, NY 10570
Robin Hill Arboretum, Platten Road, Lyndonville,
NY 14098
Sterling Forest Gardens, P. O. Box 608, Tuxedo, NY
10987
Taylor Memorial Arboretum, 10 Ridley Dr., Box 216,
Garden City, Chester, PA 19013
John J. Tyler Arboretum, 515 Painter Rd., Lima, PA
17837
Ward Pound Ridge Reservation Meyer Arboretum,
Cross River, NY 10518
Orland E. White Research Arboretum, University of
Virginia, P. 105 Public Gardens, Boyce, VA
22628
Winterthur Gardens, Winterthur, DE

＊GENERAL BIBLIOGRAPHY＊

Bush-Brown, James and Louise. *America's Garden
Book*. NY: Charles Schribner's Sons, 1958.
Carleton, R. Milton. *The Small Garden Book*. NY
Macmillan Company, 1971.
Edland, H. *The Pocket Encyclopedia of Roses*. NY:
Macmillan, 1969.
Fairbrother, Nan. *Men and Gardens*. NY: Knopf,
1956.
Hadfield, Miles. *The Art of the Garden*. NY: Dutton
Press, 1965.
Krutch, Joseph Wood. *The Gardener's World*. NY:
Putnam, 1969.
Nuese, Josephine. *The Country Garden*. NY: Charles
Scribner's Sons, 1970.
Pettingill, Amos. *The White-Flower-Farm Garden
Book*. NY: Knopf, 1971.
*Plant Buyer's Guide of Seed and Plant Materials in the
Trade*. H. Gleason Mattoon, ed. Boston:
Massachusetts Horticultural Society, 1958.

Riker, Tom and Rottenberg, Harvey. *The Gardener's
Catalogue*. NY: William Morrow and Company.
1974.
Rockland, F. F. *The Book of Bulbs*. Macmillan, 1946.
Rose, James C. *Creative Gardens*. Reinhold Publi-
shing Corporation, 1958.
Sackville-West, V. *Garden Book*. London: Michael
Joseph, 1968.
Stevens, G.A. *Garden Flowers in Color*. NY:
Macmillan, 1936.
Taylor, Norman, ed. *Taylor's Encyclopedia of
Gardening*. Boston: Houghton-Mifflin, 1961.
Von Miklos, Josephine. *The Illustrated Guide to
Personal Gardening*. Englewood Cliffs, NJ:
Prentice-Hall, Inc., 1972.
Wilder, Louise Beebe. *The Fragrant Garden: A Book
About Sweet-Scented Flowers and Leaves*. NY: Dover
Publications, 1974.
Wilson, Helen Van Pelt, *Perennials Preferred*. NY: M
Barrows and Co., 1950.
*Helen Van Pelt Wilson's Own Garden and Landscape
Book*. NY: Doubleday, 1973.
Wyman, Donald. *Wyman's Gardening Encylopedia*.
NY: Macmillan, 1973
Government pamphlets—(10 -30)
Free lists on:
PL National Parks
PL 41 Insects
PL 43 Forestry
PL 44 Plants
PL 46 Soils and Fertilizers
PL 88 Ecology
To order, write
Superintendent of Documents
U. S. Government Printing Office,
710 North Capitol Street
Washington, D. C. 20402.
Also ask for *Home Garden Brochure*
Available also from Public Document Distribution
Service Center, 5801 Tabor Ave., Philadelphia,
PA 19120.

＊BOOKS ON ORGANIC GARDENING＊

Campbell, Stu. *The Mulch Book*. Charlotte, VT:
Garden Way, 1974.
Let It Rot! Charlotte, VT: Garden Way, 1975.
Easey, Ben. *Practical Organic Gardening*. London:
Faber and Faber, Ltd., n.d.
The Calendar of Organic Gardening. Eds. of Organic
Gardening and Farming Magazine. Emmaus,
PA: Rodale Press, Inc., 1973.

Foster, Catharine Osgood. *The Organic Gardener.* NY: Knopf, 1972.
———. ed.*Terrific Tomatoes.* Emmaus, PA: Rodale Press, 1975.
Gillespie, Janet, *Peacock Manure and Marigolds.* NY: Viking, 1964.
Globus, Diane. *Digging It: How to Grow Things Naturally.* NY: The Dial Press, 1973.
Howard, Sir Albert. *The Soil and Health: A Study of Organic Agricutlure.*NY: Devin-Adair, 1947
Ogden, Samuel R. *Step-by-Step to Organic Vegetable Gardening.* Emmaus, PA.: Rodale Press, 1972.
Rodale, Robert. *The Basic Book of Organic Gardening.* NY: Ballantine, 1971.
Rodale, J. I. (ed.) *The Encyclopedia of Organic Gardening.* Emmaus, PA.: Rodale Press, Inc., 1971.
———. *The Organic Way to Mulching.* Emmaus, PA.: Rodale Press, Inc. 1972.
———. *Western Organic Gardening.* Emmaus, PA: Rodale Press, Inc. 1972.
Stout, Ruth. *Gardening Without Work.* Old Greenwich, CT: Devin-Adair, 1970.
———. *How to Have a Green Thumb Without an Aching Back.* NY.: Simon and Schuster, 1971.
———. *The No-Work Garden Book.* Emmaus, PA. Rodale Press,Inc. 1971.
Swenson, Allan A. *The Practical Book of Organic Gardening.* NY: Universal-Award House, Inc., 1973.
Tyler, Hamilton. *Organic Gardening Without Poisons.* NY: Van Nostrand Reinhold Co., 1970.
Wickenden, Leonard. *Gardening With Nature.* Greenwich, CT: Fawcett Publications, Inc., 1974.

BOOKS ON SOIL AND HOW TO CARE FOR IT: COMPOSTING

Balfour, Lady Eve. *The Living Soil.* London: Faber and Faber, 1943.
Buckman, Henry O. and Brady, Lyle C. *The Nature and Properties of Soils.* NY: Macmillan, 1969
Darwin,Charles. *Darwin on Humous and the Earthworm.* Mystic, CT: Verry, 1966.
Golueke, Clarence G. *Composting: A Study of the Process and Its Principles.* Emmaus, PA.: Rodale Press, 1972.
Ortloff, H. Stuart and Raymore, Henry. *A Book About Soils for the Home Gardener.* NY: Barrows, 1962.
Staff of Organic Gardening and Farming Magazine. *The Complete Book of Composting.* Emmaus, Pa. Rodale Press. 1971.
Waksman, Selman. *Humus:*
Waksman, Selman A. and Starkey, Robert L. *The Soil and the Microbe.* NY: John Wiley, 1931.

BOOKS ON HOW PLANTS GROW (PLANT PHYSIOLOGY)

Bold, H. C. *The Plant Kingdom.* Englewood Cliffs, NJ: Prentice-Hall, 1970.
Crafts, A. S. *Translocation in Plants.* NY. Holt, Rinehart, Winston, 1961.
Donahue, Roy L. *Soils: An Introduction to Soils and Plant Growth.* The Ford Foundation; New Delhi, India: Prentice-Hall, 1965.
Dowden. Anne G. *Look at a Flower: Botany for Gardeners.*
Galston, A. W. *The Life of the Green Plant.* Englewood Cliffs, NJ: Prentice-Hall, 1964.
Garrett, S. D. *Soil Fungi and Soil Fertility.* Elmsport, NY: Pergamon, 1969.
Greutach, Victor A. *Botany Made Simple.* NY: Doubleday, 1968.
Haring, Elda. *The Complete Book of Growing Plants from Seeds.* NY: Hawthorne, 1967.
Harlow, William M. *Patterns of Life, The Unseen World of Plants.* NY: Harper and Row, 1966.
Leopold, A. Carl. *Plant Growth and Development.* NY: McGraw-Hill, 1964.
Loeb, Jacques. *Regeneration.* NY: McGraw-Hill, 1924.
Northen, Henry and Rebecca. *Ingenious Kingdom: The Remarkable World of Plants.* Englewood Cliffs, NJ: Prentice-Hall, Inc., 1970.
The Secret of the Green Thumb. NY: The Ronald Press Company, 1954.
Slayter, R. O. *Plant-Water Relationships.* London & N.Y., Academic Press, 1967.
Torrey, J. G. *Development in Flowering Plants.* NY: Macmillan, 1967.
Vallin, Jean. *The Plant World.* NY: Sterling, 1967.
Went, P. S. F. W. *The Experimental Control of Plant Growth.* Waltham, MA: Chronica Botanica Co., 1957.
Wilson, Carl L. *Botany.* NY: The Dryden Press, 1952.

BOOKS ON GARDENING TECHNIQUES

Atkinson, Robert E. *Dwarf Fruit Trees Indoors and Outdoors.* NY: Van Nostrand Reinhold Co., 1972.

Bruning, Walter F. *Minimum Maintenance Gardening Handbook*. NY: Harper and Row, 1961.

Cruso, Thalassa. *Making Things Grow Outdoors*. NY: Knopf, 1971.

Cutler, Katherine N. *The Beginning Gardener*. NY: Gramercy Publishing Co. n. d. (A child's book, but some good hints for getting started.)

Free, Montague. *Plant Propagation in Pictures*. Garden City, NY: The American Garden Guild, 1957.

Gregg, Richard. *Companion Plants and How to Use Them*. Old Greenwich, CT: Devin-Adair, 1966.

Companion Plants and Herbs. Stroudsburg, PA: Bio-Dynamic Farming and Gardening Association.

Hartman, Hudson T. and Kester. Dale E. *Plant Propagation, Principles and Practices*. Englewood Cliffs, NJ: Prentice-Hall, 1959.

❧BOOKS ON PEST CONTROL❧

Gregg, Evelyn. *Bio-Dynamic Sprays*. Stroudsburg, PA: Bio-Dynamic Farming and Gardening Association.

"How to Kill Insects the Non-Toxic Way...with Pyrethrins." Pyrethrum Information Center, Room 423, 744 Broad Street,Newark, NJ 07102.

Hunter, Beatrice Trum. *Gardening Without Poisons*. NY: Berkeley Medallion Books, 1971.

Kramer, Jack. *The Natural Way to Pest-Free Gardening*. NY: Scribner's, 1972.

Newman, L. H. *Man and Insects: Insect Allies and Enemies*, NY: Natural History Press.

Philbrick, Helen and John. *The Bug Book*. Charlotte, VT: Garden Way Publishing, 1974.

"Plants and Gardens: Handbook on Biological Control of Plant Pests." Brooklyn, NY: Brooklyn Botanic Garden, 1972.

Rodale, J. I. (ed.) *Getting the Bugs Out of Organic Gardening*. Emmaus, PA: Rodale Press, Inc., 1973.

The Organic Way to Plant Protection. Emmaus, PA: Rodale Press, Inc., 1966.

❧BOOKS ON LANDSCAPE GARDENING❧

Brooklyn Botanic Gardens Brooklyn, NY
   Dwarf and Low-Growing or Slow-Growing Plants
   Flowering Shrubs; Kinds, Uses, Culture.
   Flowering Trees
   Japanese Gardens and Miniature Landscapes: essays by Various Experts.

Conder, Josiah. *Landscape Gardening in Japan*. NY: Dover Publications, 1964.

Crowe, Sylvia. *Garden Design*. NY: Hearthside, 1958.

Eckbo, Garrett. *The Art of Home Landscaping*. NY: F. W. Dodge Corp., 1956.

Flemer, William. *Nature's Guide to Successful Gardening and Landscaping*. NY: Thomas Y. Crowell, Co., 1972.

Gardner, Victor Ray. *Basic Horticulture*. NY: Macmillan, 1950.

Jekyll, Gertrude and Weaver, Lawrence. *Gardens for Small Country Houses*. NY: Scribner's, 1900.

Jekyll, Gertrude. *Colour Schemes in the Flower Garden*. London: Country Life, 1968.

Mansfield, L. C. *The Border In Colour*. NY: E. P. Dutton and Co., Inc. 1947. (Slanted to English gardens, and the English herbaceous border, but full of good gardening hints, fine pictures and an exhaustive list of plants to grow.)

Ortloff, H. Stuart and Henry Raymore. *The Book of Landscape Design*. N.Y.: William Harrow and Co., 1975.

Niering, William A. *The Life of the Marsh*. New York: McGraw-Hill, n.d.

Platt, Rutherford. *American Trees: A Book of Discovery*. New York: Dodd, Mead and Company, 1952.

Pratt, Richard. *Ladies' Home Journal Book of Landscaping and Outdoor Living*. (Very up-to-date, good for simple, livable, low-maintenance.)

Rodale, J. I. and staff. *How to Landscape Your Own Home*. Emmaus, PA: Rodale Press, Inc., 1963. o. p. (Lay-out, grading, what types of gardens to choose, how to make and plant them, make lawns, with exhaustive charts of most of the plant groups available for outdoor and indoor gardening.)

Sargent, Charles S. *Manual of the Trees of North America*, 2 vols.

Simmon, Alan E. *Growing Unusual Fruit*. NY: Walker and Co., 1972.

Simonds, John Ormsbee. *Landscape Gardening: Shaping of Man's Natural Environment*. NY: McGraw-Hill, 1961.

Sunset Magazine, *Ideas for Entryways and Front Gardens*. Menlo Park, CA: 1970.

United State Department of Agriculture. *Landscape for Living: Yearbook of Agriculture.* Washington: Government Printing Office, 1972.
———.Maps of frost dates and maps of precipitation available on request.
United States Forest Service. *Trees and Shrubs for Noise Abatement.* Washington: Government Printing Office, n.d.
Van Melle, P. J. *Shrubs and Trees for the Small Place.* Garden City,NY: The American Garden Guild and Doubleday and Co., Inc., 1943.
Wilson, Lois. *Miniature Flower Arrangements and Plantings.* NY: Hawthorne Books, Inc. 1963.
Wyman, Donald. *Ground Cover Plants.* NY: Macmillan, 1956.
———.*Shrubs and Vines for American Gardens.* NY: Macmillan, 1969.
———.*Trees for American Gardens.* NY: Macmillan, 1965.
Yoshimura, Yuji and Haford, Giovanni M. *The Japanese Art of Miniature Trees and Landscapes.* Rutland, VT: Charles E. Tuttle, Inc., 1957.
Youngman and Randall. *Growing Your Trees.* Available through the American Forestry Association, 919 17th Street Northwest, Washington, DC 20006.

❧BOOKS ON OLD-FASHIONED GARDENS❧

Bates, H .E. *A Fountain of Flowers.* London: Michael Joseph, 1974. (Charming, beautifully illustrated, this is an enthusiastic book about English flower gardening. Gardeners in the Pacific Northwest should find it appealing and helpful.)
———.*Gardens of Colony and State: Gardens and Gardeners of the American Colonies and of the Republic before 1840* NY: Garden Club of America, 1931-4, 2 vols.
Leighton, Ann. *Early American Gardens.* Boston: Houghton Mifflin, 1970.
Moreton, C. Oscar. *Old Carnations and Pinks.* London: Collins, 1955.
Sitwell, S. *Old Fashioned Flowers.* London: Country Life Press, 1939.

❧BOOKS ON ROCK GARDENS❧

Correvon, Henry. *Rock Garden and Alpine Plants.* NY: Macmillan, 1930.
Foster, H. Lincoln. *Rock Gardening.* Boston: Houghton-Mifflin Co., 1968.

Klaber, D. *Rock Garden Plants: New Ways to Use Them Around Your Home.* 1959.
The Rock Gardener's Bedside Book. Alpine Garden Society, 1961.

❧BOOKS ON WATER GARDENS❧

Heritage, Bill. *The Lotus Book of Water Gardening.* Middlesex, Eng.: The Hamlyn Publishing Group, Ltd., 1973.
Staff Industries, Inc., 78 Dryden Road, Upper Montclair, NJ 07043.
    Upper Montclair, NJ 07043.
(For building plastic ponds)
Three Springs Fisheries
    124 Hougar Road
    Lilypons, MD 21717
William Tricker, Inc.
    Box 398, Department H-2
    Saddle River, NJ
    (Send 25c for information on water gardens.)

❧BOOKS ON FLOWERS IN CONTAINERS FOR❧ THE PATIO AND THE INDOOR GARDEN

Baines, Jocelyn and Key, Katherine. *The ABC of Indoor Plants.* NY: Knopf, 1973.
    (Treats 300 plants, telling how to identify, grow, water, and feed.)
Ballard, Ernesta Drinker. *A Garden in Your House.* NY: Harper and Row, 1972.
Baumgardt, John Philip: *Hanging Plants for the Home, Terrace and Garden.* NY: Simon and Schuster, 1972.
Baur, Robert C. *Gardens in Glass Containers.* NY: Hearthside Press, Inc., 1970.
Brilmayer, B. *All About Begonias.* NY: Doubleday Publishing Co., 1960.*All About Vines and*
———.*All About Vines and Hanging Plants.* NY: Doubleday, 1962.
Cruso, Thalassa. *Making Things Grow: A Practical Guide for the Indoor Gardener.* NY: Knopf, 1969.
Dworkin, Florence and Stanley. *The Apartment Gardener. NY:* The New American Library, Inc., 1974.
Elbert, George. *The Indoor Lighting Book.* NY: Crown Publishers, Inc., 1973.
Faust, Joan Lee. *New York Times Book of House Plants.* NY: Quadrangle Books, 1973.

Field, Xenia. *Indoor Plants*. London: Paul Hamlyn, 1966.

Fischer, Paul. *Variegated Foliage Plants*. London: Blandford Press, 1960.

Flanagan, Ted. *Growing Food and Flowers in Containers*. Charlotte, VT: Garden Way Publishing Company, 1973.

Free, Montague. *All About House Plants*. NY: Doubleday, 1946.

Graf, Alfred Byrd. *Erotica 3*, Rutherford, NJ: Roehrs Co., 1970. (This is a pictorial and cultural encyclopedia guide to begonias, geraniums and various house plants for the advanced or serious house plant grower.)

Handbook of Succulent Plants. Brooklyn, NY: Brooklyn Botanic Garden, 1970.

Kramer, Jack. *Begonias, Indoors and Out*. NY: E. P. Dutton and Co., 1967.

———.*Hanging Gardens*. NY: Charles Scribner's Sons., 1973.

———.*One Thousand Beautiful House Plants and How to Grow Them*. New York: William Morrow and Co., Inc., 1969.

Kranz, Fredrich H. and Jacqueline L. *Gardening Indoors Under Lights*. N. Y. Viking Press, 1971.

Meachem, William L. *The Complete Guide to City Gardening*. NY: Universal Award House, Inc., 1973.

Poincelot, Raymond P. *Gardening Indoors with House Plants*. Emmaus, PA: Rodale Press, Inc., 1974.

Schulz, Peggy. *All About Geraniums*. NY: Doubleday Publishing Co., 1965.

Sunset Garden and Patio Building Book. Menlo Park, CA: Lane Book Company, 1960.

Teuscher, Henry. *Window-Box Gardening*. Toronto, Ont. Macmillan Co. 1956. (Very good for all kinds of plants in all kinds of containers.)

Walker, Marion C. *Flowering Bulbs for Winter Windows*. NY: Van Nostrand Reinhold Co., 1965.

Wilson, Helen Van Pelt. *Geraniums, Pelargoniums, for Windows and Gardens*. 1957.

———.*The Joy of Geraniums*. NY: William Morrow and Co., 1971.

BOOKS ON WILDFLOWERS AND HERBS

Birdseye, Clarence & Eleanor G. *Growing Woodland Plants*. NY: Dover Publications, 1972.

Coon, Nelson. *Using Wayside Plants*. NY: Hearthside Press, Inc., 1957.

Foster, F. Gordon. *Ferns to Know and Grow*. NY: Hawthorne Publications, Inc., 1971.

Hadfield, Miles. *Everyman's Wild Flowers and Trees*. London: J. M. Dent and Sons, Ltd., 1938.

Hatfield, Audrey Wynne. *Pleasures of Wild Plants*. London: Museum Press, 1966.

House, Homer D. *Wild Flowers of New York*. NY: Macmillan, 1936. (The state botanist back in 1918, when the two heavy, handsome volumes were published by the University of the State of New York. There are remarkably good Photographs by several skilled botanists. It is partly based on another older classic, John Torrey's *Flora of the State of New York*, 1843.)

MacLeod, Dawn. *A Book of Herbs*. London: Gerald Duckworth, 1968.

Miles, Bebe. *Bluebells and Bittersweet: Gardening with Native American Plants*. NY: Van Nostrand Reinhold Co., 1969.

The Rodale Herb Book, Edited by W. Hylton, Emmaus, PA, Rodale Press, 1974.

Simmons, Adelma Grenier. *Herb Gardening in Five Seasons*. NY: Van Nostrand Reinhold Co., 1964.

Taylor, Kathryn S. *A Traveler's Guide to Roadside and Wild Flowers, Shrubs, and Trees of the United States*. NY: Farrar, Straus, 1949.

Taylor, Norman. *Wild Flower Gardening*. Princeton, NJ: D. Van Nostrand Co., Inc., 1955.

Webster, Helen Noyes. *Herbs, How to Grow Them and How to Use Them*. Newton, Mass.: Branford, 1942.

Wherry, Edgar T. *Wild Flower Guide*. Garden City, NY: Doubleday, 1948.

SUPPLIERS

BULBS

Antonelli Brothers
2545 Capitola Rd., Santa Cruz, CA 95060
Tuberose begonias, achimenes, dahlias and other non-hardy plants.

Champlain View Gardens, 188 Asbury St., South Hamilton, MA 01982
Bulbs and lilies.

Cooley's Gardens
Silverton, OR 97381
Good catalogue. Good for iris.

Cruickshank, Ltd. C.A.
    1015 Mount Pleasant Rd., Toronto 12, Ontario,
    Canada
    Bulb house. Canadian wild plants.
Daffodil Mart
    Nuttal P. L., Gloucester, VA 23061.
    The catalogue is a list.
P. de Jager and Sons, Inc.
    South Hamilton, MA 01982
    Excellent for tulips and narcissi.
French's
    P. O. Box 87, Center Rutland, VT 05736
    Bulb importer. Extensive listings.
U. S. Representative of Holland Glory, Inc.
    1360 Stony Brook Rd.,
    Stony Brook, Long Island, NY 11790
    Tulips and crocus.
George Melk and Sons
    Plainfield, WI 54966
    Glads.
Grant E. Mitch
    Canby, OR 97013
Small business, *tops* in daffodils.
Mueller, Charles H.
River Road, New Hope, PA 18939
    Good for bulbs. The catalogue is a list.
Rex Bulb Farms
    John M. Shaver, Newburg, OR 97132
Riverdale Iris Gardens
    7124 Riverdale Rd., Minneapolis, MN 55430
    Iris.
S and K Gardens
    401 Quick Rd., Castle Rock, WI 98611
    Dahlias.
John Schleepers, Inc., Flower Bulb Specialists
    63 Wall St., New York, NY 10005
    Bulb-importers. Excellent quality, good selection.
Schreiner's Gardens, Inc.
    3625 Quimaby Rd., N.E., Salem, OR 97303
    Iris, daylilies. Excellent catalogue.
Swan Island Dahlias
    P. O. Box 800, Canby, OR 97013
    75c catalogue.
William Tricker, Inc.
    Saddle River, NJ 07458
    Water lilies and aquatic plants.

Van Bourgondien Brothers
    P. O. Box A, 245 Farmingdale Rd.,
    Route 9, Babylon, NY
    Good selection of tulips.

Wayside Gardens
    Mentor, OH 44060
    Good for tulip, narcissi, iris, crocus, as well as
    perennials and shrubs.
White Flower Farm
    Litchfield, CT
    For ornamentals of all sorts, top-notch quality.
    Charming, informative catalogue ($3.00, applied
    to order.)
Gilbert Wild and Son
    P. O. Box 337, Sarcoxi, MO 64862
    Largest source of peony, iris, and daylily.

HERBS AND WILDFLOWERS

Caprilands Herb Farm
    Silver St., Coventry, CT 06238
Casa Yerba
    Box 176, Tustin, CA 92680
Davis Cactus Garden
    1522 Jefferson St., Kerrville, TX 78028
Greene Herb Gardens
    Greene, RI 02827
Hilltop Herb Farm
    P. O. Box 866, Cleveland, TX 77327
    35c for catalogue.
K and L Cactus Nursery
    12712 Stockton Blvd., Galt, CA 95632
Knobbit Hill Gardens
    Chatham, NY
Leslie's Wildflower Nursery
    30 Summer St., Methuen, MA 01844
    25c catalogue.
McConnell Nursery
    Port Burwell, Ont. Canada
Rod McLellan Company
    1450 El Camino Real
    South San Francisco, CA 94080
    Also for unusual houseplants. An excellent
    catalogue.
Meadowbrook Herb Garden
    Wyoming, RI
Merry Gardens
    Camden, ME 04843
    25c catalogue
Midwest Wildflowers
    Box 64B, Rocton, IL 61072
Mincemoyer's Nursery
    County Line Rd., Route 526, Jackson, NJ
    25c for catalogue.

Nichols Garden Nurseries
>1190 North Pacific Highway, Albany, OR 97321
>Excellent supplier.

Putney Nursery, Putney VT: 05346

Clyde Robin
>P.O. Box 2091, Castro Valley, CA 94546
>Wildflower seeds

🌺NURSERYMEN🌺

Alpenglow Gardens, Michaud and Company
>13328 King George Highway
>Surrey, B.C. v3T - 2T6, Canada
>Hardy alpines and shrubs. Catalogue 25c.

Armstrong Nurseries
>1265 South Palmetto, Ontario CA 91764
>Old firm with good catalogue. Roses, and fruit trees.

Warren Baldsoefen
>P. O. Box 88, Bellvale, NY 10912
>Rhododendrons. $1.00 for catalogue

Carlson's Gardens
>P. O. Box 305, South Salem, NY 10590
>Azaleas and rhododendrons.

Carobil Farms
>Church Rd., Brunswick, ME 04011
>Geraniums. Catalogue 35c.

Carroll Gardens
>P. O. Box 310, Westminster, MD 21157
>Perennials, plants for the rock garden.

Conley's Garden Center
>Boothbay Harbor, ME 04538
>For Conley's Nursery Catalogue and Gardening Handbook, send $1.00 plus 25c to cover postage.

The Conrad-Pyle Company
>West Grove, PA 19390
>Star Roses and Star Mums.

Cook's Geranium Nursery
>Lyons, KS 67554
>25c catalogue.

Dooley Gardens
>Hutchinson, MN 55350
>Mums.

Edelweiss Gardens
>Box 66H, Robbinsville, NJ 08691
>Ferns.

Earl Ferris Nursery
>811 Fourth Street, Northeast,
>Hampton, IA 50441
>Large, regional firm.

Girard Nurseries
>Box 428, Geneva, OH 44041
>Dwarf conifers.

Greer Gardens
>1280 Goodpasture Island Rd.
>Eugene, OR 97401
>Rhododendrons and azaleas. 20 page catalogue.

Heirob Bonsai Nursery
>Toyo, Livingston Manor, NY 12758

Hortica Gardens
>P. O. Box 308, Placerville, CA 95667
>Bonsai. 25c catalogue.

Howell Gardens
>1587 Letitia St., Baton Rouge, LA 70808
>Day lilies.

International Growers Exchange
>Box 397, Farmington, MN 48024
>Rare Plants. $2.00 catalogue

Jackson and Perkins, Company
>RoseLane, Medford, OR 97501
>Beautiful catalogue for roses. Outstanding suppliers.

Kelly Brothers Nurseries, Incorporated
>Dansville, NY 14437
>Responsible old house; traditional material.

Krider's
>P. O. Box 193, Middlebury, IN 46540
>Shrubs and trees. Free catalogue.

Lakeland Nurseries Sales
>Hanover, PA 17331

Lamb Nurseries
>E. 101 Sharp Ave., Spokane, WA 99202
>Hardy perennials. Rock and alpine plants.

Henry Leuthardt Nurseries, Inc.
>East Horiches, NY: 11940

Logee's Greenhouses
>55 North St., Danielson, CT 06239
>Begonias. A fabulous, very old firm.

Musser Forests
>Indiana, PA 15701
>Also has vegetables.

Earl May Seed Company
>2127 Elm St., Shenandoah, IA 51601
>Shrubs, trees, vines, roses, fruit.

Mayfair Nurseries
>Route 2, P. O. Box 68, Nichols, NY 13812
>Dwarf conifers, shrubs, heather.

McCormick Lilies
>P. O. Box 700, Canby, OR 97013

McPherson Gardens
2920 Starr Ave.
Oregon, OH 43616

Sempervivums.
J. E. Miller Nurseries
    Canandaigua, NY 14424
Mission Gardens
    Techny, IL 60082
    Day lilies, peonies.
Nor'east Minature Roses
    58 Hammon St., Rowley, MA 01969
Peters and Wilson Nursery
    Millbrae, CA 94030
    $1.00 for catalogue.
Rayner Brothers
    Salisbury, MD 21801
    Berries.
Suncrest Nurseries
    Homer City, PA 15748
Stark Brothers Nurseries and Orchard Company
    Louisiana, MO 63353
    Outstanding for fruit trees, roses, trees.
Sterns Nurseries
    Avenue E., Geneva, NY 14456
    Flaming advertising, but does deliver quality
    stock.
Tillotson Roses
    Brown's Valley Rd., Watsonville, CA 95076
    Best for shrub or old-fashioned roses. $1.00 for
    catalogue.
Weston Nurseries
    East Main St., Route 135, Hopkinton, MA 01748
    Good tree and shrub selection. They do not ship
    out.
Wilson Brothers Floral Company, Inc.
    Roachdale, IN 46172
    Geraniums, african violets, unusual house plants.
Wyant Roses
    Route 84, Johnny Cake Ridge, Mentor, OH
    Old-fashioned roses.

❧GENERAL SEEDSMEN❧

Bachmans, Incorporated
    6010 Lyndale Ave.
    South Minneapolis, MN 55419
    Perennials, seeds, bulbs for the north.
Burnett Brothers
    92 Chambers St., New York, NY 10007
Burgess Seed and Plant Company
    67 E. Battle Creek St., P. O. Box 218
    Galesburg, MI 49053
    Old, regional firm. Also good for fruit and
    flowers.

Burpee Seeds
    W. Atlee Burpee Co.
    427 Burpee Building, Philadelphia, PA 19132
    Good extensive catalogue.
Dominion Seed
    Georgetown, Ontario
    Venerable seed and bulb house. Small catalogue.
Farmer Seed and Nursery Company
    Fairbault, MN 55021
Henry Field Seed Company
    407 Sycamore St., Shenandoah, IA 51601
    Excellent for farmers and gardeners in the
    midwest.
Gurney's Seed and Nursery Company
    Yankton, SD 57078
    Catalogue is tabloid. Even have vegetables for
    flavor, not just ease of harvesting.
Joseph Harris, Company, Inc.
    Moreton Farm, Rochester, NY 14624
    Good reliable seedsmen, Extensive catalogue
    with an index.
Herbst Brothers
    100 North Main St., Brewster, NY 10509
    Enormous selection—mostly wholesale
J. W. Jung Seed Company
    Randolph, WI 53956
    Good. Broad line of seeds, bulbs and plants. A
    large, regional company.
Orol Ledden and Sons
    Center Ave., Sewell, NJ 08080
    Organic seeds.
Natural Development Company
    Bainbridge, PA 17052
W. W. Olds Seed Company
    P. O. Box 1069, Madison, WI 53701
George W. Park Seed Company, Incorporated
    Box 31, Greenwood, SC 20646
    Very informative, in every area.

Seedway, Inc.
    Hall, NY 14463
R. H. Shumway
    Rockford, IL 61101
Stokes Seeds
    Box 548, Main P. O., Buffalo, NY 14240
Gamiel Story
    Box 263, Lebanon, TN
    All shades of sunflowers.
Sutton Seeds, Ltd.
    London Rd., Earley
    Reading Berkshire R G61 AB, England
    Suggestion: prepay for airmail delivery.

Thompson and Morgan, Ltd.
Ipswich, England and 401 Kennedy Blvd., Somerdale, NJ 08083
A really huge list of just about everything. Very reliable.
Vans Pines

West Olive, MI 49460
Catalogue and planting guide.
Vaughan's Seeds
Chimney Rock Rd., Bound Brook, NJ
Walnut Acres
Penns Creek, PA 17862

Index